ON THE BACK OF A TURTLE

On the Back of a Turtle

A Narrative of the *Huron*-Wyandot People

LLOYD E. DIVINE JR.
(DÁRAHǪK)

TRILLIUM, AN IMPRINT OF
THE OHIO STATE UNIVERSITY PRESS
COLUMBUS

The front and back cover artwork, along with the turtle logo, may not be reproduced without written
     permission of the author.

Registration Numbers:

TXu 1–997–063

TXu 2–022–942

Library of Congress Cataloging-in-Publication Data

Names: Divine, Lloyd E., Jr. (dárahǫk), author.

Title: On the back of a turtle : a narrative of the Huron-Wyandot people / Lloyd E. Divine Jr. (dárahǫk).

Description: First edition. | Columbus : Trillium, an imprint of The Ohio State University Press, [2019] |
     Includes bibliographical references and index.

Identifiers: LCCN 2018033982 | ISBN 9780814213872 (cloth : alk. paper)

Subjects: LCSH: Wyandot Indians—History. | Wyandot Indians—Migrations. | Wyandot Indians—Wars. |
     Iroquois Indians—Wars. | Indians of North America—Ohio—History. | Wyandotte Nation, Oklahoma.

Classification: LCC E99.H9 .D58 2019 | DDC 977.1004/97554—dc23

LC record available at https://lccn.loc.gov/2018033982

Cover design by Regina Starace

Text design by Juliet Williams

Type set in Junicode

♾ The paper used in this publication meets the minimum requirements of the American National Standard
for Information Sciences—Permanence of Paper for Printed Library Materials. ANSI Z39.48-1992.

To the girls!

Linda—the momma
our Viking princess

The four daughters:

Rebekka—skawę̓des
"voice.going.far"

Susanne—yúriẑínǫs
"wind.blows.over.it"

Sara—keyúwę̓dátah
"entreating.without.avail"

Rachel—rę̓huẑa
"pulling.down.branches.and.nipping.buds.off"

CONTENTS

ILLUSTRATIONS

Figures

Maps

PREFACE

I believe it was Macaulay who said, "A people that take no pride in the noble achievements of remote ancestors will never achieve anything worthy to be remembered with pride by remote generations." Interest in historical work is not a matter of personal gratification, nor of elegant leisure, but of public service and the discharging of a debt we owe to those who have made it possible for us to enjoy the full measure of liberty that is ours as citizens of this State, and of this Nation.

—Augustus C. Carton, 1919[1]

"The Discharging of a Debt We Owe"

Wyandottes love their turtles. Just about everywhere you look in Wyandotte, Oklahoma, you will see turtles; big turtles, little turtles, ceramic turtles, metal turtles, beaded turtles, turtles on signs, turtles on coffee mugs, turtles on pens, turtles on T-shirts, turtles on all kinds of jewelry, turtle tattoos, and of course the Turtle Stop. The mascot for the Wyandotte Nation Casino is a turtle. The mascot looks a lot like the 1960s Hanna-Barbera cartoon classic *Touché Turtle,* minus the cute little musketeer hat. While holding a handful of cash and wearing a strand of beads, the little guy comes close to convincing you are going to win some cash.

Drive a mile west to the Twin Bridges that span the Spring and Neosho rivers and you will find even more turtles, the real kind: box turtles, red-ear turtles, soft-back turtles, and snapping turtles. If you're lucky, you may even get a glimpse of a special treat, an alligator snapping turtle. The alligator snapping turtle looks like a common snapping turtle, or the moss-back turtle in the *Huron*-Wyandots' oral narratives, that the Bad Twin blew way out of proportion. These turtles are embedded with spikes reminiscent of the dinosaurs and nothing less than slow, lumbering monsters. *Watch out!* These boys and girls are big and really bad turtles that in spite of their size can bite in the blink of an eye! If you get bitten by one, just sit down and get comfortable. Think again! As if that's going to happen! This turtle will not let go until lightning strikes—that would be a thunderbolt from Hęǫ, the Spirit of Thunder.

Growing up in Wyandotte, Oklahoma, my siblings and I had turtles as pets, the little red-eared turtles you could buy at Walmart. Then someone realized they carried salmonella, and their days as pets were numbered. Still, at some point during the summer months my girls would invariably find a turtle in the back yard, and the next thing we knew it was in the living room—a box turtle in a box. The turtle quickly became the newest family pet for two or three days, and then I had the girls turn it loose. Turtles, turtles, turtles. They were everywhere.

When I chose *On the Back of a Turtle* in 1989 as the title of this book, the name derived from the fact that Earth resides on the back of the Big Turtle—the moss-back turtle. In time, as I researched and studied, I came to understand that the turtle, and the title of this book, have a much deeper meaning. From the perspective of Creation Earth resides on the back of a turtle, as do the the *Huron*-Wyandot people, reflecting an ancient position of status for the Big Turtle clan. There is little dispute of this fact even if you are a Little Turtle, Deer, Wolf, Snake, Porcupine, or Bear. All *Huron*-Wyandot clans reside on the back of the Big Turtle. William E. Connelley made a statement that still holds true to this very day: "The turtle idea was interwoven with the whole social and political fabric of Wyandot institutions."[2] *Turtles rule!* However, without the Little Turtle, Deer, Wolf, Snake, Porcupine, or Bear clans, the Big Turtle would not and could not be complete.

Growing up in *Ottawa* County, Oklahoma, in the 1960s and 70s has provided me with some very special memories. My family and I lived a little over five miles east of *Miami,* but as a kid I felt it was much farther. A drive to town every other Saturday to purchase life's necessities was both an adventure and a treat. On our way to *Miami* we drove past *Shawnee* Grocery. *Shawnee* Grocery was not the place where kids should go to hang out. It was a dark, antiquated, and dirty little store that probably hadn't changed in who knows how long. It had the feel of an old-time trading post and stood to keep the Indians from going to town, yet *Miami* was full of Indians. The Indians had nowhere else to go when they lost their land on the reservations. The reservations were full of whites. Try to figure that one out!

My brother and I had a favorite summer activity, riding our Schwinns up and down the dirt roads surrounding the section we lived in. Along the way we smashed an infinite number of whiskey bottles and caught a lot of tadpoles as we stopped to play. We lived on what remained of the *Ottawa* reservation. There were tons of bottles to smash and they were quickly replaced, more so than the tadpoles. We attended public school at *Wyandotte*, a little over seven miles away. On the ride to school we would pass the *Seneca* Indian School, and I can vividly remember admiring the kids as I hid in the shadows of the bus. They always appeared sad, but still I was mesmerized by their appearance. I did not want to be caught staring as they were Indians and looked the part. I believe most of them were *Cherokee*. When the Bears from *Wyandotte* High School played the Wildcats from *Quapaw* in a rousing and rough game of football, it was an event of the season. The rivalry was intense, and it seemed that someone would always get hurt.

On special occasions my parents would make a trip to the big city of Joplin, Missouri, to do a little shopping. Back in *Miami,* Walmart did not come to town until 1971, and even then the dime store TG&Y was still the place to purchase life's little necessities. On our annual trip to Joplin we would drive through the middle of the *Modoc's* land. It would take no more than a couple of minutes to pass through. If time did not catch us napping in the car, we would play a game. The winner was the first to spy the *Modoc's* buffalo hiding in the rolling hills. I could never understand why the *Modoc* were in Oklahoma.

Aunt Judy married Uncle Beebe, who was a *Peoria*. Beebe was a God-fearing man who could not hide his zeal for the Lord God even if he tried. Imagine that, an Indian, *Peoria* nonetheless, serving and worshiping the Lord God of the white man's Bible. As we will see, this is anything but uncommon. Let truth be known, some of the most devout Christians are American Indians.

My Grandpa Bland as a young man loved to play baseball. Grandpa was known to have an unbridled *Wyandotte* temper, at least until his heart was captured and tamed by the sweetest little white angel named Mary Mitchell. Grandpa died at fifty-three years of age, and he looked a lot like most people think an Indian should look. Unfortunately, when I looked in a mirror I did not see anything that reminded me of Grandpa Bland or the kids at the boarding school. I was blue-eyed with a fair complexion. I also had the blondest—silver blond—hair. Thankfully, over time my hair faded to a dark, dirty, and dingy brown. Now, to my slight dismay, I can see the silver returning. These are not the usual characteristics when someone thinks of an Indian. As I was growing up in *Ottawa* County, Oklahoma, in the 1960s, Indians were everywhere—as were the turtles! The Indians were dispersed among the majority whites. I was one of them, a *Wyandotte*, but would not understand what that meant for a long time.

As a young child I was taught very little about who I am as a Wyandotte. I often wondered why, and the answer is simple: There was not much to tell. Our culture and the knowledge of who we are as a people had been mixed up and much of it misplaced. I do remember my mother teaching me how to say our tribal name by circling her hand with a pointed index finger in front of me and then quickly poking my belly button. She would always say wind, as in "winding a clock"—holding the "d" for what seemed forever—and then quickly saying dot, with a precise tickle to my tummy. This was the extent of my cultural education.

Juanita McQuistion, then tribal secretary and historian, in a letter dated February 27, 1973, to Charles Garrad in Canada stated, "I am interested in learning the tribal history of our people." She continued by saying, "Most of our tribal history I have read about is in a book written by William E. Connelley."[3] Thankfully, this has changed. My four daughters know more today about who they are as Wyandottes than most citizens could have dreamed of knowing over the last one hundred years.

When my interest in my culture and history was first kindled, I inherited many beliefs that were quickly proven inaccurate. I was told we came from the Huron Tribe. My personal and passionate quest to understand who I am as a Wyandotte started once I found out there was no such thing as a Huron Tribe. Hold on, let's rethink that statement for a moment. Was there a Huron Tribe? I came to find out there was a *Huron* Tribe, but not in the context I was told. Explaining the differences between Huron and *Huron* is a complicated discussion and one of the primary goals of this book. As you read, I have tried to help you better identify these two distinct people groups who share the same name by implementing a standard throughout this book: The regular, or Roman style typeface, has been applied to the name "Huron" when generally referencing the Huron people or Huron Confederacy. In contrast, the italicized typeface has been applied to "*Huron*" when referencing the *Huron*-Wyandot people or *Huron*-Wyandot Tribe. I will explain this in greater detail in the following chapter.

I was also told the Wyandot came from Ohio, and it was our traditional homeland, but no one ever mentioned Ontario, Wisconsin, or Michigan. Before the state of Wisconsin was given its name, a proposal had been placed before the United States Congress in 1830 to name the new territory Huron.[4] The name *Huron* was referencing not the confederacy but the tribe: yes, the

Huron Tribe who would eventually become known as the Wyandot Tribe. This is an interesting fact pertinent to the Wyandot's history; most people do not know that the Wyandot were in Wisconsin. In the historical record, when the Wyandots were in Wisconsin they were known as *Hurons*. Not long before the Wyandots arrived in the Wisconsin Country, where their stay was brief yet controversial, their beginnings as a tribe could be traced back to Ontario on the Canadian side of the Great Lakes. Their origin in Ontario is the source of confusion relating to the use of the name Huron. Ontario is the Wyandot's true traditional homeland—as is Western New York.

Because the *Huron* Tribe had existed for nearly one hundred years before the name Wyandot could be found in the historical record, it is imperative to call the ancestors of the Wyandotte people *Huron*-Wyandot. The name *Huron* is often considered a derogatory name since it is believed to be a direct reference to the wild boars of Europe, or pigs. If the name Huron is ignored within the historical record, it would lead to the forfeiture of over 100 years of Wyandot history. By not understanding that the *Huron* Tribe and the Wyandot Tribe are the same people, many misidentify the *Huron* Tribe as different from the Wyandot. Because of this, I identify the Wyandot people, including their culture and traditions, as *Huron*-Wyandot throughout this book. It is also appropriate when referencing what is now considered traditional Wyandot culture and traditions to use the name *Huron*-Wyandot. Always be aware that you will not find this name in the historical record; however, *Huron*-Wyandot is a name commonly used today by many contemporary historians.

I was shocked to learn how much traditional culture had been lost in a short fifty years after a minority segment of the Wyandot Tribe left Kansas in 1857. The minority left the Territory of Kansas to relocate, *again,* to Indian Territory. I did not understand how this could have happened; it did not make any sense, especially knowing they moved with the intent to remain Wyandot. Then I learned that the loss of traditional *Huron*-Wyandot culture started long before the tribe left Ohio and Michigan in 1843. Like a leaky faucet, the loss of traditional culture began as a single drip. Over a short period of time, by the late eighteenth century the drip had progressed to a trickle. It then became a slow, steady stream until a splattering burst all but emptied the cultural reservoir in the 1820s and early 1830s. Wyandot traditions seemed to just give way to the pressure being exerted from outside forces, both Indian and white alike. In 1857 when a few Wyandot reached Indian Territory, destined to become the state of Oklahoma, the loss of *Huron*-Wyandot culture was back down to a drip. It was not the beginning of the loss—it was the end. All that remained in the *Huron*-Wyandot reservoir of traditions were just mere drops. I was seeing the process of loss in blind reverse.

As I came to understand that there were fewer than 250 Wyandot who chose to move to Indian Territory and remain Indian, it all began to make sense. *Huron*-Wyandot culture, language, and traditions were already compromised when in 1874 the tribal council tried to stop the slide to assimilation (*such a nasty word*) by requiring eligible voters to register by clan. Only seventy-six men from seven clans were found to be eligible to vote.[5] An effort to preserve the Wyandotte's traditional ways, though noble, proved futile. As a tribe the Wyandot had come to accept the loss of traditional culture as an undesirable but acceptable consequence of survival.

When the Wyandotte Tribe was reorganized in Indian Territory in the late 1860s and early 1870s, with a decimated population, there were no longer enough Wyandottes to sustain a traditional lifestyle and barely enough Wyandottes to sustain the Wyandotte Tribe. For this reason many Wyandotte went to the Seneca-Cayuga, Eastern Shawnee, and other tribes, as well as the surrounding White population, to find a husband or a wife—a mate. Survival became the primary goal of all Wyandottes. Out of attrition and not choice, my ancestors misplaced a lot of traditional culture. We cannot blame them for what happened! Shame on anyone who says my ancestors walked away from their traditional heritage and chose the white man's world. No! They adapted and survived, allowing Wyandottes to live today. At the time, my ancestors were not forsaking their heritage; it was just becoming harder and harder for them to retain and sustain it due to a number of complicated and extenuating circumstances.

The late Dr. Elizabeth J. Tooker, an anthropologist from Temple University specializing in the study of North American Indian cultures stated, "Unfortunately, no good history of the Wyandots exists."[6] Dr. Tooker did mention the work of Peter Dooyentate Clarke. Peter is the only Wyandot I know to compile a full-length history of the *Huron*-Wyandot people. Peter published *Origin and Traditional History of the Wyandotts* in 1870, and it is a classic, but it has its flaws. For example; Peter does a good job of explaining how each of the tribes has its own customs and feasts. Peter continues by saying all the tribes devote one day out of the year to give thanks to the goddess Ceres. They honor her by feasting and dancing because she is the one who gave all the Indian people corn.[7] All of this sounds pretty good except for when he mentions Ceres by name. Who exactly is Ceres, and did all the tribes have a common belief in one god or the Spirits? Absolutely not. Early in the first chapter we will see that both the Huron and *Huron* recognized a woman in their oral narratives of Creation. This woman had different personality traits and interactions with the Huron and *Huron* people, and so she could not have been the same woman in either's oral narratives. The woman was definitely not Ceres because she is the Roman goddess of fertility, mother-hood, and agriculture. Peter's universal insertion of the Roman goddess into all the Indian tribes' sacred feasts is near blasphemous.

Many years ago when I first sat down to write *On the Back of a Turtle,* my attempt turned out to be a major and disappointing flop. Within two years I stopped as I quickly realized I was not prepared to write about my amazing people: our history, culture, traditions, oral narratives, and the way the tribe fought back from the brink of disappearing into near-forgotten history. Dr. Tooker was right. There was no good history, and for good reason. The *Huron*-Wyandot's history is multidimensional and very difficult to under-stand, let alone try to write on paper, due to the whole Huron, *Huron,* and Wyandot naming mess. The many spellings, and their many contradictions, are a continuation of the age-old *Huron*-Wyandot problem—the spelling of the names and their proper usage.

Some people say that since the Wyandotte people can no longer speak Wandat, our traditional language, we no longer have the right to call ourselves Wyandotte; with the loss of our language so went our uniqueness and the right to even call ourselves an American Indian. This book will clearly show we are a unique people and we indeed have the right to call ourselves Indian—we are Wyandotte! There is much more to being an Indian than speaking a tradi-tional language. In all actuality our story is not much different from stories of most of the other tribes. Bruce Trigger, in "The Liberation of Wendake," described our cousins the Wendats as follows: "the Wendats, [Huron-Wendat of Wendake] a dynamic people who offer living proof that the survival of cultural identity does not depend on language."[8]

I have been honored to serve many years on the Wyandotte Nation Culture Committee, or historical committee as it was once known. For a majority of those years I have served as chairperson or co-chairperson, and I have had an intimate view of many debates, struggles, revelations, and glorious moments as we sought out our culture. From time to time in this book I may reference the culture committee; however, let it be clearly known that what I say I say for myself and not as a representative of the committee. This is my book, my thoughts, my opinions, my research, and my labor—not the committee's. The Wyandotte Nation Culture Committee does not hold some things I say in this book in a majority consensus, *but that's ok!* When it comes to traditional *Huron*-Wyandot culture there are many inconclusive aspects, and everyone is entitled to their opinion.

I am a Wyandotte Nation citizen, but I do not have a BS or BA, MS, PhD, ED, or Dr. in at the beginning or end of my name. I do not have a degree in any of the -ologies: ethnology, anthropology, archaeology, or sociology. I am a paramedic educator with an AS—Associate of Science. I do not have a four-year degree in American Indian or Native American studies to tell me what an Indian is or who I am as an Indian. No one has asked whether I prefer to be called an American Indian or Native American—I am first and foremost a Wyandotte. If we are identifying ourselves in the traditional way of the old *Huron*-Wyandot, then I am a Porcupine. My chosen Wyandotte name is dárahǫk, a Porcupine clan name that translates as "He throws up his quills for battle when angry." Yes, in true tradition the name describes me rather too well.

As you will see in this book, I do lean toward the American Indian side of the debate. Every individual born today in North or South America is a Native American, but not everyone born today can claim to be an American Indian. If an individual is not native to the place they are born, where do they belong? I know that Indian and American Indian are derogatory names for some people no less than *Huron* is a derogatory name for some Wyandot people. This debate and discussion will be ongoing as long as some people want to debate and *argue* the injustice of it all.

Legitimate admittance to many debates and discussions is at times restricted to the degree of your degree. Likewise, admittance to these debates at times allows entry for some people who have no business saying anything. Their voice and opinions are allowed because it's politically correct and the right thing to do. No, it's not the right thing to do! Political correctness too often excludes those who have the right, because of their heritage, to participate in discussions about themselves. As this book went through scrutiny and review, I was amazed at some of the implications that I do not know what I am talking about. Why? Because I am not a member of an academic club, and the end of my name is "Jr.," not "PhD." What you will read in this book is the very essence of who I am—Wyandotte. Nothing, with the exception of my God and my family, comes close to defining my life. Because of this I most certainly have the right to write about my heritage and my ancestors who have accomplished some pretty amazing things.

I have studied and know a lot about *Huron*-Wyandot history and culture. I am writing this book to give back to my people who have given me a very rich heritage. If by chance you sense a little attitude, as you read this book, don't let it become a distraction. The attitude is a *Huron*-Wyandot thing, part of the heritage, and adds a true *Huron*-Wyandot perspective on many things that many Wyandottes now are trying to silence. I am not a politician in search of votes. At times it's quite clear that I am telling you what you need to hear, not what you want to hear. I see myself as a historian and a realist; therefore, I will often just tell you the black and white of everything. However, you will quickly see there are a lot of gray, fuzzy areas in the *Huron*-Wyandots history, and it's likely there are some things we can never know with certainty.

It should not be the responsibility of future Wyandotte generations to search out and find for themselves who they are as Wyandottes. I have done this, and it was a very intimidating and laborious task. Likewise, it should not be the responsibility of academia to tell us where we came from and who we are as a people. It is every Wyandotte's responsibility—and Wyandottes are notably reliable—to learn for themselves and then teach their children who they are as Wyandottes. My ancestors knew this to be true!

The old Wyandot's most honored feast was the *solemn feast,* at which "the old men recite the history of their nation and their wars, and then repeat the traditions of their fathers."[9] With that being said, all *Huron*-Wyandots must embrace the ideology and commitment to being a *Huron*-Wyandot. If our generation and future generations do not sit and listen to the telling of our traditions and history, we have a problem. If academia and anyone with an interest in *Huron*-Wyandot culture are not interested in hearing who we say we are as a people, we have no less a problem. Within this book I am reciting the history of my nation and our wars, and I am repeating the traditions of my mothers and fathers. Listen to what is being said. It is a sacred and time-honored *Huron*-Wyandot tradition to listen to the telling of our history.

"They Became Known as Wyandots"

The Hurons . . . they became known as Wyandots and gradually acquired a paramount influence in the Ohio valley and the lake region. They laid claim to the greater part of Ohio.[1]

—John N. B. Hewitt, 1907

The Great Island

This narrative of the *Huron*-Wyandot people begins a long time ago in a place not so far away, yet it is a place not of our present world. The inhabitants of this place live in the Sky-world and are known as the Sky-people.[2] The Sky-world is above our present world, but it cannot be seen, and humans cannot go there. The Sky-people are not human but have human form. They are gods and godlike immortal beings endowed with powers found only in ancient oral stories such as this one. The Sky-people have no knowledge of life and death. Their villages and domain are vastly scattered throughout the Sky-world; it is comfortable and peaceful, and happiness is always abundant. Corn and fruit trees provide the people sustenance. Everything is nourished by light radiating from the wild crabapple tree. The wild crabapple tree is a sacred tree and provides light to the Sky-world; there was no sun, moon, or stars. Darkness in the Sky-world was unknown and unfathomed. Light shown forth from the many yellow flowers that grew on the tree. No one was permitted to touch the tree, especially the flowers that grew in abundance.

As with many such stories this one has a fair maiden. No, she is not a princess, yet she is the daughter of the old, strong, and wise head chief of the Sky-people. Today, as in the days of old, *Huron*-Wyandots simply and respectfully call her the Woman Who Fell from Above. It is through this woman life as we know came to the Great Island now called Earth. The Huron-Wendat people, cousins of the *Huron-Wyandot*, knew the woman as Aataentsic. The *Huron-Wyandot* people do not recognize this woman by the same name. The Huron-Wendat's woman was known to have an insidious nature. Aataentsic tried to undo all that was good upon the Great Island, and she had "charge of the souls of the dead, caused men to die, and bred epidemics."[3] *Huron*-Wyandots do not place any of these characteristics upon the Woman Who Fell from Above because she personified all that is good; therefore, the *Huron*-Wyandot people know the Woman Who Fell from Above to be a different woman.

There is no doubt the *Huron*-Wyandot's woman had a name. Since the *Huron*-Wyandot people of olden days remembered the names of her twin sons, they would have also remembered the mother's name; however, it appears the *Huron*-Wyandot people rarely if ever spoke her name. It is possible the name of the Woman Who Fell from Above was too scared for the *Huron*-Wyandot's to speak, or her actions in the Sky-world brought them too much shame. Knowing that Aataentsic was a different woman, I will not call the Woman Who Fell from Above "Aataentsic," because this would be most disrespectful; I will not do this to her—not now, not ever.

Unlike many such stories this one does not end with happiness. It is not convenient that a handsome young warrior should carry our young woman away on a silver stallion to his lodge in the forest and they live happily ever after. Unfortunately, fate, or an act of willful choice, will lead our story down an unexpected path. In the Sky-world it can be said there was nothing good and there was nothing bad. Every citizen was equally respectful of all citizens and willfully cared for the needs of their fellow citizens. There were laws and there was order, yet there was no need for the laws to be spoken, as they were written on the hearts of every citizen and everyone just enjoyed life. However, one day, for no apparent reason, our young woman did what was unthinkable—she touched the wild crabapple tree, and, worse, she plucked and then ate one of its radiant flowers.

The instant our young woman touched the tree, its light faded and twilight began to settle upon the Sky-world. For the first time, darkness could now be seen above the Sky-world. The young woman became sick after eating the flower. She had just singly introduced many unknowns to the Sky-world, and the Sky-world would be forever changed unless her wrong could be quickly undone. The chief called forth the medicine men to heal the tree and save his daughter. All their medicines and charms were unsuccessful. The chief sent forth a moccasin, the fastest runner and messenger of the Sky-people, with a commission to find and bring back the oldest and most knowledgeable medicine man of the Sky-people. This old man lived alone somewhere in the Sky-world, and he had to be found quickly. The moccasin searched everywhere and finally found the old medicine man. Since twilight could now be seen within the Sky-world, the old medicine man knew something was amiss. The old medicine man agreed to return with the moccasin to the village where the tree of light grew and many Sky-people had assembled.

Immediately upon seeing the faint tree of light and the sickly young woman, the old medicine man knew exactly what needed to be done to heal the land of this mysterious and troublesome disease. The old medicine man instructed the young people of the Sky-world to start digging. The young woman's medicine would be found buried within the roots of the tree. Heal the young woman, and the tree would likewise be healed. Not knowing what this medicine was, or what it looked like, the young woman was laid next to the tree. The old medicine man said the young woman would recognize her own healing once it was found. The young people began to dig, and as they became tired, they were replaced with others who wanted their home to be healed. The young people continued to dig, but unfortunately the young woman never found her healing.

Suddenly, as one last scoop of dirt was lifted, a loud and mighty crash sent the tree of light falling through the bottom of the Sky-world. As the tree of light fell, the sickly young woman became entangled within its branches and she instantly disappeared into the hole. Heno, the Thunderer, Spirit of thunder and lightning, bellowed a massive roar upon the dark and lightless abyss of the underworld as the tree and the young woman quickly fell into thick darkness. Heno accompanied the young woman into the underworld.

The violent and sudden burst of Heno's voice had startled two great Swans swimming upon the water's surface of the underworld. No such violence had ever been heard before. The tree of light, though dimly lit, cast its radiance upon the deep, but the two Swans could see the young woman falling from above. The rift in the bottom of the Sky-world suddenly closed behind the unpropitious and unfortunate young woman, leaving her no hope of return. The underworld was nothing but darkness and water as far as the young woman could see to the outer edge of light cast by the tree's radiant flowers.

Swimmers, zoological gods with innate special powers and humanlike personalities, inhabited the underworld. These animals were not the same as we know them today; they were enormous. The Swans were half as tall as a tree, or when standing about forty feet tall. All the animals of the underworld would have been proportionally the same—they were very big and possessed supernatural powers. All the animals were members of the Great Council of the Underworld.

As the tree of light splashed and then quickly disappeared below the water, the two Swans knew the young woman would suffer the same fate. They hurriedly swam to the place the young woman would also splash into the water. There they caught her upon their backs. Turning and looking upon her face they exclaimed, "What a beautiful creature it is. But what shall we do with it?"[4] As the young woman settled upon the backs of the Swans, she had no fear and was not in despair. Heno watched and did not interfere. A sense of peace was upon the young woman, and she knew she was in good care. The young woman was no longer ill, nor did she possess any of the supernatural powers she once held in the Sky-world—she became a mortal being with an immortal spirit.

The Swans, realizing they could not support the young woman upon their backs, decided to go see the Big Turtle, head chief of the animal gods. The Big Turtle immediately sent forth the fastest swimmer of the animals to convene a council of the underworld swimmers. Upon assembling, and having never seen a creature such as the young woman, the council just floated in silence and looked upon her with great wonder. The Big Turtle, finally calling the council to order, informed them as to what needed to be done. They could not let the young woman fall from the backs of the Swans into the water and die, for she must have been sent to them for a reason. The Swans, with the woman still upon their backs, led the council to the place where the tree of light had disappeared below the surface of the water. Upon reaching the tree, the Swans could still see it below the water's edge, and its flowers appeared to be flickering.

The Big Turtle called for the best of the divers to assemble; the Otter, Muskrat, and Beaver quickly swam forward to be the first to dive. The council determined that if one of the divers could reach the tree of light, they could obtain some dirt that was undoubtedly entangled within its roots. As an incentive the Big Turtle offered her back to be used as an island once the dirt was retrieved. If the divers were successful in retrieving a little dirt, the back of the Big Turtle would forever become the young woman's home.

Writhing with anticipation the Otter was the first to dive. In a deluging splash she excitedly and anxiously disappeared out of sight below the water. The otter was gone for a long time, and all the other animals began to think she was dead and would never return. Then they saw her across the way returning to the water's surface; however, she had been unsuccessful in obtaining any dirt, and terribly exhausted, she died.

The Muskrat was next to dive. As she prepared to dive, she was a little slower, more cautious, and more methodical as she also passed out of sight below the water's surface. She remained below the water longer than the Otter. Upon returning to the water's surface, she too met the same fate as the Otter. The Big Turtle then summoned the Beaver. Confident of the power she possessed in her tail, the Beaver slapped the water's surface, imitating Heno's thunder as she dived out of sight. Yet the dirt remained elusive at the bottom of the water's edge, and she also died in her attempt. Retrieving some dirt from the tree of light was beginning to look like an impossible task since the three best and strongest divers had met their demise. More divers of less skill followed the Otter, Muskrat, and Beaver, yet they also died in their noble attempts to retrieve some dirt from the roots of the tree. The flowers on the tree were progressively becoming dimmer and dimmer with each sputtering flicker. Time and hope were about to be lost, as was the life of the young woman.

The Big Turtle, unwilling to sacrifice any more lives, summoned the remaining animal gods and asked for a courageous volunteer. No animal swam forward. After a long while the ugly, warty old Toad volunteered as she prudently and slowly pushed herself forward. The animals parted as she came from the back of the council, and they looked upon her with worrying sighs and disdain. The old Toad took a deep breath and then dived below the water. She was gone the longest of all when a small bubble of air blipped onto the water's surface. It startled all the remaining swimmers as they bobbed in silence waiting in hopeful, expectant anxiety. The Big Turtle said, "Let us swim right to the place where the bubble has burst, and if the Toad comes back we shall hold her up for fear that she may fall back."[5] The animals swam to the place just as the Toad rose from the darkness of the deep water's edge. The current pulled the Toad to the side of the Big Turtle where she was found to be dead; however, a few small grains of dirt were in her mouth. The old warty Toad was successful in retrieving the dirt when all the other divers had failed, and she was given the greatest honor and would forever be revered as Grandmother Toad.

The council was concerned that Grandmother Toad had retrieved too little dirt to be of any use. The Little Turtle, second chief of the underworld swimmers, felt otherwise and recommended the dirt be taken from her mouth and placed on the shell of the Big Turtle. The Little Turtle swam forward and spread the grains of dirt. An island began to slowly grow around the edge of the Big Turtle's shell. After awhile the two Swans moved close to the island, and a most grateful young woman stepped from their backs to the back of the Big Turtle. When she was safe upon the back of the Big Turtle, the council dismissed and each returned to their respective lodgings within the underworld. Before long, how long no one knows, the few grains of dirt became a Great Island upon the Big Turtle's back. It was then that the young woman could walk about, but not without the risk of a fall. After the last ember from the tree of light died, overwhelming darkness, so thick the young woman could touch and feel no differently than water did, again existed in the underworld.

The council of the underworld swimmers was again convened to see if they could find an answer to the prevailing darkness. After great deliberation no answer was found. Then the Little Turtle, full of confidence after spreading the grains of dirt stated, "Let me go up to the sky; I will put a light there for the Woman."[6] The council agreed and they called forth Heno, who quickly came to assist with this most important and difficult task to carry the Little Turtle into the sky.[7] As a terrible cloud approached full of thunder and lightning just above the surface of the water, the animal gods could see that it contained a dreadful mixture of rocks, trees, streams, and lakes. Fearlessly the Little Turtle swam into one of the streams, and Heno quickly carried her into the dark and lifeless sky.

The Little Turtle began to gather Heno's lightning as it flashed throughout the cloud. Forming the lightning into a great ball, she placed it into the sky, thereby creating the sun. The sun was not alive and he could not move. The sun shone forth a great amount of light, and the young woman could now see the vastness of the Great Island upon which she lived. The sun proved too hot and uncomfortable for the young woman. The great council of swimmers decreed the sun should be given life and a spirit so that it could freely move about the sky from water's edge to water's edge. After the council had given the sun a spirit and the freedom to move within the sky, he would not go below the water's edge. The sun knew that by going below the water's edge, he would cause the water to quench his fire and his light would die. The Mud Turtle was asked by the great council to dig a hole through the Great Island so that the sun could move through a passageway without the risk of losing his life. The Mud Turtle dug a vast hole, and the sun could freely move within the sky along the path established by the Little Turtle and the Mud Turtle. Along this path the sun could pass through the Great Island without being harmed by the water.

In his freedom the sun ventured to the back of the Great Island and would often take too much time in returning. While he was gone, the Great Island would again be filled with darkness. The Little Turtle decided it would be good to make the sun his mate; therefore, she created the moon to be the sun's mate. They were very happy together, and over a great span of time she bore him many children. The sun and the moon filled the vast dark sky with many stars. The moon and her children, the stars, gave light to the Great Island when the sun was away. The young woman would not live in darkness. As in the Sky-world from which she fell, there was always light in the sky. In the underworld, the Great Island was bathed in light from the sun, moon, and their countless children, the stars.

After a long while the sun became jealous and displeased with his mate, for she was as bright as he in the sky. One day the sun enticed his mate into the Mud Turtle's passageway and severely chastised her to the point of death. The sun stole from the moon much of her light, and she severely shrank in size. The moon was weakened to the point where she could no longer keep pace with the sun in the sky. The Little Turtle, noticing the moon was gone, went looking for her and found her alone in the passageway. She was severely hurt, and her light could no longer shine as brightly. All that remained was a small crescent of light. The Little Turtle encouraged her and helped mend her wounded pride. After encouragement the moon felt better and fully recovered, but not for long. The sun still treated her poorly and no longer gave her the attention she once enjoyed. As the moon realized the sun no longer cared for her as he once did, her brightness again began to fade. To this day she has never given up hope that the sun will return to her and their relationship will be as it was in the beginning. This is why at times her light shines bright and at other times it can be seen only as fading crescents of light. The Little Turtle remains in the sky to encourage her month, after month, after month. This is why the Little Turtle is the Keeper of the Sky.

The Great Island was a good and perfect place for the young woman to live, and the animal gods continued to make her world even more comfortable. One day, as the young woman was exploring her island world, she found a lodge in the forest. Inside the lodge was an old woman whom she called her Grandmother. From where the old woman came no one knows. The old woman taught the young woman everything she needed to know. The old woman also provided protection as the Great Island continued to grow. The young woman was happy, yet she felt alone. She wished for children and then she became pregnant—indeed the young woman was pregnant with two boys.[8]

While her twin boys were still in the womb, our young mother could feel them continually struggling one with the other. She could also hear them taunting and bickering, but she could not understand what they were saying. One of the Twins said to his brother, "I shall not be born in the manner of other children. Indeed, I shall kick my way out through her side."[9] His brother responded with great and immediate anger saying, "It should not be so! For this would injure, or even kill, our mother."[10] When it was time for the Twins to be born, the first was born the natural way and his mother held and looked upon him with affection and pride. However, the second Twin cared about neither his brother's feelings nor his mother's life; therefore, he violently kicked his way through the armpit of his mother, killing her instantly.

In death, the Woman Who Fell from Above was placed on a scaffold. As the young woman lay on the scaffold, drops of her decay fell to the dirt; corn sprang from the droppings of her breasts, beans from those of her limbs, and pumpkins from those of her head. Other vegetables also grew from the droppings of her limbs. From her also sprang tobacco. For this reason, corn, the life-giving food from her breasts, is called our mother, and tobacco grows on its own without care or cultivation.[11, 12] In her death she became nourishment and life for all her future grandchildren. The young woman's body died, yet her spirit still lives. The Woman Who Fell from Above now stands at the entrance to the great underground city located somewhere in the far northern lands of the Great Island.[13] The Woman Who Fell from Above still assists all *Huron*-Wyandots as they make their journey after death to the Land of the Little People.[14]

After the Woman Who Fell from Above died, the old woman took charge and care of the Twins. She raised them in the absence of their mother. The old woman taught them of their destiny and how they were to expand and prepare the lower world for the coming of the people. As she raised them, she could easily see that although they were twins, they were absolute opposites. It has been said that the elder Twin was good, the younger Twin bad. The old woman favored the younger bad Twin. The Twins were gods, as they possessed the same supernatural powers found in the Sky-world. Their grandfather, the wise, old chief of the Sky-world gave them their names. He called the elder Good Twin tséhstaʔ, and the younger Bad Twin tawéskare.[15] The names translate from the traditional language of the *Huron*-Wyandot as "Man Made of Fire" and "Man Made of Flint," respectively. In this book I will call them as most Wyandottes do today, the Good Twin and the Bad Twin. Their names do not express good and evil, as some believe. Their names are best expressed as our friend and our enemy.

As time passed the Twins grew in strength and stature. The Twins' powers eventually surpassed those of their grandfather.[16] The elder Good Twin was stronger and possessed more power than his younger brother, the Bad Twin. The Good Twin had no desire to argue and fight with the Bad Twin; therefore, he made many accommodations and concessions to try to appease his brother as they ventured forth to expand the lower world. Their differences were often manifested in open conflict and hostility, much to the dismay and disapproval of the animal gods. The taunting and bickering, which started before their birth, never ceased and only increased.

The Twins decided the Great Island should be divided and the best way to keep from fighting was to stay in their designated realms. The Good Twin made a great river to separate the land into east and west. This great river still exists and is now called the Mississippi River. The Good Twin chose east of the river as his realm and made the land flat with gentle rolling hills, and watered with cool, refreshing rain. Throughout the land he also made springs and clear, flowing rivers with two currents flowing side by side so that traveling up and down the river would be effortless. Into the rivers he put numerous fish without scales. The Good Twin also made abundant fruit trees, and the blackberry, strawberry, and raspberry vines did not have thorns. Nuts could be picked and eaten straight from the tree. The Good Twin made the pumpkin and vegetables abundant. He made the corn, which had sprung from the breasts of his mother, grow with hundreds of ears on each stalk. The syrup of the maple was made to flow thick, rich, and sweet straight from the tree. The smoke of the tobacco he made to carry the prayers and requests of the coming people into the sky so that he could hear all their needs and supply their all their wants. For the hunt the Good Twin made the animals: buffalo, deer, turkey, raccoon, rabbits, and other small game. Everything the Good Twin made was very good.

The Bad Twin went west of the river and pulled up great mountains that reached into the sky. He then threw flints, rocks, and boulders across the land. Great patches of thorns and briars grew thick and stretched as far as the eye could see. Dark swamps were full of mosquitoes the size of turkeys.[17] Marshes of mud would serve to impede the coming people. He made trees with leaves and berries of poison to entice and sicken the people. There was no water to drink, no food to eat. Deserts of sand stretched to the horizon with no shade from which the people could hide from the heat of the sun. The heat was intolerable, much like the heat his mother had once had to endure. Animals for the hunt he did not make; instead he made wolves, panthers, snakes, owls, ravens, and monsters. These animals, especially the monsters, were hunters and eaters of flesh like the people who had yet to be created. Everything the Bad Twin made was very bad.

The Twins agreed that once their work was finished, they would give each other time to inspect and make adjustments to the other's Creation. Any changes made by one could not completely undo the Creation of the other. This time the Bad Twin went first. The rivers he swirled with his hand mixing the currents into one. He also created rapids and waterfalls. Many of the fish he gave flinty scales, making them difficult to eat. The fruit trees he made no taller than shrubs and covered the vines with thorns. The nuts he encased within a hard, nearly impenetrable shell. Mother corn now bore two, three, and often no more than four ears of corn. The syrup of the maple he mixed with water, turning it into a weak milky sap. The animals made by the Good Twin were caught and frightened until their innocence was gone and fear of the coming people placed in their hearts. Many more things were done to undo the good work of the Good Twin.

The Good Twin went west and turned many of the Bad Twin's mountains into foothills. He also turned much of the desert into prairie and placed refreshing springs throughout. Streams drained many of the swamps and flowed into rivers watering the land. The rivers also provided a path upon which the people could travel. The Bad Twin created his animals to be enormous and ferocious; the Good Twin shrank them down to a normal size. Like the Bad Twin, the Good Twin made many changes to the Creation of his brother. As the conflict between the brothers turned into an outright fight, much of what they created was destroyed, rebuilt, and destroyed again and again for countless ages. The Bad Twin did not honor the river's boundary; therefore, he tossed all the bad of his Creation into the good of his elder brother. The original Creation of the animal gods was destroyed.

In time the council of the animal gods was led into the sky by the Deer. They ascended the rainbow to escape the carnage and to live in peace with the Little Turtle. Today only four of the animal gods still live upon the Great Island. The Big Turtle holds the Great Island upon her back and will do so for eternity. The weight she carries is extreme, yet she bears it with magnificent strength and humility. Every so often she shifts her position to support the weight. This causes the Great Island to quake. After digging the subterranean passageway, the Mud Turtle never returned to the surface of the Great

Island, for inside the passageway she created a perfect world. The Mud Turtle lives within this passageway and for the time has been appointed ruler over the interior of the Great Island. The two Swans stand guard over the northern and southern boundaries of the Great Island. One of the Swans now resides in the Arctic Ocean, the other in the Gulf of Mexico.[18]

The name the Twins gave their Creation in the lower world was Nature. After the animal gods left the lower world, Nature cried out to the Good Twin to bring them back. The Good Twin agreed to go into the sky and bring them back to the lower world. The Good Twin was strong and entered the sky. The Good Twin could also enter the land the Mud Turtle made. Before going into the sky, the Good Twin took the soft, white down from the breast of the two Swans and scattered it behind him as he entered the sky. This created the Milky Way seen in the sky at night, and the path the Good Twin could use to find his way back home.[19] After the Good Twin found the animal gods, they refused to return with him to the lower world. The Good Twin returned to the lower world alone to the grief and sorrow of Nature.

It was not until the animal gods ascended into the sky that the Twins created people to populate and fill the lower world. The Good Twin made all the Indians, and the Bad Twin all the other people found throughout the lower world. Many of the people created by the Bad Twin are enemies of the Indians. To assist in the fight with his younger brother, the Good Twin created the tátikéah, also known as the Little People. The Little People were given supernatural powers to protect and fight alongside the Indians. The Little People are a twin Creation of the Wyandot, but they are not human. They were unlike dwarfs, as they were true little people, humanlike yet very diminutive in size, standing around two feet tall. They never fought a monster unless they were in pairs, and the team was always two males. In spite of their very small size, the Little People were formidable warriors.

The Bad Twin created the hústrẹdú, also known as Flinty Giants or, as more commonly known by Wyandots, the Stone Giants. The Stone Giants were as tall as trees and covered with sheets of stone, making them nearly impossible to kill. The only weakness in their armor could be found in their armpits. The Stone Giants were cannibals and craved the flesh of the Indians. Over time the Stone Giants killed and ate many Indians; however, with the help of the Little People, and with the knowledge the Indians obtained that a weapon made from the basswood tree would kill Stone Giants, the monsters were defeated.

As war waged between the Twins, and deadly confrontation was becoming inevitable, the Good Twin hid and protected his Indians by placing them in a large underground city. The Indians stayed there in a state of hibernation for a very long time. The Woman Who Fell from Above stood watch over the Indians as they slept. She was given a torch of lightning by Heṇǫ to assist her during her vigilant guard.

One day in an attempt to kill Nature, the Bad Twin collected all the water upon the Great Island. After taking the water hostage, he placed it in a large skin bag.[20] The Bad Twin carried the bag of water upon his shoulder, hindering the Good Twin from rescuing the water and safely returning it to the springs, rivers, and lakes. This angered the Good Twin, as he knew all of Nature would certainly die without the water. The Good Twin finally came to the realization he and the Bad Twin could not coexist and their differences would never be mended. The Good Twin challenged his brother to a fight, with the death of one the prize for the other.

Before the final battle began, the Good Twin constructed a great bow and used the trunk of a tall pine tree as the shaft for his arrow. The Good Twin knew if he could ever so slightly pierce the bag holding the water, it would trickle back into its proper abode. The arrow had a point made from flint, one of the Creations of his brother. As the Good Twin drew back his bow and released the water's champion, the Bad Twin stepped aside trying to dodge the arrow's head. He knew if the arrow struck the bag of water the arrow would set the water free. In his hurry the Bad Twin stumbled, causing the bag of water to be directly hit by the arrow. A deluge and a great flood covered all of Nature. The Good Twin, much to the euphoria of the Bad Twin, had destroyed everything upon the Great Island.

The death of Nature, caused by his own doing, severely angered the Good Twin, and a fight to the death with his brother commenced. The Bad Twin, realizing his elder brother was stronger, feared for his life and fled to the West where he was convinced he could hide in the mountains. The Good Twin, knowing the path his younger brother would take, scattered many horns— antler sheds of the Deer along the way. By chance the Good Twin came to know that the antler sheds were the only things that would kill his brother. As the Bad Twin fled, he tripped and became entangled in the sheds. During the Bad Twin's struggle to stand and resume his flight, his body was pierced by many sheds. His wounds were numerous, and a quick death was his fate. With the death of the Bad Twin a sense of peace and finality settled upon the lower world like a cool, thick mist. Yet the mist covered nothing as nothing remained. Everything had been destroyed, and the lower world could no longer sustain Nature and the Indians who blissfully slept in the underground city unaware of the carnage above.

The Good Twin did not rest, nor did he mourn the death of his brother; he immediately began recreating the lower world so that it could again sustain Nature and the Indians. The Good Twin could not recreate the lower world in its original perfection. The lower world was recreated back to the place agreed upon by the Twins. The noble integrity of the Good Twin was so strong that he still honored the agreement made with his brother back in the ancient days of their original Creation. The new Creation contained both good and bad, and it took the Good Twin a long, long time to finish his work.

Upon completion of his work the Good Twin traveled throughout Nature. The Good Twin was inspecting and admiring all he had done. While walking, the Good Twin saw something he did not recognize. As he walked closer he could see it was alive and it was a Naked Man. The Good Twin spoke to the Naked Man, saying, "I am walking to see the creation, which I have made, but who are you?" "Clothed man," said the Naked Man, "I am as powerful as you, and have made all that land you see." "Naked Man," replied the Good Twin, "I have made all things, but do not recollect making you."[21] The Good Twin and the Naked Man agreed to test their powers and see who was stronger by speaking to the mountains. Each was to try calling forth the mountains, standing far on the distant horizon, to the place they now stood.

The Naked Man was the first to try. He fell to his knees and began to pray. He too read from a large open book. His efforts were not successful, as the mountains only partially came to the place they stood. The Good Twin was next to try. He took a turtle rattle from his belt, shook it, and softly spoke some words, so softly the Naked Man could not understand. The mountains then stood next to them and were so tall they pierced the sky. The Good Twin resumed his rattling, and the mountains returned to the place they originally stood. The Naked Man became frightened and ran away, never to be seen again.

After a long time, how long no one knows, the Naked Man sent His messengers—His preachers to the Indians who lived upon the Great Island. However, the Naked Man is believed to have never returned to the Indians Himself. Some of the Indians listened to the message of the Naked Man's preachers, and the Good Twin could not convince them to stop listening. Over a short period of time the Indians learned to pray and read from the Naked Man's Big Book. They also believed the stories it told. Many of the Indians were compelled to go and tell the other tribes the Good News which the Big Book proclaimed; hence, they also became preachers of the Naked Man.[22] It did not take long for the Naked Man, and the true power He possessed, to cause the Indians' recollection of the Good Twin, and all he had done, to become hazy with many forgotten details.

Back in the ancient days of the Great Island, after prevailing over the Naked Man, the Good Twin finished his walk through Nature. The Good Twin was pleased with the work he had done. Returning to the cabin of his grandmother, he found her in a terrible mood, for she was very angry he killed his brother. No longer desiring to listen to her rants and the stories of why she favored the Bad Twin, he picked her up and threw her to the moon. She hit the moon with such great force that the impression of her face can still be seen on the surface of the moon to this day.[23]

Nature had been ripened by the sun and was now ready to once again receive the Indians. The Good Twin returned to the underground city where his mother kept watch over the Indians while they continued to sleep. Upon seeing her son approach, and knowing why he had returned, the Woman Who Fell from Above said, "Lead my children forth. Scatter them abroad in the lower world. I will remain in this city. At death each Wyandot shall pass through the Yoowatayo [the underground city] on the way to the land of the Little People, there to remain forever."[24] The Good Twin asked the Big Turtle, upon which his Creation stood, to shake the land. Likewise, Heno shook the sky with great thunder and lightning. The dirt above the underground city was ripped open, the sun shown into the underground city, and the Indians were gently wakened. They were then called forth tribe by tribe, each tribe with its own chief. The first tribe called forth was the *Huron*-Wyandot, who were placed at the head of all the tribes. The *Huron*-Wyandot's chief was to be the chief of chiefs. Each tribe went from the underground city to its assigned place on the Great Island, and their numbers began to multiply.

As the different tribes went forth upon the Great Island, some of them found people, bad people created by the Bad Twin. How these people were able to withstand the destruction of the lower world during the War of the Twins, and how the Good Twin did not find them as he reviewed his Creation, are not understood. It does not matter where they came from. The children of the Bad Twin were found upon the Great Island and eventually brought death and destruction to many of the tribes. Against great odds the *Huron*-Wyandot survived the deceitful and mischievous deeds of the bad people as they contrived to gain control of the Great Island. As history attests, the children of the Bad Twin eventually overcame the children of the Good Twin. The Indians of the Good Twin may have been defeated, but they were never conquered. The Great Island to this day still resides *on the back of a turtle.*

The Tribe with No Name

Over an expanse of great time the tribes migrated throughout the Great Island, and many of them began to change. North America is the name by which the Great Island is known today. In their changes, the tribes formed many unique cultures. Also in their change many of the tribes forgot about the Good Twin. They fell into deceit by some of the monsters that yet lived on the Great Island. The monsters told these tribes they were their gods, and many believed the lie. As the tribes changed, many of them retained special kinships and bonds, in spite of their now-unique cultures and identities. Many languages and dialects emerged, further dividing the tribes. When common interests were shared with neighboring tribes, they created regions of similar culture. Over time there became many regions of similar cultures throughout the Great Island.

In the ancient days of the Great Island the tribes settled into their respective areas and began to live a productive life. Nature provided more than enough to sustain the tribes, yet the people had to work hard to create stores for the harshness of winter. In their abundance vast networks crossed the Great Island, and the tribes traded goods, ideologies, and technology. As time passed, the Great Island began to fall into disarray and strife rose among the tribes. Open conflict between the tribes made life that much more difficult. The ensuing battles were in conflict with Nature, and they also conflicted with the very nature of the Indians as given by the Good Twin.

The *Huron*-Wyandot never forgot the Good Twin. They continued to remember all he had done and honored him by telling the stories of his great deeds from generation to generation. Upon departing the underground city, the *Huron*-Wyandot remembered their travels, and they also remembered, although with uncertainty, where the underground city was located. It's believed that the underground city is located in an inhospitable land in the far northern regions of the Province of Quebec.[25] When did the tribes come forth from the underground city? No one knows because it was so long ago and through the passage of time all sense of time has been lost.

The head chief of the *Huron*-Wyandot was a man named Sastaretsi, whose dignity, stature, and greatness surpassed those of all the chiefs of the Great Island.[26] [27]Sastaretsi was then the chief of chiefs of all the many different tribes. His name became a title and was worn with unsurpassed honor by many men. One day, although the actual date is uncertain, Sastaretsi indicated to his people that they were to go west, and he led them on a journey as far as the Great Lake now named Huron.[28] He told his people that this stage of their journey was but the first and there would be many more. Soon after the *Huron*-Wyandot reached their destination, Sastaretsi died. However, before he died, he drew a map on a piece of birch bark to further guide his people to their final destination. He also told his people to make an oak image of himself, in his royal attire, and stand his image at the head of his grave so it would always face the sunrise. When the sunrise fell upon his image, it would turn and face the direction his people were to continue in their travels.

As prophesied, the image of Sastaretsi turned as the sunrise struck his face. So powerful was the force from the rays of sun that his image groaned as it turned between the large logs that held it upright. Upon turning, the image of Sastaretsi faced south, and without hesitation the *Huron*-Wyandot followed his gaze. Twelve of the best warriors were sent by canoe to first locate their new and final home. They traveled along the eastern shore of Lake Huron, through Lake St. Clair and the narrow passages north and south of the lake, until they finally drifted into Lake Erie. Upon entering Lake Erie, they turned back and returned to the narrow streams near Lake St. Clair. The leader of the warriors then stated, "This is the place which King Sastaretsi meant to be the home of our nation."[29] The warriors returned to where the tribe waited and then led all the people to their new home. The place this warrior led his people is today located on both sides of the river near Detroit, Michigan, and Windsor, Ontario.

Mondoron, also named Joseph White, was chief of the Canadian Wyandots. It was he who told this folktale. Chief White told his narrative to Horatio Hale before making his journey to the Land of the Little People in 1885. In the latter half of the nineteenth century many of the *Huron*-Wyandot's oral traditions had been clouded by the haziness of time. Chief White's narrative of the *Huron*-Wyandot's migration has proven to be an unreliable narrative for historical purposes; however, the hope of Sastaretsi's prophetic gaze remained a powerful religious and motivational force for many *Huron*-Wyandot who claimed the territory around Detroit as their final home.

As the English, who were children of the Bad Twin, gained knowledge of the Indian people living upon the Great Island, they used oral traditions, such as the *Huron*-Wyandot's claim of the territory around Detroit, against them for their own ill-favored gain. As the children of the Bad Twin fought their wars for control of the Great Island, the *Huron*-Wyandot were compelled to stay in the area of Detroit and be used as expendable pawns. Many *Huron*-Wyandot would not leave the area around Detroit because of the prophetic decree of Sastaretsi. For Chief White the journey of his Wyandots ended at Detroit; however, the journey for many other Wyandots did not end until the final leg of their journey took them to Indian Territory (Oklahoma). As late as the mid-nineteenth century many *Huron*-Wyandot thought that the oak image of Sastaretsi was still standing somewhere in the Canadian forests.

The *Huron*-Wyandot's narrative of migration is uniquely their own. However, all the various tribes on the Great Island have their own accounts. Of course we know today that emerging from an underground city after being placed in a state of hibernation is a fanciful concept of the imagination. Yet it is still a brilliant attempt to explain an innate desire to belong and fit into Nature. It too gives an explanation that all humans and civilizations struggle to understand—where did they come from? The process of all the different tribes migrating, changing, and settling into their respective places in North American is complex and very difficult to understand. Archaeologists and anthropologists struggle as they try to piece together the past. Much of their obtained knowledge is based upon speculation and oral traditions of the various tribes and is complemented by science as sifted from grains of dirt through a mesh hoping to catch even the smallest fragmentary evidence. Noted Canadian archaeologist James V. Wright, specializing in Ontario Iroquoian archaeology, stated of the tribes' development and maturity over the course of 11,000 years since the last ice age: "To present a general picture it has been necessary to make the complex appear simple, to present the poorly known as well known, and to favour one interpretation when, in fact, several conflicting interpretations exist."[30]

Digging through permafrost, mud, dirt, and stones does not produce many absolutes. However, in the hundreds of years to come, like in the countless years that preceded today, the beliefs in which the *Huron*-Wyandot people found contentment, belonging, and the hope of their origin will remain unchanged. Like today, and in the countless years to come, the Wyandotte people will be telling the stories of the Woman Who Fell from Above, the Big Turtle, Grandmother Toad, the Twins, and Sastaretsi. All of academia's speculations and theories of how this and that came about, their maps show-ing that these people moved from here to there and these people became these people, are all subject to change. In ten years, fifty years, one hundred years, there will be more theories to replace today's theories, and the cycle will con-tinue—the *Huron*-Wyandot's oral traditions will not change.

The name the *Huron*-Wyandot people called themselves is without doubt the most difficult and confusing element of their history. Simply saying they are Wyandot is making the complex appear simple. The name by which the *Huron*-Wyandot people called themselves after the dispersal of 1652 is unknown. A name was not recorded in the historical record, which says *'this name'* is what the people called themselves. The *Huron*-Wyandot people were essentially a tribe with no name. This tribe of people who had no name came to be called by many names, as historians tried to figure out who they were. Not all of the people in Sastaretsi's tribe came from one tribe; they were an amalgamation of no fewer than three tribes, as they ventured south to the region around Detroit. By default, Sastaretsi's people came to be known as *Huron*. Over the course of about one hundred years they would also come to be known as Wyandot.

Historically, the name Huron sometimes does and sometimes does not correctly represent the *Huron*-Wyandot people. Whether the correct repre-sentation is being used or not depends upon when and how the name Huron is used. Yes, I know the statement is a little confusing; this is why I want to again emphasize the system I have developed. This system will hopefully make the names easier to understand and identify as we encounter the three variations throughout this book. *Take note: This difference is very important!* When the name Huron is used to identify an indigenous people or tribe of North America erroneously named Huron by the French, and specifically four of these Huron tribes who formed the Huron-Wendat Confederacy, the name will be displayed in a regular typeface as Huron. If the name *Huron* is used to represent the Huron people who would eventually become known as the *Huron* Tribe, who in turn became known as the Wyandot Tribe, the name will be displayed in an italicized typeface as *Huron*.

As we will see, the French initially called most of the newfound tribes in New France Hurons, making little to no differentiation of their tribal or cul-tural differences. The French came to recognize that four of these tribes were united in a confederacy, and they have historically been known as the Huron Confederacy. There were three other Huron tribes who were not members of the Huron Confederacy; these tribes united as one, forming the *Huron* Tribe.

History has wrongly assumed the *Huron* Tribe are the remnant people who survived after the Huron Confederacy had been destroyed and dispersed by the Iroquois Confederacy.

There is one exception to this rule. Throughout this book if the name Huron is found in a quote that is referencing the *Huron* Tribe, the chances of its being italicized in the original text is highly unlikely. For the sake of preserving the integrity of history, I will not italicize the name *Huron* in these instances. Therefore, if you are reading a quote and the name Huron is used, it will be a good opportunity to train yourself to understand the context in which the name is being used. You must determine if the name is or is not referencing the *Huron* Tribe. Another good clue is to look at the time period in which the name is being used. The Huron-Wendat Confederacy was defeated and dispersed by the Iroquois Confederacy in 1649. If you see the name Huron being used to identify an organized and cohesive people after the year 1649, you can assume that the name is referencing the *Huron* Tribe; however, always be aware of the context in which the names Huron and *Huron* are being used.

Using this system helps to ensure that the name is used and understood in its proper context. More important, the system is used so you can clearly understand which people group is being referenced—the Huron who are not Wyandot, or the *Huron* who are Wyandot. On many occasions the name Huron has represented two people groups who technically did not split one from the other, nor did one pass the identifying name to the other. They were truly two different people groups.

The remainder of this section concentrates on identifying the names *Huron* and Wyandot in history. It can be a complicated and confusing discussion as we connect both names as one; therefore, we must take the advice of James V. Wright and try to make the complex appear simple. What follows are several examples taken from the work of six very influential historians: Francis Parkman, Henry R. Schoolcraft, John Hewitt, Horatio Hale, Charles Barbeau, and Bruce Trigger, all of whom initially tried to identify the *Huron* and Wyandot. However, as we will see, they each had similar analyses but varied in their final conclusions. Since the name *Huron*-Wyandot is a relatively new way of expressing the name of the *Huron* and Wyandot people, in order to preserve the integrity of history, for the moment we will revert back to just using *Huron* or Wyandot.

All of the historians but Trigger made the common error of stating, or implying, that the *Huron* were the same people as the Huron. It wasn't until the recent works of gentlemen such as Bruce Trigger, Georges Sioui, Charles

Garrad, James Clifton, and John Steckley, and the emergence of some of my own theories, that the names became a little clearer in the historical timeline. Let's begin with Parkman and see who the *Huron*-Wyandot people are in the historical record.

Francis Parkman, a deeply respected historian from the nineteenth century, begins his book, *History of the Conspiracy of Pontiac,* published in 1868, with a brief historical overview of the various tribes. Much of Parkman's work was indeed pioneering and has been well respected; many of his conclusions about the various tribes are readily accepted as historical and factual. Parkman's use of the names Huron and Wyandot, directly implying they are names for the same people, was so blatant that it's hard to deny what he said. When he printed the following statement, it appeared decisively clear that the two were the same people.

> The peninsula between the Lakes Huron, Erie, and Ontario was occupied by two distinct peoples, speaking dialects of the Iroquois tongue. The Hurons or Wyandots, including the tribe called by the French the Dionondadies, or Tobacco Nation dwelt among the forests which bordered the eastern shores of the fresh water sea, to which they have left their name.[31]

Parkman indicated that the Huron, referencing the Huron Confederacy, are the same people as the Wyandot. As we study the two names Huron and Wyandot, we will see that the name Wyandot does not enter the historical record until around 1747. Therefore, they could not have been the same people. Technically, the two people groups never crossed in the historical timeline. It would have been impossible and impractical to call the two people groups by the same name. However, Parkman did, it stuck, and here we are today, nearly one hundred fifty years later, with many people believing the Huron and Wyandot are one and the same. My argument is all about historical semantics and the proper use of names. For this reason, if you did not know any better, you will read and take what Parkman said word-for-word: that the Huron, referencing the Huron Confederacy, are the same people as the Wyandot Tribe.

I am not going to say the confusion regarding the use of the names Huron and Wyandot is alone Parkman's fault, but he did publish the one sentence that was very persuasive. After the Iroquois Confederacy's extermination, adoption, or dispersal of many tribes in the Great Lakes Region in the mid-seventeenth century, the complications of trying to understand the movement of the various tribes was difficult if not impossible. Unfortunately, many of the various tribes were adopted into other tribes, and their ancient names discarded and forgotten. Afterward there was a lot of confusion and speculation as to who came first, who went where, and who became who.

Parkman is not the only historian to suggest that the name Wyandot is the same as Huron, and vice versa—there have been many others. From time to time Henry R. Schoolcraft made the same assumption. Schoolcraft's six-volume behemoth, *History of the Indian Tribes of the United States,* published between 1851 and 1857, once served as a respected and definitive source of history for many of the various tribes well into the early twentieth century. It was an incomparable and monumental project that is plagued with many inaccuracies, such as the one I have chosen to reference below. In this quote Schoolcraft calls the Wyandot an ancient tribe:

> Fishing vessels of the leading maritime nations of Europe, appeared on the banks of Newfoundland in the early part of the 16th century. Denis commanded one of these, in 1506, and Aubert in 1508. Cartier, who coasted along the rugged and barren shores of Newfoundland, the "Heluiland" of the Scandinavians, in 1534, having discovered the gulf and river St. Lawrence, ascended the latter, the following year, to Lake St. Peters, in one of his ships, whence he proceeded, in boats, to the island of Hochelaga, the present site of Montreal. He found a large and populous town of Indians at this place, who, it is perceived from his short vocabulary, were of the Iroquois stock. These were subsequently found to be the ancient tribe known to us as Wyandots, whom the French, as Charlevoix tells us, named Hurons, from the wild manner of dressing their hair.[32]

One of the best early observations that came close to getting everything correct was written in 1907 by John N. B. Hewitt and published as *Handbook of American Indians North of Mexico,* Part 1. The handbook, in two volumes, was also a major work much like Schoolcraft's; however, the two volumes were well organized and well written by then-experts on each tribe, without the sporadic information found in Schoolcraft's work. Hewitt wrote several tribal histories contained in the two volumes. If you analyzed all his work and overlaid each tribal history with histories of other tribes who had a close and codependent relationship, the history and positions of the Huron and Wyandot finally begin to make sense. However, even Hewitt literally and linearly combined the histories of the Huron Confederacy and *Huron* Tribe into one section as though they were a transition, one from the other. Again, if one reads Hewitt's account from a literal perspective, the Huron and *Huron* appear to be the same people.

John Hewitt in "Huron" indicated that the name Wendat was corrupted into "Wyandot" by the English. The English did not have contact with the tribes of the Wendat Confederacy, or, better known in history, the Huron Confederacy, before their dispersal. It was the French who recorded the name Wendat, and it was the English who recorded the name Wyandot in various spellings about 124 years after the French. By the time the English colonies began to make their push into North America, the Wendat had long dispersed and ceased to exist. The name Wendat was no longer being used to identify a tribe or a people group. The name Wendat had disappeared into the historical record and was rarely, if ever, used. If the people and name ceased to exist, then how could the English have known or heard the name Wendat to corrupt it into "Wyandot"? Hewitt stated the following:

> After the destruction of the Huron or Wendat confederation and the more or less thorough dispersal of the several tribes composing it, the people who, as political units, were originally called Huron and Wendat, ceased to exist. The Tionontati, or Tobacco tribe, with the few Huron fugitives, received the name "Huron du Petun" [the Tobacco Huron] from the French, but they became known to the English as Wendat, corrupted to Yendat, Guyandotte, and finally to Wyandot.[33]

Hewitt's description is an excellent analysis of the names Huron, Wendat, Tionontati, Tobacco, Petun, and Wyandot all rolled up into one complex yet very enlightening paragraph. Unfortunately, to clearly understand who the Wyandot people are, you must first possess a good idea as to whom each of the names represents. Let's take a moment and study each name and see how they are related or are synonyms one to the other.

Huron

The name Huron is believed to have first been used somewhere around 1600 by early French traders. As the Native populations of the Great Lakes Region began coming to French outposts along the St. Lawrence River to trade, the name generally referenced all the Native peoples.[34] Samuel de Champlain and Father Gabriel Sagard are believed to be the first ones who officially used the name in text around 1623.[35] The name was undoubtedly used in casual conversations and initially applied to all the various Iroquoian tribes in the region, commonly known today as the Ontario Iroquoians. There are some contemporary historians who are not fond of the name Iroquois. From time to time, you will see them use a new name to describe the Ontario Iroquoians—Nadouek. It is also possible that the Algonquian-speaking tribes of the St. Lawrence River and Great Lakes Region were also generally referred to as Hurons.

For early French explorers it would have been difficult, if not impossible, to initially determine the differences between the various tribes. In time this would change. This is why from time to time you may see Huron rendered in various forms to describe the various tribes such as "Huron de la Nation Neutre" and "Hurons de la nation du Petun."[36] These names reference the Attiwandaronk and Tionontati, respectively. For early French explorers all the Native peoples of the Great Lakes Region were just a bunch of Hurons.

Over time the name Huron came to represent, in a very specific way, just four of the many tribes—the four tribes were a confederacy. After the French initially named and called the confederacy Huron, it took them several years to truly know who the confederated people were—they called themselves Wendat. By then it was too late, for the name Huron had stuck and was difficult to replace within the historical record. In addition, I'm not so sure the French really cared what the various tribes called themselves. They had their own names such as Huron, Tobacco, and Neutral, or they just used the names the Huron Confederacy called their neighbors. This naming convention simplified the complexities of trying to keep the various tribes sorted and contained within their unique cultures and traditions, a task which was nearly impossible for the French to have done back in the day.

The men of the various tribes often plucked their heads to create a hairstyle known today as a Mohawk. The Mohawk is also at times referred to as a roach; however, the contemporary roach has come to represent a headdress often worn in conjunction with or in the absence of the Mohawk. Some of the men wore their hair as a scalp lock, a single lock of hair on the crown or temporal region of the head. The roach headdress is commonly made of moose or deer hair and porcupine quills, adorned with golden eagle feathers. The roach headdress can be quite colorful. It is much more than decorative, for it serves as a symbol of status, courage, conquest, and honor for those who earn the right to wear it.

The French turned the Mohawk and the roach into a mockery. The Mohawk and its bristling hair is said to have reminded the French explorers of the wild boars—wild pigs— in Europe. Unfortunately, Huron is a historical name that has stood the passing and test of time. Huron, when referencing the various tribes, specifically the four tribes of the Huron or Wendat Confederacy, is by far more recognizable today than other less offensive names many contemporary historians are now choosing to use.

Throughout this book when referencing the Huron, I will do something I have rarely done in the past: I will call these people Huron. In the past I would use the name Wendat, but I have come to realize I was doing this in error. When you read about these people in historical texts, more times than not they are always referred to as Huron. The name Huron, a derogatory term from the Old French word *hure,* is commonly defined as a boar's head, bristling hair, or similar variations. In Charlevoix's *History and General Description of New France,* Vol. II, the following was stated of the name: "The word Huron comes from the French, who seeing these Indians with the hair cut very short, and standing up in a strange fashion, giving them a fearful air, cried out, the first time they saw them, *Quelle hures!* (What boars' heads!) and so got to call them Hurons."[37]

Dr. Bruce Trigger indicated that the acceptance of the name Huron as referencing a boar's head might be nothing less than folklore.[38] He continued by noting that the name Huron predates the discovery of the New World. The name was a slang term meaning "ruffian" and "rustic." Long before Dr. Trigger, John Hewitt also stated, "The name Huron, frequently with an added epithet, like *vilain,* 'base,' was in use in France as early as 1358 as a name expressive of contumely, contempt, and insult, signifying approximately an unkempt person, knave, ruffian, lout, wretch."[39]

From the perspective of the early French traders, even the roughest of the lot, this name seemed to be appropriate. In comparison to the many luxuries found in refined, proper, and Renaissance-inspired France, the Indians, and their cultures and way of life, would have appeared very rough, very rustic, and very primitive. The various Indians would have been continually bombarded with insults from the sophisticated Frenchmen as they would, *in paraphrase,* shout, *"you Huron!"*

Wendat

The four tribes of the Huron Confederacy collectively called themselves Wendat. Father Lalemant, a Jesuit missionary, recorded the name in 1639. Father Lalemant had a brilliant idea: He simply asked the people what they call themselves. Father Sagard, in his dictionary of Huron names, gives Houandate as the name by which the people called themselves.[40]

John Hewitt attempted a translation of the name Wendat. Hewitt stated, "In the Huron tongue the common and general name of this confederation of tribes and dependent peoples was *Wendat* (8endat), a designation of doubtful analysis and signification, the most obvious meaning being 'the islanders' or 'dwellers on a peninsula.'"[41] John made his doubtful analysis and translations of the name around 1907. Until recently the translation has stood firm as the accepted translation of the name. As the linguistic evidence has been studied over time, there are now contemporary linguists who have made different hypotheses as to what the name Wendat actually means. Preceding Hewitt's work some of the most ludicrous explanations were attempted.

Many contemporary Wyandottes are familiar with Dr. Charles Marius Barbeau, but they are not familiar with many of the other earlier historians who attempted to identify their ancestors. Dr. Barbeau visited Wyandotte, Oklahoma, in 1911 to 1912 under the auspices of the Anthropological Division of the Geological Survey of Canada, which eventually became a division of the Canadian Museum of Civilization. Dr. Barbeau's intent was to collect folk stories and songs. What he found in Oklahoma was more than could be imagined and the usual fulfillment of an old ethnologist's lifelong career. Dr. Barbeau was a very young twenty-eight years old and just starting his long productive career. Before traveling to Oklahoma, Dr. Barbeau did a little background research on the Wyandot. It's likely he was already familiar with the Huron since they lived just down the road from him in Quebec, and it's likely he studied much of what the earlier historians were writing on the Wyandot. Dr. Barbeau was aware it is good to know the people you are interviewing—a little of their history, customs, and how they came to be where they now lived. In 1915 when *Huron and Wyandot Mythology* was published, the following is what Dr. Barbeau said of the Wyandotte people:

The present-day Hurons and Wyandots are the half-breed descendants of the once powerful Huron nation, whose country was situated between Lake Simcoe and Nottawasaga bay, Ontario, at the time of the discovery of America. As a result of the destruction of their villages by the Iroquois and their final dispersion (1648–1650), a few hundred survivors sought the protection of the French and settled near Quebec city, while the others fled northwestwards. After incessant migrations about the Great Lakes, the western bands of the Hurons, there-after described as Wyandots, definitely established their settlements, in 1701, along the shores of the Detroit river. Early in the eighteenth century most of these Wyandots moved to the southern shore of Lake Erie, to the present site of Sandusky, Ohio. The Ohio band of Wyandots was transferred, in 1843, to the site of the present Kansas City, Kansas, and, in 1868, to Wyandotte reservation, Oklahoma. Six or seven hundred half-breed Hurons and Wyandots are still to be found; about three hundred and fifty of these live at Indian Lorette, over two hundred and fifty on Wyandotte and Seneca reservations, and a small number in Anderdon township, Ontario, Detroit, Michigan, and Kansas City, Kansas.[42]

Dr. Barbeau just repeated, with a little more linear detail, what everyone else had already stated—the Wyandotte people are Huron with the implication they are a direct descendent of the Huron-Wendat Confederacy. Most of the early historians did nothing but exacerbate the *Huron*-Wyandot's problem of proper identification. Since the *Huron*-Wyandot people are not Huron proper, anything associating the Wyandottes with the confederacy is irrelevant, correct? No, not exactly. If not for one tribe, the Attignawantan, who was a founding member of the Huron-Wendat Confederacy, there would be no need to specifically mention the four tribes of the Huron Confederacy. After the dispersal of 1649, and the likely inclusion of a small number of Attignawantan citizens into the amalgamation that became *Huron,* the Attignawantan were an important tribe for the *Huron*-Wyandot people. Another, more important, reason that the Attignawantan need mentioning is their relationship with the Wenroronon Tribe, whom we will look at momentarily.

As noted, the Huron-Wendat Confederacy comprised four tribes who lived on the eastern shore of Lake Huron on the Penetanguishene Peninsula of Georgian Bay. The founding tribes of the Huron-Wendat were the Attignawantan and Attingueenongnahac who are believed to have formed the confederacy around 1450.[43] The Arendaronon were first admitted to the confederacy, in 1590, and the Tahontaenrat were the last admitted, in 1610.[44] Along with the four confederated tribes there was a fifth people group called the Ataronchronon. They are believed to have been an extended segment of the Attignawantan, or a hodgepodge of segments from the various other tribes.[45] The Ataronchronon do not appear to have been a seated member of the Huron-Wendat Confederacy.

Upon the dispersal of the Huron-Wendat Confederacy in 1649, the people who composed the Ataronchronon simply disappeared and remain unaccounted for in history. It is believed many of the Tahontaenrat were killed or adopted into the Seneca Tribe. Many Arendaronon were also killed or adopted into both the Seneca and the Onondaga tribes. The Attignawantan, the once-powerful founding tribe of the Huron Confederacy, were routed by warriors of the Iroquois Confederacy and many citizens were killed or adopted into the Mohawk Tribe. It is believed that a few Attignawantan citizens were absorbed into the Tionontati. These people, and only these people, can legitimately be called Huron as part of the Huron Confederacy and *Huron* Tribe. In 1652 they fled westward with the two tribes of the Tionontati and the remnants of the Wenroronon Tribe; they eventually became known as citizens of the *Huron* Tribe.

The name Huron-Wendat is today reserved for the descendants of the Attingueenongnahac tribe of the Huron-Wendat Confederacy. These are the true descendants of the Wendat people. After abandoning Christian Island in Georgian Bay between April and June of 1651, approximately three hundred survivors fled to the regions around Quebec. Predominately Catholic, in Quebec they sought the protection of the Jesuit missionaries. Initially occupying various places, they settled in 1697 at the small village of Lorette on the outskirts of Quebec City and eventually became known as the Huron of Lorette. In 1985 their name was changed from the Huron of Lorette to the Huron-Wendat of Wendake.[46] The Huron-Wendat still live in the vicinity of Lorette to this day and have a thriving community.

Wyandot-Wendat

In years past when lecturing or writing, I often referred to the *Huron*-Wyandot people as Wendats. Since doing so, I have had many regrets and have since stopped using the name. I must assume responsibility for promoting a rather compelling theory and movement as being the truth among citizens of the Wyandotte Nation. The *Huron*-Wyandot people have not been proven to be Huron-Wendat. Unfortunately, the use of the name Wendat is controversial because contemporary agendas are trying to designate the name as the parent name for many historic and contemporary tribes. Use of the name Wendat has recently been labeled as a "transnational movement," a term that illustrates the degree of the effort to put forth the name as valid.[47] Using the name Wendat in this way takes it out of its historical context based upon theories of ancient relationships through unprovable linguistic analyses and *personal feelings* of individuals both native and non-native.

The historic tribes I once promoted as being Wendat were obviously the four tribes of the Huron-Wendat Confederacy: Attignawantan, Attinguee-nongnahac, Arendaronon, and Tahontaenrat—the true and historic Wendat Confederacy. In addition to the Wendats, I promoted all the Ontario Iroquoian tribes of the Great Lakes Region, minus, of course, what were then the five tribes of the Iroquois Confederacy. In addition to the historic tribes, I promoted the Wyandotte Nation, Huron-Wendat of Wendake, Wyandot of Anderdon Nation, and Wyandot Nation of Kansas. These four contemporary tribes have been referred to as Wendats due in part to the contemporary 1999 Wendat Confederacy.

Janith (Jan) English, Chief of the Wyandotte Nation of Kansas, is the author of the 1999 Wendat Confederacy. This contemporary confederacy exists in name and spirit only. Chief English was commissioned to compose a document of friendship symbolically binding the three contemporary bands of the *Huron*-Wyandot and the Huron-Wendat. The document was a simple token confirming renewed tribal relations, which had been lost or stressed over the preceding decades and centuries. Many people have taken the purpose and intent of the 1999 Wendat Confederacy out of context and have since applied undue social and governmental responsibilities upon something that was never intended.

The definition of this new contemporary confederacy stands in stark contrast to John Hewitt's 1912 definition of the historic confederacy. Hewitt's description and definition of the historic Wendat Confederacy was expressed this way: "A confederation of 4 highly organized Iroquoian tribes with several small dependent communities, which, when first known in 1615, occupied a limited territory, sometimes called Huronia, around L. Simcoe and s. and e. of Georgian bay, Ontario. . . . In the Huron tongue the common and general name of this confederation of tribes and dependent peoples was *Wendat*."[48]

In my quest to search out and study the name Wendat I recently sent an email to Dr. Craig Kopris asking his opinion on the name. I was curious if the name could possibly hold a universal religious or social covering that was applicable to the many Ontario Iroquoian tribes, which might justify Chief

English's use of the name. A search in Dr. Kopris's database collection of Wandat and Wendat words could possibly determine if the old Iroquoian languages held any references or clues to the name being used outside the four tribes of the Huron-Wendat Confederacy. As commonly happens with Dr. Kopris (which I have come to deeply appreciate), I received a long and elaborate answer to my question as he grammatically and linguistically broke down the name Wendat. Dr. Kopris also looked into the known language databases of the Iroquoian-speaking tribes and could not find one match outside the four tribes of the Huron-Wendat Confederacy. In short, Dr. Kopris's answer was "As far as I know, no one was ever actually referred to as "Wendat" except for the Wendats themselves."[49]

I agree. In all my research I cannot find one source confirming that the name Wendat was used by any tribe other than the four tribes of the Huron-Wendat Confederacy. My peers, who believe the Wyandot and Wyandotte are Wendat, have been misinformed and hold on to their belief in that error. Dr. Bruce Trigger, in *Children of Aataentsic,* indicated that Wendat may have actually referred "to the Huron country," which was not necessarily a direct reference to the people or tribes of the confederacy.[50] If this is true, the name referenced the place where the Wendat Confederacy was located. The Wendats lived on the small Penetanguishene Peninsula between the Georgian Bay of Lake Huron and Lake Simcoe. This is the historic Wendake, that is, Huronia, and its residents exclusively called themselves Wendats.

All of this seems pretty simple and straightforward, but clearly the name Wendat has recently become a point of contention and division. Such division is disappointing given the fact that the name once unified the four Huron tribes into the strong and powerful Wendat Confederacy. After their defeat and dispersal in 1649 the name seemed to all but disappear for 350 years until the 1999 Wendat Confederacy helped revive the name and to some degree gave it credence. Since the signing of the 1999 Wendat Confederacy, there has been a precise effort to promote the name Wendat well beyond the name that once solely and uniquely identified the four tribes of the Huron-Wendat Confederacy. A cooperative effort between fragments of Wyandot, Wyandotte, and Wendat tribal communities, and emerging scholars within academia, has embraced the name Wendat and liberally promoted its use.

A recently published book, *From Huronia to Wendakes: Adversity, Migration, and Resilience, 1650–1900* (2016), could easily serve as the manifesto of those promoting the use of the name Wendat. A theme found throughout the book's essays speaks of multiple Wendat communities scattered from Lorette to Wyandotte, Oklahoma. The idea of multiple Wendat communities, both historical and contemporary, throughout North America is understood and accepted by only a microfraction of Wyandotte Nation citizens. Leadership of the Wyandotte Nation does not officially support a latent argument within the book which states Wyandottes are Wendats. This fact was known by the editors and justified with their statement, "Although in most cases we worked through the structures of tribal governments in approaching representatives to read and comment on our work, when this was impossible due to already stretched resources, we asked friends and colleagues from these nations to serve in this role. In all cases their comments mark neither the official opinion of tribal governments nor their sanction."[51]

During a speech in Midland, Ontario, in the year 2000, Dr. Bruce Trigger gave a brief overview of how the name Wendat was revived. Today's emerging scholars have not revived the name; however, they have in essence become the name's champion. In his speech Dr. Trigger indicated that unearthing the history was a rather long and indirect process, and he identified religious interests as playing a primary role in the resurrection of the name. He did not acknowledge the signing of the 1999 Wendat Confederacy. His speech was published in *Ontario Archaeology* in 2001 under the title "The Liberation of Wendake," in which he stated the following:

> The Euro-Canadian mythographization of Wendake was initiated by the return of the Jesuit Order to Canada in 1842. Jesuit missionaries from France began to study early Jesuit history in Canada in an effort to re-establish their priority among Roman Catholic religious orders. . . . The work of these Jesuits revived interest in the Huron mission and initiated a movement that resulted in the erection of the Martyrs' Shrine near Midland, in 1926, and the canonization of the seventeenth-century Jesuit martyrs in 1930.[52]

Dr. Trigger continued by identifying Canadian archaeologists and ethno-historians. Their recent work with the Ontario Iroquoian cultures furthered an interest in Wendake and the Wendats. All of this renewed interest in the name Wendat proved to be an inspiration for Chief Jan English to choose the name when she composed her document of friendship. The assumed need for such a document was the renewed peaceful relationship between the Wyandotte Nation and the Wyandot Nation of Kansas. For the preceding decade Chief Leaford Bearskin and Chief English had been locked in a battle of words and political maneuvering over the fate of the *Huron* Indian Cemetery in Kansas City, Kansas. Chief Bearskin, when proposing that a casino be built over the cemetery property, indicated that the graves of the Wyandots would be exhumed and their bodies moved to Oklahoma. This sparked a long, heated battle that became horribly divisive and further damaged an already contentious relationship.

Before the signing of the 1999 Wendat Confederacy the Wyandotte Tribe of Oklahoma and the Wyandot Nation of Kansas reached an agreement on July 11, 1998. This agreement ceased all confrontations, as concessions were found to mutually protect and preserve the *Huron* Indian Cemetery. Without this initial agreement, and a renewed peaceful relationship, the 1999 Wendat Confederacy would not have been possible. The situation between the two chiefs was still contentious, and Chief Bearskin did not attend the ceremonies and Second Chief Jim Bland was sent in his stead. Ever since the document was signed, reconciliation between the Wyandotte Nation and the Wyandot Nation of Kansas has continued, with positive steps made in the relationship.

The 1999 Wendat Confederacy was inspired by the renewed religious interest in everything Wendat and Wendake, the archaeologists and ethnohistorians, and the renewed relationship between embattled chiefs. In the past, Wendat and Wendake would have been written as Huron and Huronia, but since the names have an origin within the French explorers and Jesuit missionaries, they now needed to be sociopolitically corrected. It's too bad Chief English did not choose to use the name "1999 Huron Confederacy." If she had done so, knowing the French universally called all Ontario Iroquoian tribes Hurons, we likely would not be having this discussion.

Of course Chief English did not use the name Huron due to obvious derogatory connotations associated with the name. In many ways the contemporary use of the names Wendat and Wendake is similar to how the names Huron and Huronia came about. When the French declared the many tribes of the Great Lakes Region to be Hurons, they made a cardinal mistake in thinking they and their cultures were all one and the same. The same principle applies to contemporary religious enthusiasts, archaeologists, ethnohistorians, and emerging scholars. Generously and erroneously stating, without cultural or historical proof, that all Wyandots, Wyandottes, and Wendats are Wendats is no less than the French calling all the people Hurons—minus the negative connotations of course. Leadership of the Wyandotte Nation does not embrace the name Wendat because the name has no applicable purpose for the *Huron*-Wyandot people to embrace.

Dr. Kathryn Magee Labelle is one of the emerging scholars promoting the use of the name Wendat. Dr. Labelle's work is highly acclaimed, and I personally respect her work, although I do not always agree with all of her opinions. In Dr. Labelle's doctoral thesis, published in 2013 under the title *Dispersed but Not Destroyed,* she said the following: "In the aftermath of The Great Peace of Montreal of 1701 and the beginning of the eighteenth century most of the Wendats from Michilimackinac migrated to Detroit and began to identify themselves separately from other Wendats by calling themselves the "Wyandot." This division departs from the seventeenth-century notion of one collective Wendat identity and deserves its own unique study."[53] This present book, *On the Back of a Turtle,* is a unique narrative that studies the history of the *Huron*-Wyandot people. It is fine, and actually desirable, that Dr. Labelle and I at times hold differing opinions on certain elements of *Huron*-Wyandot history. This allows for people interested in the history to have differing perspectives, which allows for a much broader study. Remember what I said in my preface? "When it comes to traditional *Huron*-Wyandot culture there are many inconclusive aspects, and everyone is entitled to their opinion." Dr. Labelle has the degree and I have the heritage. My opinions and perspectives on the history just happen to be that of a Wyandotte Nation citizen.

Tionontati

From here on we will center the focus of our discussion of names directly upon the Huron who became Wyandot. As we saw with the old historians, many of the new historians continue to try to label the *Huron*-Wyandot as Wendats. Before the tribe became known by either *Huron* or Wyandot, Tionontati, and its many various spellings, is the most common name found in the historical record. However, from time to time you will now see the name Sastaretsi Tribe being used to recognize the *Hurons* who became known as Wyandot. Since the name *Huron* has been deemed offensive, some contemporary historians have chosen to adopt the title of the Tionontati's hereditary chief as the tribal name. Clearly, I choose to use the name *Huron* because if it's stricken from the historical record one hundred years of *Huron*-Wyandot history is in jeopardy of being overlooked. How a tribe goes from being called Tionontati to *Huron* and eventually Wyandot is complicated, but hopefully this explanation will make the complicated appear simple.

The Tionontati were commonly known as the Hurons de la Nation du Petun and Tobacco Nation by the French. Note that the umbrella name Huron is used in conjunction with the more specific and locally identified name Petun. Petun has a Brazilian origin and means "Tobacco People." "Tobacco Nation" was first used by Champlain in 1632 and is a direct reference to the tribe as cultivators and traders of tobacco.[54] The Tionontati were known and named by the four tribes of the Huron-Wendat Confederacy as the Khionontateronon, or similar spellings. The name is translated as *"People of the Mountains,"* or similar translations. The actual name the Tionontati called themselves is unknown. Many historians believe that the Tionontati were a confederacy of two tribes—the Oskenntonton and the Hannaariskwa.[55] Many people also believe the Tionontati were members of the Huron-Wendat Confederacy; however, as we have already noted, they were never admitted to the Huron-Wendat Confederacy in spite of living but a stone's throw away.[56] The two tribes of the Tionontati were actually members of the Attiwandaronk Confederacy, known as Hurons de la Nation Neutre [Neutral Confederacy] by the French.

Jesuit missionaries observed the Tionontati and Attignawantan as having a very similar dialect of the Iroquoian language. It is believed the Jesuits unfortunately did not preserve within their handwritten manuscripts any examples of the Tionontati's language. Their traditions and cultures were also noted as being very similar. Some anthropologists and linguists have speculated the reason is that at some point they may have been one people who split into two different people groups. Some theorize their split could have recently occurred not long before the arrival of the Europeans to North America. No one knows with absolute certainty, but I find the notion doubtful.

Like the two tribes of the Tionontati, the Wenroronon Tribe was another member tribe of the Attiwandaronk Confederacy. A clan segment of the Wenroronon Tribe was adopted into the Attignawantan Tribe after the Iroquois Confederacy defeated and dispersed the Wenroronon in 1638. The Wenroronon are a very important tribe for the *Huron*-Wyandot people. This clan segment of the Wenroronon was *technically adopted* into the Attignawantan; however, I do not believe they gave up their personal and unique identities as Wenroronon. After the destruction of the Huron-Wendat Confederacy by the Iroquois Confederacy in 1649, the Wenroronon fled to the Oskenntonton and Hannaariskwa seeking protection. These tribes would quickly abandon the

Blue Mountains and themselves seek protection among the greater tribes of the Attiwandaronk Confederacy.

Again, these three tribes would eventually flee their Ontario homelands in 1652 and seek asylum in the far western Great Lakes Region, where they become known as the *Huron* Tribe. It is believed that in the summer of 1660 the French first named the dispersed amalgamation of Oskenntonton, Hannaariskwa, and Wenroronon the "Tobacco-Huron"; hence, the name Tionontati-Huron is a contemporary version of the same name. Although the French called this new amalgamation Tobacco-Huron, the name by which they called themselves remains unknown. I like this statement by Gordon Sayre: "In practice the name depended more on the identity of the namer than of the named."[57] When writing about what the Wyandots called themselves, Charles Aubrey Buser, an amateur historian of the Wyandotte Nation, stated, "In any case, the tribe had more to worry about than just what someone else called them."[58]

In the mid-seventeenth century, the three tribes of the Attiwandaronk Confederacy were dispersed from their homelands by the warlike actions of the Iroquois Confederacy. As they fled to resist adoption or extermination, the Iroquois continued to pursue their flight. Fleeing westward these people sought asylum and protection in the vast regions of the western Upper Great Lakes among their Algonquin allies, primarily the Ottawa. The French, eventually by default, began calling these people the *Huron* Tribe. Over time the Tobacco segment had been dropped and only *Huron* remained. The name *Huron* is not a direct reference to the Huron-Wendat Confederacy; it is referencing the fact all the tribes of the Great Lakes Region were once universally call Huron by the French. When the French found the dispersed people of the old Huron Mission living in the far west, they were speaking a dialect of the Iroquoian language. The French identified the dialect among the ocean of Algonquian and Siouan languages that dominated the region. The French had no idea who these people were and likely did not care. They were *Hurons*. The name stuck, and no one argued anything different.

Could it be that the amalgamation accepted *Huron* Tribe as their new de facto tribal name as a calculated and blatant play upon the Huron-Wendat's old position of authority with the French? Absolutely! The new *Huron* Tribe stepped up and stepped into the trading relationship the Huron-Wendat Confederacy once dominated throughout the Great Lakes Region. The *Huron* Tribe kept exploiting the French as if they were the Huron-Wendat, and everyone was happy, except for the Wenroronon.

Huron-Wyandot

The Huron did not reveal their name, or maybe since they were not yet at this time a tribe of people, they did not have a name to share. It would take time for the three tribes to unite as one and identify as a tribe of people. Until this happened, their identity remained in their individual clans. By not expressing a name, other than what the French were calling them, they would not lose their new and very profitable trading relationship with the French. I have no doubt that many Oskenntonton converted to Catholicism to consummate this new relationship. The two tribes of the Tionontati tried to obtain a trading relationship with the French when they were sent as emissaries to the Huron-Wendat Confederacy by their parent confederacy, the Attiwandaronk. The four tribes of the Huron-Wendat Confederacy forbade this trading relationship. The tribes of the Attiwandaronk Confederacy no longer existed, with exception of the Oskenntonton, Hannaariskwa, and Wenroronon, and the tribes of the Huron-Wendat Confederacy had also been eliminated. Thus, the new *Huron* Tribe now had everything to themselves.

The Oskenntonton were likely more than content with being called *Huron*. It's also likely that the Wenroronon weren't so pleased with the name; however, they were not then in a position to contest much of anything. The Wenroronon had been weakened to the point where they were in much need of the mutual protection as given by the Oskenntonton, the Hannaariskwa, and the Ottawa. The Wenroronon grudgingly went along with the scam of pretending to be Huron-Wendat. Why weren't the Wenroronon pleased? Maybe they had suggested or initially contributed a name to this new tribe, and now it was just being tossed aside for something a little more grandiose. The Wenroronon were an unhappy bunch of Indians. Unhappiness can last only so long before something gives. In all actuality, their anger did give in, and the Wenroronon would venture out and defiantly call themselves Wyandot. In a radical turn of events, it would be the *Huron* who joined the Wyandot's newfound, yet reestablished, position of power and authority in the Ohio Country. At last the name Wyandot is beginning to have historical relevance.

In the late 1730s to early 1740s a division began to emerge within the political alliance that formed the *Huron* Tribe. Disenchanted bands began venturing south into the Ohio Country, which had been left vacant after the Iroquois Confederacy displaced or destroyed the original inhabitants. The Iroquois claimed the Ohio Country, and any tribe entering did so only with express permission. The bands of *Huron* who went into the Ohio Country shunned the name *Huron,* and they also initially shunned the French by seeking a trading relationship with the English. Oddly enough, at this time the *Huron* band that ventured into the Ohio Country was on very friendly terms with their ancient and deadly enemy, the Iroquois—primarily the Seneca Tribe. This rogue *Huron* band sought the unthinkable, that is, inclusion within the Iroquois Confederacy as an independent tribe. However, the Iroquois insisted upon adoption, and the *Huron,* who were now calling themselves Wyandot, said no!

Over the years I have come to believe that the band of the *Huron* who ventured into the Ohio Country were predominately descendants of the Wenroronon. Distancing themselves from their cousins, brothers, and sisters who remained in the vicinity of Detroit, they reclaimed their ancient name as Wandat along the Sandusky River. This is the name the English initially heard and transcribed as Wondot in September of 1745, or thereabouts. Now, in the Ohio Country the Wyandot began to forge a trading relationship with the Pennsylvanians.[59] Some historians want to say that the name they used was Wendat, which was incorrect. I have no doubt the name they expressed to the Pennsylvanians was Wandat which eventually came to be spelled as Wyandot.

In "Huron" John Hewitt lists seventy-eight different names for the Huron and Wyandot, but, unfortunately, in "Huron" John fails to differentiate the *Huron* Tribe from the Huron-Wendat Confederacy, and all the various names for each are intermixed. Two of the names listed are "Owandats" and "Wandats,'" both of which were referenced as recorded by Conrad Weiser in 1748.[60] Colonel Johann Conrad Weiser Jr. was Pennsylvania Dutch and led one of the first official expeditions for the English colonies west of the Appalachian Mountains into the Ohio Country. It was then that Conrad Weiser first heard and preserved two names—Wandat and Wondat. The name *Huron,* which had previously represented the Wenroronon, was about to be discarded by the English for their true ancient name—Wandat.

On September 6, 1748, Colonel Weiser noted in his journal, "Had a Council with the Wondats, otherways called Ionontady Hagas [an Iroquois name for the Wyandot], they made a fine speech to me to make me welcome, & appeared in the whole very friendly."[61] Two days later Weiser referenced the Wondats as the Owandaets.[62] Why? Was someone else translating that day, and this was his take on the name? What a mess the Wyandot's name truly has become because of situations such as this. Remember what Gordon Sayre said: "In practice the name depended more on the identity of the namer than of the named."

Wandat, sometimes spelled as Waⁿdat or Wandát, is the true traditional name for the Wyandot people. Dr. Charles Marius Barbeau has translated the name as "Villagers."[63] Dr. Bruce L. Pearson, who served as tribal linguist for the Wyandotte Nation for nearly twenty years, stated, "The name, sometimes given Wyandot or Wendat, actually comes from Wandat, the term used for both the people and the language. The name, commonly translated as "the people," comes from the third person prefix *wa-* ('they') and the root *-(n)dat(a)-* from earlier *-nat(a)-,* meaning to have a village or settlement. It is frequently translated as "the villagers."[64]

Wandat, now Wyandot, is the name the *Huron* band called themselves upon moving into the Ohio Country; however, it was not a new name. They just made it up for the occasion. They had undoubtedly known themselves by this name for a long, long time. Yes, Wandat was initially transcribed by the English and recorded as Wondot, Wondat, and Owandaet, along with many other different spellings. The English were listening and made a lot of mistakes, but we need to give them credit, for at least they were trying to get the name right. I have no doubt the name Wandat originated within the people who continued to identify themselves as Wenroronon. Why? James A. Clifton in *The Reemergent Wyandot,* explained things this way:

> Since we know that the ancestral Petuns were organized in two great localized divisions, the Deer and Wolf phratries, and because we know, in comparison to the fragmented Huron experience as refugees after 1649, that the Petuns migrated west as a more intact society, it seems evident that after 1653 or so the surviving Hurons [Wenroronon] were incorporated into the Petun system as a separate phratry, the Turtles, with their subdivisions identified by place— likely village—names rather than totemic eponyms.[65]

The Turtles, who were the Wenroronon, possibly still mixed with a few Attignawantan, who were also Turtles. Dr. Barbeau indicated that the name Wandat translates as "the Villagers." Clifton had just stated that the Turtles likely identified themselves as belonging to a place, likely a Village. I choose to believe that the name translates as the Villagers, for the name was clearly defined by practice pre- and postdispersal. Both the Tionontati and Wenroronon originated within the Attiwandaronk, or Neutral Confederacy. Charles Garrad in "The Petun and Paired Villages" discusses the recurring pattern of a Village, which belonged to one of the tribes of the Attiwandaronk Confederacy, having its smaller satellite villages. This practice continued in Ohio, as there were a number of larger Wyandot villages surrounded by smaller villages often inhabited by single-family units who identified themselves as belonging to a single clan. The Wyandot did not put all of their resources in one place; they spread it around in many smaller satellite villages that varied in distances from the parent village. Each one of these satellite villages had its own village chief. The village was an important cultural identity marker for the *Huron*-Wyandot people. Therefore, it is not only appropriate to believe that the Wenroronon called themselves the Villagers; it is also appropriate to believe that the Tionontati could have called themselves by a variation of this same name.

As we have seen, there are some strong and credible references to the name Wandat as early, or maybe it is best said as late, as 1748. I have no doubt the name is a most ancient name that somehow failed to be recorded by the French, Dutch, or English until about this time. Dr. Charles Marius Barbeau obtained some of the most compelling evidence while visiting the Oklahoma Wyandotte during 1911 and 1912. Dr. Barbeau recorded the traditional name as told to him by the elders—the last living link to the old ways of the Wyandots. The Wyandottes name was recorded as Wandát. Why should we doubt the elders?

As we have seen, Wyandot is an English corruption of Wandat. One of the first printed references to the name Wyandot can be found in J. Hinton's 1761 edition of "An Accurate Map of Canada." On this map the name is spelled as Winandot. This undoubtedly was one of those early attempts to properly translate the sound of Wandot. Historically, Wyandot is the most recognized and used spelling of the Wyandot Tribe's name, but there are many variations of the spelling.

The name Wyandot, or one of its many various spellings, was not recognized and written on paper until the mid-eighteenth century. Bruce Trigger, like James A. Clifton, indicates it was the Pennsylvanians, namely, Conrad Weiser, who first documented and began calling the *Huron* "Wyandot."[66] After the name went through a series of noted spelling variations, it was finally established as Wyandot somewhere and maybe as late as the 1760s or early 1770s. This is absolutely amazing! Does this make the Wyandot's name an ancient name as indicated by Henry Schoolcraft? Yes, it could indeed be a most ancient name, but not in the context by which Schoolcraft chose to use the name.

From time to time you will see Wyandot spelled with a double t—Wyandott. To my knowledge the Wyandot Tribe has never officially used this spelling to represent the tribe. For a brief time in the mid-nineteenth century this spelling appeared and may have been influenced by William Walker Jr. Much of William's correspondence and personal writings show that when he referenced the tribe, he used Wyandott. Since William was elected and served as the Provisional Governor of Nebraska Territory, his influence would have been quite strong. In addition, William was often alluded to as being the tribal historian. During this same time The Reverend James B. Finley used the spelling of the name Wyandott in his *History of the Wyandott Mission,* as did Peter Dooyentate Clarke in his *Origin and Traditional History of the Wyandotts,* both contemporaries of William Walker Jr.

Kansas officially became a territory of the United States on May 30, 1854. After signing the Treaty of 1855, the Wyandot Purchase was quickly allotted to tribal citizens. As the territory progressed into obtaining statehood, the various counties were established, with Wyandott County, Kansas, being one in 1859. Many old maps from this era show the new name for the county spelled as Wyandott. In 1857 Wyandott City was officially established, and the village quickly became a thriving little boomtown. In 1886 Wyandott City, Kansas City, and the city of Armourdale gave up their individuality and merged into one city while retaining the name Kansas City, Kansas.

In references to Wyandott County and Wyandott City, it appears that not many official rules were honored or enforced. Throughout the era there were many conflicting uses of the names Wyandott and Wyandotte; however, one spelling that does not appear in the record, or at least not very often, is Wyandot County or Wyandot City. The spelling, and its many contradictions, are a continuation of the age-old Wyandot problem—the spelling of the name and its proper usage.

"Wyandotte" has its origin as a variation of Wyandot with a French twist and flair—Guyandotte.[67] You can almost hear a French diplomat saying Guyandotte—Wyandotte—as the name rolls off the tip of his tongue. However, today the name is pronounced no differently than "Wyandot" is—the extra t and e are silent. One of the first places the spelling was seen in print is the 1807 treaty with the Ottawa. The spelling of the name appears again in 1867 in a treaty with the Seneca, Mixed Seneca and Shawnee, and Quapaw. It was then the US government reinstated the Wyandot as a federally recognized tribe comprising citizens who did not wish to retain their US citizenship as given in the Treaty of 1855. As a reward for being Refugee Indians and supporters of the Union cause during the Civil War, the Wyandotte Tribe was reinstated after the Treaty of 1855 terminated the historic Wyandot Tribe.

As designated in the Treaty of 1867, land was purchased from the Seneca Tribe in Indian Territory, and the Wyandots, who had moved from Kansas and elsewhere, were adopted back into the reinstated and reorganized Wyandotte Tribe. This spelling of the name gave separation and differentiation from the Citizen or Absentee Wyandots who chose, or who experienced unfortunate circumstance, to retain their US citizenship in lieu of seeking adoption back into the Wyandotte Tribe.

The Oklahoma Indian Welfare Act of 1936 required that a new constitution be written for the Wyandotte Tribe. In the Constitution of 1937 the tribe's name was again changed with a geographical designation, the Wyandotte Tribe of Oklahoma. In the late twentieth century, as the tribe grew under the leadership of Chief Leaford Bearskin, self-governance was obtained. The tribe's relationship with the US government and the state of Oklahoma became more complex and demanding. This great complexity again necessitated that additional considerations be given to the name. A new constitution was adopted in 1999, and today the Wyandotte in Oklahoma are simply known as the Wyandotte Nation. All geographical references have been dropped. The Wyandotte Nation is the only federally recognized band of Wyandots. The other two bands of Wyandots are the Wyandot of Anderdon Nation, or Canadian Wyandot; and the Wyandot Nation of Kansas, historically known as the Citizen, or Absentee, Wyandot.

Children of the Bad Twin

Many people seem to believe that all the Indians upon the Great Island are the same. Not even close! Even though many tribes share similar cultures, they have fundamental differences that cannot be easily explained or ignored. Before the bad children of the Bad Twin were found upon the Great Island, all the different tribes had settled into their respective areas. Who were the tribes? What were their names? What were they like? There is no way to adequately answer these questions in this book because time and space will not permit me to do so. It is not wise or historically possible to singly present the history of the *Huron*-Wyandot people, or any tribe of the Great Lakes Region, without mentioning the other tribes. Many of their histories and relationships were so entwined that it would be painful to try to differentiate them one from another.

After the Europeans established contact, their written documents and records of the various tribes did not make sorting and separating the tribes any easier. There was still much speculation about who some of these tribes were, where they came from, where they went, and who they eventually became. There were and are still today hundreds of Indian tribes spread throughout the Great Island. At this moment we are concerned with just a few who lived in the Great Lakes Region in the sixteenth and seventeenth centuries. When you begin reading about the Indians of the Great Lakes Region, you quickly realize there was a lot of interaction, some good and some bad, between the various tribes. Their relationships were made exponentially more complex when the children of the Bad Twin—French, Dutch, English, Spanish, Russian, and so on—were found upon the Great Island. There was fighting among the various tribes, but fighting and all-out war among the tribes may not have always been commonplace. Fighting and disagreements may have been more commonly found among smaller groups such as individual clans, family groups, or groups of individuals acting outside any governing body.

On many occasions disagreements and fighting did not take place at the tribal level. Disagreements usually sought revenge for a death; however, those with disagreements too often sought captives for the purposes of torture or of adoption of members of the other tribe to replace losses within their own clans. A warrior could also obtain his status and prestige by taking the life of a worthy combatant. Before the arrival of the Europeans, unless there was a need to expand hunting grounds for the procurement of food, there appear to be few motives for conquest of territory; and blood feuds at the tribal level were generally not bent on extermination or genocide. When one person was killed, another of the opposing combatants now had to pay with his life. The cycle was almost never-ending but very rarely erupted into an all-out war with the displacement or disappearance of an entire tribe or people group. However, the St. Lawrence Iroquoians, a group of related people, completely disappeared shortly after the arrival of the Europeans. No one knows for sure what happened or where they went. Their existence upon the Great Island was completely erased, and not by the hands of the Europeans.

The *Huron*-Wyandot have two stories that may explain how blood feuds, skirmishes, and wars may have been started upon the Great Island. One of the stories was recorded in 1822 at Detroit, and the second in 1827 at Upper Sandusky. Both oral traditions detail a blood feud that turned into a brutal war between the Wyandot and the Seneca.[68, 69] The storytellers use the name Wyandot in the narrative, and I will continue the tradition. At the time of this tale the Wyandot did not technically and historically exist. The Wyandot and Seneca are said to have been very close friends before the war and lived next to each other on the banks of Lake Ontario—but maybe this is a narrative of the Wenroronon and the Seneca. The war between the Seneca and the Wyandot turned out to be a long, complicated, and costly war that started several years before the arrival of the Europeans in the first quarter of the sixteenth century. For the Wyandots this narrative may have explained how the Wenroronon migrated to the Nottawassaga Bay of Lake Huron. Archaeologists believe the Wenroronon and Tionontati were relative newcomers to the area shortly before their dispersal in 1652. Gary Warrick indicates that their presence may have been a meager thirty years or less.[70] Charles Garrad agrees it had been a recent migration but says it lasted a little longer than thirty years. Charles explains the geopolitical circumstances and the ensuing game of chess that dictated as to why and how the Tionontati came to call the hills east of Georgian Bay along the Niagara Escarpment their traditional homeland. As Charles explains,

> The Neutrals wanted trade goods but could not go directly themselves up Lake Ontario and the St. Lawrence because the south side of the lake and river was occupied by tribes enforcing the Great Peace ("Iroquois"). So they had to reach the French overland via other tribes en route. The Rock [Arendaronon], then in the Trent River Valley, could supply the French goods in return for beaver. So c. 1575 the first Neutral tribe, the Wolf, moved to a point well south of Nottawasaga Bay where it could trade with the Rock in one direction, and the Neutral tribes (possibly ten) in the other. When the Rock moved to Huronia closer to the Bear ca.1580 the political/trade system began to change until eventually the Bear took over. The Neutral response was to send a second tribe, the Deer, to settle nearer to Nottawasaga Bay north of the Wolf, closer to the Bear (they could see each other's territories across the Bay). Their archaeological sites give a date of ca. 1600 for the development. The Huron collectively called the two tribes the Tionontati. They dispersed [in]1650. So the Wolf were in Tionontati country perhaps 75 years, and the Deer 50.[71]

In the early nineteenth century the Wyandots were not concerned with archaeological evidence to explain their movements. They had their oral traditions and memories, some of which were ancient, some newer in origin. The following narrative appears to be one of the newer stories. It has a Wyandot woman as its central character; she is said to have been beautiful and to have started a war. All the men of her longhouse wanted her as their mate, but she was not inclined to be anyone's mate. The young woman did not reject their offers, but neither did she accept them. She remained stubborn and all but ignored their proposals. The young men finally gave up and went to the war chief of their longhouse to settle their despair. The rejected young men proposed that their chief seek the hand of the young beautiful maiden himself. They pledged him their loyal assistance in his endeavor with no less fervor than if they were following him into war. The war chief accepted their offer to try and obtain the beautiful maiden as his mate with great hesitation, as he was a fighter not a lover. The chief painted and then dressed himself for the purpose of trying to impress his quarry. However, he was not fully committed to the scheme—especially a strategic battle to gain the favor of a woman. For several days the chief tried different plans and strategies until, surprisingly, the young beautiful maiden accepted his proposal to be his mate. However, she continued to remain obstinate until one of her conditions was agreed upon and fulfilled. This one condition she would not divulge until he swore on his reputation and honor as one of the finest warriors of the Wyandot to do her bidding. Again with great hesitation and the coaxing of the young men of his lodge, the chief eventually succumbed to her beauty and accepted his fate, not knowing what his fleeting challenge was. Swearing to fall upon the vengeance of hawędížuʔ (*God, or the Almighty*), and the persecution of dehšurunǫ (*the devil, or wicked one*), the chief cast his lot. It was then she told him his fate. She requested that he kill a Seneca war chief she despised and bring his scalp to her. She indicated she had lost her brother to the Seneca war chief; therefore, she was now alone and demanded revenge.

The Seneca war chief she sentenced to death was the best friend of the Wyandot war chief. They had grown up together and were inseparable. Unwilling to do her bidding, the chief asked for the forgiveness of his pledge. The young maiden would not accept his plea and forgive his pledge. She threatened to cast him as a coward and a man of dishonor to all the Wyandot people if he did not fulfill his commission. The chief had no choice in the matter; he had to fulfill his pledge no matter what the cost. Infuriated by what he had to do, the war chief blackened his face and entered the Seneca village. Entering the lodge of his best friend, he tomahawked and scalped him in front of his family, whom he knew all too well. After identifying himself to the Seneca, enraged as though he was inflicting vengeful justice upon his devious mate, he entered the fight, and many Seneca warriors were killed. The Seneca, bent on revenge, dispensed a war party to the village of the Wyandot to uphold the honor of their murdered war chief.

The Wyandot initially suffered greatly at the hands of the Seneca. The young woman who started the war was mercilessly killed, as were many others under the tomahawk and scalping knife of the Seneca. Fleeing the eastern banks of Lake Ontario, where they had lived for so long, the Wyandot are said to have briefly lived in the vicinity of Toronto before eventually settling on the eastern shore of Nottawassaga Bay. There the attacks of the Seneca slowly diminished, but they never ceased. The blood feud turned into a war unlike any other experienced upon the Great Island as the warriors hunted each other as wild animals of the forest. Eventually the Wyandot gained the advantage in the war, and the Seneca sued for peace.

During the interview at Detroit when Henry Schoolcraft asked Charlo, a chief of the *Huron*-Wyandot, how the Wyandot could have been so soundly defeated and driven from their homeland by the Seneca, Charlo answered, "The Wyandots were proud. God had said that such should be beaten and brought low. This is the cause why we were followed from the east, and went up north away to Michilimackinac, but as we had the right before, so when we came back, the tribes looked up to us, as holding the council fire."[72]

Charlo's response to Schoolcraft not only answered his question but also gave confirmation of and insights into the events and migrations of the Wyandot. What remains unclear is when and from where the dispersal occurred. Were the Wyandot driven from their homelands in southern Ontario, or was it possibly Upstate New York? During this interview, and in a very rare account as given by a Wyandot chief, Charlo's response also confirmed that the Wyandot were Keepers of the Council Fire for the Lakes Confederacy. This confederacy, consisting of the Wyandot, Ottawa, Chippewa, and Potawatomi, successfully defeated the onslaught of the Iroquois Confederacy. Among the Iroquois Confederacy, the keepers of their council fire were the Onondaga.

Remember the children of the Bad Twin? How can we forget them? They are about to be found—again—upon the Great Island, and things are going to get messy really fast. Knowing this, we are again going to take the advice of James V. Wright and make the complex appear simple. We now have all of the tribes in their various places upon the Great Island and the year is 1534. Some Micmac and Huron-Iroquois have just seen some very unusual animals swimming on the distant horizon of the great sea, and they are coming this way.

When the children of the Bad Twin—*the Europeans*—were found on the Great Island, there were not many, and initially they did not prove to be a threat to the children of the Good Twin—*the Indians.* Many believe the first Europeans found by the Indians on the Great Island were the Vikings, but that is a totally different narrative from what we are now concerned with telling. Our narrative first tells of the arrival of the French; however, the Dutch, English, and Spanish were also found on the Great Island. I do not want to spend much time discussing the Europeans, but we have little choice—it must be done. If we completely skip or overly minimize their presence on the Great Island, not telling about their early activities would leave such a gaping hole in this narrative that what eventually follows would make little sense. If it were not for the coming of Europeans, the Indians would have continued to advance in their cultures and presence upon the Great Island. Over time, likely a long period of time, their cultures would have continued to mature, morph, and merge. Undoubtedly, there would have been a lot of change.

The Europeans came to North America for several reasons, but their primary reasons were their quests for wealth and freedom. By this time in Europe the governments were tapped of funds, the people were oppressed, technology was exploding, the plague was diminishing, and conflicts between the various countries were ongoing with no apparent peace in sight. Something had to give. The Spanish were the first to arrive in the New World. We all know Christopher Columbus's story and his discovery of the New World in 1492. It was such a momentous day in history that we celebrate the discovery of the New World annually on Columbus Day—*yeah, right!* The discovery of the New World was inevitable, and we could easily be celebrating Hudson Day or Cartier Day. Whatever the case, Columbus set foot on an island, but it was not the Great Island, and it was a long way away from where our narrative is taking place. The problem is that Columbus's success was inspirational to other Europeans.

Many of the European kings and queens wanted their share of the New World. As they sent forth their emissaries and explorers, they naturally and unknowingly brought all their troubles along with them. Some of their troubles were in the form of diseases. The virgin-soil epidemics that burst across the Great Island were as devastating to the Indians as the Black Death was to the Europeans. The coming plague of people and pestilence upon the Indians in the Great Lakes Region alone would kill more Indians than anyone can begin to count. Gary Warrick indicates one theory of what led to depopulation of the tribes: It could have been widespread, starting around 1519 and quickly progressing. A second proposed theory is that depopulation was localized and occurred only after the Indians maintained contact with the Europeans.[73] How

many Indians died? No one knows. The carnage from the diseases was horrific. Bruce Trigger states, "The Algonkin were dying in such numbers that
the living were unable to bury the dead, whose bodies were eaten by dogs."[74]
It is believed that once the epidemics had subsided, all the tribes had suffered
nearly equal losses. Eventually, the diseases would lie relatively dormant; however, the pestilence of people persisted and ever increased.

First contact by the Indians with the Europeans upon the Great Island,
excluding the Vikings, took place along the gulf of the St. Lawrence River in
1534. The Indians found Jacques Cartier, a French explorer. Yes, the Indians
found Cartier—Cartier did not find the Indians. Cartier was conducting a
quick assessment of the gulf, after which he promptly returned to France with
two Huron-Iroquois captives as gifts for his king.[75] The next year Cartier
returned, and, with the aid of his two Indian captives, sailed down the St.
Lawrence River where he made contact with the residents of Stadacona and
Hochelaga, two large, fortified, and prosperous Indian villages. Who were the
residents of Stadacona and Hochelaga? No one knows for sure; therefore, they
are simply known today as the St. Lawrence Iroquoians.

Troubles in France ceased all meaningful expeditions financed by the
crown, and very little exploratory progress of the New World took place for
nearly fifty years. However, by 1580 professional fur traders had established
trade with the Indians, and European trade goods were beginning to make
their way into the interior of the Great Lakes Region.[76] It wasn't until the
arrival of Samuel de Champlain in 1603 that organized expeditions to explore
New France resumed. The same year Champlain ventured to Stadacona and
Hochelaga to find the two villages abandoned and all but destroyed. The
destruction of the two villages and the dispersal of their residents could possibly be the first casualties of the virgin-soil epidemics, or evidence of the
forthcoming wars for control of the fur trade and economic wealth among the
Indians.[77] Champlain officially founded New France and Quebec City in July
of 1608, whereas Champlain built the small village of Quebec in the general
vicinity of where Stadacona once stood. Hochelaga is now covered by the
modern, bustling city of Montreal.

The concept of economic wealth was foreign to the Great Island prior to
the coming of the Europeans. Bruce Trigger eloquently describes the moti-
vation of the Iroquois people prior to the arrival of the Europeans: "The
Iroquoians believed that no community member should go hungry or lack
necessities while others had more than they needed. The principal motive for

accumulating surplus food stuff and obtaining rare goods from other groups was to be able to give them away to fellow tribesmen."[78]

According to Trigger, the very essence of this social concept did not change; however, it was stressed and tested and went through a radical metamorphic change. Eventually and quickly, greed, power, jealousy, and the need for confederated protection went viral in the Great Lakes Region, seemingly overnight. The complexion of the Great Island was changing from the status quo that had existed for centuries. Once the tribes were routed and dispersed, they had no choice but to revert to the power of community in order to survive.

Before the arrival of the Europeans, blood feuds and skirmishes had been fought hand to hand and face to face by the various tribes—the fighting would have been simply brutal. Clubs, bows and arrows, and knives made of stone or bone were the main implements of war. Both Huron and Iroquois warriors wore body armor made of wood planks. This technology was made obsolete overnight when Dutch traders began selling and trading guns to the Iroquois. The French refused to do the same with their Huron allies unless they were Christians, and only then a small number of converts received the very expensive reward.[79]

The moment the Dutch began selling the Iroquois guns, the balance of power between the tribes that had existed since the Creation of the Great Island was kicked off axis and tossed into a spiraling spin. Alliances between the tribes were formed to better protect themselves from neighboring tribes. Tribes also began uniting into confederacies, combining their individual resources while retaining their unique tribal identities. Fighting for territorial control within the Great Lakes Region erupted and intensified, all over the procurement of beaver pelts—or so we are led to believe. The fur of the mighty beaver was as good as gold, and the Beaver Wars were now in full atomic mass. All the tribes of the Huron and Iroquois Confederacies quickly depleted their supply of beavers within their traditional hunting grounds and territories. The need to acquire more beaver pelts, in order to obtain more French and Dutch goods, sent raiding parties into the territories of the opposing tribes. Total annihilation of villages and their inhabitants was now becoming a common and accepted practice.

As the Beaver Wars, or properly named French and Iroquois wars, intensified, bands, segments of tribes, and whole tribes were displaced. From these displaced tribes many refugees sought adoption into the tribes of the Huron, Tionontati, and their Algonquin neighbors. Whole tribes disappeared from the Great Island and the historical record. Many citizens of the displaced

tribes were taken captive and forcefully adopted into the tribes of the Iroquois to replace their losses incurred by the war. The Wenroronon, one of
the first casualties of the Beaver Wars, were displaced from their traditional
homeland in Western New York in 1638 after the Attiwandaronk Confederacy
recanted their alliance of mutual aide from and protection against the Iroquois
Confederacy.

Wenroronon

The Wenroronon, a favored child of the Good Twin, had the unfortunate
and deadly fate of being next-door neighbors to the Seneca. Interesting. This
sounds a little reminiscent of the tale we told a few moments ago when the
Great War erupted over a beautiful woman and her evil request. Could it
truly be that the Wenroronon are indeed the Wyandot? Even without a lot
of archaeological evidence, it is generally accepted that the Wenroronon were
initially very close neighbors to the Seneca, and they were one of the first
casualties of the Beaver Wars.

Very little is known of the Wenroronon prior to the dispersal from their
original homeland. Their name as given by the Huron, "*Oneronon*" (and other
various spellings), has traditionally been translated as "*People of the Place of
Floating Scum.*"[80] Recently, John Steckley proposed that the name translates as
"*moss-backed turtle*" people.[81] The original translation of the name is suggested
to reference an oil spring in the vicinity of Cuba, New York, which is believed
to have been within the Wenroronon's traditional homeland. Steckley's proposed name is derived from material collected by Charles Marius Barbeau
from 1911 to 1912 in Oklahoma. There Barbeau discovered that the name for
the Big Turtle clan was the "moss-back turtle." Steckley continued by stating,
"The 'moss-back turtle' people are known in the historical literature as the
Wenro." This is yet another compelling argument, and a much more scientific
one, for the Wenroronon to be the Wyandot people. The actual name the
Wenroronon called themselves is unknown; however, I have proposed their
traditional name *may* have been "Wandat," or its traditional spelling today of
Wyandot.

The Wenroronon's original homeland has never been officially confirmed
by archaeological evidence. They are said to have lived east of the Attiwandaronk and beyond the Erieehronon.[82] This would place them on the southern
side of Lake Ontario somewhere west of the Seneca. It would also place them

close to Niagara Falls, which is said to be the home of Henǫ. The ancestors of the Wyandots believed the roar of the falls was the thunderous voice of Henǫ.

The dispersal and travels of the Wenroronon have been followed through archaeological evidence, primarily through a style of pottery named Genoa Frilled. In 1973 archaeologist Frank Ridley first observed this type of New York pottery in Ontario and collated it with the known distribution of the Wenroronon refugees among the Attignawantan. Later archaeological evidence has found the same style of pottery in two predispersal villages of the Tionontati.[83] The pottery style has also been noted on Rock Island in the Green Bay of Wisconsin, where the Wenroronon, Tionontati, and Ottawa refugees are known to have resided for a brief time in their westward migrations.[84] Evidence of Genoa Frilled pottery in Ontario has been generally accepted by many archaeologists to be Wenroronon; however, not everyone agrees. Dr. Alicia Hawkins, anthropological archaeologist at Laurentian University, recently stated, "At this time, the issue of the identity of the makers of frilled pottery in Huronia remains unresolved. A plausible argument can be made for production by Wenro refugees, the main shortcoming being that we have not identified their homeland on the basis of appropriate pottery types."[85]

Two theories exist as to the causing agent of the Wenroronon's dispersal from their homeland—for all we know it could have been the beautiful woman. After their dispersal, and upon their arrival in Huronia, the Wenroronon refugees were noted as being "ill from the epidemic which was primarily the occasion of their flight."[86] It is believed that the Wenroronon may have been displaced due to a severe epidemic of smallpox in their country. Possibly at this time the other tribes of the Attiwandaronk Confederacy withdrew their warriors from the Wenroronon because they did not want to catch the pox. Often referred to as Neutrals, the Wenroronon were once a part of the larger Attiwandaronk Confederacy. Some historians speculate that this confederacy could have comprised up to ten different tribes, or lesser bands. The Wenroronon are believed to have been one of the larger and stronger tribes of the Attiwandaronk. If allied warriors were withdrawn from the Wenroronon's homeland, it could have opened and weakened the Wenroronon for a direct attack from the Iroquois Confederacy.

A second theory is that the Seneca were in need of fresh land to trap more beaver, and the marshy lands of the Wenroronon were known to be rich with them.[87] The Wenroronon may have been dispersed for territorial gain. In the process people were acquired for adoption to replace Seneca losses. Whatever the cause of their dispersal—a woman, an epidemic, a conquest, or a combination of all the above—really doesn't matter. What is important is that the refugees from the Wenroronon sought the permission of the Huron-Wendat for inclusion into the Attignawantan Tribe. Permission was granted, and approximately 600 Wenroronon settled in Ossossané, the largest village of the Attignawantan, and in a few of their lesser villages.[88] Charles Garrad indicates that the process was relatively easy because the Attignawantan included a clan segment of Turtles, and the Wenroronon were also Turtles. They would have viewed each other as family and essentially absorbed, or universally adopted, each other as one. The remaining Wenroronon who did not make the trek to seek adoption into the Attignawantan were either killed or adopted into the Seneca, or they found protection and adoption within the various tribes of the Attiwandaronk.

Before the Wenroronon left their homeland, the Huron sent a delegation of warriors to assist them and to provide protection from the Iroquois during their migration. Many of those making the migration were women and children, and due to fatigue and hardships many died during the trek of about two hundred forty miles through Canadian wilderness. Arriving ill and fatigued in Ossossané, the Wenroronon would have initially been a heavy burden upon the Attignawantan; however, they were received as family, and the Jesuits were noted to have stopped all their activities to assist in caring for the sick. As the Jesuits assisted in providing care, they noted that "wherever they were received, the best places in the cabins were assigned them, the granaries or caches of corn were opened, and they were given liberty to make such use of it as their needs required."[89] The Wenroronon were clan family, and the Attignawantan received them with no limitations.

The Attignawantan's investment proved more than worthwhile. Father Paul Le Jeune described the Wenroronon as "those strangers who recently arrived in this country," but to the Attignawantan they were no strangers. Father Le Jeune continued by saying that they "excel in drawing out an arrow from the body and in curing the wound, but . . . the efficacy of the prescription avails only in the presence of a pregnant woman."[90] What in the world could a pregnant woman have to do with the removal of an arrow? I found this very interesting. The Wenroronon medicine men would prove to be an invaluable asset to the Attignawantan, and to the Huron in whole, during the war with the Iroquois.

The migration and absorption of the Wenroronon into the Attignawantan was well documented by the Jesuit missionaries. Even after absorption into the Attignawantan, the Wenroronon must have retained the knowledge of their original tribal identity, when a short twelve years later they again sought asylum among the Tionontati after the Attignawantan disintegrated from the exerted pressure placed upon them by the Iroquois Confederacy.

A few of their adopted brothers and sisters from the Attignawantan likely stayed with them as they fled with the Tionontati into exile in 1652. At that moment in time everything in the homelands was nothing less than a state of chaos. Boundaries between the various Huron tribes had been shattered, and the mix-up is obvious.

The majority of the Attignawantan are believed to have moved with the Jesuits to Christian Island for one last stand against the Iroquois. That stand failed, and a majority of the surviving Attignawantan were adopted into the Mohawk. After the fall of the Attiwandaronk Confederacy in 1652 the Tionontati, Wenroronon, and fragments from various tribes fled west to Michilimackinac, where they obtained asylum among their Algonquin friends and allies. In spite of the Jesuits' tedious documentation, no such documentation exists for this new amalgamation's initial flight west. What sense we can glean from it today is anyone's best guess. What really happened? Who knows? Dr. Hawkins states it best: "It is a truism to state that relations among Iroquoian groups in the seventeenth century were complex."[91] Yes, they were complex then, and they remain complex to this very day.

The Huron-Wendat's Confederacy proved a difficult and cumbersome arrangement for the four tribes, as explained by Bruce Trigger. "The Iroquoians valued self-reliance. Every person prized his or her independence and resented being given orders: hence chiefs, having to rely on public opinion to support general policy, had to consider the wishes of their people carefully before proposing a particular course of action."[92] This personal and individual trait of self-reliance was powerful and noble, but unfortunately it would prove detrimental to the political and military unification of the Huron Confederacy.

The Iroquois Confederacy had no such issues. The individual tribes of the Huron manifested similar characteristics; for example, they too prized their independence. Then why commit to the confederacy? Could the tribes have committed to the confederacy for personal economic reasons rather than for the contribution of resources for the whole and good of the confederacy? Though a confederacy, and still quite powerful amid their faults, each tribe of the Huron too often acted independently and paid the consequences against a united and inseparable Iroquois. Throw in a little religious intolerance between the dividing factions of Christianity and the traditional Huron religions or way of life, and the Huron-Wendat Confederacy was doomed. They could not act or react as a cohesive unit, and when the attacks of the Iroquois intensified, the confederacy seemingly crumbled overnight.

The Iroquois were also a confederacy of five Iroquoian-speaking tribes who lived south of the St. Lawrence River and the Great Lakes. The five tribes of the Iroquois are Seneca, Cayuga, Onondaga, Oneida, and Mohawk. "The Algonquian allies of the French called the Huron and the Iroquois tribes Nadowek, 'adders,' and *Iri^n khowek*, 'real serpents,' hence, 'bitter enemies.' The singular *Iri^n kowi,* with the French suffix -ois, has become the familiar 'Iroquois.'"[93] The Iroquois called themselves Haudenosaunee, meaning *"people of the longhouse."* I am not going to get into a long discussion of the Iroquois Confederacy, as they, other than antagonists, have no other immediate role in this narrative. Always remain cognizant of the fact the Iroquois were and are still today a marvelous people. Their confederacy, a true form of democracy, is one of the oldest on Earth. The traditional date for the formation of their confederacy has been in the mid-fifteenth century, the same as for the Huron-Wendat. New theories are proposing that the confederacy could be much older than originally thought, going back to as early as the mid-twelfth century.[94]

The histories of the Huron-Wendat and Iroquois Confederacies are so entwined that a study of their extended relationship would be a complex and difficult task. Long after the destruction of the Huron-Wendat Confederacy, the Iroquois Confederacy remained a dominant and decisive force upon the North American continent. The unity of the Iroquois, their cultural stability, and their military force are arguably unparalleled by those of any other tribe or tribes upon the Great Island. It wasn't until another confederacy came along that their power base was toppled—the thirteen colonies of the United States of America. Francis Parkman in *The Conspiracy of Pontiac* gives a good narrative of the Iroquois mindset that thrust them into being a preeminent power upon the Great Island. Parkman stated, "Their war-parties roamed over half America, and their name was a terror from the Atlantic to the Mississippi. . . . We stand amazed at the folly and dissension which left so vast a region the prey of a handful of bold marauders."[95]

As war between the two powerful confederacies erupted, and all the other tribes found themselves caught in the middle, a second and no less devastating war ensued. In the middle of the war to obtain territorial control to feed the vicious and voluptuous appetite for beaver, a war of cultural and religious intolerance was also being pursued within the Huron. With the arrival of the Recollects and Jesuits in New France, our narrative takes a decisive turn from which there can be no return. Because the Recollects and Jesuits spread Catholicism, traditional ways of life quickly came into direct conflict with Catholicism. There were a relatively large number of Catholic converts among the Huron, and very few if any among the Iroquois. As the Huron fought the Iroquois externally, they also fought themselves internally.

The Recollects, and especially the Jesuits, were driven by the need to obtain Indian converts—at all cost. The heathen Indians were dying and going to hell by the droves. Baptizing them into Catholicism was the only way to save their poor, unfortunate, and ignorant souls. All of this was taking place right in the middle of the war for economic superiority and conquest of territory. What the Jesuits did with the tribes was both very bad and very good. What did they do that could have ever been considered good for the Indians? Not much, but their writings contained within *The Jesuit Relations* is the definitive cultural and historical resource by which we know these tribes today. Their preservation of the various histories and cultures—and, yes, while you learn you will need to tiptoe through the land mines of intolerance and flamboyant propaganda—is an irreplaceable treasure. In spite of the actions of the Jesuits, and the many Indians who died at their hands, their writings are beyond valuable. Bruce Trigger in "The Liberation of Wendake" states, "Thanks to Champlain, Sagard, and Jesuit missionaries, the Wendats are the best documented aboriginal society that lived north of Mexico prior to the second half of the seventeenth century."[96]

Often called Black Robes, because of their ever-present full-length black robes, or cassocks, the Jesuits arrived in New France in 1611 but did not initially engage in missionary work. The Recollects arrived in 1615 and quickly established their first mission among the Huron that same year. The Recollects next established a mission among the Tionontati in 1616; however, that mission was quickly abandoned. They too established a mission among the Attiwandaronk in 1626. By 1632 the Recollects' work and resources in New France were tapped, and they were way over their heads. In 1634 the Recollects requested that the Jesuits take over all their missionary efforts within the Huron Mission. Charles Garrad indicates that the name Huron Mission is a term collectively applied to all the Ontario missions in New France from 1615 to 1650: Huron, Tionontati, Attiwandaronk, Algonquin, and so on.[97] After 1634, work among the various tribes and their missions was exclusively a Jesuit endeavor.

The Jesuits not only busied themselves in obtaining Catholic converts; they also by design possessed great governmental power. Upon their arrival in

New France, the Recollects forged an alliance with Champlain; however, the Jesuits circumvented Champlain's authority and took control of the highest echelons of the colonial administration in France itself.[98] In doing so, they obtained control of all the trade and the appointment of government officials, and they insured that no other religious entity could oppose or contest their work. What happened in New France, or traveled to New France, first had to pass through the Jesuits. Oppose them and pay the price.

Indian children, who were not yet fully "corrupted" with traditional beliefs, were identified by the Recollects as having the highest prospects for long-term conversion to Catholicism.[99] The Jesuits embraced this philosophy, and by 1635 one of their primary goals in the Huron Mission was to obtain the rights to Indian children. They believed that with just one or two years of instruction they could make a profound difference in the lives of the children; however, they first had to separate and isolate them from their parents. This was no easy task. It sounds very similar to the Indian policies of another country three hundred years later. It was proposed that the children be sent all the way to France or at least to Quebec.[100]

The Huron children were instructed in the ways of Catholicism, and they were taught to speak, read, and write French. The hope was to turn these children into little French boys and girls. Again. The French enticement of their plan was to exchange Indian children for French soldiers to defend the Huron against the marauding Iroquois.[101] Being a matrilineal society, the Jesuits had a difficult time accessing the right to the little girls. In addition, making the trip all the way to Quebec was a life-threatening proposition for the girls, in more ways than one. When all was said and done, very few children were actually sent to France and Quebec because it was more practical and feasible for them to be instructed at their mission churches located within their homelands.

Turning the Indian children into little French children and obtaining converts with baptisms were critically important to the Jesuits. A nationality calamity helped the Jesuits with this task when many Huron were baptized during the epidemics of 1636 and 1637. The act of baptism was believed by the Huron to be a healing practice, and many readily accepted baptism; however, of the survivors, many renounced their conversions once they recovered. Converts were also obtained by the Jesuits from Indians who wanted a deeper relationship with the French and the freedoms granted them as trading partners—just for accepting Catholicism.[102]

If the Huron had know how dependent the French were upon them, maybe more so than the Huron were upon the French, things may have been totally different in Huronia—and the Huron Mission. The French held a heavy hand over the Huron, indicating that if any harm ever befell the missionaries, they would leave and take their trading relationship elsewhere. If the Jesuits had fulfilled this threat and relieved the Huron of their trading relationship by taking it to the Tionontati or Attiwandaronk, the Huron-Wendat Confederacy could have been destroyed as quickly as the Iroquois Confederacy. The safety of the Jesuit missionaries was dependent not upon French military power but upon the power and value held over the Indians in the form of luxury items they obtained through trade. The Indians were addicted to French goods, and giving up the goods was not an option for a moment's consideration.

The Huron-Wendat initially repelled the Iroquois invasions; however, after the palisade walls were finally breached on March 16, 1649, many Huron-Wendats were indiscriminately slaughtered. After the destruction of the great Huron-Wendat village of St. Louis, the next day the Iroquois advanced deeper into the heart of Huronia and attacked the French fort and mission of St. Marie. There, all three hundred Huron warriors who had been sent to repel the attack were killed. It is estimated that during three battles over two days the Iroquois lost at least one-third of their army. With such a loss the Iroquois decided to withdraw to Iroquoia, for they were aware the Huron could amass an army and kill every last one of their warriors. Unknowing of the Iroquois retreat, the Huron, fearing another attack, scattered, essentially abandoning Huronia and leaving it a desolated and haunted country. The Iroquois had unknowingly accomplished a decisive victory and did not negotiate any terms of surrender. In the time it took the Huron to collect their personal belongings and flee, likely a matter of hours, the once-all-mighty Huron-Wendat Confederacy ceased to exist.

Keith Otterbein, author of "Huron vs. Iroquois: A Case Study in Inter-Tribal Warfare," stated, "I regard these battles of 1649 as being among the most important fought on this continent."[103] In 1649 the war did not end. The war continued to rage for another fifty-plus years, as the *Huron*-Wyandot became a primary target of the Iroquois Confederacy. Acquiescence, annihilation, and adoption were the only choices given the *Huron*-Wyandot by the five nations of the Iroquois Confederacy. The *Huron*-Wyandot chose the opposite—defiance, life, and freedom—and won the war!

CHAPTER 2

"They Act Like Foxes"

For they [*Hurons*] are malicious, intriguing, and evil-intentioned men, capable
of great undertakings; but fortunately their sword is too short. Nevertheless,
as they cannot play the part of lions, they act like foxes, and spare no effort
to embroil matters between us and our allies.[1]

—Sieur de Lamothe Cadillac, 1718

"People Are Dispersing in Every Direction"

In the early months of 1649 if you ran into a Huron-Wendat village and yelled,
"The Iroquois are coming," you may have been trampled to death as everyone
tried to get out of town. If the village had decided to stand and fight, you may
have been killed for inciting terror among the living. The same would have
been true of an Iroquois village if you had shouted, "The Huron are coming!"
The fear instilled in all villages north and south of the Great Lakes had everyone on edge, and nerves were nothing less than coiled springs of anxiety. Life
was anything but normal. Hope had become fleeting.

A long, horrible war had razed complete villages, and their inhabitants
were slaughtered or led away into captivity and adoption. Tribes were displaced
and many annihilated. However, today there is no accounting for many of the
various tribes that once existed. They were either destroyed or adopted into
other tribes, and their names lost in history.

A deadly balance of power had been established, and casualties were
mounting as neither the Huron-Wendat nor the Iroquois could find an advantage to defeat the other. Huron-Wendat and Iroquois military tactics had
slowly evolved to reflect European precepts of war: total defeat and unconditional annihilation with club, spear, arrow, stone, fire—and rifle. Wars with
savage brutality unlike any before upon the Great Island. The French often

stood on the sidelines unwilling or unable to help their extorted allies in New France—the many various tribes they called Huron. The war was seemingly unwinnable, yet neither the Huron-Wendat nor the Iroquois Confederacy was willing to accept defeat.

Everything changed when from March 16 to 19, 1649, an estimated 1,000 Iroquois warriors shattered the Huron-Wendat's will to stand and fight.[2] The event was a moment in history when decisions made within minutes or hours forever changed history. If only the Huron-Wendat had known the Iroquois were retreating back to Iroquoia, and if they had attacked them in their retreat, they could have routed and defeated them. The Huron-Wendat did not know the Iroquois were retreating; therefore, in fear, citizens of the Huron-Wendat Confederacy fled Huronia. The people left the land all but uninhabited for the unknowingly victorious Iroquois to quickly claim as their own.

After the fall of the mighty Huron-Wendat Confederacy, fear reigned and a state of chaos ensued. The vacuum left by the Huron-Wendat's demise was no less than an imploding black hole in the vastness of space. The Huron-Wendat's fall and the resulting shock waves were felt across the whole of the Great Island. "On the night of March 19, 1649, the Turtle-dominated people of Ossossane learned that the Iroquois enemy could be approaching. They abandoned Ossossane . . . and fled to the Petun."[3]

Father Ragueneau witnessed the dispersal: "The blows dealt by the Iroquois have filled the Huron land with consternation, and its people are dispersing in every direction."[4] He continued by describing the directions of their flight: "Fifteen villages have been abandoned by their inhabitants, who have fled some westward, to the Tobacco tribes; others to St. Joseph (Charity) Island in Georgian Bay; others still talk of going to the Manitoulin Islands."[5]

The first waves of shock and fear would have struck the Huron-Wendat's neighbors to the west, the Tionontati, with full force. Watching the Huron-Wendat's demise was an unimaginable nightmare. The Tionontati must have known that their turn to embrace the wrath of the Iroquois was quickly approaching. The first wave of weary Huron-Wendat refugees is believed to have crossed the frozen expanse of Nottawasaga Bay. Charles Garrad explained why he believes the majority if not all of the refugees, were Wenroronon.

The Iroquois invasion of Huronia in early 1649 provided the Wenros the opportunity to escape the control of the French and possibly to restore their national identity. On the night of March 18, 1649, fearing imminent attack by the Iroquois, the "Hurons" of Ossossane and district, both born and adopted, principally the "women, the children, and many centenarian old men," the male warriors being elsewhere, abandoned the village and overnight crossed on the ice of frozen Nottawasaga Bay to take refuge in the two Petun villages near the shore at the present Craigleith. With them travelled Father Chaumonot, representing the Mission of La Conception, at least one other Frenchman. Father Chaumonot and his Christian followers stayed with the Petun only until spring and on May 1, 1649 they departed for Christian Island, leaving an unknown number of Ossossane migrants with the Petuns. These may have been entirely Wenros.[6]

After the Wenroronon refugees were absorbed into the Tionontati, their inclusion could not be overlooked or ignored by the Iroquois. In December of 1649 the southernmost village of the Hannaariskwa was attacked and destroyed. The village, containing up to six hundred families, was burned, and all the children, women, and elders were massacred. The men, young and old warriors alike, were not in the village to defend the people. Knowing the Iroquois warriors were making their way to their village, a decision was made to set an ambush and stop the attack. Unfortunately, the Hannaariskwa warriors took a wrong route and missed the advancing Iroquois army who "after giving all to the flames, retired in haste."[7]

On December 7, 1649 Etharita, the principal village of the Hannaariskwa, was dealt a mortal blow. The complete loss of one village was an unexpected and crippling blow for the whole of the Tionontati. All the remaining villages were evacuated, and the citizens fled to two smaller villages on the shore of Nottawasaga Bay—near the city of Collingwood, Ontario. The Tionontati, accompanied by the Wenroronon, fled back to the territory of the Attiwandaronk Confederacy where they hoped to find refuge. The Hannaariskwa, Oskenntonton, and Wenroronon were all still estranged members of the greater Attiwandaronk Confederacy.

The Ottawa, who were at the time of dispersal resident guests and longstanding friends of the Tionontati, struck out on their own and headed to Mackinac Island, a comfortable distance from the Iroquois. The Hannaariskwa, Oskenntonton, and Wenroronon went the opposite direction and found tentative shelter among their fellow Attiwandaronk tribes. Charles Garrad believes the Hannaariskwa, Oskenntonton, and Wenroronon were given food, water, and shelter by tribes of the Attiwandaronk. The Wenroronon, who were already resident among the various tribes of the Attiwandaronk, quickly took among themselves the dispersed Wenroronon. Not all of the

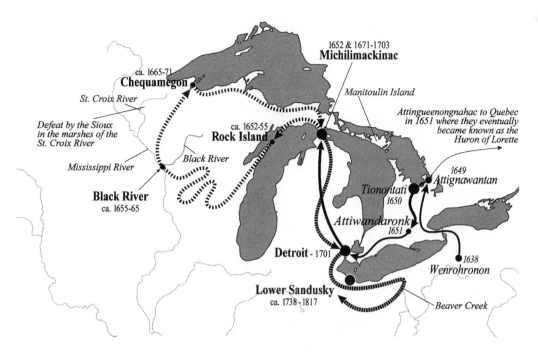

MAP 2.1. The *Huron*-Wyandot Dispersal and Migrations

Wenroronon chose to leave the Attiwandaronk Confederacy in 1638 to seek shelter within the Attignawantan Tribe of the Huron-Wendat Confederacy. When the displaced Wenroronon returned in 1650, their fellow Wenroronon, who never left their homeland, likely received them into their homes.

By mid-1650 pressure was being placed upon the Attiwandaronk Confederacy by Iroquois spies, and attack seemed inevitable. Knowing an invasion was forthcoming, the Wenroronon, Hannaariskwa, and Oskenntonton did not want to lose their individuality to something worse than death—adoption into the Iroquois Confederacy, where their individuality would not be permitted. It is believed that at this time many tribes of the Attiwandaronk Confederacy were freely giving themselves to the Iroquois. The choices were few, and the Wenroronon, Hannaariskwa, and Oskenntonton chose the only option—*life and freedom.* Simply because the Wenroronon, Hannaariskwa, and Oskenntonton had chosen to resist the tribes of the Iroquois Confederacy, their fate would have been no less than the tribes of the Huron-Wendat Confederacy.

The Huron chief detailed the barbarous act of their brethren, and narrated in glowing language their cruelty; that their allies had driven them from their lands; that their children had been thrown on the blaze of their own fires in their own wigwams, and that the wigwams, beneath which they had resided for years, had been reduced to ashes. Some were compelled to drink the blood of their own children, while those who were carried away into their own brethren's country were denied food and were offered their own childen's [sic] flesh in its stead. They said the graves of their people were desecrated and that the bodies of their women and children lay unburied on their battlefields.[8]

Unimaginable horrors can be committed when the resident evil in men's hearts is released with no moral restraints. When war comes to an end, the compassion also found inside men's hearts is capable of forgiving unforgivable sins, and enemies can become friends. Yet the memories of all the bad can never be truly forgotten. Such would happen with the *Huron*-Wyandot's ancestors and the many Algonquian and Iroquoian tribes they chose to call both friend and foe.

When the Iroquois Confederacy launched attacks in 1651 against the tribes of the Attiwandaronk Confederacy, they also abandoned their homelands. The only route of escape was to the southwest across the land that surrounds Lake St. Clair to the north and south. It would be in this general area in about fifty years that Antonie Laumet de La Mothe de Cadillac would build a new fort, Pontchartrain du Detroit, now simply called Detroit. Arriving at this juncture, the remaining tribes of the Attiwandaronk Confederacy would separate. The Hannaariskwa, Oskenntonton, and Wenroronon would travel north to find shelter within the Ottawa Tribe, now comfortably living in the vicinity of Mackinac Island. The remaining tribes of the Attiwandaronk Confederacy submitted to the Iroquois Confederacy, at which time they were adopted and dispersed namelessly into history. It is believed that in about one hundred years descendants from these tribes would again find freedom and become nominally known as the Mingo. These people were allowed to live independently in the far western regions of Pennsylvania, where they retained their identity but answered to the rule and the name of Seneca.

Be on Your Guard against the *Hurons*

Moving as far from the Iroquois Confederacy as possible, the refugees initially settled in the region around Mackinac Island known as Michilimackinac. There they reluctantly, and in dire need, joined the Ottawa in 1652. This move met very stiff resistance from the other Algonquian tribes, specifically the Ojibwa, Potawatomi, and Menominee, who could have destroyed the refugees with little to no effort. It was said the proud and noble Grandfathers, as the three refugee tribes were anciently know and acknowledged by many of their neighbors, sent their chiefs—emaciated, begging, painted black, and dressed in ragged clothes—to the council of the Ojibwa. It was in this condition the Ojibwa set aside the history of transgressions and seated the humbled chiefs at their side.

> Remembering the Hurons and their many barbarous acts, [Wah-boo-geeg] shook the war club over their heads, and said that it was not fear which had led them to give them such a reception, but it was pity for their children that induced them to open their arms and receive them. He told them that henceforward none should molest them; that the war club of the Ojibways [*sic*] should protect them, and that they were as numerous as the leaves of the forest toward the setting sun.[9]

For the sake of identification within this text, I will at this moment in time, and prematurely, call these refugees with no name *Huron*. At this point the refugees had formed a very loose alliance and, better yet, an understanding of cooperation based upon three primordial needs—food, water, and shelter. The people had just obtained much-needed protection and shelter among the vastly populated Algonquian tribes; the Ottawa, Potawatomi, and Ojibwa. It appears the Menominee did not forgive past transgressions and defiantly resisted seating the chiefs at their council fire.

Antonie Laumet de La Mothe de Cadillac, while commander of the French post of Michilimackinac from 1694 to 1696, indicated that Michilimackinac translated as "*Isle de la Tortue* [Turtle Island]."[10] Turtle Island was a most fitting name and location for the *Huron* to settle down and regroup. Thwaites continued by speculating the "name may be due either to its shape or to the fact that a turtle was found in the vicinity." It is likely that the people at Michilimackinac, who would become known as the *Huron* Tribe, completed and perfected the unification of their three phratries. As we will see over the next few decades, the refugees, who humbly submitted themselves to former enemies with the hope of acceptance and forgiveness, grew into a powerfully influential tribe of people. Cadillac stated of the *Huron,* "They are malicious, intriguing, and evil-intentioned men, capable of great undertakings; but fortunately their sword is too short. Nevertheless, as they cannot play the part of lions, they act like foxes, and spare no effort to embroil matters between us and our allies."[11]

In 1652, after rendezvousing with the Ottawa, the *Huron's* stay was brief in the vicinity of Michilimackinac. The Iroquois closely followed the Hannaariskwa, Wenroronon, and Oskenntonton with deadly intent. At the mercy of their Algonquin friends who had far superior numbers, the *Huron* looked upon the Ottawa for protection. This sense of reliance would lead to an unhealthy relationship in spite of the positions and honor held by the three tribes. To make their condition worse, their European ally, the French, had abandoned them to their mortal enemies with no hope of support. This would come back and haunt the French, who would later come to realize their mistake. "The Huron never forgot the way in which we abandoned them, on that occasion, to the pleasure of their enemies."[12]

Moving further west, the *Huron* settled at Rock Island, or the Noquet Islands, located in Lake Michigan off the northern tip of the Door Peninsula. The peninsula separates the southern part of the Green Bay from the whole of Lake Michigan. Spending close to three years at Rock Island, the *Huron* would find little rest. Iroquois spies kept everyone unsettled and on edge. Anxiety settled not only upon the *Huron* but upon the Ottawa as well, who were accompanying the *Huron* in their westward travels.

The Iroquois still followed. In 1653 they sent an eight-hundred-man army into these hiding places and drove the *Huron* even further west, but not without suffering severe losses. Within the Iroquois army an unexpected surprise was found and retrieved. "In their army were many Hurons who were the offspring of the people whom they had come to attack—men whose mothers had escaped from the ruin of their tribe when the Iroquois had invaded their former country."[13] An influx of children, assumed killed during the Iroquois invasions, was encouraging and welcome. The Iroquois had forced their adopted prisoners to fight against their own people. Their recovery and inclusion back into the *Huron* was a day of celebration and strengthening of the people. However, the villages at Rock Island, on the eastern shore of Wisconsin, were eventually abandoned around 1755 as lack of game and continued Iroquois pressure pushed the people further westward.

As the *Huron* moved further west into the Wisconsin Country, they eventually came to the Mississippi River where they first met the Sioux. Profusely welcomed by the Sioux, the *Huron* presented them "articles of iron obtained from French fur-traders who had not yet penetrated to the Sioux."[14] Still in obvious retreat from the Iroquois, but not having felt the scorn of defeat for a few years, the *Huron* were feeling pretty good about themselves. They held off the attacks of a frightfully large Iroquois army and in the process obtained peace—although fleeting. Peace agreements were frequently made when needed; however, they allowed for an honorable escape to regroup and fight another day.

Upon meeting the Sioux, and seeing they were still living in conditions not unlike those of the Stone Age, a sense of superiority swelled in the hearts of both the *Huron* and the Ottawa. The Ottawa were an ever-present companion of the *Huron*. Small gifts of iron were given to the Sioux, but nothing of great value. As the Sioux and their allies came to meet the *Huron* and Ottawa, they were looked upon as spirits, and their iron tools and weapons as gifts from the gods. The *Huron* and Ottawa were not amused. The Ottawa, "seeing these people weeping over all who approached them, began to feel contempt for them, and regarded them as people far inferior to themselves, and as incapable even of waging war."[15]

For years I was convinced the Sioux attacked the *Huron* without provocation. In actuality, the opposite occurred, and the results were nothing less than disastrous. "But the impolitic fugitives repaid their kind hosts with base treachery, and the latter turned upon them with fury."[16] When the Sioux were observed weeping, the *Huron* and Ottawa viewed them with disdain and contempt. They were convinced with blind certainty these people were morally weak and incapable of defending themselves and their homeland. As the *Huron* crossed eastern Wisconsin looking for suitable land to settle upon, they found land that "was destitute of woods, and contained only prairies and level fields, although buffaloes and other animals were found there in abundance."[17] The Sioux proved to be hospitable hosts, and there was plenty of land for everyone. However, the *Huron* became greedy and coveted all the land for themselves, and they attacked the Sioux without provocation.

With so much contempt being held for the Sioux, and no less found among the Ottawa, a plan was devised to obtain the whole of the Wisconsin Country. Fueled with a pride of possessing guns, metal knives, tomahawks, and all the modern skills and implements of war, the *Huron* were convinced, in spite of their small numbers, that the Sioux could easily be defeated and run out of the territory. Without making adequate preparations, and scouting to see that the Sioux were very populous, "the Hurons attacked the Dacotas [*sic*], but being defeated and harassed in turn by this tribe, retired to the sources of the Black River, the Ottawa continuing their retreat to Chagoimegon."[18]

With hurt pride in the face of clear defeat the *Huron* settled near the confluence of the Black River and the Mississippi River, a respectably safe distance from the Sioux. There they began to make the best of their new home. The *Huron* were clearly out of their natural elements and about 180 miles from Green Bay.[19] "Here and there in these gloomy depths was a cluster of starveling [*sic*] Algonquians, or a band of Huron from east of Georgian Bay, still trembling from fear of a return of the Iroquois, who had chased them from Canada into this land of swamps and tangled woods, where their safety lay in hiding."[20]

This was not the life for the *Huron*. They were miserable, alone and without the French trade goods they had come to need and covet. Eventually a few of the *Huron* would pull up stakes and move to Chequamegon Bay, where the Ottawa had ventured. Others *Hurons* would walk the 180 miles to Green Bay just to be near the sound of crashing waves and sweet smell of water. On the Black River a sea of prairie grass and swamps surrounded the people, and they were drowning in the vastness of the sky.

In 1659 or thereabouts, French fur trader and explorer Pierre Esprit Radisson found his way to the isolated shores of Chequamegon Bay on the far western shore of Lake Superior. There he found several tribes: "Chippewas, Potawatomis, Kickapoos, Sauks, and Foxes, native to Wisconsin, together with Hurons and Ottawas from the Huron country."[21] The various tribes had been attracted to the area because the fish were plentiful and its remoteness gave a sense of security and protection from the Iroquois in the east and the Sioux in the west. Radisson and Medard Chouart des Grosseilliers, along with six other traders and a "band of Huron Indians, explored the southern bays of Lake Superior."[22] The French had arrived, built a fort, and made plans to stay. The remaining band of the *Huron* chose to remain relatively isolated on the Black River where concerns of Sioux attack remained minimal.

After Radisson arrived to the far western shore of Lake Superior he did a lot of exploring with the *Huron* among his guides—or, I have often wondered, did they actually serve as bodyguards? Upon Radisson's return to New France, the world the *Huron* had come to deplore would change. "On the 19th of August, 1660, there arrived at Montréal 60 five-man canoes with 300 Ottawa tribesmen and Pierre Esprit Radisson and Médard Chouart Groseliers, with furs valued at 200,000 livres, or $1,000,000.00."[23] At this time in history it was an unimaginable fortune. After suffering a severe setback after the fall of the Huron-Wendat Confederacy, the French were more than ready to again exploit the riches found in New France. However, a French priest by the name of Father René Menard saw a greater treasure than dead fur. Father Menard saw "remnants and refugees of the old Huron mission."[24]

In a very short eight days Father Menard assembled an expedition to head west. On August 27, 1660, just a few hours before departure, Father Menard wrote to his Father Superior: "I write you the last word and I desire it to be the seal of our friendship into Eternity. In three or four months, you may put me into the memento of the dead."[25] Father Menard knew in his heart the expedition west did not allow for a return trip home.

Upon reaching Chequamegon Bay, Father Menard asked the whereabouts of the Tobacco-Huron who had taken refuge in the vastness of the Wisconsin wilderness. The Father insisted on seeing the refugees, as he was certain of their identity as being from the Huron Mission. Having access to records of the Jesuit priests who preceded him, he was convinced they were Hurons. The Huron Mission was initially inclusive of all tribes in the Great Lakes Region. When the French first came to North America and began to make contact with the various tribes, they too often failed to identify and bestow rightful individuality and recognition to each unique group of people. For many of the Jesuits and Frenchmen the various tribes were all simply and universally Hurons.

A few Frenchmen had already made the round trip to the *Huron* living on the Black River. They reported it was too hard to traverse and urged the Father not to go—yet still Father Menard insisted. He possessed a direct invitation from the *Huron* to come, and he would not refuse their invitation. While in route to rendezvous with the *Huron,* Father René Menard died in August of 1661 due to hardships encountered in the wilderness.[26]

It was a mere ten years postdispersal. The destruction or adoption of the various tribes was a chaotic blur for the French to try to understand. One day there were literally several Huron tribes, not just the four commonly known as the Huron Confederacy, and the next day they were all but gone. The name Huron was inclusive of the many tribes in the region, because they were all equally looked upon as rough, rustic, and a very primitive people. When the war between the Huron-Wendat Confederacy and the Iroquois Confederacy came to an abrupt end, where did all the Huron people go? Father Menard believed he found them living as an exiled people within the solitudes of the Wisconsin wilderness. This is how the *tribe with no name* would come to be known as the *Huron* Tribe. Since Father Menard and the French chose to call these people *Huron,* and the people did not dispute the name, in time the *Huron* Tribe would wrongly come to be called remnants of the Huron-Wendat Confederacy.

Quickly following in Father Menard's footsteps was Father Claude Allouez who arrived at Chequamegon Bay in 1665. Father Allouez served the various tribes of Chequamegon Bay a total of four years, including the *Huron,* when a younger priest, Father Jacques Marquette, relieved him.[27] When Father Allouez first built his chapel at Chequamegon Bay, the *Huron* promptly abandoned their Black River villages to enjoy the advantages of French trade and French protection against the Sioux and Iroquois. Peace had not been established between either, and fear of attack was a daily concern. Upon first meeting the *Huron,* Father Allouez observed, "They numbered from four to five hundred souls, but from long mingling with pagan tribes had almost lost all traces of Christianity."[28]

With the French back in the region, life became a little more familiar, comfortable, and tolerable for the *Huron*; however, the Sioux were not equally impressed with their new French neighbors. Sure, the Sioux liked the goods the French had to trade, but the Sioux seemed determined not to become addicted to them, as did many of the other tribes. The *Huron*'s resentment over being defeated by the Sioux ten years earlier began to burn within their hearts. They found the presumed inhospitality of the Sioux to be unacceptable and again began to devise a plan. Approaching their good friends the Ottawa, the *Huron* were enticed to seek revenge, start a winnable war, and get a little payback—not to mention the whole of the Wisconsin Country to themselves. Trade with the French was now good and very profitable. Much like the *Huron*'s archenemies, the Iroquois, who sought conquest for the procurement of land, the *Huron* now employed the same policy of conquest.

Not long after Father Jacques Marquette established his mission at Chequamegon Bay, his half-naked parishioners provoked a war in 1671 with their powerful western neighbors, the Sioux. As a result of this ill-fated war all the various tribes at Chequamegon Bay, including the *Huron,* with Father Marquette in tow, were "driven like leaves before an autumn blast eastward along the southern shore of the great lake."[29]

After suffering terribly and being driven from their own homeland by the Iroquois, it makes one wonder—what were the *Huron* thinking? Where were their compassion and understanding? Why would the *Huron* want to drive the Sioux from their homeland and turn them into refugees? It's hard for us to imagine, but war, fighting, pillaging, kidnapping, and murder had become a way of life—it was just life and it was all too normal.

Over the centuries many *Huron*-Wyandot warriors died in battle. It is clear that not every offensive action taken by the *Huron*-Wyandot can be considered noble, pure, and justified. The following account, written by Reuben Gold Thwaites, illustrates the magnitude of defeat suffered by the *Huron* when one hundred of their warriors unknowingly challenged an army of 3,000 Sioux. Of the one hundred warriors, only one would escape capture. This excerpt also illustrates why the *Huron*-Wyandot people deplore and would rarely eat wild rice in later years.

The hundred Hurons became involved among these swamps, and without canoes; they were discovered by some Scioux, [*sic*] who hastened to spread the alarm everywhere. That was a populous nation, scattered along the circumference of the marshes. . . . More than 3,000 Scioux came together from every side, and besieged the Hurons. The loud noise, the clamor, and the yells with which the air resounded showed them that they were surrounded on all sides, and that their only resource was to make head against the Scioux (who were eagerly striving to discover their location), unless they could find some place by which they could retreat. In this straitened condition, they concluded that they could not do better than to hide among the wild rice, where the water and mud reached almost to their chins. . . . They [the Sioux] bethought them of this device: they stretched across the narrow strips of land between the lakes the nets used in capturing beavers; and to these they attached small bells, which they had obtained from the [Ottawa] and their allies in the visits which they had made to those tribes. . . . This scheme indeed succeeded; for the Hurons slipped out under cover of the darkness, creeping on all fours, not suspecting this sort of ambuscade; they struck their heads against the nets, which they could not escape, and thus set the bells to ringing. The Scioux, lying in ambush, made prisoners of them as soon as they stepped on land. Thus from all that band but one man escaped . . .

The captives were conducted to the nearest village, where the people from all the others were assembled in order to share among them the prey. It must be observed that the Scioux, although they are not as warlike or as crafty as the other tribes, are not, like them, cannibals. They eat neither dogs nor human flesh; they are not even as cruel as the other savages, for they do not put to death the captives whom they take from their enemies, except when their own people are burned by the enemy. . . . The Scioux, having shared the prisoners, sent back part of them, and made the others objects for their sport—delivering them, as I said, to their boys to be shot to death with arrows; their bodies were then cast upon the dung-heap. Those whose lives they spared were condemned to see their comrades die, and were then sent home. . . . The Hurons, recognizing the smallness of their numbers, made up their minds to meditate revenge no longer.[30]

The Sioux called forth their hordes fully armed and ready for war. In a frightful scurry to escape, "the Ottawas retired to Ekaentouton [Manitoulin Island], and the Hurons to Mackinaw, founding the Mission of St. Ignatius."[31] Like a tornado sweeping across the Great Plains, the Sioux were determined to destroy everything and everyone in their path—especially those disrespectful and intolerant *Hurons*. The mutual disdain they held toward the small band of dispersed Indians from the east was complete. The *Huron* were no longer welcome, nor were the Ottawa and the French. The Sioux expelled everyone with little to no effort.

That was a hard lesson to learn and a turning point in the policy and practice of the *Huron* Tribe. Rather than try to use brute force, much like the tactics of the Iroquois, with only a handful of warriors the *Huron* would turn to multilayered diplomacy and craftiness.

After sustaining a convincing defeat the *Huron* now had relentless enemies on both their front and back—the Iroquois to the east and the Sioux to the west. The small band of *Huron* were stuck in the middle and exposed on all sides. After the *Huron* moved such a distance from the Sioux, peace was nominally established; however, being out of sight did not necessarily mean the *Huron* were out of the Sioux's thoughts and minds.

When the *Huron* returned to Michillimackinac, it looked a lot more like home—no, it was home. In 1672 Father Marquette noted that the population of the *Huron* was an astonishing 380.[32] The war with the Sioux had been very costly, and it was time to settle down, replace the many good men and women who were lost, and start anew amid a land of plenty. With experience in the west, and a hard-obtained knowledge of the various tribes, it was a natural for the *Huron* to partner with the French and act as brokers and middlemen with the tribes on the Plains. "While the Hurons and Ottawas, gathered about the old mission of Michillimackinac, acted as factors for the Sioux, the Winnebagoes, and many other remote hordes. Every summer they brought down their accumulated beaver skins to the fair at Montreal."[33]

Once reestablished back in Michilimackinac the *Huron* were busy collecting a lot of beaver pelts from the far west. Countless premium pelts were making their way east to Montreal, and the Iroquois could not help taking note. The Iroquois wanted a piece of the action. Unfortunately, it was those pesky *Huron* they couldn't eliminate from the face of the Great Island who hit the mother lode. The *Huron* were like a mosquito, buzzing and buzzing, and no matter how hard the Iroquois tried, they could not swat and kill them. A measly little tribe of four hundred people came close to stopping the expansion of the Great Peace in its tracks—but not quite.

In an unexpected move somewhere around 1676, the Seneca sent a delegation to the *Huron,* bearing gifts and offering assistance in their war with the Sioux. Did the Iroquois truly want to assist in the war, or did they want to tap into the monopoly of fur being exploited from the Great Plains and the vast regions northwest of Lake Superior? Were they going to help the *Huron* for free? Of course not. The Iroquois, especially the Seneca, at this time were bent on conquest and territorial gain.

What the Seneca really wanted was to entice the *Huron* further east and via adoption make them Seneca. If this could be achieved, the Iroquois would freely obtain all the wealth the *Huron* had stumbled upon in Wisconsin. They wanted the *Huron*'s beaver circuit, they wanted the racket, and they wanted the money. The French, especially the missionaries, saw through the charade. Over the next several years the relationship grew deeper, and the Seneca's visits to Michilimackinac increased. It began to look like the *Huron* and Seneca were becoming best friends, but then again you just cannot shake the history of being mortal enemies from the relationship. When you play with flint and steel around a keg of black powder, all it takes is one spark to make everything go kaboom!

In 1681 when the Illinois Tribe killed a Seneca chief named Annanhac, the growing relationship between the *Huron* and Seneca came to an immediate halt. The *Huron* did not commit the murder; the Illinois did. However, the *Huron* just happened to be present when Annanhac was killed. It's possible, and the Iroquois believed, that the *Huron* might have instigated the whole event.[34] Everything the Iroquois had been working so hard to accomplish by trying to convince the *Huron* people that adoption into their league was a noble gesture instantly disappeared into nothingness. Tension and concerted acts of violence, along with an unhealthy number of kidnappings in the woods, once again became the norm. The old war resumed with no less ferocity. "They [the Iroquois] made the valley of the Illinois a desert, and returned with several hundred prisoners, of whom they burned those that were useless, and incorporated the young and strong into their own tribe."[35]

Michilimackinac quickly became a hornet's nest and lion's lair. But no, it became a den of foxes—it was home of the *Huron* Tribe. It was at Michilimackinac that all the various tribes came to plot and align against the Iroquois. It was also at Michilimackinac that they brought their prisoners to display, or trade, and get drunk. The dangers at Michilimackinac were obvious and severe, the conditions were surreal, and the stew of Indians mixed with a sprinkling of French and English became quite volatile. There were many long and ancient histories between the various tribes that read of raids, coups, abductions, and cannibalism. Loyalties were always in question, and the French were on constant guard of revolt.

One day the *Huron* may have been friends with this tribe or that tribe and at war with them the next. Even the inseparable *Huron* and Ottawa "were far from harmony among themselves. Each was jealous of the other, and the Ottawas charged the Hurons with trying to make favor with the common enemy at their expense."[36] The *Huron* were also beginning to feel they were slaves to the Ottawa. It felt as though the Ottawa were always forcing *Huron* warriors to fight their wars. Many of their bravest and strongest warriors were losing their lives to the Ottawa's enemies—it was time the Ottawa fought their own wars. It was time the *Huron* stood on their own and controlled their own destiny.

Trying to contain and restrain the various tribes from fighting each other was a daily challenge for the French. Focusing their rage, talents, and power toward the Iroquois, and the English, was an even more difficult challenge. Many of the tribes did not want to provoke the Iroquois, as they knew any challenge would invoke their wrath. Dangers were everywhere, and the only law was treaties of convenience and the honor of those in agreement. Unfortunately, many of the tribes who struck agreements with each other, or the French and English, had little intent to honor those agreements—all the agreements did was buy a little time. The swirl of politics, intrigue, contempt, and duplicity made understanding what was happening shy of impossible. Keeping the various tribes aligned and their loyalties dedicated to the French cause became a daily task of near-impossible diplomacy. Much-needed information and intelligence usually came a day late and one hundred dead people short.

In the middle of the chaotic mobocracy life was cheap. It was impossible for the French to keep abreast and in control of the politics and diplomacy of the various tribes. With so many assembled tribes the *Huron* showed more stability and loyalty to the French; however, it was clear to the French that some within the *Huron* "were bent on allying themselves with the Senecas and the English."[37] There seemed to be a difference—two distinct *Huron* peoples—that continued to identify as one, yet they too often shared uncommon loyalties, political agendas, and religious affiliations.

It took much effort for the French to retain control of the various tribes at Michilimackinac due to the meddling and interference of the fur traders. These men would come into the region and prey upon the women of the various tribes, taking for themselves mates, usually against their will. They also brought alcohol, mostly French brandy, which numbered well into the hundreds of barrels. Intoxicated revenge against the fur traders was always a concern; however, for the French "the most pressing danger was the defection of the lake tribes."[38] The four lake tribes—*Huron,* Ottawa, Potawatomi, and Chippewa (Ojibwa)—formed an alliance, the Lakes Confederacy, that was near-impossible to defeat. The Lakes Confederacy, with the *Huron* as Keepers of the Council Fire, would fight the Sioux to a standstill and force the mighty Iroquois Confederacy to concede to peace.

The Rat

In 1682 Adario, or Kondiaronk, also known as Le Rat or The Rat, was considered the chief speaker of the *Huron* Tribe. Technically, he was not the head chief, since Sastaretsi was the head chief, but Kondiaronk exerted considerable influence. When we say The Rat, let's clarify what The Rat is referencing. No, it is not referencing the Bad Twin upgrade to the little field mouse—The Rat references a Muskrat. Throughout the oral narratives of many American Indian cultures, the Muskrat holds a place of great honor. Remember from the *Huron*-Wyandot's Creation story that the Muskrat was one of the divers who attempted to retrieve dirt from the roots of the Tree of Light. In spite of the Muskrat's failing at the task, honor has always been given to the noble effort. For Kondiaronk to bear the name The Rat shows that his people held him in a position of great honor.

Kondiaronk, the Rat, is recognized as one of the greatest chiefs in the history of the *Huron*-Wyandot people. First stepping into notoriety when attending an Indian congress at Montreal, August 15, 1682,[39] for the next twenty years Kondiaronk would dominate the *Huron* political and military scene: "Kondiaronk, one of the most able and influential savages of his time."[40]

Time can heal bruises and hard feelings. After the Seneca set aside hard feelings over the killing of Annanhac in 1681, by 1686 they were back in Michillimackinac, secretly bringing more British agents to meet their cousins the *Huron.* They were again trying to win the *Huron* over to the English cause. If only the *Huron* had been as dedicated to either the French or the

English as the Seneca were to the English, much failed diplomacy and much conniving could have been avoided. The *Huron* were momentarily "won by the persuasions of the Senecas, and the cheapness of English goods, [the Hurons] could scarcely be restrained from removing *en masse* to New York, but the missionaries and French officers succeeded in retaining them."[41] Again, if not for the Jesuit missionaries, the French would have lost their greatest and most powerful ally. Plus Kondiaronk's influence was gaining momentum, and he did not trust the Seneca. There was no way Kondiaronk was going to allow his *Hurons* to become Senecas or any other tribe of the Iroquois Confederacy.

One of the deterrents to the *Huron* moving en masse to New York was the request they be admitted to the Iroquois League and stand alongside the Seneca, Cayuga, Mohawk, Oneida, and Onondaga—as *Huron*. The Iroquois League rejected the request; however, they would welcome the adoption and ensuing dispersal throughout the existing tribes of the league. This was never going to happen. Why? It's likely the five nations of the league knew that if the *Huron* were admitted to the league, they would quickly ascend to a position of prominence. This proposition was unacceptable under any circumstance; after all, the *Huron*'s very existence was built upon the determination to live free, not as adopted second-hand citizens or worse—slaves.

It was becoming clear the *Huron* were not completely committed to the French cause. There seemed to be a difference of opinion within the *Huron* as to whom loyalty should be accorded: the French or the English. By this time it appears Kondiaronk may have ascended to serve as head chief of the *Huron* Tribe, without possessing and having a right to the title of Sastaretsi. Kondiaronk's first loyalty was to his people, second to the interest of the various tribes, and then to the French, but only as long as they played by his rules.

One of the greatest acts of *Huron* duplicity and treachery occurred in 1688 when the French came close to obtaining peace with the Iroquois. There was a long and nonnegotiable agreement between Kondiaronk and Governor Louis de Buade de Frontenac that peace would never be obtained with the Iroquois unless the Iroquois Confederacy was first utterly destroyed or severely weakened. Kondiaronk was opposed to any form of peace with the Iroquois, for he knew that only the continuation of the war would preserve his people. Unaware the French had conspired with the Iroquois to achieve peace, Kondiaronk set out to go Seneca hunting in the mid-summer of 1688. By happenstance Kondiaronk stumbled upon knowledge of the French conspiracy and quickly devised a plan to spoil the peace process. Francis Parkman in *Count Frontenac and New France* explained the events. Parkman began by giving praise to a most noble *Huron* savage.

> Among the Hurons of Michillimackinac there was a chief of high renown named Kondiaronk, or the Rat. He was in the prime of life, a redoubted warrior, and a sage counsellor. The French seem to have admired him greatly. "He is a gallant man," says La Hontan, "if ever there was one;" while Charlevoix declares that he was the ablest Indian the French ever knew in America, and that he had nothing of the savage but the name and the dress.[42]

With the hope of giving justice to an otherwise long and complicated story full of brilliant diplomacy and tactics, I will keep this story as short and simple as possible. The French were always accusing the *Huron* of dabbling in duplicity; however, as the French pointed a finger at the *Huron,* they had four, plus a big thumb, pointing right back at them. Kondiaronk expressed his position rather too clearly: He and his *Huron* would never seek peace with the Iroquois until the Iroquois were soundly defeated. The French agreed with this position and gave Kondiaronk their support in his war; however, behind his back they sought their own peace. One day as Kondiaronk was visiting Fort Frontenac, located at the mouth of the Cataraqui River where the St. Lawrence River leaves Lake Ontario, the French were caught in a lie, and Kondiaronk would learn of the French plot to secure peace with the Iroquois. The location of this fort was highly strategic, for it controlled the waterway into the heart of New France.

Without causing alarm or showing the French his anger and disdain, Kondiaronk left for home. Quickly changing his route, Kondiaronk planned to intercept the forthcoming Onondaga emissaries. Setting an ambush along their route, he waited for their arrival, upon which he and his warriors killed one of the three chiefs and wounded everyone else in the Onondaga's party with only one escaping, but not without severe wounds. With the situation well under control Kondiaronk informed his captives he was acting on the orders of Governor Denonville. The Onondaga were infuriated, for they had come in peace and Denonville was well informed of their mission. Kondiaronk then gave a stellar performance in which he appeared to be angry at the French. Turning his sympathy to the Onondaga, who because of Denonville's treachery were wrongly attacked, Kondiaronk appeared to take their side in the misunderstanding.

Kondiaronk promptly released his prisoners, with the exception of one whom he kept as a traditional replacement for a *Huron* killed in the skirmish. The Onondaga peace party would return home to tell their brethren of the French's treachery, and the war would continue unabated. Promptly returning home to Michillimackinac, Kondiaronk surrendered his prisoner to the French commander who had yet to be informed of the pending peace with the Iroquois. The Onondaga prisoner detailed the events of the ambush and their mission of peace. Kondiaronk laughed the story off as nothing but a delusion. The prisoner, who thought he was going to be adopted into the *Huron,* was marched outside and shot by the French. Another Iroquois who had long been a prisoner of the *Huron* was called forth, released of his captivity, and told to return to his people with a report of French cruelty and betrayal.

The one Onondaga who escaped the ambush did make his way back to Fort Frontenac and told the French of the disastrous events. Expressing their deepest regrets and apologies, the French told him to return home; however, it appears they did not deny the conspiracy as their concoction. Instead, they tried to convince the Iroquois that peace was still obtainable. Peace was not obtained, as the Iroquois boldly attacked the small French village of Lachine on August 5, 1689, near present-day Montreal. In one night of revenge they indiscriminately butchered many of the men, women, and children. Most of the village was burned and all hope for peace obliterated. Kondiaronk's bold plan of treachery was a total success, and the Iroquois never suspected it was anything but a French conspiracy.

In true *Huron*-Wyandot tradition there was an opposite, or an enemy, of Kondiaronk within the tribe, a man named Escoutache, or the Baron. It is clear the Baron never served as head chief, and, given his position within the clans, he could never have served as chief. The relationship between Kondiaronk and the Baron can be described as good and bad, yin and yang, a balance of opposites, much in the same way as the Good Twin complemented the Bad Twin, and vice versa. The *Huron*-Wyandot was noted as having balance—a nature of good and a nature of bad. This character trait can be seen within the tribe throughout history and was believed to be a reflection of the Good Twin's compromised Creation of the Great Island after the death of his twin brother. This balance, or constant opposition, could also reflect the incomplete union of the Tionontati and Wenroronon people who composed the *Huron* Tribe.

As we have just seen, Kondiaronk hesitantly supported the French in their war against the Iroquois. Kondiaronk was committed to a continuation of the war; however, the French were not as committed to war as was Kondiaronk. Even though his support prolonged the war, Kondiaronk knew if peace were achieved between the French and Iroquois, the Iroquois would then turn upon the *Huron* along with their friends and allies. This could never be permitted; therefore, it was in the best interest of the Lakes Confederacy to keep the French and the Iroquois Confederacy fighting themselves.

The Baron supported the English, which required him to cast his lots with the Iroquois. The Baron was not content with the arrangements between Kondiaronk and the French; therefore, he enticed his followers, an estimated three or four families, to leave Michilimackinac and go live with the Miami Tribe.[43] The three to four families were extended families or households, possibly accounting for more than one hundred citizens. From the Miami Country the Baron planned to continue his negotiations with the Iroquois with the hopes of bringing the English into the western countries.

In July of 1696, the Baron represented the *Huron* in a congress of the various tribes at Montreal. There he outwardly and falsely professed a desire to carry on the war with the Iroquois; however, in reality he withheld the *Huron* braves from taking the warpath. His true intent was to send his son along with thirty *Huron* braves to the Senecas with the hopes of obtaining peace. This caused an extraordinary amount of trouble for Cadillac.[44] Antoine Laumet de la Mothe, sieur de Cadillac was then commander of Fort de Buade. It was during this time at Michilimackinac, between 1694 and 1696, that Cadillac would form an enduring respect for the *Huron* people. During this time Cadillac would also lay the foundation for his life's dream, the establishment of his own, new fort.

The Baron's grandest scheme was to cause a magnificent diversion from the French and Iroquois War and swirl chaos throughout the whole of the Great Lakes Region. The Baron wanted to upend the work of Kondiaronk and the Lake Confederacy's alliance against the Iroquois. The Baron's conspiracy was an attempted renewal of the war between the *Huron* and the Sioux. A renewal of this war would have proven disastrous for the *Huron,* the French, and the three Algonquian tribes of the Lakes Confederacy. All the various tribes of the Great Lakes Region would have suffered greatly with a renewed war between the Sioux and their allies. Cadillac discovered the Baron's conspiracy and acted quickly, promptly averting disaster.[45]

It has been said the Baron was a master strategist no less than Kondiaronk. After the failure of his conspiracy with the Sioux, the Baron's next tactic appears to have been an all-out coup. Of course the coup also failed, but not without exacting a heavy and personal toll for Kondiaronk. The Baron's last attempt to upset Kondiaronk's policy of war for peace came while returning prisoners to the Seneca. Noble and frequent gesture was given by both the *Huron* and the Seneca. As the Baron was exchanging prisoners and presenting wampum belts of peace, the following statement was relayed from the Baron to the Seneca through his son:

> Our Father [the French governor] has vexed us, he has long deceived us. We now cast away his voice; we will not hear it any more. We come without his participation to make peace with you to join our arms. The chief at Michili-mackinac [Kondiaronk], has told us lies; he has made us kill one another. Our Father has betrayed us. We listen to him no more.[46]

The Iroquois readily accepted the Baron's belts of peace in spite of an intense effort from Antoine de la Mothe Cadillac to ensure his failure. Kondiaronk also unsuccessfully attempted to destroy the Baron's quest for peace. Trade and diplomatic relations between the Baron's band of *Huron* and the Iroquois promptly ensued. Cadillac convinced the Ottawa to attack a delegation of Iroquois who were returning to their homeland with a mass of fur, and also *Huron* representatives from the Baron's band. In the ensuing attack the Ottawa killed and scalped many of the *Huron* in the party while others were taken prisoner and eventually released. Still under the influence of Cadillac, the Ottawa were enticed to continue their attacks. In these attacks the Ottawa did not discern any differences between the Baron's band of *Huron* and Kondiaronk's band of *Huron*. In one such attack it was a son of Kondiaronk who became a victim.[47]

Kondiaronk bridled his temper and did not seek revenge against the Ottawa, nor did he seek revenge upon his fellow *Huron* citizens. Knowing the true source of the fault, he unleashed his fury upon the Iroquois. The acts of the Ottawa, a longtime friend of the *Huron,* did not go unnoticed but added to an already stressed relationship that was destined to end in disaster. Until that fateful day the *Huron* and Ottawa warriors continued to rain destruction upon the warriors of the Iroquois Confederacy

That same year the Ottawa, Potawatomi, Sac, and *Huron* organized parties against the Iroquois, and more than one hundred Seneca were killed or captured. During this campaign one of the great water battles occurred on Lake Erie, a battle that helped expedite an end to the long war between the Iroquois and French. The war between the *Huron* and the Iroquois resulted in an untold number of *Hurons* losing their lives, primarily to the hands of the Seneca.

During this battle on the water, fought aboard canoes, fifty-five Iroquois were killed during the battle that lasted about two hours. The *Huron* and the Ottawa fought this battle against the Seneca and lost only four men in the battle. In one of the few documented descriptions of the battle on water, Henry Rowe Schoolcraft provided some chilling details to the bloody and historic actions of the *Huron* and Ottawa.

It is somewhat remarkable, as no other tradition makes mention of an Indian battle upon water, that one of these, said to have occurred on Lake Erie, between Long Point and Fort Talbot, was fought in canoes. Of this the following detail is given.

A large body of Wyandots accompanied by two Ottawas left Lake Huron in birch canoes, on a war excursion into the country of the Senecas, who had settled at this time, near the head of the Niagara river. They put ashore at Long Point to cook, when one of the Ottawas and a Wyandot were sent out as spies to reconnoitre. They had proceeded but a short distance from the camp, when they met two Senecas, who had been despatched by their party for the like purposes, and from whom they instantly fled. The Ottawa finding his pursuers gaining upon him, hid himself in the branches of a spruce tree, where he remained till the Seneca hail passed. The Wyandot, fleeter of foot, succeeded in reaching his camp and gave the alarm, when the whole body embarked and pushed out into the lake. In another moment a party of Senecas was discovered, turning the nearest point of land in wooden canoes. Immediately the war-whoops were sounded and the hostile bands began to chant their respective songs. As they slowly approached each other, the Wyandots struck a fire, and prepared their gum and bark to repair any damage which might occur to the canoes. The battle was fought with bows and arrows, and after a furious and obstinate contest of some hours, in which the carnage was dreadful, and the canoes were beginning to fill with blood, water and mangled bodies, the Senecas began to give way. The encouraged Wyandots fought with redoubled ardor, driving the Senecas to the shore, where the conflict was renewed with unabated fury. The Wyandots were victorious, and few of the surviving Senecas escaped to tell the story of their defeat. One of the prisoners, a boy, was spared and adopted by the nation. Two Wyandots are now living who profess to have seen him, when very far advanced in years.[48, 49]

This one historic defeat, a battle fought by Indians on water with birch-bark canoes, and canoes hewn from logs, ended the Baron's public career of antagonism and duplicity. The Baron permanently left the *Huron* people to go live among the Miami. More importantly, the Baron's conspiracy to use the Iroquois for the destruction of the Miami was diverted. Under cover of negotiating peace with the Miami, the Baron was actually planning their extermination. After the battle on water ended, Kondiaronk, who was in command, notified the Miami to be on guard and not trust the Baron.[50] The Baron would eventually settle among the Mohawk, where he disappeared into the pages of history.[51]

Kondiaronk committed his life to war in order to obtain peace. This is such a novel idea that it confounds logic, but it worked as designed. As long as the French and Iroquois were fighting each other, the Iroquois would be distracted and unable to focus their assembled might against his beloved *Huron*. The French were paying a heavy price, and all they wanted was peace for New France. Peace finally came in 1701 under the terms of the Great Peace of Montreal.

The venerable, well-respected, and feared Governor Louis de Buade de Frontenac, who had initiated the peace process, died in November 1698 leaving his work unfinished. Two Onondaga and four Seneca chiefs announcing their desire for peace approached Frontenac's successor, Governor Louis-Hector de Callières, in July 1700. Throughout the ensuing year gestures were exchanged, and peace now appeared to be obtainable. Throughout the deliberations and gestures Kondiaronk kept warning, that in spite of the Iroquois's sense of good faith, they could not be trusted. Governor Callières summoned all the tribes to Montreal in the summer of 1701 with the hope lasting peace could finally be obtained. While making his way to the peace conference, Kondiaronk made the following discovery:

We have found many of our brothers dead along the river. . . . Word has spread that the sickness was great in Montreal. All these corpses eaten away by the birds which we found at every moment were sufficiently convincing proof of it. But we made a bridge of all these bodies on which we marched firmly.[52]

On August 1, 1701, Kondiaronk was seriously ill with a fever from the influenza that consumed Montreal.[53] Yet this did not stop Kondiaronk from speaking for two hours in favor of a peace treaty to be guaranteed by the French. "Peace, then, was made. 'I bury the hatchet,'" said Callières, 'in a deep hole, and over the hole I place a great rock, and over the rock I turn a river, that the hatchet may never be dug up again.'"[54] The peace treaty was signed, and there would be no more war between the French and the Iroquois Confederacy. Thirty-eight nations signed the treaty, including the *Huron* Tribe and the five tribes of the Iroquois. For the French, obtaining peace was a great victory, yet the faint rumblings of inevitable war with the English were being heard in the not-so-distant future. The Iroquois promised to remain neutral in any future conflict between the French and the English. "The power of the Iroquois was so far broken that they were never again very formidable to the French. Canada had confirmed her Indian alliances, and rebutted the English claim to sovereignty over the five tribes."[55]

Allotted for the Wiandóts

The Great Peace of 1701 clearly left the French in control of the Great Lakes Region. Unfortunately, the French had already made bad decisions that would compromise their victory. Prior to the Great Peace of 1701, King William's War of 1688–96, a prelude to the French and Indian War of 1754–63, coincided with an Algonquin offensive against the Iroquois. During this period when the Iroquois were on the retreat, an excess of beaver pelts flooded the European markets, causing a dramatic drop in prices. The French crown, under pressure from the Jesuits, revoked all trading licenses in 1696, resulting in the suspension of the fur trade in the western Great Lakes. The fur trade was the French government's greatest tool in New France to keeping the various tribes happy and aligned with France. Overnight the relationship that tenuously held the various tribes and the French together began to fall apart.

With the French and their ever-present threat of pulling the trading relationships from the various tribes, Cadillac found himself with a little problem—actually a huge problem. How was he going to defend his new fort? French troops were scarce, and against a powerful tribe he did not stand a chance. Then he remembered the *Huron* Tribe and their immediate allies. They were invited to move and help defend his fort; however, not all the *Hurons* were keen on the idea, as they did not trust the French. Finally, the prophetic homeland of the *Huron* was now theirs to forever keep.

La Motte Cadillac's great project was to establish a post at Detroit, and, in 1701, he began Fort Pontchartrain at that place, inducing a portion of the

Hurons to accompany him, which they did readily. . . . Thirty more followed, in 1703, leaving only twenty-five at Mackinaw. Before 1706 all had departed, and the missionaries, burning their house, descended to Quebec.[56]

The tiny little tribe called *Huron* was a major force in the Great Lakes Region. Plus they proved beyond the shadow of a doubt they were survivors. The greatest military force to slash, burn, and pillage upon the face of the Great Island could not conquer them. The *Huron* never succumbed to the Iroquois's Great Peace. Cadillac would have been a fool not to want the *Huron* on his side of the fort's walls. "The Hurons, the Ottawas, the Pottawattomies were gathering in strong villages round his fort and he could train them for defense against the English and the prairie tribes," whose trade he desired, but whose treachery kept him ever watchful."[57]

What kind of man was Cadillac to recruit the *Huron* to defend his fort? He was desperate and the *Huron* were greatly needed. Why would he trust their savage, unpredictable nature and uncanny intelligence to protect his life's dream? Cadillac did not trust the *Huron* any more than he trusted a single fox in his personal henhouse. However, give him a handful of foxes, and he could hold back all the savage hordes that would undoubtedly contest the legitimacy of his dream. All he had to do was keep the foxes happy, but with foxes in his henhouse this proved to be an immense challenge. "He [Cadillac] regards the Hurons and Ottawas as mischievous brutes never loyal even to their missions. They 'play the fox but never the lion.'"[58]

The Great Peace of Montreal did not bring lasting peace to the Great Island. The English did not sign the peace agreement. Queen Anne's War erupted in 1702 and would last until 1713. This was a European war that splashed across the Atlantic into the New World. During the war, England, the League of Augsburg (an alliance of several small European states), Denmark, Portugal, and the Netherlands declared war on France and Spain to prevent a union of the French and Spanish crowns. A unification of the two European powers would have resulted in dire global consequences for England and the whole of Europe, but King Charles II of Spain died on November 1, 1700. As a result of the war in North America, France ceded the Hudson Bay territory, Newfoundland, and Nova Scotia to England. Another victory for England was their obtaining protectorate status over the Iroquois Confederacy from the French. This would prove to be an uneasy alliance, and at times it makes one wonder who was actually protecting whom.

Cadillac's first challenge to his new fort would come in 1703 during the outbreak of Queen Anne's War as the English tried to entice the western tribes to burn the fort. The attempt was unsuccessful; however, the English did sow a lot of dissension among the western tribes. After attending a conference at Albany in 1702, a delegation of Ottawa returned to Detroit with an instilled sense of mistrust for the French. Initially Cadillac was able to defuse the situation and everything appeared to be status quo; however, while Cadillac was away on business, the Ottawa revolted and did manage to cause a little damage. "A portion of the palisades, Cadillac's house, Ste. Anne's Church, the residence of the priest and another building were burned to the ground, but no lives were lost."[59]

As the war between France and England sputtered along the Atlantic coast, little of its effects were felt in the far west around Detroit. However, the various tribes gave Cadillac little rest as their constant bickering with each other never ended. Another test for Cadillac would quickly come in 1706 as the *Huron,* still jealous of the Ottawa, sided against them when they attacked the Miami at Detroit. In the confusion the Ottawa killed Recollet priest Father Nicholas Bernardin Constantin de L'Halle. This would prove to be a breaking point in the long, and forced loyalty between the *Huron* and Ottawa, which had too often proved a one-sided relationship. It is believed the ensuing riot was started over a dog. The Ottawa became furious when *Huron* warriors refused to again fight at their beckoned call. Not only did the Ottawa continue their rant upon the Miami, but they also openly attacked the *Huron* in their own village and longhouses!

On June 6, 1706, a party of six Miami Indians were set upon by some of the Ottawa, and five of the six were killed. The one who escaped gave the alarm in the Miami village, the inhabitants of which hurried to the fort for protection. The immediate cause of this trouble lay in the fact that an Ottawa was bitten by a dog belonging to a Miami and, when he kicked the dog, was so severely beaten by the commandant, De Bourgmont, that he died. (Some writers say the dog belonged to De Bourgmont.)

Father de L'Halle, the beloved Recollet priest, was walking in his garden at the time of the outbreak. He was captured by some of the Ottawa, probably with the intention of holding him as a hostage to protect themselves from punishment. One of the chiefs, however, ordered his release and the priest started for the fort. Just as he was about to pass through the gate he was shot to death by an Ottawa. His body was carried inside the fort, the gates of which were then closed, and De Bourgmont ordered the garrison of fifteen soldiers to fire upon the insurgents. In the melee which followed about thirty of the Ottawa were killed. Then they tried to induce the Huron braves to join them in making an assault upon the fort. Failing in this, they made an attack upon the Huron village, but were repulsed. For nearly a month the fort was kept practically in a state of siege, when the Ottawa grew tired of the warfare and sued for peace.

Cadillac wrote plainly to Governor Vaudreuil, urging the capture and execution of Le Pesant, the Ottawa chief at Michilimackinac, whom he accused of being the instigator, if not the actual leader, of the outbreak which resulted in the death of Father de L'Halle and the attack on the Huron village.[60]

The politics, alliances, deception, and acts of blatant treachery kept the region around Detroit a hornet's nest of warring and marauding tribes. The tribes were pitted one against the other, as well against the hands that instigated them—the French and English. It would have been impossible to know where trust and security could be found. Stuck in the middle of all the games of chance and war were the *Huron*. The *Huron* were Cadillac's secret weapon, which wasn't so secret, and he used the *Huron*'s warriors to no end. In addition, the Ottawa used *Huron* warriors as their elite warriors, their special forces if you will, to finish many of the fights they started.

The pressure and toll of always being used by the Ottawa finally ruptured when in 1706 the *Huron* stood their ground against the Ottawa with a vengeance. In one dramatic change of stressed loyalty that had existed since joining the Ottawa at Mackinac in 1652, the *Huron* struck hard, fast, and decisively to finally win their freedom. Evidently there was a price to pay for the Ottawa's friendship and protection—something a little shy of slavery. The Ottawa kept the *Huron* in a state of unrelenting servitude. Still outnumbered by a significant margin, the Ottawa could not have mistaken the message delivered by the *Huron*'s warriors, and their freedom earned was never relinquished.

The quarrel had been simmering, and often resulted in cuts and bruises, one to the other, for over fifty years when it finally erupted into open hostilities. By the time the move to Detroit was made, the strength of the *Huron* had improved. It was time to stand alone without the heavy hand of the Ottawa always trying to manipulate the tribe as a puppet. The tipping point, or possible excuse, was the death of Father de L'Halle. After the quarrel had subsided, it would take several years for the relationship to again show signs of candor and friendship; however, an underlying mistrust would always exists between the two near-inseparable allies.

To illustrate the intense nature and importance of Fort Detroit, and also how quickly alliances and enemies can change, the following account is from a dispatch to the Governor General of Canada in the spring of 1712.[61] After six years the relationship between the *Huron* and Ottawa had been tentatively restored. At this time a combined force of Mascoutin and Fox Tribes defiantly set up camp not fifty paces in front of the main gate of Fort Detroit. There they proceeded to build a fort of their own with a very powerful palisade.[62]

Their mission, as commissioned and dispatched by the English, was to destroy Fort Detroit, along with the French, Ottawa, and *Huron*. With a small detachment of thirty French soldiers Commandant Dubuisson was powerless to repel their insulting and imprudent claim to owning all the surrounding country. While waiting for arrival of Kickapoo reinforcement, the Mascoutin and Fox laid siege to the fort and threatened to burn it to the ground. Their plans were intercepted and delivered to Commandant Dubuisson by a Fox named Joseph, who had long left his people to live with the French.[63] Treacherous spies were abundant and noted as being everywhere. Over the preceding and following years prying ears and lying tongues would foil many Indian revolts.

In need of his allies Commandant Dubuisson sent for the *Huron* and Ottawa, who were still at their hunting grounds, as were the Chippewa and Mississauga. On May 13 the *Huron* and Ottawa arrived at the fort. The Potawatomi were also outside the fort and requested council. An emissary was sent to the Potawatomi, and their chiefs indicated that "six hundred men would soon arrive . . . to eat those miserable nations who had troubled all the country."[64]

With a significant army amassed, the French were content with running off the Mascoutin and Fox; however, the *Hurons* were too irritated. Anything less than destroying the Mascoutin and Fox was unacceptable. The *Huron* were in charge of the amassed army, and the Mascoutin and Fox were to be utterly destroyed. In a display of *Huron* political prowess and multilayered diplomacy it was reported by Jacques-Charles Renaud Dubuisson, commander of Fort Detroit, "This great affair had been too well concerted during the whole autumn and winter with all the nations."[65] It was useless to speak of accommodations and peace. It was clear to the French that if the Mascoutin and Fox were not destroyed, the amassed army could easily turn upon them.

As preparations were being made to repel the Mascoutin and Fox, another army was seen approaching from the woods. This army consisted of the Illinois, Missouri, Osage, Ottawa, Potawatomi, Sacs, Menomonie, and other nations yet more remote. "This army marched in good order, with as many flags, as there were different nations, and it proceeded directly to the Fort of the Hurons."[66] Multilayered diplomacy? The reach of the *Huron* was vast, and vastly powerful unlike any other force upon the Great Island.

During the siege the Mascoutin and Fox were forced to dig holes four to five feet deep to gain protection from the lead balls that rained as hail. Two large scaffolds twenty feet high were erected from inside the walls of Fort Detroit, and from the towers lead balls rained. Four to five hundred warriors from the amassed army encircled the village of the Mascoutin and Fox; no one left and no one entered.[67]

Still in defiance the Mascoutin and Fox covered their palisades with scarlet blankets. The blankets indicated they intended and wished the earth to be covered with blood. The red blankets were a charm with significant meaning to the Indians. The French also knew this was a signal from the English. Infuriated by the display the war chief of the Potawatomi requested to address the Mascoutin and Fox from the erected towers. He stated, "Wicked nations that you are, you hope to frighten us by all that red color which you exhibit in your village. Learn, that if the earth is covered with blood, it will be yours."[68]

Ignoring the words of the Potawatomi war chief, the Mascoutin and Fox successfully constructed a scaffold that was protected by an earthen embankment. From this shelter the Mascoutin and Fox began to enact a heavy toll upon the warriors within Fort Detroit. Commandant Dubuisson was forced to make a difficult decision and employ his cannon from the exposed reaches of the two towers. The cannons were so well aimed that the enemy scaffold was destroyed. After the volleys of cannon fire, the Mascoutin and Fox requested a conference with Commandant Dubuisson. All the assembled chiefs of the alliance agreed that the conference was desirable, and the Mascoutin and Fox would be allowed to make their plea.

The next morning of the planned conference the red blankets had been removed from the palisade, and white ones were placed in their stead. Chief Pemoussa of the Fox, indicating obvious defeat with the white blankets, requested a two-day cease-fire to negotiate the terms of peace. Commandant Dubuisson indicated that if terms of peace were to be considered, and if the Mascoutin and Fox truly desired peace, three hostages within their palisade would be immediately returned.

Within two hours three chiefs—two Mascoutin and one Fox—came bearing a white flag along with their three hostages. They spoke: "My father, here are these three pieces of flesh that you ask of us. We would not eat them, thinking you would call us to an account for it."[69] Commandant Dubuisson was pleased the hostages were returned uneaten and was now content to establish a final truce; however, the assembled Indian alliance had yet to speak their terms. The head chief of the Illinois was appointed by the chiefs of the other nations to speak these words:

> Now listen to me ye nations who have troubled all the earth. We perceive clearly by your words, that you seek only to surprise our father, and to deceive him again, in demanding that we should retire. We should no sooner do so, but you would again torment our father, and you would infallibly shed his blood. You are dogs who have always bit him. . . . We shall see from this moment, who will be master, you or us; you have now only to retire, and as soon as you shall re-enter your fort, we shall fire upon you.[70]

As they returned to their palisades, the battle commenced and raged for another three to four days. Intent on burning Fort Detroit, the Mascoutin and Fox sent three to four hundred arrows at a time into the fort with their points aflame. This caused such disarray among the assembled tribes, with the exception of the *Huron* and Ottawa, that they wished to abandon the fight. The surviving French also wanted to retreat to Michilimackinac. Having gained a conference with the allied chiefs, Commandant Dubuisson rebuked their decision to flee. "What, my children! when you are just on the point of destroying these wicked nations, do you think of retreating shamefully. . . . All the other nations would say, are these the brave warriors, who fled so ignominiously, after having abandoned the French?"[71]

After nineteen days of siege it began to rain. Seeing a chance for escape, the Mascoutin and Fox slipped from their palisade around midnight. Both the Indian allies and the French pursued the fleeing survivors. After running about five miles, the vanquished stopped and prepared to make one final defense. It was then Commandant Dubuisson called for the two cannons to be brought forward. After another four days of siege the Mascoutin and Fox surrendered to the wrath of the allied tribes. "All were killed except the women and children, whose lives were spared, and one hundred men. . . . Their amusement was to shoot four or five of them every day. The Hurons did not spare a single one of theirs."[72]

With such a convincing victory the French were grateful for the help of the allied tribes, especially the *Huron*. Unfortunately, during the battle Iroquois warriors were seen within the ranks of the *Huron*. This spread doubts among the French concerning their loyalty. After all, they were *foxes* and noted as playing all sides with politics and alliances that were horribly complex and nearly impossible to discern. They too had assembled a powerful army of the various tribes. Their persuasion to compel the various tribes to fight, or not to fight, was an ominous power.

By the mid-1730s certain factions within the *Huron* ventured south into the near-vacant Ohio Country and claimed it as their own. They began to explore and exploit the vast country that lay as a buffer between the western tribes and English colonies. It is safe and appropriate to assume that as the *Huron* pressed south and east, clan factions settled small villages and never returned to Detroit; however, a relationship was always kept intact with the rest of the clan family that would remain in Detroit.

It's also clear the *Huron*'s relationship with the Ottawa suffered many setbacks. It was like a classic, elementary school playground struggle between the bully and the skinny kid. Unfortunately for the Ottawa, by the time the skinny kid in third grade had reached sixth grade, he had packed on some muscle and had grown about a foot taller. In 1738 there was another quarrel between the *Huron* and Ottawa.

In 1738 the *Huron* offered a belt of peace to the Ottawa. A long war between the Flathead of the West and the *Huron* had been concluded. The Ottawa were also known enemies of the Flathead, and the *Huron,* wanting to protect their newfound allies, requested the Ottawa to honor their peace. The Ottawa refused and became resentful that the *Huron* would entertain such a request. To make matters worse, the Chippewa and Pottawatomi sided with the Ottawa, placing an extreme strain upon the longstanding confederacy that defeated the Iroquois.

In response to the *Huron* chief's request, the Ottawa promptly sent a war party against the Flathead. While making their way to the Flathead village, two *Huron* war parties were dispatched and first reached the Flathead village, warning them of impending attack. "The raven cry was distinctively a Huron signal and had two meanings, a warning of impending danger and a call of hunger. It appears, however, that the Flathead Indians understood it and when the Ottawa made their attack they found themselves between the Flathead warriors on one side and the Huron on the other."[73]

Nearly one-half of the Ottawa war party was killed. Upon returning to Detroit, the Ottawa chiefs and warriors confronted the *Huron* and accused them of betraying their friendship. Of course the *Huron* chiefs denied the accusation, and the Ottawa called the *Huron* dogs. This would have been an insult worthy of war. The Ottawa also indicated that the cry of the raven during battle was a clear sign that *Huron* warriors participated in their defeat. The disagreement persisted and hostilities ensued. The Ottawa still possessed a greater population than the *Huron*. As a result, many *Huron* were forced to leave the area around Detroit to seek shelter on Bois Blanc Island. The *Huron* stayed on the island for several years until their differences with the Ottawa were mended.

Differences of opinion, skirmishes, and wars seemed to be never-ending among the various tribes. Political intrigue and complex diplomacy never stopped. For a small tribe such as the *Huron* it was very important to always be on guard, especially knowing that many of the tribes could field more warriors than the *Huron* had citizens. Similar quarrels, as noted with the Ottawa, persisted to no end. C. C. Trowbridge, in his journal, provided a list of the various tribes the *Huron*-Wyandot fought. When listing the various tribes with whom the *Huron*-Wyandot declared war, it would have been easier to list the tribes with whom they did not fight.

> They have fought with, the Cherokees, Chickasaw, Yankeshaw, Foxes, Sacs, Creeks, Menominies, Winnebagies, Sioux, Chippewaws, Ottawas, Potawatomie. Six nation of W. [New] York—Kickapoos, and indeed with every other nations with whom they are acquainted, except the Miamies, Delewares, Shawnees, the Nations of Canada, and through others on the Wabash Weas, We-a-te-nong's, and Peoria's. In these different battles they conquered all the nations with whom they fought. They attributed their remarkable success to the goodness of the Great Spirit in giving them a War Chief, who was half as tall as a tree, and whose presence at the head of the armies always ensured victory.[74]

Nicholas: Full of Savage Cunning

Nicholas Orontony is thought to be a war chief, possibly the warpole. The warpole was chief of the war chiefs, or commanding general of the *Huron*-Wyandot's military branch of the tribe. He appears to have first reached a prominent role within the *Huron* Tribe in or around 1739.[75] Nicholas was described as "a wily fellow, full of savage cunning, whose enmity, when once aroused, was greatly to be feared."[76] Dr. John Steckley indicated that his name first appeared in 1730 and he was of the Porcupine clan. Nicholas, like most other *Huron* of the time, would have been baptized into the Catholic Church. His baptized name was Nicholas; his given name Orontony. Nicholas's clan citizenship would have allowed him to obtain the position and title of warpole.[77] Nicholas's grandson Dunquat, or Pomoacan, would also achieve a noted place in the history of the *Huron*-Wyandot people where he is known as the Half King.

In 1739 Nicholas approached the French and asked for resettlement of his band of *Huron*. Nicholas wanted to move north along the St. Lawrence River. Frustrated with the French and their fickle, unpredictable disloyalties, he wanted change. The French obviously denied his request. Why did Nicholas ask for permission to move, and why were the French in a position to dictate where he lived? Nicholas was frustrated with the Jesuits' intolerant demands for penance, loyalties to the Virgin Mary, and everything and anything Catholic. The Jesuits' religion was in direct conflict with his identity as a Porcupine. It can be a little scary how Porcupines can become very prickly, and rather quickly, when they become irritated or their security and identities are questioned and challenged.

For unknown reasons Nicholas changed his mind and led his disgruntled band of *Huron* permanently south into the Ohio Country. Nicholas's move would have brought his band of *Huron* into a direct and sustained relationship with the Iroquois. For the French any influence from the Iroquois Confederacy was undesirable, but obviously the Iroquois already had a direct influence on Nicholas's actions. The Iroquois may have inspired his move around 1740 to the Sandusky River. It was around this same time the Iroquois, who claimed the whole of the Ohio Country via conquest, gave Nicholas's *Huron* settling rights to nearly the whole of the Ohio Country. This move eventually allowed the English to establish a very discreet presence outside Detroit's own front door within Nicholas's villages on the Sandusky River.

Nicholas's proposed changes were a radical, severe, and abrupt departure from previous *Huron* loyalties to the French; however, signs of change had been evident and growing for a long time, going back to the days of Baron. The problem was that most of the previous signs of possible defection to the English were subtle, with the exception of Baron, and were quickly denied or recanted as rumors. For the French it was hard to know exactly where those *foxes* stood and their loyalties lay. Nicholas and his actions were undeniable when in 1743 he traveled to Albany, New York, and publicly proposed an alliance with the Iroquois Confederacy and English colonists.[78] The

Iroquois Confederacy, in particular the Seneca Tribe, did not accept the Wyandot's proposed alliance; however, Pownall's 1755 map of the "Middle British Colonies" does indicate that a preliminary agreement of inclusion into the confederacy was obtained. The map states, "These Parts were by the Confederates allotted for the Wiandóts when they were lately admitted into their League." Nicholas wanted his Wyandot recognized as a tribe with equal standing to the other tribes of the Iroquois Confederacy. Inasmuch as the Tuscarora were admitted into the Iroquois Confederacy in 1722, Nicholas wanted the same for his Wyandot. The Iroquois still proposed adoption for the Wyandot—an unacceptable proposal for Nicholas.

About this time the English, especially the Pennsylvanians, began calling this *new* tribe in the Ohio Country the Wiandót. Within a few years Nicholas, with a strong and productive trading relationship with the Pennsylvanians, would promote a revolt and direct assault upon the French. It is now estimated the *Huron* could muster a little over two hundred warriors; however, they were divided, and Nicholas commanded but half the warriors. The hereditary head chief of the *Huron,* Sastaretsi, still commanded a sense of historical power, authority, and influence—but not for much longer.

The Nicholas Orontony Affair, Conspiracy, or Uprising technically began in 1747 when Nicholas and his allies, the Miami and Wea, attacked French trading posts and burned the Jesuit mission on Bois Blanc Island, located in the Detroit River. Nicholas was then centering his operations from the village and stronghold of Sandosket (Sandoski or Sandusky) on islands off the southern shore of Lake Erie where the Sandusky River empties into the lake. It was here Nicholas gave permission for the first fort or blockhouse, Fort Sandoski, to be built in the Ohio Country in 1745.[79] It was also here in 1747 that Nicholas's Wyandot killed five French traders and robbed them of their goods when they entered his village uninvited.[80] Nicholas's village was then known to be populated with English traders and officials—and so close to Detroit! Still in negotiations with the Seneca and English, Nicholas plotted a direct assault upon Fort Detroit.

Fearing an all-out war, the *Huron,* led by Sastaretsi from the Deer phratry and chief Taeehiaten from the Wolf phratry, immediately endeavored to clear themselves of all guilt and association with Nicholas. However, Chief Angwirot from the Turtle phratry stood with Nicholas in his revolt.[81] Being a Porcupine, Nicholas was of the Turtle phratry. Fearing a war with the French, Sastaretsi and Taeehiaten traveled to Montreal in August of 1747 to pledge their allegiance to the French. While in Montreal they also requested a return of the Jesuit missionaries and pledged they would deliver Nicholas to the French. This would prove to be impossible as Nicholas was "powerful, and gathering many around him, besides influencing those at Detroit."[82]

The Sastaretsi, hereditary chief of the *Huron* Tribe, died in 1747 and hence never returned to Detroit. This Sastaretsi was likely the last to hold any true power and authority over the *Huron* Tribe. Once they sensed their independence, the Wyandot, the name by which Nicholas was now calling his band, never relinquished their freedom or acknowledged any ancient authority of the Sastaretsi. Sastaretsi's young nephew, who is thought to have been a child, claimed the ancient title, but now for the first time since the dispersal did not have a unified tribe to lead.

Nicholas's desire to separate himself and his band from French control was continually strengthened; for example, he sent wampum belts to the various tribes urging them into a general uprising. The Ottawa and Potawatomi, who had promised the French to destroy the *Huron* village on Bois Blanc Island in revenge for Nicholas's attack on the Jesuit mission, set aside their promise for various reasons. They instead joined Nicholas's uprising. The Miami attacked the French in their lands, and they were cut off from their fellow countrymen. "The Miamis and Wyandots were to exterminate the French from the Maumee country; to the Pottawattomies were assigned the Bois Blanc Islands, while the Foxes were to attack the settlement at Green Bay. Nicholas reserved to himself and his followers the fort and settlement at Detroit."[83] The day set for this uprising and massacre was one of the holidays of Pentecost.

The Wyandot devised a plan to massacre the French at Detroit. Nicholas's plan may have succeeded if a woman had not overheard the details. This woman ran and confessed to the Jesuit priest what was about to transpire. The priest in turn ran to the French commander of Fort Detroit, and the plot was spoiled. Evidently the sanctity of confession was no longer considered a private affair between the parishioner, priest, and Lord God. Could this be one of the reasons Nicholas despised the priests? Nicholas's plan was simple: He and his warriors were going to spend the night inside the fort, which was not an unusual occurrence, and when the inhabitants were asleep, they were going to be killed. Each warrior had been assigned a home and ordered "to kill the people of the house where he was."[84]

The French response to Nicholas's actions forced him into a truce. In 1748 Nicholas and his followers, numbering about one hundred nineteen warriors,[85] burned their villages along the Sandusky and then sought protection among the Miami in the Illinois Country. Nicholas did not stay long in the

Miami Country. He and his band eventually moved to the White River, or Cuyahoga, near present-day Cleveland, Ohio. There Nicholas put a lot of distance between himself and the French in order to recuperate and to rethink his actions. Nicholas was still determined to rid Fort Detroit and the Ohio Country of the French pestilence. Unfortunately, many of Nicholas's followers would quit his cause and return to Detroit.

From the White River Nicholas would continue on to Kuskusky on Beaver Creek in Western Pennsylvania.[86] This area was likely once inhabited by the Wenroronon, and Nicholas was instinctively leading his Wyandot to their true homeland. For unknown reasons, probably differences of opinion with the Seneca, Nicholas would not stay long at Beaver Creek. Still on the move, Nicholas would travel to the forks of the Muskingum in Southeastern Ohio and settle for a while at Conchaké before finally settling upon the Sandusky plains.[87] It was about this time in the summer of 1748 that Conrad Weiser made contact with the Wyandot and became very impressed by this small yet powerful tribe, the band of the *Hurons.*

> The Wyandots, a powerful group of Indian tribes, at one time in the French interest, and recently avowed friends of the English, were reported to Weiser as weakening in their new resolution and inclined to go back to the French. These Wyandots, says Weiser, were called Ionontady Hagas, and were an exceedingly influential body of Indians. He at once called a council of their chiefs and asked them why they had left the French. They replied that it arose from their hard usage. The French had treated their young men in the wars as they would slaves. And for some years French goods had been so dear that the Indians could not buy them. They further said that all the Wyandot Tribes were dissatisfied with the neutral action of the Six Nations and desired that they would take a decided stand against the French. . . . Weiser gave these Indians some tobacco and whiskey, and made them the warm friends of the English.[88]

It is believed that Nicholas Orontony died in the spring of 1750. Even in death his personification as a defiant legend still urged his followers to resist the French and the Jesuit missionaries. For the first time the *Huron* and Wyandot were divided and in disagreement as to their profession of loyalties and alignments with the European powers. Throughout the whole of Nicholas's affair the *Huron* at Detroit remained loyal to the French. After things began to quiet down, many *Huron* and Wyandot moved to Lower Sandusky.

It was here that Father de la Richardie established a mission at the town of Sunyendeand on a creek of the same name, meaning Rockfish.[89] Here the Wyandot would also extend their claim and authority over a good portion of the Ohio Country. This claim would go uncontested—not even the Iroquois would refute the bold claim.

So what happened to the warm friends of the English? What changed their minds? In spring 1751 a French army of about five hundred men threatened to invade the Ohio Country. Their mission was to drive out the Wyandot and Shawnee. The French assumed these two tribes were contaminating the other resident Indians and enticing them over to the English cause. If the Wyandot and Shawnee did not stop their mischievous dealings with the other tribes, the French were going to kill them.[90] Still being small in number, though powerful, to sustain a direct attack of five hundred men would have been devastating. The Wyandot pledged their loyalties to the French, but only after the French flexed their military muscle of intimidation with threats of complete extermination.

The English would not sit idly by and let the French gain control of such a powerful and desirable ally. Colonel George Croghan, the prince of Pennsylvania traders and English Indian agent, was sent to try to retain Wyandot loyalty to the English. He was not successful.[91] In his attempt to retrieve the Wyandot's loyalty Croghan stated,

> I understand that the French, whom you call your father, won't let you rest in your towns in peace, but constantly threaten to cut you off. How comes this? Are you not a free and independent people? Have you not a right to live where you please on your own land, and trade with whom you please? Your brethren, the English, always considered you a free nation, and I think the French, who attempt to infringe on your liberties should be opposed by one and all the Indians.[92]

The Wyandot had just moved into the Ohio Country and claimed it as their own, and now the French and English, and a little later the Americans, were trying to claim the land as theirs. Not without a fight! Long before the fight over the Ohio Country persisted, skirmishes began in Central and Western Pennsylvania. The Delaware and Shawnee initially declared war due to the invasion of the Juniata Valley in Central Pennsylvania. At that time the British Colonial government did what was right. The government expelled the settlers rather than risk war with the tribes.[93] Unfortunately, their efforts would prove too little and too late to divert the inevitable war. It's a shame those same sentiments and expulsions did not happen in the Ohio Country. In actuality, the opposite occurred, as the British and then the Americans began to use the land as payment and reward for their soldiers who fought their wars.

Joseph Pritts stated in *Incidents of Border Life,* "The Indians who here resisted the advance of civilization, were certainly the most heroic and warlike race that ever claimed a portion of the territory we now call our own, and they kept up a more prolonged border warfare than was elsewhere witnessed in defence [*sic*] of it."[94] What Pritts and the Americans did not know in 1841, when the preceding quote was published, is that all the various tribes in the far West would make the same heroic and defiant stand to protect their own homelands. The closing of one era in the Indian Wars would lead to the opening of another that would persist until the end of the century. In the east it was the Wyandot who led the fight. In the west it was the Sioux who led their fight. Two former enemies had the same common goal: to protect a way of life and ensure the hope of future generations.

"This Continent Is Not Wide Enough for Us Both"

In life we may choose to live, or inadvertently find ourselves living, in a bubble. At times it may be possible to successfully live in the bubble, a protected and wonderful little place, for a short or long while. Unfortunately, as things happen outside the bubble, the bubble can be gently cradled or tossed about with turbulence. If things become too turbulent, like what happened when Europeans first made contact with the resident tribes of the Great Island, the bubble can be distorted out of its traditional shape. This can happen with no extenuating circumstances causing fault to be placed upon residents of the bubble. No matter how much the residents try to mind their own business and live in harmony with Nature, there is a competing and contrasting life outside the bubble. This outside life, seemingly populated by a small number of people easily ignored, can at times squeeze and distort the bubble until life becomes uncomfortable and in threat of change.

If and when the bubble bursts, its residents can be thrown into someone else's bubble, bringing catastrophic consequences to their way of life. To make matters worse, it is disheartening and troublesome for the people to know they did nothing to cause their bubble to burst. Such is life, and this is what happened when the English first came knocking on the front door of the *Huron*-Wyandot's cabins in the middle-of-nowhere Ohio Country. The *Huron*-Wyandot's cabins, and the land they claimed as their own, would quickly become the bull's-eye of a global war full of many swirling bubbles that could now no longer be ignored.

About the same time as the French and English began their struggle for dominance of the Ohio Country, land they truly did not own, Nicholas Orontony gave grief to the French at Detroit. It was at this same time the Pennsylvanians were venturing deep into the Ohio Country, where they knocked on the front door of the Wyandot's newly built cabins. The Wyandots and Pennsylvanians initially established a wonderful relationship, but something went desperately wrong. In about five to seven years, the Wyandots went from being friendly with the Pennsylvanians to killing hundreds of their brethren at the Battle of the Monongahela. Without making this story too complicated or time-consuming, simply put, it was all about the land. The various tribes knew the value of the land. The European governments were slowly learning of the land's value and vastness. This time the coming war was not about the possession of beaver pelts worth their weight in gold, but something much more valuable—dirt.

In the early to mid-eighteenth century the various tribes of the Great Island, at least those living within the Great Lakes Region, Western Pennsylvania, and the Ohio Country, were on rather friendly terms with the French and the British. Before the turn of the eighteenth century the Dutch had been defeated and driven from North America by the British. The Dutch had no choice but to abandon their colonial efforts in North America. In their absence, the British essentially took everything over as though nothing had changed—but change had most certainly come to the Great Island.

Taking over what the Dutch had already established, an uneasy relationship with the Iroquois Confederacy, the principal Indian allies of British were the Seneca, Cayuga, Oneida, Onondaga, and Mohawk. They were uneasy and restless allies, for they had just been forced into a peace treaty by the French and their Indian allies. For the tribes of the Iroquois Confederacy to have had near free rein over most of North America east of the Mississippi River only to now be corralled did not settle too well with their ambitions. Doubts were creeping in, and the strength they once possessed was beginning to show signs of weakness.

The principal Indian allies of France were the four dominant tribes of the Great Lakes Region: *Huron*, Ottawa, Potawatomi, and Chippewa. The four lake tribes had a very powerful alliance that could stand toe-to-toe with the

Iroquois any day of the week. "Their anxiety to open the road to the white traders, in order to procure fire-arms and their much coveted commodities, induced the Ojibways, Ottaways, Pottawatumies, Osaukies, and Wyandots to enter into a firm alliance. They sent their united forces against the Iroquois, and fighting severe and bloody battles, they eventually forced them to retire from Canada."[95]

By right of discovery the French claimed all the land from the Allegheny Mountains to the Rocky Mountains. They too claimed everything north of Spanish Mexico and Florida all the way to the North Pole, with the exception of a minor and chilling toehold the British held on the Hudson Bay.[96] The French controlled all the major rivers: Mississippi, Ohio, St. Lawrence, Missouri, and so on. "Canada at the north, and Louisiana at the south, were the keys of a boundless interior, rich with incalculable possibilities."[97]

The British had thirteen colonies that were as diverse as the French territory was vast. Their claim to the land was through conquest of both their European competition and the Native inhabitants. Their colonies stretched along the Atlantic coast from New France to Spanish Florida. Outside the Hudson River Valley in New York, which once stood as the pride of Dutch colonial expansion in North America, there were no major waterways into the slender interior they colonized. The English possessed but a fraction of the vast continent. Francis Parkman stated of the thirteen colonies, "The differences among them were great. Some were purely English; others were made up of various races, though the Anglo Saxon was always predominant. Some had one prevailing religious creed; others had many creeds. Some had charters, and some had not."[98]

It seems the loyalty of the various tribes was won or lost by the French and British with the value of and accessibility to trinkets and through intimidation. "The French could not compete with English presents and trade, the effect of force and numbers could intimidate the Indians allied to the English and eventually bring them to the French side."[99] The French were initially more adept at trading and creating sustainable relationships than the British; however, the cost of the French goods was enormous compared to the cost of the British goods. It also appears the French had a deeper respect for the Indians and the value they shared for the land, whereas the British just wanted the land. With political issues in France it was becoming harder for trade goods, which the various tribes had come to expect and relish, to make it from France to the interior of the Ohio Country. This is why gentlemen such as Conrad Weiser and George Croghan began to persuade the Indians to come over to the British side. The various tribes' accessibility to a steadier flow and cheaper trade goods was convincing enough for many of the tribes to begin casting their lots with the British.

The flash point of the French and Indian War was the Ohio Country. The French laid claim to the land, yet they had never inhabited the land, nor did they build forts, except for Detroit, which technically did not lie within land designated as the Ohio Country. Detroit was initially built to protect interests deep in the heart of the western realms of New France. As the battleground began to shift to the Ohio Country, Fort Detroit would serve as the cornerstone of defense of the Ohio Country for the French, British, Indians, and eventually the Americans. Other than Fort Pitt, there was no more important fort than Fort Detroit.

The British settlers, primarily Pennsylvanians and Virginians, were beginning to press deep into the Ohio Country. Both the Pennsylvanians and Virginians claimed the land, and a little healthy competition between the two colonies expedited their consumption of all obtainable land. Many of the other New England colonies also claimed their stakes in the vastness of the Ohio Country; however, their active presence in the land grab appears to be rather weak and passive. It was at this same time Conrad Weiser, George Croghan, and others were tickling the hearts of the tribes deep in the Ohio Country itself.[100] The Wyandot were interested and intently listening, as proven by Nicholas in 1747. For the French this was an unacceptable arrangement, and little skirmishes began to lead to open conflict. As previously noted, the Wyandot were actively recruiting allies in their opposition to the French. One ally, the Delaware, would prove to be both a great friend and a fickle ally. The Delaware's duplicity was noted by their initial reluctance to join the upcoming war and pick a side—French, British, or Indian. The persuasiveness of the Wyandot was clearly shown as the Delaware chose to fight alongside the Wyandot, *their uncles,* as an ally of the Wyandot and not as an ally of either France or England. The persuasiveness and the intrigue of the Wyandot were firm, compelling, and strong. "The western Delawares' sequential plan for the war provides context for Tamaqua's later claims that the western Delawares had never accepted the 'French hatchet,' but instead had reached an accord with the French allied Wyandots and Caughnawaga [Mohawk] Iroquois."[101]

Some historians believe it was not the French or the British who persuaded and pushed the Wyandot and other tribes into the French corner of the duel— it was the Iroquois. Regardless of who was guilty of the shove, it was clear to the tribes that "the two white nations had conspired to destroy them, and then divide their lands."[102]

Yes, both the French and the British were placing untold and unnecessary pressure on all the tribes. The pushing, shoving, and threats were beginning to take their toll. The Great Island was vastly richer and bigger than both France and England could imagine. Yet still they chose to fuss over a very small corner, and the cost would be extreme. The Reverend Jonathan Mayhew would say it best in 1754: "This continent is not wide enough for us both."[103] His statement referenced the ongoing British and French disagreement. The continent was indeed wide enough for them both, but greed and pride prevailed. Unknown at the time, Mayhew's statement would quickly prove to be prophetic, as the continent would prove to be equally narrow for the Indians and the Americans.

In the summer of 1754, from June 19 to July 11, representatives held a conference in Albany, New York, as delegates from seven of the thirteen British American colonies participated. The Albany Congress was attended by Connecticut, Maryland, Massachusetts, New Hampshire, New York, Pennsylvania, and Rhode Island. Oddly enough Virginia was notably absent from the congress. The colonies assembled in response to a recent incident earlier that spring perpetrated by a young lieutenant colonel in the Virginia militia named George Washington. The conference served two purposes: (1) unify the colonies for the inevitable war with the French and (2) strike a treaty with the Iroquois to gain their support or neutrality.

During the Albany Congress, representatives of the seven colonies in attendance also met with chiefs representing the Iroquois Confederacy and a few other tribes. The English colonies needed to reaffirm the Iroquois as being on their side in the coming war or persuade them to remain neutral. One of the stipulations found in the 1701 Great Peace of Montreal was that if and when war broke out between France and England, the Iroquois would remain neutral. This stipulation and agreement were French, not English. The Iroquois were the Iroquois and they did as they wished. The British desperately needed to secure a new treaty. Two previous treaties were in existence, one from 1701 and the second from 1726.[104] This new treaty was paramount due to recent differences between the Iroquois Confederacy, primarily the Mohawk, and the British colony of New York.

During the Albany Congress a treaty of friendship and alliance was secured with the Iroquois; however, ultimately the Iroquois determined it would be the choice of the individual tribes to fight with the British or remain neutral.[105]

The British colonies were in attendance, and each had its own agenda. While all the tribes were gathered, the noble Pennsylvanians took the opportunity to enlarge their domain. Coveting the Susquehanna Valley, the Pennsylvanians wanted to make it their own before the other colonies noticed its wealth and value. The problem was that the other colonies, especially Connecticut, had already taken note of the Susquehanna Valley, and they wanted it too.

Conrad Weiser was in attendance representing the Penn family. Weiser made a desperate and public attempt to purchase the valley. It just so happened that the Mohawk came to the conference, with a tomahawk to grind, and proved to be worthy negotiators. Weiser was concentrating his negotiations with the Oneida and Tuscarora; however, at that time the Shawnee and Delaware occupied the land that was on the bargaining table.[106] When the Mohawk became involved, Weiser tried to keep them at bay, as they had no traditional claim to the land—and neither did the Oneida and Tuscarora. Ultimately, a deal was penned, and the Pennsylvanians obtained everything they had come to Albany to purchase. As Conrad Weiser was concluding his deal with the Iroquois, John Henry Lydius, a representative hired by the Colony of Connecticut, was conducting his own negotiations for much of the same land Weiser just purchased.[107] Lydius's tactics were very harsh compared to Weiser's and were concealed behind closed doors, or so Lydius assumed. Lydius's tactics did not go unnoticed by the Shawnee and Delaware or the other tribes of the Ohio Country. When the settlers came rushing into the Juniata Valley and adjacent lands, it was pretty clear to the Delaware and Shawnee what had taken place. The Iroquois had again betrayed their existence and sold them out to the Europeans. The Delaware and Shawnee were left with no options. Timothy Shannon explained in *Iroquois Diplomacy on the Early American Frontier*:

> The land purchases conducted at the Albany Congress reflected the harsh reality of Iroquois diplomacy at midcentury. Once again, the Iroquois enriched themselves, at least temporarily, by selling distant lands inhabited by other Indians. . . . The Pennsylvania and Susquehanna Company deeds became controversial during the Seven Years' War, as Shawnees and Delawares in the Susquehanna Valley fought to defend homelands sold out from under them at the Albany Congress.[108]

The Iroquois's selling of Shawnee and Delaware land in the Susquehanna Valley would be a leading cause for Nicholas's Wyandot to realign their efforts back to those of the French and Detroit *Huron*. It would be assumed by the Wyandot, and most of the other Ohio Country tribes, that the British had one purpose and goal—to take all the land the Indians possessed as their own. The *Huron*'s alliance was still strong with the French against the British. The reunion of the *Huron* and Wyandot, along with their persuasive influence to rally the various tribes, was a critical weapon for the French. In addition, the French promoted the decisions of Lieutenant Colonel George Washington to the various tribes as being the manifest nature of British aggression on the Great Island. The French were at that moment victims of British aggression, and the Indians would be next. The French convinced the tribes that what happened in the remote wilderness on the far eastern edge of the Ohio Country would be played out time and time again until not one of them, French and Indian alike, would be left alive.

Battle of the Monongahela, 1755

According to many firsthand and contemporary accounts of the Battle of the Monongahela, the Wyandot did not participate in the battle. Thus, when doing research on the Wyandot, it is imperative to always look for the name *Huron*. Although an exact list and number are disputed, history records the participating tribes as being Ottawa, Potawatomi, Chippewa, *Huron*, Delaware, Shawnee, and Mingo. It has been said that the largest number of warriors in the battle arrived from Detroit, was represented by approximately eight hundred Ottawa, Potawatomi, and *Huron* commanded by Ensign Charles Langlade.[109]

> As fast as these bands were ready they gathered their canoes and sped over the waters of Lake Michigan and Huron, past Detroit and through Lake Erie to the French post at the present City of Erie; whence Langlade led them over the hills and through the woods to the little fort Duquesne at the head of the Ohio, where they were soon destined to make important history. With them there were also the Hurons or Wyandots of Lake Huron. . . . Langlade's motley throng of savages, about four or five hundred, with his border partisans arrived at Fort Duquesne about the 1st of July, 1755.[110]

Lyman C. Draper stated, "De Beaujeu organized a force of about two hundred and fifty French, and six hundred and fifty Indians."[111] Ronald D. Martin indicated, "Captain Beaujeu led 192 French and 637 Indians, all that could be persuaded or shamed into joining the seemingly hopeless attack."[112] The actual number of Indian participants is disputed, but it's clear the various tribes acted with minimal leadership from the French officers. Regardless of the number of Indians in the battle, the lopsided victory was convincing.

The little spark that ignited the major battle on the Monongahela occurred in the wilderness somewhere near the confluence of the Mononga-hela and Allegheny rivers. Lieutenant Colonel George Washington ambushed and killed a French commander, Sieur de Jumonville, on May 28, 1754. The French cried foul, and, knowing war was imminent, the British dispatched General Edward Braddock from the port city of Cork on the southern coast of Ireland on January 15, 1755, to be commander-in-chief of the army in the American colonies.

Arriving at Hampton Roads, Virginia, in March, and his command rein-forced with colonial militia, General Braddock's army grew to nearly three thousand men. By early May, General Braddock reached Wills Creek, his base of operations for the campaign. His objective was to capture Fort Duquesne and drive the French back across Lake Erie and end their claim to the Ohio Country. General Braddock had his mind trained for European modes of warfare. Looking good was part of the strategy, and, as we have seen, the appearance of Indian warriors was no less strategic. In the Ohio Country, war was savage and quickly made the European gentleman wars obsolete. Red uni-forms in the wilderness accomplished two things: They made the soldiers easy to see, and they masked the blood of the soldiers who wore them. The Eng-lish traveled in style: "The baggage train was four miles long. All this seems ridiculous, when it is known, the savage and borderer, under de Langlade, wore only breeches and hunting shirt, some of them carrying a blanket for night use. They had their guns and spears, but no baggage train or baggage."[113]

It would take General Braddock nearly a month to hack his way through the Pennsylvania wilderness with nearly one thousand three hundred troops in addition to supporting men, women, and tons of equipment. With knowledge of the slow-advancing British army, Captain Daniel Hyacinthe Liénard de Beaujeu organized his small army of French and Indians to ambush General Braddock's convincingly superior army. To allow a direct frontal assault and siege of Fort Duquesne would have been suicide. Captain Beaujeu abandoned European tactics of war, donned war paint and the clothing of his Indians (or lack thereof), and planned his attack. Reluctant to attack and fight a much superior army, the Indians had their morale boosted, and their resolve to fight strengthened, as Beaujeu became one, in a figurative and literal sense, with his troops. It was determined that an ambuscade at the crossing of the Monongahela or some other favorable spot was the best mode of stopping the advancing army. Beaujeu proposed the plan to the Indians, received communion, dressed himself like a savage, and joined his ravenous army.[114]

Leaving approximately one hundred men to burn Fort Duquesne if his mission failed, on the early morning of July 9, 1755, Captain Beaujeu left the false security of his fort for the forest. "They [Indians] numbered six hundred and thirty-seven; and with them went thirty-six French officers and cadets, seventy-two regular soldiers, and a hundred and forty-six Canadians, or about nine hundred in all."[115] With General Braddock's army a short ten miles from Fort Duquesne, the action plan had to be quickly deployed. Within moments of attacking the advanced guard of the British column, Captain Beaujeu was struck in a volley and instantly killed. His Canadian militia turned and abandoned the field. However,

the Indians alone remained and "Their awful war-whoop rang out on the mountain side. The fierce savage growl of the bear came from the Ottawa; mingled with the blood curdling screech of the Winnebago, imitating the panther of Wisconsin; mingled with the venomous cries of the Menomonee; the treacherous scream of the Pottawattamies; and the long wail of revenge from the Wyandots.[116]

Captain Jean-Daniel Dumas, Beaujeu's second in command, rallied the Indians and broke the British advance guard. The Indians then encircled the confused soldiers and began killing them hundreds at a time. Within three hours the battle had been won. By nightfall the British were retreating from the battlefield with a mortally wounded General Braddock, who would die in three days from a wound to his chest.[117] The Indians had won a decisive victory. They took a lot of scalps and a lot of contraband from the bodies of the fallen soldiers. "'I cannot describe the horror of that scene, no pen can do it. The yell of the Indians is fresh in my ears, and the terrific sound will haunt me till the hour of my death,' wrote one of Braddock's officers, three weeks after."[118]

British and colonial militia: twenty-six officers killed, thirty-seven wounded; four hundred thirty soldiers killed, three hundred eighty-five wounded. "Responsibility for the disaster [was placed] on the unnecessary panic shown by the enlisted ranks. . . . the failure of colonial governments to provide requisite supplies on time and the alleged perfidy of Native Americans."[119] It is believed the French and Indians lost fewer than thirty men, with an unknown number of wounded.[120]

> Word of this startling and unexpected calamity spread quickly throughout the British mainland colonies causing grim forebodings—particularly along the generally unprotected frontier. Many of the settlers there subsequently deserted their holdings seeking greater security in locales in less exposed areas to the east. The French and their Indian allies, aware of their strategic advantage, began ravaging exposed outlying settlements.[121]

Pontiac's War, 1763–66

Before the French and Indian War came to a close, the Spanish, taking notice that the French were losing the war, came to their aid. Their effort was to no avail and eventually resulted in their loss of Spanish Florida to the British. At the beginning of 1763, negotiations were underway between Great Britain, France, and Spain to find concession and cease hostilities. The Treaty of Paris was signed on February 10, 1763, officially bringing the French and Indian War in North America to a close. Article VII of the treaty gave Great Britain the grand prize—most of the North American continent—and a bunch of very unhappy Indians as a bonus—all for free.

The Royal Proclamation of October 7, 1763, would come too late, prove too ambiguous, and be too insincere to prove any value in keeping the various tribes of the Ohio Country happy and secure. On May 7, 1763, the Ottawa's Chief Pontiac rebelled, thinking the French would soon return to North America. It was then clear, even before any proclamations had been declared, that the "loving Subjects" of King George III would ignore any boundaries to the Indians' claim of land.

Long before the Treaty of Paris was signed, Major Robert Rogers and his rangers arrived on November 29, 1760, in Fort Detroit to accept the unconditional surrender of the French.[122] Upon their arrival, it did not take long for a party of Ottawa to intercept and inform Major Rogers that their chief, the great Pontiac, was the king and lord of this country.[123] Within minutes Pontiac arrived and demanded to know why Major Rogers came into his country with troops without his permission. Inspired with great caution to choose his words carefully, Major Rogers responded that he came in peace and only to accept the surrender of the French garrison of Fort Detroit. Pontiac was doubtful that this was his true intent, but he received his words and smoked the calumet of peace. Pontiac also gave him free passage throughout his country without fear of being harassed or attacked and killed.

The tribes at Detroit watched in amazement as the French capitulated. All the French commanding officers and soldiers were promptly sent away as prisoners. The Indians were appalled at the weakness displayed by their French allies and appalled that the victors, the British, did not kill their French captives with gallant pleasure. To add even more confusion to the charade all the French citizens were allowed to stay and retain possession of their homes, farms, property, and livestock. Before being allowed to stay, they first had to swear allegiance to the "Most Serene and Most Potent Prince, George the Third."[124] Observing the spectacle from afar, and in silent protest, Pontiac knew that the raising of the British flag over Fort Detroit indicated "the downfall of Indian supremacy in America."[125]

Pontiac and his allies had not been conquered or forced to swear loyalty to the unseen British king. The British had conquered, or were in the process of trying to conquer, a vast and troubled realm they knew very little about. Sir William Johnson, distinguished soldier, diplomat, politician, and overall smart guy on everything there was to know about the various Indian tribes, was appointed Superintendent of Indian Affairs for Great Britain in the whole of the Northern Colonies. The problem was that the various tribes were thinly scattered, and a person could travel for days through pristine forests, rolling prairies, and dark muggy swamps without seeing a living soul. Finding the tribes, if they did not want to be found, would be like trying to find a porcupine quill in a forest of pine needles.

The British did not have to go searching through the forests to find the tribes, many had settled in the area of Fort Detroit and their presence was well known. The Ottawa were there as were the *Huron*. The Wyandot were also deeply entrenched along the Sandusky River in the Ohio Country. "The Wyandots of Sandusky and Detroit far surpassed the surrounding tribes in energy of character and in social progress. Their log dwellings were strong and commodious, their agriculture was very considerable, their name stood high in war and policy, and they were regarded with deference by all the adjacent Indians."[126]

Unfortunately, Pontiac did not hold much regard for the *Huron*. His disregard was surpassed only by his jealousy. The longstanding history of friendship had been bruised with many spats. Pontiac and the Ottawa challenged the *Huron*'s unquestioned position of leadership among the tribes. It would be the Ottawa who would lead the coming attack on the British in a brilliant and masterful way. Chief Pontiac seemed to ignore tradition and challenged the *Huron*'s reputation with disdain and threats of reprisals. For many of the *Huron* the recent memory of how the Ottawa once held them in a state of vassalage would forbid their immediate response to Pontiac's demand to join his confederacy against the British.

Sir William Johnson was dispatched to Fort Detroit to ascertain the whereabouts and loyalties of the various tribes in the west. He too was to assess the state and condition of the fort itself. Sir Johnson's primary goals during the expedition were twofold: "first to conclude a solid and lasting treaty with the western tribes . . . and secondly, to regulate the fur trade, and settle the prices of clothes and provisions."[127] When Sir Johnson arrived at Detroit on September 3, 1761, the Indians were not impressed; however, he received a lukewarm yet friendly welcome. Upon his arrival the various tribes came bearing gifts and many questions. To the chagrin of Sir Johnson, he and his officers were woefully unprepared. "The Hurons, the Pottawatamies, the Wyandots, the Chipewas, and the Ottawas were all present. Indians from regions far beyond the Superior also came, that, with their own eyes, they might behold the man, whose house was the fire place of the dreaded Iroquois."[128]

Herein lay the problem with Sir Johnson and his ability to obtain a viable and lasting treaty with the Western tribes—all the various tribes knew of Sir Johnson's longstanding relationship with the Iroquois Confederacy. In their mind's eye Sir Johnson could be trusted no more than his villainous bedfellows. Also in attendance from the east were the Shawnee, Delaware, and Seneca. The Shawnee and Delaware had recently felt the burn of the Iroquois's treachery, and the atmosphere was charged with tension. However, the Seneca did not come as allies of Sir Johnson and the British. They came as allies of Pontiac and the alliance he was quietly assembling. The Seneca arrived at the conference days before Sir Johnson and made contact with their Wyandot cousins. They came bearing a special request, and they knew their cousins were the best tribe to accomplish the task.

After one day of speeches, negotiations, and compromises, the assembly was excused. Sir Johnson was promptly pulled aside by the *Huron* and a recommendation was made that a treaty be presented the next day. There were obvious concerns; for example, "some of the Indians, loitering around the fort, might get drunk."[129] A drunk Indian creates a bad day for Englishmen. Taking the advice of the *Huron,* the next morning the tribes were assembled, and a treaty was quickly presented, and the response of the many tribes was very satisfactory.[130]

However, before the tribes could retire to their various places, Kaiaghshota, a Seneca chief, and two Wyandots stepped forward to address the assembled Englishmen and Indians. Earlier, before the conference had been convened, the Seneca had been accused of recruiting the Wyandot to kill all the Englishmen at Fort Detroit. Kaiaghshota wanted to try to dispel the accusations in spite of overwhelming evidence the accusations were true. "In the midst of his speech, however, Adariaghta, the chief warrior of the Hurons, coming forward, confronted him, and disclosing everything that had occurred, revealed to all present the Seneca's duplicity."[131] An Ohio Indian named White Mingo, whose tribe was not disclosed, accused the *Huron* of trying to incite a massacre of the British troops. Sir Johnson quickly adjourned the conference and distracted the various tribes with the giving of gifts. This likely averted a major disaster with monumental consequences for Sir Johnson.

The preceding account was provided to reiterate two interesting observations. First, there seems to have been contention and a little irritation between the *Huron* and the Wyandot. The *Huron* looked to favor a peaceful relationship with the British, while the Wyandot, who may have seriously entertained the Seneca's offer, look to be hostile toward the British. Second, it also appears that the *Huron* from Detroit may have been looked upon and treated as a tribe separate from the Wyandot on the Sandusky. Why else would the Wyandot at Detroit still be referred to as *Huron* while the Wyandot from Sandusky were now being called Wyandot? The *Huron* and Wyandot were truly evolving into becoming two separate Wyandot bands with a common origin and identity.

Sir William Johnson spent the next few days at Detroit celebrating and socializing with the fort's garrison and civilian residents. As Johnson headed east, the attitude of the garrison and the obvious reality of what just happened were quickly made clear. Without two superpowers to compete and vie for the attention, friendship, and alliance of the various tribes, they and their interests became a secondary concern for the British. In short order the gifts the tribes had come to expect became scarce. Variances in the price for trade goods became common, and the traders were taking advantage of the Indians. Behind the traders came unwelcome and illegal settlers to occupy the land that had been deemed by his Most Serene and Most Potent Prince George III to be exclusively reserved for the Indians.

The various tribes along the Eastern frontier had no choice but to defend their homeland. After all, if the British were not honoring the official proclamation of their king and the treaties of his agents, who else would protect and defend the homeland? That's right: no one but the Indians themselves. With unquestionable rights to protect what rightfully belonged to them—their families, lives, way of life, and land—they quickly and earnestly began taking matters into their own hands.

> During the fall of 1762 he [Pontiac] traveled many miles through the forests or in his canoe, visiting the various tribes, and succeeded in enlisting most of those northwest of the Ohio River in his scheme. The Pottawatomi chief, Ninivois, was a weak character and fell easy prey to Pontiac's seductive oratory, but the Huron presented a more complex problem to the wily schemer. The Huron were of two branches, which were led by Takay and Teata, the former a match for Pontiac in character, but the latter a shrewd, discerning man who was not persuaded to Pontiac's way of thinking. Consequently, the Ottawa chief had to be content with the aid of only half of the Huron band, [th]at under Takay.[132]

Pontiac's plot was simple: At a given signal the tribes were to gain access to the forts (not just Detroit but all British forts), fall upon the unsuspecting garrisons, and massacre everyone to the last man, woman, and child. The most difficult task was aligning the many different tribes to act in unison. However, the plot was revealed to Major Gladwin on May 6 by his mistress, an Ojibwa girl,[133] and steps were immediately taken for the safety of Fort Detroit. Other forts throughout the Ohio Country, however, did not have the luxury of an advanced warning and suffered terrible fates.

With his plot near fully exposed, Pontiac tried to act as though nothing was happening and everything was normal with a boring and monotonous status quo. After being forbidden entrance to the fort on May 9, Pontiac attacked all the "English dwellings, built outside the palisades, and having tomahawked their wretched inmates, bore the reeking scalps to their camp, and spent the entire night in dancing and carousing."[134] Thus the siege of Fort Detroit officially began on May 10, 1763. The time had come to relieve Detroit of the British menace.

The Ottawa would not attack alone; at least half of the *Huron*-Wyandot Tribe, under the leadership of Takay, also joined the attack. The Potawatomi and Ojibwa also participated—the old alliance of the four Lake Tribes was still holding strong. Balls of lead slammed hard against the fort's palisades; however, the British entrapped behind the walls could not find targets at which to return the fire. The warriors of the four tribes hid behind every means of protective cover and were no less invisible than if they were fighting in a forest and hiding behind trees. With the fort's garrison having provisions for no more than three weeks, Pontiac was content to starve the occupants of the fort or force them into surrendering.

As the siege ensued, Pontiac came to the realization that not all the *Huron*-Wyandot were at his side joining his alliance. Infuriated, and with several of his chiefs in tow, Takay likely being one, Pontiac was determined to rectify the injustice. Nearly half the *Huron*-Wyandot had come under the influence of Jesuit Father Pierre Potier. These *Huron* living in the general vicinity of Detroit were the *Huron* under the leadership of Teata.

I can see Pontiac, just shy of a state of delirious rage, standing nose-to-nose with Teata. While Pontiac was screaming, little spitballs hit Teata square in the face, yet he did not blink. In the middle of Pontiac's rant, Teata, with a defiant and mocking smile, squeezed the drops of spit from his own lips. Following his convictions, and with knowledge and wisdom of the ongoing political implications, Teata chose to remain firm but not incite Pontiac beyond his own self-induced condition. Unfortunately, with threats of destruction Teata did not have much of a choice. It's clear, and disappointing to see, that the old Ottawa way of forcing the *Huron* to fight their wars had not changed in over one hundred years.

Father Potier consented, allowing his flock to fight in the last war, as it was then the Catholic French against the heretic Anglican English. It was necessary to use every means available to defeat the English, even to the extreme of going to war. This time, though, things were different and war was an unacceptable risk. One of the means to ensure that his *Huron* would not fight was to threaten the withholding of the holy sacraments. For the nominal Catholic *Huron* this was a serious offense. Now that Pontiac threatened their destruction and was deathly serious about its effect, it was either fight or die. Of course Teata chose to fight, but not without first holding mass and getting the blessing from Father Potier. "These nominal Christians of Father Pothier's [*sic*] flock, together with the other Wyandots, soon distinguished themselves in the war; fighting better it is said than all the other Indians—an instance of the marked superiority of the Iroquois over the Algonquin stock."[135]

Across the whole of the frontier, synchronized attacks erupted with intensity never before experienced by the British or any other European power. Nearly all the Algonquian-speaking tribes banded together, as did the Iroquoian-speaking *Huron,* Wyandot, Seneca, and Cherokee. Several tribes of the lower Mississippi also joined the alliance. The Seneca were not the Seneca of the Iroquois Confederacy but rather the Mingo. The Iroquois remained neutral under the influence of Sir William Johnson.[136] Fort Pitt was laid siege by the Seneca, Shawnee, and Delaware. Like at Fort Detroit, all the civilian inhabitants outside the protection of the fort's walls were mercilessly and horridly hacked to death with tomahawks and knives. Pontiac's plan was simple, effective, and perfectly timed to coincide with a certain change of the moon in May of 1763. Every military post of the English was simultaneously attacked, and hundreds of soldiers were killed, no less than the civilians, in the most brutal and horrific ways imaginable.[137]

Pontiac's plan also included the purging of unscrupulous English traders from the Ohio Country who were literally raping and pillaging the various tribes. Throughout the whole of the Ohio Country nearly every trader was killed in all the Indian villages. The first two and three days of the war saw some of the most horrific killings in the most barbaric and treacherous ways known to savage warfare. The fury of an abused and vengeful Indian had been fully released. The Moravian missionary George Henry Loskiel relates the story of one such attack in the villages of the Wyandot. The following event likely occurred at Lower Sandusky.

> The traders were so numerous that the Indians were afraid to attack them openly, and had recourse to the following stratagem: They told their unsuspecting victims that the surrounding tribes had risen in arms, and were soon coming that way, bent on killing every Englishman they could find. The Wyandots averred that they would gladly protect their friends, the white men; but that it would be impossible to do so, unless the latter would consent, for the sake of appearances, to become their prisoners. In this case, they said, the hostile Indians would refrain from injuring them, and they should be set at liberty as soon as the danger was past. The traders fell into the snare. They gave up their arms, and, the better to carry out the deception, even consented to be bound; but no sooner was this accomplished, than their treacherous counsellors murdered them all in cold blood.[138]

Over time, the ensuing stalemates and uneventful, boring sieges of Forts Detroit and Pitt began to sputter. Under Teata, the Potawatomi and *Huron* sued the English for peace, which was promptly granted. The Seneca also sued for peace, and they too were allowed to retire. On June 10, 1764, Teata arrived at Detroit bearing a dispatch from Sir William Johnson.[139] After Teata had delivered Sir Johnson's message, another Wyandot chief from Sandusky named Big Jaw thanked Teata for his troubles. The council deliberated after Teata advised them to come to their senses. Four days later Teata was summoned to deliver the tribe's decision to Sir William. One of the questions asked by Sir William was Why did the tribes attack the British? The council responded, "Tell him it was them that just embroiled the Earth and were the first cause of what has been done."[140] This was a simple and pointed response to a very complicated and multilayered problem. This was not the answer Sir William expected and hoped to hear.

Sir William and the Iroquois Confederacy wanted Pontiac's alliance to assume full responsibility for the unjustified uprising.[141] The council instructed Teata to deliver a wampum belt of peace and recite the following: "What is past is past, that we have yet done no harm since last summer, we have kept our Young Men quiet for which reason we think the breach may be easily mended."[142] Two Mohawk who traveled with Teata tried to incite the council by stating that the Shawnee and Delaware were again on the warpath. The council knew better, and the Wyandot from Sandusky laughed and mocked Teata behind his back. They called him a fool for believing what Sir William sent him to relay.[143]

During the war forts Detroit and Pitt were besieged for more than a year. The frontier settlements of New York, Pennsylvania, and Virginia were ravaged with tomahawk and fire. Countless and defenseless settlers fled from the frontier to the interior of the colonies; however, even the furthest-removed settlements and towns were not immune to attack. The war lasted for over two years and created widespread horror and destruction. It was not until the British marched an army to the far outposts of Kaskaskia and Cahokia, on the banks of the Mississippi River, and raised the red flag did the war end.[144] Pontiac's war came to an end in the fall of 1764, yet Pontiac did not concede to the British until July of 1766.

After the close of the war Pontiac removed himself from the political scene and sought personal exile in the Illinois Country. It is believed that here in April of 1769 Pontiac was brutally assassinated with a tomahawk by a drunken man of the Kaskaskia Tribe. This nameless man was bribed with a barrel of liquor to kill the great chief.[145] In retaliation and vengeance many of the tribes who had followed Pontiac in his recent war with the British rose up against the tribes of the Illinois: Peoria, Kaskaskia, and Cahokia. The fate of each tribe was desperately severe as Pontiac's avengers nearly killed every last citizen.[146]

For a brief period of time after Pontiac laid down his tomahawk, peace reluctantly and superficially prevailed. The relationship between the British and the various tribes improved, but it never quite achieved the level of comfort once experienced with the French. The French never returned to the Great Island as many of the tribes had been deceived into believing.

As citizens of the British colonies began to express their dissatisfaction with having the burden of paying for the cost of the last war through excessive taxes, hints of another war loomed on the horizon. It was then that once-bitter foes slowly and cautiously became precarious allies. The various tribes sided with the British Empire against the American colonies in their War of Independence. It was for the various tribes a matter of choosing the lesser of two evils. Having personally experienced the brutal and barbaric power the various tribes possessed for war, the British army recruited and inflamed the tribes against their rebelling colonists—their fellow citizens. This would command harsh rebuke from the British Parliament. The British made promises to the tribes they could never keep, but during times of war, friends are often made out of convenience and necessity, knowing that promises are often words of appeasement and flattery. The British turned loose their horrible hell-hounds of savage war—and indeed it was savage war.

CHAPTER 3

"Wyandots Will Not Be Taken Alive"

The Hurons, alone among the Indian tribes, held it disgraceful to turn from the face of an enemy when the fortunes of the fight were adverse.[1]
—Henry Rowe Schoolcraft, ca. 1884

"These Horrible Hell-Hounds of Savage War"[2]

A popular read back in the mid-nineteenth century was Joseph Pritts's *Incidents of Border Life*. The book detailed the lives and circumstances of many whites who were captured, adopted, or escaped from Indian captivity. With so many whites finding fame for suffering, or glorious deeds of valor, the book seemed to convince the reader that only whites suffered during the Indian wars of the Ohio Country. Actually, white and red alike performed valiantly and suffered greatly on both sides of the frontier. From 1755 to 1813, war seemed never-ending in the Ohio Country. The loss of life was extreme. No one was safe. Men, women, children, and infants—white and Indian alike—would suffer and die in some of the most horrific ways imaginable. For the Indians, desperate measures demanded desperate tactics, and brutality met brutality while both races perpetrated savage warfare. The Indians did terrible things as did the whites. The whites pushed hard and the Indians pushed back even harder. Of course after the wars ended, the victors forgot all the bad things they had done, and the Indians were solely to blame for all the spilled blood.

> We are too apt to think of the Indian as a lurking, dangerous, unrelenting savage, infesting the forest and living without laws or restrictions of any kind, and with no intentions but of evil. This view is both erroneous and unjust. It is true that they were alert and dangerous as enemies when once they were

made enemies, but when we shall have learned a broader charity, and truth instead of prejudice and fiction shall be recorded as history, it will be found that the Indian has not always been the aggressor, and was not by nature the cruel savage as generally assumed and represented. We, the white people, have written all the history so far, but a more impartial review will yet be made when it will appear that the cruel and vindictive acts of the Indians were largely the result of the cruel and vindictive acts of the white men.[3]

Colonel Edward Livingston Taylor, in September of 1897, could not have said the preceding statement any better or with greater conviction. What he said was politically incorrect for his day. Just a little less than seven years earlier on December 29, 1890, the massacre at Wounded Knee occurred in South Dakota. It was there that old men, women, and children were mercilessly murdered by soldiers of the US Army. The plight and continued killing of the Indians had not improved in the fifty years since Summundowat's barbaric and unprovoked assassination at the hands of white men. Summundowat was the Wyandot's head chief in Ohio. He was a defiant yet peaceful man who was also an ordained minister of the Methodist Church. Summundowat paid dearly for his resistance to removal in 1840. It cost him his life.

Of all the Indian wars fought upon the Great Island, it is believed more people lost their lives in the frontier wars of Western Pennsylvania, Virginia, and Ohio than all the other Indian wars combined. This includes people killed during the French and Indian War, the American Revolution, and the many numerous uprisings in between, ending with the War of 1812. Many on both sides of the frontier would remain unaccounted for as they were killed on small plots of land in the unknown wilderness or were captured and adopted into many of the various tribes including the *Huron*-Wyandot. Pritts continued by stating of the people who ventured west into the land of the savages, "Almost every one knows something . . . of desperate conflicts between the white settlers and their savage foes, sometimes one party victorious, and sometimes the other.[4]

During this time relationships were very complex, not only between the English and French or the English and Americans, but also between the Indians and their European allies. The relationship between the various tribes was also complex, and they frequently disagreed on how to align their efforts against the white invasion. Throughout much of the border wars the Wyandot had *issues* with both the Shawnee and the Delaware, two of their closest and most trusted allies. The Wyandot never declared war on the Shawnee or

Delaware, but at times stress in the relationship may have come very close to creating all-out war, even as they were fighting the Americans. There were also ongoing wars within the wars. As the standing European armies fought each other on the North American battlefields, the colonial militias of the British, and then the Americans, fought the various Indian tribes on separate battlefields.

In the fall of 1763 or 1764, during Pontiac's War, about fifty Delaware and Mingo warriors descended the Great Sandy River deep into Virginia. The warriors had fully intended to attack Roanoke, Catawba, and Fort Young, which is near present-day Covington, Virginia. As the war party approached Fort Young, they came across a stockade fort on the land of William Carpenter. The stockade was managed and under the care of a man named Brown. Approaching the stockade, Carpenter was killed. Carpenter's son, two sons of Brown, and one woman were taken captive. All three boys were noted as small children. The elder of the two Brown boys was about six years old.[5]

Returning to the Ohio Country, the two sons of Brown were sold to the Wyandot. "Brown's youngest son, (the late Col. Samuel Brown of Greenbrier) was brought home in 1769—the elder son never returned."[6] The elder son, Adam Brown, stayed with the tribe and eventually took a Wyandot woman as his mate. Adam became well respected, wealthy, and very influential within his adopted people. Until the War of 1812, Adam lived a happy and fulfilled life at Brownstown, named in his honor, just outside Detroit. There were many whites who despised the name Adam Brown. What did the whites have against Adam? He "acted a conspicuous part in the late war and died in 1815."[7] Adam clearly stood with his adopted people against the people of his birth. There are stories in Wyandot tradition telling of Adam's participation in many war parties against the whites. For Adam, he was an Indian—a Wyandot— and unlike his younger brother he chose to stay with the Wyandot and live the life of an Indian.

Adam was just one of many white children who were adopted into the Wyandot Tribe and rose to prominent positions. There are many interesting events in the life of Adam Brown. One such event involves another white captive named William Walker. When William came into the Wyandot Tribe as a child, he was initially purchased by Adam. Yes, an adopted white man purchased another white boy to be his slave. Adam did this as an intervention to save his life and likely never put or held William in the position of bondage. William lived with Adam until he took a mate somewhere around 1789. From this union William Walker Jr. was born.

William E. Connelley told the story of another white child's adoption into the Wyandot Tribe. The child's English birth name is unknown, as would have been the case with infants or young children adopted into the tribe. This very young boy was taken captive during the Revolutionary War when the Wyandot were raiding the Cherokee in Eastern Tennessee. Yes, as noted earlier, while fighting the British colonists, the Wyandot were still fighting other Indian tribes. As the Wyandot war party was descending the Big Sandy River, they came across an abandoned cabin. A warning of the warriors' approach had been extended to its inhabitants, and the occupants fled; however, they forgot something of great value—a very young boy. As the Wyandot warriors were walking through the valley, they saw the young boy running to find a place and hide.

When they arrived at the homestead, a search ensued and the young boy was found hiding in the bed of a muddy stream. By chance a Wyandot warrior looked under a mass of tangled roots extending over the stream bank where the boy was found pressed deep into the mud. Grabbed by the foot, the young boy was pulled kicking, but not screaming, from the roots where he was hiding. Since he pressed himself deep into the bank of the stream, his mouth was full of mud. From that day onward he was called Mud Eater.

The young boy was given food and taken back to Detroit where he was adopted into the Wyandot Tribe. Mud Eater's son, Russia Mudeater, took for his mate a daughter of Adam Brown. It's interesting how stories often come full circle. Matthew Mudeater, their son, would become one of the greatest chiefs of the Wyandot and Wyandotte people.[8]

In 1755 during the Battle of the Monongahela, James Smith was an eighteen-year-old captive of the Indians.[9] During the battle James was kept inside Fort Duquesne as his wounds healed from being forced to run the gauntlet just days earlier. Unlike Adam Brown and Mud Eater, years later James Smith would eventually leave his adopted people and return to the people of his birth. James was an adult when captured and, unlike many adopted children, could not be completely washed of his white blood. As Colonel James Smith, he would write his memoirs detailing his stay with the Indians to dispel the common belief they were something less than undisciplined savages. Colonel Smith explained his opinion based upon his personal experiences.

I have often heard the British officers call the Indians the undisciplined savages, which is a capital mistake—as they have all the essentials of discipline. They are under good command, and punctual in obeying orders: they can act in concert. . . . When they go into battle, they are not loaded or encumbered with many clothes, as they commonly fight naked, save only breech-clout, leggins and moccasins. There is no such thing as corporal punishment used, in order to bring them under such good discipline: degrading is the only chastisement, and they are so unanimous in this, that it effectually answers the purpose. Their officers plan, order and conduct matters until they are brought into action, and then each man is to fight as though he was to gain the battle himself. . . . Could it be supposed that undisciplined troops could defeat Generals Braddock, Grant, &.c. . . . The Indians had no aid from the French, or any other power, when they besieged Fort Pitt, in the year 1763. . . . They had no British troops with them when they defeated Colonel Crawford, near the Sandusky, in the time of the American war with Great Britain; or when they defeated Colonel Loughrie, on the Ohio, near the Miami, on his way to meet General Clarke; this was also in the time of the British war. It was the Indians alone that defeated Colonel Todd, in Kentucky, near the Blue Licks, in the year 1782; and Colonel Harmer, betwixt the Ohio and Lake Erie, in the year 1790, and General St. Clair, in the year 1791; and it is said that there were more of our men killed at this defeat, than there were in any one battle during our contest with Great Britain.[10]

At the outbreak of the French and Indian War the *Huron*-Wyandot people had been in a state of constant war for well over one hundred years. How did the *Huron*-Wyandot prepare for war? Why were they so successful against the greatest military powers—the Iroquois Confederacy and the British Empire—to then exist upon the face of the Earth? As I reflect on the question, it is easy to compare the *Huron*-Wyandot to ancient Spartans in their battles against the Persian Empire. Both Spartan and *Huron*-Wyandot warriors were fierce, always outnumbered, highly respected, and regarded as elite warriors. Did the *Huron*-Wyandot have a special military academy that produced such noted warriors? No, they were just ordinary boys who grew into ordinary young men who would become extraordinary legends on the battlefields. Always outnumbered, always fearless, always noble in their defense of the homeland, they lost many warriors: mates, fathers, sons, brothers, grandfathers, uncles, and nephews.

Consul W. Butterfield in *An Historical Account of the Expedition against Sandusky* stated, "The Wyandots were the most powerful. This arose not so much from the number of their warriors, as from their superior intelligence."[11] When *Huron*-Wyandot warriors took to the battlefield, they were more than capable of employing tactics and strategy that confounded and overwhelmed their enemies—on both a military and a diplomatic level. When combined with an ancient tradition of never turning their backs and giving up the fight, *Huron*-Wyandot warriors were a terrible and dreadful foe. In addition to their intellect, *Huron*-Wyandot warriors used the ancient practice of employing the Spirits, and their services, for courage, strength, guidance, and leadership.

To best illustrate this practice, in 1911 Star Young recited to Dr. Charles Marius Barbeau a "Wyandot War Adventure."[12] Star's narrative is centered on a *Huron*-Wyandot village that had been attacked by an Indian enemy with many citizens killed. Many citizens were also found to be missing and presumed taken captive. Star's narrative is a rather fanciful and unconventional story that easily illustrates the old belief in Spirits and the shamanic lifestyle that once permeated the *Huron*-Wyandot's way of life. The narrative begins with the head chief entreating the Spirits for a terrible revenge with words of honor and a gift of sacred tobacco. The *Huron*-Wyandot warriors painted their bodies; gathered their spears, bows, arrows, and tomahawks; and prepared themselves for the war dance. Along with these traditional implements of war, other magnificent weapons were also gathered.

After dancing, and before taking to the warpath, the head chief would shake a dried wolf skin and throw it to the ground. The dead skin would turn into a live wolf. The head chief would then address the wolf, "Now, Cousin Wolf," said the chief, "you have to follow their trail!" Pointing in the direction taken by the hostile Indians, the wolf would howl and jump until the head chief ordered him to rush ahead, and the warriors would promptly follow. When their enemy was near, the head chief would catch the wolf, shake it, and once again it would become a dried skin. Next the head chief would take a dried crow that represented a mystical bird much larger than a raven. This dried crow when shaken would turn into the powerful raven and soar into the sky, giving the warriors an eye from above. As the raven flew back and forth, tightening its path, the warriors then knew the enemy was very close. Again the chief would catch the raven and shake it, and it would also turn back into the dried resemblance from where it came.

Before the enemy would be attacked, another fire was kindled and another dance celebrated with more sacred tobacco burned as an offering. At this fire the chief would again make the noble request to the Spirits for honorable revenge. Once again a dried skin would be employed to help seek out the enemy—this time, that of a small bird. After being shaken and thrown to the ground, the small dried bird would turn into a quail who with precision would lead the war party to their unsuspecting prey. When the quail would return and fall to the feet of the head chief, the warriors knew that their enemy was ready to be vanquished. For many people this is an amazing story that holds little validity, but can they say with confidence that it is not true? Did Sparta and Persia also employ the Spirits in the many battles they fought? Ancient civilizations perceived their relationship with Nature much differently than most contemporary civilizations do today; however, there are still remote civilizations in the world who rely on Nature, and their chiefs, to seek help from the Spirits, in ways many people cannot fully understand today.

The *Huron*-Wyandot's shaman sought guidance from the Spirits, and the clan chiefs were charged with teaching and training their citizens in the arts of war. During times of great stress and imminent danger, the whole of the Wyandot Tribe would unite against common enemies and consent to the leadership of the warpole, the war chief, and his war chiefs (usually numbering about two). Even the head chief of the tribe would submit to his warpole's decisions. Before being taught the skills to fight their most dangerous foe, their fellow man, *Huron*-Wyandot children, only the boys, were taught the skills of hunting small game. *Huron*-Wyandot girls and women were not permitted to touch implement of war in anger or vengeance, for they bore life and did not invest themselves in the taking of life; however, at times women were known to accompany their men during war and the chase. Reverend Elliott in 1822 observed the passion *Huron*-Wyandot boys held for the chase.

> The passion of the boys for hunting was strong and unconquerable. All of them came equipped with bows and arrows, in the use of which they were very dexterous. The bows were made of the toughest hickory, the strings of which were of the sinews of deer. It was rarely any would miss the mark. . . . The rabbit hunt was an amusing sight. He who first saw the rabbit uttered the well known war whoop, at which every one in the company joined in the pursuit; and unless the animal was near his hole, nothing was more certain than that an arrow soon laid him on the ground. Squirrels and birds of every description were killed by their arrows. Whenever any one killed anything in hunting, the first trophy of his victory was to tinge with the warm blood of the victim some prominent parts of the face, as the cheeks, chin and forehead. Thus from their childhood they are assiduously trained for the chase.[13]

It would not have been uncommon to see young *Huron*-Wyandot boys participating in skirmishes, battles, and all kinds of acts of war. C. C. Trowbridge

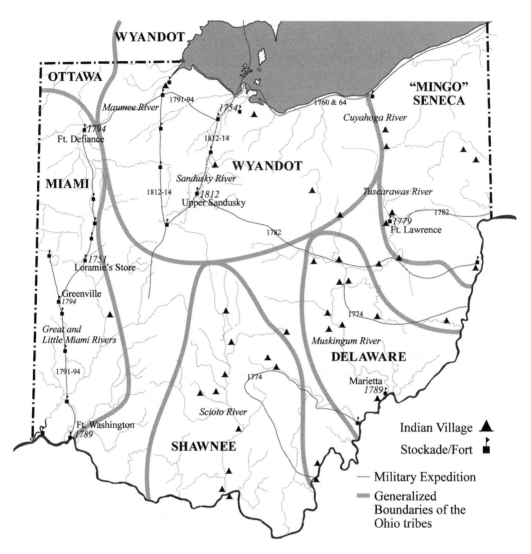

MAP 3.1. General Location of the Tribes in Ohio

indicated, "The young men go to war as early as the age of 10 years, so young that in presenting his rifle it almost falls to the ground, and then continue to bear arms until they are 70 years old."[14] The bow and arrow was their weapon of choice and they were experts in its use.

There is a longstanding tradition among the *Huron*-Wyandot people that a common, everyday tool of the chase and war was engineered to be unique among the various tribes. The nock on Wyandot arrows was a dimple, not a slit. The strings of Wyandot bows were tied in the middle with a knot. The dimple on the shaft of the arrow easily fit over the knot. This allowed only Wyandot warriors to shoot their arrows; however, the Wyandot could return the arrows of their enemies with their own knotted strings and the enemies' slit arrows. The warriors of the Wyandot's enemies could not easily pick up Wyandot arrows and return them, as they would not stay on their bowstrings. *Ingenious.* Development of the skills required to use a bow began at a very early age—with and without nocked arrows. C. C. Trowbridge also noted, "They also used spears, which were pointed like their arrows, with flint. They did not practice throwing the spear, but always retained it in the hand and thrust in the body of their enemies."[15] Trowbridge continued: "They assembled the nation and instructed the young in the art of war. They sometimes placed the youths in two parties opposed to each other for the purpose of training them, and these sham fights frequently produced unfortunate results, as some of the boys being wounded, in their endeavors to perfect themselves."[16]

The face paint of a Wyandot warrior was within itself a weapon. Reverend Elliott described the Snake clan's painting of their face. "The most striking kind of painting was that of the face, with the appearance of rattlesnakes. By a reddish kind of paint, the snakes, with their scales, head, tails, and hissing tongues, were drawn always to the life, in bunches on their faces, writhing and folding in each other, and emitting their poisonous venom, so as to present to a beholder at first sight a most shocking spectacle."[17] Each Wyandot clan possessed certain markings that easily identified each warrior's clan. Each warrior likely had his own style of painting that would have brought him special protection, power, and courage. Many of the warriors' faces and bodies were often painted red, and thus the name redskin was given to the Indians. The painting of the body with red ocher was an indication of life, and the painting of the body black with charcoal was an indication of death.

Over time the rifle would begin to replace the bow and arrow, and Wyandot warriors would become equally skilled with its use. However, in just about every account given, from the smallest raids on individual cabins to laying siege on nearly impenetrable forts, one implement of war stands far above the rest—the tomahawk. The tomahawk became the weapon of choice during a war that was often fought hand-to-hand and face-to-face. "It is not in Indian nature to stand quiet in the midst of war; and the defeat of Braddock was a signal for the western savages to snatch their tomahawks and assail the English settlements."[18]

Most, but not all, of the excursions into the British and American settlements originated from villages around Detroit or along the length of the Sandusky River. This was land claimed by the *Huron*-Wyandot. By 1747 Nicholas and his band had claimed nearly the whole of what would become the state of Ohio; however, there were several tribes who also called the Ohio Country home. The tribes who permanently lived on the land that became the state of Ohio did so at the invitation and blessing of the *Huron*-Wyandot.

Where did the various tribes live in the Ohio Country? In the early to mid-eighteenth century the Wyandots claimed nearly the whole of what later became the state of Ohio. There were no fences or walls erected to indicate the Wyandot lived here and everyone else lived over there somewhere; however, the rivers did provide a measure of indicating whose territory you may be passing through. Although the Wyandot laid claim to so much land, there were six nations who occupied or claimed a piece of the land: Wyandot, Mingo (Seneca), Shawnee, Delaware, Ottawa, and Miami. There were other tribes who passed through, and even stayed for awhile, but these six tribes wholly dominated the Ohio Country by the mid-eighteenth century.

As the Shawnee and Delaware moved into the Ohio Country, they were assigned a place and given permission to stay. During the Albany Congress of 1754 and the Treaty of Fort Stanwix in 1768, when tribes of the Iroquois Confederacy gave to the British land where the Shawnee and Delaware were residing, they had no choice of where to go: They had to go across the Ohio River onto land claimed by the *Huron*-Wyandot. The Shawnee and Delaware were welcome to stay only as long as they never sold or traded the land to the whites. The Mingo, or Seneca, already had a presence in the Ohio Country, as did the Miami and Ottawa tribes to lesser degrees.

With much disapproval and rebuke, almost to the point of declaring war, several tribes surrendered to the Americans land that the Wyandots had given them. Yet still after the Shawnee and Delaware gave away their land, the Wyandot again gave them even more land upon which to reside. The Wyandots are a generous and patient people, but only to a certain point. In an article found in the Treaty of 1789, signed at Fort Harmar, the following was stated to remind everyone of the Wyandot's rightful claim to the land. It also served as a warning to the Wyandot's displeasure and pending rebuke of the Shawnee Tribe:

> Be it remembered, That the Wyandots have laid claim to the lands that were granted to the Shawanese [*sic*], at the treaty held at the Miami, and have declared, that as the Shawanese have been so restless, and caused so much trouble, both to them and to the United States, if they will not now be at peace, they will dispossess them, and take the country into their own hands;

for that the country is theirs of right, and the Shawanese are only living upon it by their permission.[19]

As a result of the many various ongoing battles and wars, the six Ohio tribes suffered a terrible toll. Over time the tribes began to lose interest in the fight. One such instance during the Revolutionary War was noted when the Mingo approached Pomoacan, or the Half King, for advice after inciting the Virginians during a raid. The Virginians were now seeking revenge. Half King's advice to the Mingo was "Be strong & fight as men."[20]

By the early nineteenth century all the tribes chose to leave the state of Ohio, with the exception of the Wyandot Tribe. The Wyandots were the last tribe to leave the state of Ohio. They continued to defy the Americans; however, they did not send warriors to shed their blood on a battlefield. The Wyandots fielded a different kind of warrior—home-raised tribal attorneys and intelligent leading men of great capacity. When the Wyandot Tribe finally consented to sell the Grand Reserve in Ohio, and the *Huron* River Reserve in Michigan, leaving their beloved Ohio and Michigan would not be an easy or welcomed task. After defiantly standing in opposition to removal for twelve years, there were few, if any, choices but to move west. The Wyandot Tribe freely consented to leave the Ohio Country; however, the eviction notice was written in the blood of Chief Summundowat. The Wyandot Tribe did exactly as they advised their friends—they long stood strong and fought as men.

The following narrative on the defense of the Wyandot's chosen homeland is at times quite graphic and reflective of a time when death was all but imminent for those living on the frontiers. The Reverend James Bradley Finley stated the following on the savage and cruel barbarity often displayed by the Wyandot and their Indian allies: "Much has been said about the barbarity of these tribes in their mode of warfare. But let it always be recollected that they were nobly engaged in the defense of their country, their families, and their natural rights and national liberties. Never did men acquit themselves with more valor, nor, according to their means, make a better defense."[21]

As I describe what happened, I am not trying to glorify the carnage or make light of the lives lost on either side of the battlefields. The truth of history needs to be told and not misrepresented with pleasant, benign superlatives or hidden under pretty words and perfume. Obviously, my perspectives of the battles are different from what has been written thus far in most history books. My eyes are looking from the Indians' side of the battlefields. After the battles there were many widows, on both sides of the frontier, Indian and white alike.

When discussing the defense of the homeland, how could we begin to describe every skirmish, battle, or expedition? It would be impossible within the confines and intent of this book. I have chosen twelve different events to detail the border war as fought by the *Huron*-Wyandot. From a hand-to-hand wrestling match, merciless raids, and major battles, hopefully you will be able to see how involved, devastating, and fearless the *Huron*-Wyandot warriors were. The year 1777 alone has inspired complete books on the war that transpired within this one year. "This 'year of the three sevens,' as it was called, was long known as 'the bloody year' of border history."[22] Sure, during all the years of bloody warfare the Wyandots killed a lot of whites, but the whites also killed a lot of Wyandots.

The Death of Miss Jane McCrea, 1777

It has been said that history is written by the victors. Thus, the histories of the Border Wars largely ignore the white man's cruelties and mistakes. One such story is the killing of Miss Jane McCrea. Actually, there are many stories that tell of Jane's death, and most are as flamboyant and as far from the truth as nightmarish fairy tales. In spite of an apparent knowledge of truth, the outlandish stories were allowed to instill fear and disdain within the hearts and minds of the Colonial Americans. This fear was expressed toward both the British and their allies, and the allied tribes of the Ohio Country—in particular the Wyandot.

The one account relevant to this story that is most often ignored is the one told by the accused who was present when Jane died. Let's look at two of the more prominent versions of Jane's death. Why is Jane's death so important? After all, she is but one of thousands to die during the American Revolution at the hands of the Indians. This is the problem: Jane did not die at the hands of the Indians, yet still the Wyandot were blamed for her death.

It is known that Jane's fiancé was a Tory officer by the name of David Jones. Tories were American colonists who supported the British efforts during the American Revolution. David was attached to the army of British Lieutenant General John Burgoyne. One version of the story says that on July 27, 1777, Jane's fiancé commissioned two Indian scouts, Wyandot nonetheless, to escort Jane to their appointed wedding near Fort Edward. It was also said that while in route Jane was brutally killed by one of the scouts named Le Loup. Supposedly, a disagreement occurred between the two Wyandots over a keg of rum paid to them for their services.[23] In the ensuing argument Le Loup, for no apparent reason, decided to tomahawk and scalp Jane. Afterwards Le Loup is said to have proudly displayed his trophy for all to see while confessing to her murder. He supposedly made his confession in the presence of General Fraser, who was cousin to another captive also reportedly taken by Le Loup. Mrs. McNeil was returned to her people alive but was stripped naked and publicly ashamed. As a result, General Fraser was convinced Le Loup killed Miss McCrae.

In a second version of the story Jane was to be escorted by a detachment of British soldiers for a getaway excursion on Lake George, where David Jones had intentions of taking Miss McCrae as his wife. Before the marriage party could leave for the short trip to Fort Edward, the detachment of British soldiers were distracted due to the unexpected presence of American soldiers in the general vicinity.[24] While the British soldiers were absent from their protective care of Jane, and chasing rebel soldiers, Indians took her and her friend Mrs. McNeil captive. The two unfortunate young women were dragged from their hiding place in the cellar of Mrs. McNeil's home where Jane had been staying. In flight they were pursued by a few of the Americans who, upon firing at the fleeing Wyandots, mistakenly hit Jane and instantly killed her. During the flight Jane had been separated from the company of Mrs. McNeil.

Lieutenant General Burgoyne was infuriated and in an ensuing investigation identified Jane's supposed captor and murderer as Le Loup. It was suggested La Loupe viciously tomahawked and scalped Jane, in spite of no wounds on her body to substantiate such a brutal attack. Le Loup argued it was the Americans who had shot and killed Jane as they attempted to stop his flight. No one at the time was willing to believe the Wyandot's version of what occurred. After much to-do Lieutenant General Burgoyne eventually failed to punish Jane's supposed killer due to pressure from his superiors not to upset and antagonize the Indians. If Le Loup had been wrongly punished for the accusation and Jane had truly been killed by the Americans, the Indians, especially the Wyandot whom the British desperately needed as allies, would have revolted and declared war on both the British and the Americans.

Regardless of what truly happened, the killing of Jane McCrea was a rallying cry for the recruitment of Patriot forces against the British. Many Tories, realizing the British could not protect nor likely had any desire or intent to protect them from the Indians, switched loyalties and supported the colonists' quest for independence. The story of Miss Jane McCrea's brutal murder at the hands of the Wyandot warrior spread throughout the colonies in many fanciful variations. Jane quickly became a martyred legend, which only inflamed an already blistering hate for the cruel and savage Wyandot.

Nearly fifty years later, in 1826, the killing of Miss Jane McCrea was still a big story and legend of folklore. It was then that James Fenimore Cooper first published his classic novel *The Last of the Mohicans*. It is believed the killing of Jane was inspiration for the killing of Cora in his literary masterpiece. Of course it's clear that Cooper took many creative liberties with the event, as his narrative of 1757 was during the French and Indian War, not the American Revolution.

By the time all the evidence surrounding Jane's death was being compiled in 1853, David Wilson wrote Jane McCrea's biography. Her body was exhumed, examined, and reburied. The evidence did not support a brutal tomahawk attack by La Loup, but rather her body did possess the presence of bullet holes as obtained from musket balls just as La Loup first indicated. As Wilson began to write, he summarized Jane's death, "In the history of the Revolutionary War, perhaps no single incident is recorded which, at the time of its occurrence, created more intense sympathy, or aroused a spirit of more bitter indignation, than the massacre of Jane McCrea."[25]

Siege of Fort Henry, 1777

The Siege of Fort Henry is well discussed in many books; however, the details of and inconsistencies in the story of this two-day siege vary greatly. The Reverend Joseph Doddridge in *Notes on the Settlement and Indian Wars* sidestepped the event, as there was then a lack of correct information regarding the siege and ambush near Grave Creek. After Doddridge's death a manuscript was discovered by Dr. Lyman Draper that detailed the occurrences, but unfortunately the manuscript was incomplete with pages missing. The following account of the attack on Fort Henry is based on Alexander Withers' *Chronicles of Border Warfare*.

First published in 1831, Winthers's work was a very important piece for early historians of border warfare. Annotated and republished in 1895 by Reuben Gold Thwaites, many of Withers's errors or points of confusion were resolved. Thwaites in *Frontier Defense on the Upper Ohio 1777–1778* published many manuscripts, letters, and notes from the men who were directly involved in the year's events. It was customary in all of Thwaites's works to give many extra details in his footnotes not found in the original text. One such detail set the background to Fort Henry's siege.

> As a rule, Indian war-parties against the American frontier were small. They sought to elude the garrisons, penetrate into the settlements before discovery, strike a quick blow, and then retire. During 1777, however, considerable forces of the aboriginal enemy twice appeared on the border, prepared for hostile operations on a larger scale than usual.[26]

The siege of Fort Henry was exclusively an Indian operation. The Indians engaged in the attack were chiefly Wyandot and Mingo, with a few Shawnee and Delaware. There was a total of about two hundred Indians. One Wyandot was killed, nine wounded.[27] A few months prior to the Siege of Fort Henry, an increased Indian presence was noted in the outlying area. Settlers were being openly and brutally killed, including children. Many if not all attempts to intercept and kill the marauding Wyandot proved to be a futile endeavor. The taking of captives did not appear to be a motive for the increased attacks. The Indians were plundering everything considered valuable for their need and cause. More important, and even more discreetly, Wyandot spies were assessing the strengths and defenses of the area. An accounting was being made and preparations laid for something big.

The Wyandot clan chiefs, somewhere around 1775, installed Pomoacan as the new Wyandot head chief. Pomoacan's tactics of warfare would prove to be remarkably different. Instead of the characteristics commonly attributed to the Wyandot as *foxes*—sneaky, sly, and stealthy—Pomoacan assumed the persona of a Wyandot *wolf*: diplomatic, yet bold, in-your-face open tactics that comprised overwhelming strength, which naturally instilled fear. Pomoacan was strong and tactically brilliant. He too was compelling and commanded authority over the other chiefs and tribes. For this Pomoacan was given the rightful title of the Half King.

If the Moravian Delaware had not alerted the frontier settlements about an amassed Wyandot army preparing for attack, settlements from Fort Pitt to Fort Henry may have been obliterated. As we will see later in this chapter, Pomoacan would eventually rebuke the Moravian Delaware or, better, their missionaries for being American spies. If the element of surprise had been assured, the Wyandot and Mingo force was so great that open conflict with the whites would have resulted in grave casualties for many of the settlements.

Fort Henry, also known as Fort Wheeling, was indeed a fort; however, it enlisted neither soldiers nor militia to garrison the fort. Instead, nearby residents from the village of Wheeling served as its garrison. The security of their village and homes was entrusted to free-roaming scouts who scurried the countryside in search of signs of an approaching enemy. If an Indian does not want to be seen, no white scout at the time was going to find him or his signs. The residents of Fort Henry were oblivious to the approaching danger of an Indian army who made a war party look laughable.

For several days Captain Ogal and twelve men had been watching the trails and roads leading to Fort Henry. Returning to the fort, Ogal was comfortable to report there were no Indians in the area. Unbeknownst to Ogal, Pomoacan had snuck and placed an Indian army of three hundred eighty-nine warriors just outside the front gates of the fort. Instead of a full-frontal assault, Pomoacan positioned his warriors for an ambuscade the next morning. When morning broke, six Wyandot warriors were used as bait when they just happened to stumble out of the woods to catch the attention of two men who had ventured outside the fort. Throughout the night Pomoacan strategically placed his warriors in two parallel lines hidden within a large cornfield that extended to the Ohio River. The trap had been set and was ready to spring.

As the two hapless men from Fort Henry spied the six warriors, one was immediately killed with a single shot from a musket, while the second was allowed to miraculously escape back into the fort. Sounding the alarm, and thinking there were only six Indians, Captain Mason sent a party of fourteen men to quickly dispose of the six warriors; however, all fourteen soldiers were literally shredded to pieces as the occupants of the fort watched in horror. Only Captain Mason escaped the carnage as he hid behind a fallen tree and listened to the screams of his men. As Captain Mason crawled from the field to find the shelter of the fallen tree, he killed the only Wyandot warrior to die in the battle.

Hearing the screams of the dying men and the sound of muskets, Captain Ogal led his twelve scouts to rescue their friends and neighbors. However, the Indians again fell upon these men, and, unlike the other fourteen, all but three were shred to pieces. Two of the three men to escape death sustained severe wounds. Like Captain Mason, Captain Ogal also survived the carnage by hiding; however, this time the captain hid in a patch of briars and did not kill anyone.

As the twenty-three men were being destroyed, residents in the village of Wheeling fled for the safety of Fort Henry. As the gates were being closed, both Captain Mason and Captain Ogal also made it safely back into the fort. There the two men came to a conclusion that a substantial Indian army was attacking the community. Yes, this is why both men were being paid captain's wages for their services.

Much has been said about how the residents of Wheeling, thirty-three men plus women and children, held off and defeated the attack of a three-hundred-eighty-nine-man Indian army. Yes, they successfully withstood a twenty-four-hour siege behind the fort's walls, but they did not defeat Pomoacan's army. Time did not allow Pomoacan the comfort and ease to wait and starve out the fort's inhabitants. The siege would likely have bred a rescue army of militia that could have inflicted many unnecessary casualties. Because of this, Pomoacan withdrew his forces after razing the village of Wheeling and killing all its livestock. The inhabitants of the fort lost everything but the clothes on their backs.[28]

After abandoning the siege of Fort Henry, Pomoacan returned to the Sandusky and waited. Not knowing the whereabouts of the Indians, the residents of Fort Wheeling continued to live under an unrelenting siege of fear. After a few weeks life began to return to a guarded normal for the captive residents. Routine was reestablished and scouting parties renewed their pointless forays into the frontier. It was then Pomoacan initiated the second phase of his attack. He left the comforts and security of Sandusky with about forty warriors. He returned to Fort Henry and waited for an opportunistic moment. This time no one was aware of his presence, for he avoided the Moravian Delaware.

On the morning of September 26, captains Foreman and Ogle set out with forty-three men to scout the land south of Fort Henry near present-day Moundsville, West Virginia. It was here they discovered the settlement abandoned and then ransacked by the Indians. Due to prevailing darkness, they spent the night and made plans to return to Fort Henry the next morning; however, Pomoacan had different plans.

> They camped for the night, and the next morning (the 27th) started to return along the river bank, to Wheeling. Linn, apprehensive of Indians, marched along the hill crest, but Ogle and Foreman kept to the trail along the bottom. At a point where the bottom narrows because of the close approach of the hills to the river—a defile then known as McMechen's (or McMahon's) Narrows—they were set upon by Half King's party, awaiting them in ambush. Foreman and twenty others were killed, and one captured.[29]

Battle of Little Mountain, 1782

The Battle of Little Mountain, or Estill's Defeat, is a good illustration of a classic Wyandot incursion far behind enemy lines. Humphrey Marshall, in his 1824 *The History of Kentucky,* was just forty-two years removed from the battle. With the incident still relatively fresh on the minds of many Kentuckians he stated the following of the Wyandot and their allies:

> Their determined bravery; their obstinate perseverance; the promptitude, with which they seized on the absence of the detachment, to advance on their enemy; and thus, by a step not less bold, than judicious, to ensure to themselves a victory, of immortal renown: conduct alike bespeaking the possession of skill in war, and a training to command, which could but render them formidable, and even victorious, . . . the Shawnees, Delawares, and Wyandots, in particular, were the more terrifying to the exposed stations; as their depredations were frequent: It was thought, that they fought with more than usual obstinacy; and were even likely to derive an increased audacity, from repeated success.[30]

The following account gives intimate details into a single battle that no doubt played out countless times across the frontier behind enemy lines. The Wyandot were unique in that an extended campaign could be strategically developed with all the logistics in their proper place. The Wyandot could safely advance into enemy territory, enact terror, defeat the militia and settlers, win a battle, lose a battle, and escape with acceptable casualties back into Wyandot territory across the Ohio River. It's assumed in this particular battle significant casualties were sustained—more than the whites, yet technically the battle was still won. The winner, in spite of losses, is the one left holding the battlefield once the fighting stops. Again, always remember—the whites have written most of the history thus far.

On March 20, 1782, a party of twenty-five Wyandot attacked Estill's Station located approximately three miles southeast of Richmond, Kentucky. As usual the surrounding area was razed and all the livestock killed. During the attack one woman, Jennie Gass, was killed and scalped. A slave named Monk, owned by the station's captain, James Estill, was captured and taken prisoner. Monk was loyal to his master and deceived the Wyandot war party into believing the station was heavily garrisoned with forty men. The presence of the war party had been discovered, and Captain James Estill, with twenty-four men, was hunting the Wyandot war party. A few days earlier a raft used by the war party had broken loose from its moorings and floated past Boonesborough. However, it was fortunate for the people in Estill's Station that the Wyandot war party abandoned their attack and went looking for other prey as the station was defended by four old men along with women and children.

After being informed of the attack on his station, Captain Estill finally overtook the Wyandot on March 22, 1782, at Little Mountain almost forty miles northeast of his station near the city of Mount Sterling in Montgomery County, Kentucky. The Kentuckians initially held the elements of surprise and strategic ground as the Wyandot warriors were caught crossing a streambed at the bottom of two adjacent hills. The Kentuckians spied the warriors as they walked out of the woods into a clearing on the opposite hill of the stream. One of Captain Estill's men fired the first shot which is said to have instantly killed two Wyandot warriors. The most improbable shot rallied and inspired the Kentuckians to fight; however, as the battle commenced, seven of Captain Estill's men deserted the battlefield, leaving their friends and neighbors to their fate.

Compromised by the terrain, the Wyandot warriors had but one choice: they turned and faced their enemy and fought like Wyandots. "In this position they returned the fire, and entered into the battle, which they considered, as inevitable; with all the fortitude, and animation of individual, and concerted, bravery; so remarkable in this particular tribe."[31] The third Wyandot to be shot was the war chief of the party, who would eventually die of his wound but not before conducting his warriors in a vicious fight to the death. Remember, a Wyandot warrior never deserted a battlefield or turned his back to an enemy, no matter how dire the circumstances. The battle would rage for two hours, initially fought behind trees at fifty yards, until the fighting became hand-to-hand.

Captain Estill was also killed in the hand-to-hand combat. When his previously broken arm again snapped, a Wyandot warrior was able to bury his knife in Estill's heart. The warrior would also die, as a bullet from one of Estill's men took his life. After about three hours only four of Captain Estill's men were able to continue the fight. They fled, abandoning the battlefield and their dead to the victorious Wyandot. Some accounts say the dead were scalped; others say they were not scalped, nor were any of the dead's belongings taken. How many Wyandot died in the battle is unknown; however, not one Wyandot warrior was found dead on the battlefield when the Kentuckians returned to claim their dead. Clearly several Wyandots survived as Monk remained a captive and would not escape for some time. Various reports state that anywhere between twelve to seventeen Wyandot warriors were killed and two wounded; however, it is believed the war party did not immediately return to the Sandusky, and some warriors could have been killed in other engagements. The Kentuckians had seven killed, ten wounded, and seven to a fate much worse than death—cowardice.[32]

Gnadenhutten Massacre, 1782

One of the most fiendish massacres during all the border wars occurred on March 8, 1782, in Gnadenhutten, a small Moravian Delaware village. Gnadenhutten was one of three Moravian settlements on the Tuscarawas and Muskingum rivers in Eastern Ohio. Indian warriors did not perpetrate the massacre; instead, colonial militia from Pennsylvania under the leadership of Colonel David Williamson has the heinous distinction of committing the hellish crime.

The combination of events—the Gnadenhutten Massacre and the Battle of Sandusky, or Crawford's Defeat, which we will look at next—are likely the two most noted and discussed combination of events during the whole of the border wars. The horrific details of Colonel Crawford's torture and death became a battle cry against the Wyandot and all the tribes within the Ohio Country. Initially the Wyandot bore much of the blame because the torture took place on Wyandot land. Unfortunately, the massacre of the Moravian Delaware garnered very little rebuke for the murders of men, women, and children.

Soon after the Moravian Christians, who were from Eastern Bohemia in the present-day Czech Republic, immigrated to the New World, many Delaware Indians began to convert to their form of Christianity. Why? The Moravian tenets were very appealing due to their philosophy of creating self-sufficient communities isolated from the whole of society. The isolated villages shunned both Europeans and non-Christianized Indians, creating what can easily be described as Delaware and Moravian utopias. The first village of Gnadenhutten was established in 1744 about thirty miles from Bethlehem, Pennsylvania, near the junction of the Mahony and Lecha rivers.[33] The community grew to about five hundred and is said to have made a good impression on surrounding tribes. Yet still, during the French and Indian War the village was destroyed in 1755 with many killed and the survivors fleeing to Bethlehem.

In 1772, after an uneasy relationship with whites and Indians alike, about two hundred forty of the Christian Indians moved deep into the Ohio Country with The Reverend David Zeisberger. Here on the Tuscarawas branch of the Muskingum River the second Moravian village named Gnadenhutten was established.[34] Upon the outbreak of the Revolutionary War, the Moravian Delaware declared their neutrality, not wishing to again move or be victims of hostile Indian attacks—they just wanted to be left alone.

The Moravian Delaware's declared neutrality did not appear to last when in 1777 to 1778 the Wyandot began to suspect that they, *or their missionaries,* were acting as spies for the American colonies. Positioned in the middle of the land given to their pagan brethren, the village of Gnadenhutten was a little less than halfway between Sandusky and the settlements the Wyandot were relentlessly attacking. It became commonplace for frontier settlements to be forewarned as Indian war parties passed near the Moravian settlements on the Tuscarawas River.

As the Wyandot began to suspect that the Moravian Delaware were alerting the Pennsylvania and Virginia frontier towns, the reverse was also happening. The Pennsylvanians and Virginians also began to suspect that the Moravian Delaware were allowing their villages to serve as staging areas for attacks on the frontier. The Half King paid several visits to the Moravian Delaware and expressed dire warnings that they were alerting the frontier towns of pending attacks, dire consequences would be forthcoming—if the warnings were found to be true. The Moravians always denied the accusations; therefore, the Half King struck a covenant with the Moravian Delaware in return for their pledge of neutrality.

Early in 1781 Pachganchihilas, the war chief of the Delaware, and a party of eighty warriors paid their Christian brethren an unexpected visit. Arriving at the Moravian village, Pachganchihilas stated, "If you stay where you now are, one day or other the long knives (Virginians) will, in their usual way, speak fine words to you, and at the same time murder you."[35] As the Pennsylvanians were apparently preparing for an attack on Gnadenhutten, the British Governor of Detroit decreed that the Moravian Delaware be removed from the frontier. This prompted a visit from the Wyandot. Fully aware of his covenant with the Moravian Delaware, the Half King was reluctant to forcibly remove them from their village to a distant place; however, the Half King did not have a choice in the matter. On August 20, 1781, the Half King delivered the following message to the Moravians:

Two powerful, angry, and merciless Gods (said he) stand ready, opening their jaws wide against each other: you are sitting down between both, and thus in danger of being devoured and ground to powder by the teeth of either one or the other, or of both. It is therefore not advisable for you to stay here any longer. Arise and follow me! Take also your teachers with you, and worship God in the place to which I shall lead you, as you have been accustomed to do . . . and on the 21st the latter replied to the Half King: "Uncle! we have heard your words; but have not yet seen the danger so great, that we might not stay here.[36]

As expected, the Moravian Delaware refused to go peaceably and of their own freewill. Mixed among the Indians were also a sizable number of white Moravians. Given an opportunity to change their mind or to be forced into making the appropriate decision, the Half King and his warriors decided to make themselves comfortable and stay awhile. While forcibly taking advantage of the Moravian's hospitality, "small parties of them made inroads into the neighbouring country, bringing prisoners to Gnadenhutten, which was thus rendered a theatre of war and pillage."[37]

The Half King was trying to force their decision while making the Pennsylvanians' suspicions true. But in due time, enough was enough. The patience of the Half King was all used up, and Gnadenhutten and her two sister villages, Salem and Shoenbrunn,[38] were no longer afforded a choice—it was now time to leave. "The savages now drove them forward like a herd of cattle. The white Brethren and Sisters were usually in the midst surrounded by the believing Indians."[39]

After a long, hard winter in Sandusky the Moravians were starving, most of their livestock dead. "The savages [Wyandots] who came on a visit to Sandusky, seeing such numbers of cattle lying dead by the way side, laughed, and reviled the believing Indians, expressing great joy at their sufferings. "Now," said they, "you are become like us, and certainly you ought not to fare better."[40] The famine presented the Moravian Delaware no choice but to return to Gnadenhutten, Salem, and Shoenbrunn, for there they knew food had been left both in storehouses and standing in the fields. The trip was risky and the food may have spoiled, but it was much better than what was sold in Sandusky at an enormous price. Unfortunately for the Moravian Delaware, their choice to return for the food in the fields would lead them face-to-face with an unimaginable nightmare. "Colonel David Williamson . . . raised a force of about a hundred men, and went to the Tuscarawas in November, with the intention of compelling the Moravians either to migrate into the country of the hostile Indians or to move to Fort Pitt."[41]

The following is a long account of the Gnadenhutten massacre as preserved by The Reverend George H. Loskiel, then presiding bishop of the northern district of the American province of the Moravian Church. There are many accounts given by many historians and authors, but this one is given from the perspective of those murdered. It's raw, it's brutal, and it's savage barbarism at the hands of the whites against an unarmed and peaceful people—the Moravian Delaware.

Next day the murderers arrived at Gnadenhutten. About a mile from the settlement they met young Shebosh in the wood, fired at him, and wounded him so much that he could not escape. He then, according to the account of the murderers themselves, begged for his life, representing that he was the son of a white Christian man. But they paid no attention to his entreaties and cut him in pieces with their hatchets. They then approached the Indians, most of whom were in their plantations, and surrounded them, almost imperceptibly, but feigning a friendly behaviour, told them to go home, promising to do them no injury. They even pretended to pity them on account of the mischief done to them by the English and the savages, assuring them of the protection and friendship of the Americans. The poor Indians, knowing nothing of the death of young Shebosh, believed every word they said, went home with them and treated them in the most hospitable manner. The Americans then informed them that they should not return to Sandusky, but go to Pittsburg, where they would be out of the way of any assault made by the English or the savages. This the Indians heard with resignation, concluding that God would perhaps choose this method to put an end to their present sufferings. Prepossessed with this idea, they cheerfully delivered their guns, hatchets, and other weapons to the murderers, who promised to take good care of them, and in Pittsburg to return every article to its rightful owner. The Indians even showed them all those things which they had secreted in the woods, assisted in packing them up, and emptied all their bee-hives for these pretended friends.

The defenceless Indians at Gnadenhutten were suddenly attacked and driven together by the white people, and without resistance seized and bound. . . . Soon after this, the murderers held a council, and resolved, by a majority of votes, to murder them all the very next day (March 8). Those who were of a different opinion wrung their hands, calling God to witness that they were innocent of the blood of these harmless Christian Indians. But the majority remained unmoved, and only differed concerning the mode of execution. Some were for burning them alive, others for taking their scalps, and the latter was at last agreed upon; upon which one of the murderers was sent to the prisoners, to tell them, that as they were Christian Indians, they might prepare themselves in a Christian manner, for they must all die tomorrow. . . . Immediately after this declaration the carnage commenced. Neither women nor children were spared, all, without exception, were knocked down [killed] and scalped.

Fourteen were knocked down by one man with a cooper's mallet, which he found in the house; he then handed the instrument to a fellow murderer, saying, "My arm fails me! go on in the same way! I think I have done pretty well."—A sister called Christina, who spoke English and German well, fell on her knees before the captain of the gang, and begged her life, but was told that he could not help her.

Thus ninety-six persons magnified the name of the Lord, by patiently meeting a cruel death. Sixty-two were adults, one-third of whom were women; the remaining thirty-four were children.[42]

Battle of Sandusky, 1782

The Battle of Sandusky "is to be considered as a second Moravian campaign, as one of its objects was that of finishing the work of murder and plunder with the Christian Indians at their new establishment on the Sandusky. The next object was that of destroying the Wyandot towns on the same river."[43] It was clear to the Pennsylvanians that most of the war parties originated from the Sandusky Plains. This revelation did not indicate that all the Indians were Wyandot; however, it implied that Wyandot or not, Sandusky was used as a staging area for excursions across the frontier.[44]

Sandusky must be destroyed, and Colonel William Crawford was chosen by five votes over Colonel David Williamson to lead the expedition deep into the heart of Indian country.[45] The defeated Colonel Williamson, perpetrator of the Gnadenhutten Massacre, would be second in command of the expedition and appointed as first field major. Two other men of historical renown who participated in the expedition are Dr. John Knight, appointed expedition surgeon, and John Slover, one of two pilots, or expedition scouts.[46] Both men had a *wonderful* escape from captivity and would return to write their own memoirs of the expedition. Published in July of 1782, *Narratives of a Late*

Expedition against the Indians first told the world of Colonel Crawford's torture and execution.

Colonel William Crawford would lead his hastily prepared and self-supplied army of eager Pennsylvania and Virginia volunteers from Mingo Bottom, their point of rendezvous. The opportunity to strike and give a little payback to the Indians in their own homes was an adventure in need of little recruiting. The militia included most of those who had taken part in the murderous expedition at Gnadenhutten. This fact, and the men's general character, made it clear that any Indian, including one professing Christianity, "would be slaughtered as pitilessly as their hostile brethren."[47]

Colonel Crawford appeared to be the best man to lead the expedition. A veteran of the French and Indian War he survived the massacre on the Monongahela to receive both an accommodation and a promotion. General George Washington was a good friend, as were many of the Indians he had become familiar with since his presumed retirement from the army. Colonel Crawford was considered an expert on the Delaware, Shawnee, Wyandot, and Mingo—their customs and modes of warfare. Colonel Crawford had a reputation of being an Indian fighter. Before being recalled back into active service, he served as justice of the peace in Cumberland County where he was living a quiet and comfortable life at the crossings of the Yochaghany River.[48]

No matter how comfortable Colonel Crawford may have been in his retirement, and no matter how close the British were to suffering defeat in the Revolutionary War, war still loomed on the frontier's horizon. By circumstance of reputation Colonel Crawford would be handpicked to lead the expedition. With reluctance he again would lead men, many dishonorable, back into the bloody work of war. Fulfilling a lifelong dream of advancing upon and defeating the tribes of the Sandusky, primarily the Wyandot, Colonel Crawford left Mingo Bottom on May 25, 1782. Crawford's four-hundred-eighty-man army marched north and westward as they quietly snuck upon the unsuspecting Wyandot and their allies. After a four-day walk the army camped near the devastated Moravian villages where corn was again found on the stalks from the previous year's planting. It was here that Colonel Crawford believed he was first discovered, as two Indians were spotted and fired upon. Little did Colonel Crawford know, but Wyandot spies had actually spotted him at Mingo Bottom, and his presence was fully known and reported to the Half King.

On June 4, after a week of sneaking the expedition through the Ohio forest, John Slover cautiously stepped onto the Sandusky Plains. Slover had been a captive of the Miami and Shawnee for twelve years[49] and was not surprised to find the Moravian village they sought deserted. He knew that traveling so far over so many days and seeing only two Indians was an ominous sign. When riding into the heart of Indian Country, one would have expected to see Indian spies on the perimeter; but Indians had not been seen, and Slover was deeply concerned. The village was abandoned and looked to have been so for quite some time.

Perplexed and not knowing what to do, Colonel Crawford called for a war council to seek advice. The second scout on the expedition was Jonathan Zane. "He was, perhaps, the most experienced hunter of his day, in the frontier country."[50] He and his brother settled Wheeling, Virginia, also known as Fort Henry, and he was considered an expert in Indian war tactics. His advice to Colonel Crawford was to immediately retreat, for he knew with certainty the Wyandot were amassing a formidable force not only to repel their army but to completely wipe it from the face of the earth. Did Colonel Crawford take the advice of the most experienced scout then in the Ohio Country? Yes and no. Colonel Crawford agreed that the likelihood of an overwhelming Indian army lay ahead; however, the decision was made to forge ahead just a few more hours and then they would halt. Sending a small party of scouts in advance of the main army, they trudged deeper into Wyandot country knowing what likely lay ahead. The problem was that no one knew where the Wyandot were and when they would spring their trap.

The Ohio forest dissolved into the Sandusky Plains, and all that remained was a large grove of trees in the middle of a tall sea of grass. The scouts were unaware that to the west lay a marshy swamp that was all but impassable to both man and beast. Not long after passing the island of trees, sure enough the Wyandot and the Delaware were waiting. Naked and painted warriors poured from nearby timber, their objective being to surround the scouts.[51] Two scouts immediately peeled from the party and darted back to the main army to inform Colonel Crawford the Indians had finally been found. The remainder of the scouts fought their way back to the island of trees, which served as the only protection in the near endless sea of grass.

On occasion, a warrior would come close enough to throw a tomahawk at the Americans. When both the scouting party and the main army reunited in the grove of trees, the location became known as Battle Island. Throughout the remainder of the afternoon, until nightfall, a lively exchange of gunfire was observed as Battle Island was surrounded: Wyandots to the north, Delaware to the south, and swamp to the west. About a mile to the east across open prairie lay the Sandusky River.

Approximately two miles north of Battle Island the Half King's village was strategically placed near the Sandusky River. The Half King's warpole, Zhau-Shoo-To, believed by many to be an adopted white man named Abraham Kuhn (in time Kuhn was changed to Coon), was able to assemble approximately four hundred Wyandot warriors to confront the Americans.[52] The great Delaware war chief Captain Pipe brought approximately two hundred of his warriors to the battle. Among Captain Pipe's men was Wingenund, a lesser war chief of the Delaware who personally knew Colonel William Crawford.

Also with the Delaware was Simon Girty, the infamous white man who was a deserter from the Continental Army and traitor to his own people; Girty had used the cause of the Indians defending their homeland as an excuse to become one of the most hated and vicious villains of the border wars. "His influence [Girty] was as great with the war-chief of the Delawares as with Zhaus-sho-toh, or the Half King."[53] An associate of Simon Girty, Matthew Elliott, received the commission of captain from the British, whereas Girty never received a commission.[54] Captain Elliott was an Indian agent throughout the duration of the Revolutionary War. He was also married to a Shawnee and proved to be a very strong and influential leader of the Shawnee, Delaware, and Wyandot warriors. During the Battle of the Sandusky, Elliott was in command of the Indian warriors and British Rangers. As the battle commenced, Captain Elliott held the Wyandot warriors in reserve and sent the Delaware to initiate the attack on the Americans. In a slash-and-reposition tactic, the Delaware flanked the Americans and took the southern guard on the siege of Battle Island.

As night fell over the Sandusky Plains, the air grew quiet as all the combatants tried to rest and get a little sleep for the coming day. For the Americans the need for water became a pressing and dire issue, but thirst did not quench the need for sleep. As the morning sun shone forth on June 5, the smell of bacon and biscuits filled the air, as did the zing of rifle balls. Rifles began to smoke and boom from distances that resulted in few casualties. Throughout the day shots were returned from both sides as the Indians began to taunt the Americans with insults and a sense that something was happening behind their lines. Many of the Americans noted that the Indians seemed to become careless, and several were killed because of foolish mistakes. As uneasiness began to settle over Battle Island, the unthinkable happened, which confirmed what Colonel Crawford suspected: The Indians were stalling for the arrival of reinforcements.

To the dismay and shock of Colonel Crawford, reinforcements arrived early in the afternoon. To the rear of the Wyandot's line a sentinel spotted mounted troops. As the troops approached it became clear they were British—Butler's Rangers.[55] As if the arrival of the British Rangers weren't enough, just before dusk approximately one hundred fifty Shawnee warriors arrived to the south and reinforced the Delaware's line. Upon the Shawnee's arrival their warriors taunted their opponents and waved a red flag while firing volley after volley into Battle Island.

The defense of Battle Island was now impossible. Colonel Crawford called a war council, and a plan was devised to retreat after nightfall; however, not all of the officers were in agreement, and dissension prevailed. Their escape called for retracing their route back to the south, thereby splitting the camps of the Delaware and Shawnee. This would take them back along the old Indian trail they had followed to Battle Island. Some wanted to take their chances and head due east through open prairie. Colonel Crawford sternly objected to this plan. Running the gauntlet between the Delaware and Shawnee warriors seemed the lesser of two evils. Striking east across the prairie meant having to face the Wyandot's warriors. It seemed best to try to sneak past the combined force of Delaware and Shawnee than tangle with the Wyandot.

In and around the fast-emptying grove, the scene was chaotic. It's possible that the Wyandot, Delaware, and Shawnee warriors stood in stunned amazement watching Colonel Crawford's men give a stellar vaudevillian-like performance of classic renown. Stumbling and falling over each other, the American army disintegrated and scattered under the cover of darkness. Colonel Crawford was left standing in a nearly empty grove, looking for family members and wondering where his army had disappeared. By mid-morning on June 6 approximately two hundred fifty men from his army had assembled at the old abandoned Wyandot village, now under the command of Colonel Williamson.[56] From there the band headed east along the trail they earlier traversed. On their way home the trip was filled with dread, for this time the Wyandot were just about everywhere they turned, and the hunter became the hunted. No one knew the whereabouts of Colonel Crawford.

Colonel Crawford, Dr. Knight, and John Slover were captured by the Delaware, and their fates sealed. The barbaric murder of the Delaware's Christian brethren had to be avenged, and these three men would meet a death equal in torment and torture endured by the ninety-six Christians. The Delaware had hoped to capture Colonel Williamson, and with his escape Colonel Crawford would stand in his stead. It did not matter that Colonel Crawford had no part in the Moravian massacre. Painted black, all three men were to be burned at the stake; however, the Delaware had one major problem.

As the burning of prisoners was an obsolete custom with the Wyandots, the Delawares did not dare to inflict the death penalty in that manner upon their territory without obtaining permission from the Half King (the Delawares were tenants at will in the Sandusky country, under the Wyandots).

Fearing a refusal if application direct was made to the Wyandot sachem, the two Delawares resorted to stratagem. A messenger, bearing a belt of wampum, was dispatched to the Half King with the following message: "Uncle We, your nephews, the Lenni Lenape, salute you in a spirit of kindness, love, and respect. Uncle! We have a project in view which we ardently wish to accomplish, and can accomplish if our uncle will not overrule us! By returning the wampum, we will have your pledged word!"

Pomoacan was somewhat puzzled at this mysterious message. He questioned the messenger, who, having been previously instructed by The Pipe and Wingenund, feigned ignorance. The Half King, concluding it was a contemplated expedition of a Delaware war-party intending to strike some of the white settlements, returned the belt to the bearer with the word "Say to my nephews, they have my pledge." This was a death-warrant to the unfortunate Crawford.[57]

Dr. John Knight and John Slover miraculously escaped the fate Colonel Crawford had to endure. The Delaware burned Colonel Crawford. Yes, there were Wyandots in their company, and they did participate in the burning; however, all responsibility was attributed to the two Delaware war chiefs Pipe and Wingenund. When the sun broke the next morning, all ninety-six Christian Delaware who lost their lives to Colonel Williamson had been avenged.

When we were come to the fire the colonel was stripped naked, ordered to sit down by the fire and then they beat him with sticks and their fists. Presently after I was treated in the same manner. They then tied a rope to the foot of a post about fifteen feet high, bound the colonel's hands behind his back and fastened the rope to the ligature between his wrists. The rope was long enough either for him to sit down or walk round the post once or twice and return the same way. The colonel then called to Girty and asked if they intended to burn him?—Girty answered, yes. The colonel said he would take it all patiently. Upon this Capt. Pipe, a Delaware chief, made a speech to the Indians, viz. about thirty or forty men, sixty or seventy squaws and boys.

When the speech was finished they all yelled a hideous and hearty assent to what had been said. The Indian men then took up their guns and shot powder into the colonel's body, from his feet as far up as his neck. I think not less than seventy loads were discharged upon his naked body. They then crowded about him, and to the best of my observation, cut off his ears: when the throng had dispersed a little I saw the blood running from both sides of his head in consequence thereof.

The fire was about six or seven yards from the post to which the colonel was tied: it was made of small hickory poles, burnt quite through in the middle, each end of the poles remaining about six feet in length. Three or four Indians by turns would take up, individually, one of these burning pieces of wood and apply it to his naked body, already burnt black with the powder. These tormentors presented themselves on every side of him, so that which ever way he ran round the post they met him with the burning faggots and poles. Some of the squaws took broad boards upon which they would put a quantity of burning coals and hot embers and throw on him, so that in a short time he had nothing but coals of fire and hot ashes to walk upon.

In the midst of these extreme tortures he called to Simon Girty and begged of him to shoot him! but Girty making no answer he called to him again. Girty then, by way of derision, told the colonel he had no gun, at the same time turning about to an Indian who was behind him, laughed heartily, and by all his gestures seemed delighted at the horrid scene.

[. . .]

Col. Crawford at this period of his sufferings besought the Almighty to have mercy on his soul, spoke very low, and bore his torments with the most manly fortitude. He continued in all the extremities of pain for an hour and three quarters or two- hours longer, as near as I can judge, when at last being almost spent, he lay down on his belly: they then scalped him and repeatedly threw the scalp in my face, telling me "that was my great captain."—An old squaw (whose appearance every way answered the ideas people entertain of the Devil) got a board, took a parcel of coals and ashes and laid them on his back and head after he had been scalped: he then raised himself upon his feet and began to walk round the post: they next put a burning flick to him as usual, but he seemed mere insensible of pain than before.[58]

The Wyandot had prisoners of their own and they were likely tomahawked and beheaded. Estimates of American casualties were obtained by way of military accounting. The Americans minimized and the British exaggerated their losses. There are sixty-five names listed as casualties for the Battle of Sandusky—forty-one were killed, seventeen wounded, and seven captured.[59] As for losses sustained by the Wyandot, Delaware, Shawnee, and British Rangers, tradition states only about half a dozen.

The Struggle of Big Foot and Adam Poe, 1782

The encounter of Big Foot and the Poe brothers—Andrew and Adam—is one of the most celebrated events in the history of the border wars. It also has the most contradictions, almost equal to those in the death of Miss Jane McCrea. "Adam Poe himself wondered that narrators of the occurrence could be led into such mistakes."[60] At times the telling of the adventures on the frontier were stories spun from the imagination and hope the war had not been lost to the Indians. As the tales were told, they often became wildly outlandish and were spun in the most inexcusable manner. Such is what happened when Big Foot and his brother were killed by famed Indian fighters Adam and Andrew Poe. This event in the history of border warfare could easily be just another instance where seven Wyandots raided the frontier and only one returned home. Unfortunately, this story is different. As humans, sometimes it helps lessen our fears when we can make the monsters of our nightmares bigger than reality: hence the name Big Foot. It also helps when the monster that is killed happens to be the prince of an evil king. In this particular story, our prince was the son of the greatly feared and respected Half King.[61] No, Half King was not an evil king, but the whites and their many fears made him out to be evil.

The Wyandot were already the subject of many conversations around the taverns, blockhouses, trading posts, community gatherings, and cemeteries. A little hope and inspiration were much needed. To be alone in a cabin made of sticks and stones on the frontier brought never-ending stress. Then why go? To kill a Wyandot in hand-to-hand combat was considered a great achievement, a very, very rare one, but one that could bring you much fame. This made for stories of fairy tales and folklore, and lists were accumulated of great men such as Daniel Boone, George Rogers Clark, Davy Crockett, William Crawford, and of course the Poe brothers, Adam and Andrew—you know, Indian fighters.

The exploits of Adam and Andrew can be found in just about every book published on the tales of border warfare between the Indians and the whites. At the time of the famed struggle, "Adam, [was] more intent upon securing the scalp of Big-Foot as a trophy, than upon his own safety."[62] Adam was not interested in becoming a folk legend among the whites; he was just trying to stay alive and obtain a rare trophy—an Indian scalp. Obtaining an Indian scalp would have been no different than shooting a big twelve-point "buck" and mounting its head above the fireplace on your living room wall.

The terrible encounter of the Poe brothers brought fame not only to themselves but to their children and grandchildren as well. Adam's daughter, Sarah Kuffel, relayed the story of the encounter to Ben Douglass in *History of Wayne County, Ohio.* The following account is based upon Mrs. Kuffel's narrative of one of the most famous encounters between Wyandot warriors and the whites. Something like this did not happen every day, and it was indeed reason to celebrate, but be careful: There are a lot more Wyandots out there to seek revenge. The Wyandot never forget; it may take a generation or two, but you can be assured that in due time retribution will be obtained.

A small war party of seven Wyandots, led by Scotosh, the eldest son of the Half King, made their way to a settlement on the Ohio River near Fort Pitt. Upon entering the village, one of the first to be killed was an old man. The news of his death quickly spread across the community, upon which Adam and Andrew Poe, along with six other men, responded and began the difficult task of trying to locate and stop the war party. Intercepting the Wyandot at night proved fruitless. It would not be until the next morning that the Poes would locate the war party. The Wyandot trail led to the Ohio River and escape back to the safety of the Sandusky.

Andrew left the main party of searchers to scout ahead through the thick brush with the hope of surprising the ever wily and vigilant Wyandots. It was looking as if the war party was not expecting an encounter with the whites, as an uncharacteristic number of signs pointed to their presence—and their presence was everywhere. Still unable to see the Wyandots, Andrew quietly snuck ahead until he spied Big Foot, a son of the Half King. Accompanying Big Foot was another smaller Wyandot, and both were well armed with rifles, tomahawks, and knives. Hoping to quickly dispatch the large, intimidating, and powerful Big Foot, Andrew prepared his rifle, but when he fired, only flint met steel. The rifle did not discharge and Andrew Poe was now in a lot of trouble.

The snap of the rifle alarmed Big Foot and his companion, and they quickly located Andrew in the thicket. Knowing he could not outrun the two, Andrew decided to try his best to outwrestle Big Foot. Charging them both, Andrew dove headfirst, knocking them to the ground in a big body-slamming pile. While focusing upon trying to keep Big Foot subdued, the smaller Wyandot slithered loose, grabbed his tomahawk, and started for Andrew. Seeing his companion approaching with the raised tomahawk, Big Foot gave Andrew a bear-hug and turned him for a better position to give the smaller Wyandot one swing at Andrew's head. Andrew in desperation kicked for the tomahawk, and luckily it went flying from his hand. Retrieving the tomahawk, he again came for Andrew who this time was unable to stop his assault without taking a blow to his wrist.

Somehow Andrew was successful in releasing himself from the grasp of Big Foot, and he quickly grabbed one of the Wyandot's rifles and shot the smaller Wyandot. Big Foot quickly recovered from being tossed aside, and he bulldozed Andrew into the Ohio River. They both immediately went underwater, upon which Andrew grabbed Big Foot's scalp lock and held him under the water with the hope of drowning his intimidating foe. After a long struggle Big Foot went limp, Andrew released his grip, only to find that Big Foot was playing possum. Big Foot again came at Andrew with a massive lunge only to find they were in deep water and the river's current was about to drown them both. All efforts were made by both men to quickly and safely return to the river's bank. Big Foot proved to be the better swimmer of the two.

Big Foot first reached the muddy shore and, lunging for his rifle that had yet to be fired, secured it in his gigantic hands. Andrew was now certain he had no other choice but to try to swim for deep water and dive below the penetration of the lead ball. Big Foot, while pointing the rifle at Andrew, noticed he grabbed the wrong rifle, as it had already been discharged. At about this same time, Adam Poe arrived at the scene of the frantic struggle. Unfortunately for Adam, he too was holding a discharged rifle. In harmony he and Big Foot proceeded to quickly reload their rifles. The first to reload would live to see tomorrow. As Big Foot pulled the ramrod from the muzzle of rifle, his wet and big fingers lost grip of the rod, and it went flying a few yards down the riverbank. As massive as Big Foot was, he was quite agile and quickly recovered his rod. This fleeting moment gave the advantage to Adam, who was able to shoot Big Foot by the time he was raising his rifle to shoot. Mortally wounded, Big Foot fell into the mud of the Ohio River.

Seeing his brother also wounded and floating in the river in what looked to be helpless and hopeless despair, Adam entered the river to save his brother. Andrew, coveting the trophy of Big Foot's scalp, screamed at his brother that he was fine but told him to get the prized trophy of Big Foot's scalp. Big Foot, who was not yet dead, heard Andrew's request and rolled into the Ohio River's current and disappeared below the muddy water. As Big Foot slipped below the water, one of the Poes' companions arrived at the riverbank and mistook Andrew for Big Foot. With one shot Andrew was struck in the shoulder, causing a severe wound.[63]

Adam Poe was also wounded in the struggle with the five Wyandots. Five of the seven Wyandots in the war party and three white men were killed. In one skirmish the great Wyandot chief lost two of three sons engaged in the skirmish—revenge must be obtained. Adam's daughter told him that the struggle between her father and uncle with Big Foot had occurred at the mouth of the Little Yellow Creek. The Half King's eldest son, Scotosh, returned to the Sandusky and told their father of his brothers' fate.

The Wyandots never forgot the fate of the Half King's sons. In their hearts vengeance burned and was never quenched, nor could it be until Adam Poe was dead. Many years after the encounter, an assassin was quietly dispatched across the border to seek revenge. The chosen man for the task was Rohn-yen-ness, who, if not for Reverend Finley, may have passed into forgotten history. Rohn-yen-ness's task and ensuing adventure to kill Adam was preserved in *History of the Wyandott Mission*. Reverend Finley recorded the deed to show how kindness, when bestowed upon a Wyandot, can have profound results and can even squelch the lingering burn for revenge. This adds a powerful twist and unexpected ending to one of the greatest and most popular stories ever told of the fighting upon the borders.

> I will here give an instance, as related by the man himself, to me and others. The reader will easily recollect the great conflict of Adam Poe, in 1782, with the Wyandott Indian, Big-foot, and the victory he then achieved. The Wyandott nation's loss in this conflict, was two of their greatest warriors; and knowing that Adam Poe was the man who killed them, they always meditated his destruction. Poe then lived on the west side of the Ohio river, at the mouth of Little Yellow creek. The Wyandotts determined on revenge. They chose Rohn-yen-ness as a proper person to murder him, and then make his escape. He went to Poe's house, and was met with great friendship. Poe not having any suspicion of his design, the best in his house was furnished him. When the time to retire to sleep came, he made a pallet on the floor for his Indian guest to sleep. He and his wife went to bed in the same room. Rohn-yen-ness said they both soon fell asleep. There being no person about the house but some children, this afforded him a fair opportunity to have executed his purpose; but the kindness they had both shown him worked in his mind. He asked himself how he could get up and kill even an enemy, that had taken him in,

and treated him so well so much like a brother? The more he thought about it, the worse he felt; but still, on the other hand, he was sent by his nation to avenge the death of two of its most valiant warriors; and their ghosts would not be appeased until the blood of Poe was shed. There, he said, he lay in this conflict of mind until it was about midnight. The duty he owed to his nation, and the spirits of his departed friends, aroused him. He seized his knife and tomahawk, and crept to the bed side of his sleeping host. Again the kindness he had received from Poe stared him in the face; and he said, it is mean, it is unworthy the character of an Indian warrior to kill even an enemy, who has so kindly treated him. He went back to his pallet, and slept until morning.

His kind host loaded him with blessings, and told him that they were once enemies, but now they had buried the hatchet and were brothers, and hoped they would always be so. Rohn-yen-ness, overwhelmed with a sense of the generous treatment he had received from his once powerful enemy, but now his kind friend, left him to join his party.

He said the more he reflected on what he had done, and the course he had pursued, the more he was convinced that he had done right. This once revengeful and powerful savage warrior, was overcome by the kindness of an evening, and all his plans frustrated.[64]

Big Bottom Massacre, 1791

Even a tentative, hopeful peace after the close of the American Revolution did not come to fruition. Open hostilities between the British and the Americans concluded; however, the British did not abandon their western forts as agreed upon in the Treaty of Paris. The British stayed and continued to agitate the various tribes, and the Wyandot were more than happy to carry on the fight. Excursions deep into and well beyond the frontier continued relentlessly. Americans were dying, yet the settlers kept coming, wave after wave. It was near impossible to defend against the war parties. No one knew where the Indians would strike, and as swiftly as they came, they left, masking their escape.

In response to the continued attacks, President George Washington planned an offensive expedition into the Ohio Country. Outrage from the continued Indian attacks necessitated that something be done; the plan was to take the fight to the Indians and combat the tribes head-on. General Harmar's defeat at the Battle of Kekionga on October 20, 1790, was devastating and a complete failure. This American loss only incited and inflamed the tribes to higher levels. As a result of this victory one of the most infamous massacres occurred, the Big Bottom Massacre.

The winter of 1790–91 was very cold. Because of the cold, rarely did the Indians venture out of their villages on raiding parties, as the danger was twofold: the whites and the weather. The Indians were concerned about the weather, more so than the whites, and often stayed home—but not in January of 1791. A blockhouse, near present-day Stockport, Ohio, capable of accommodating twenty men, had been built on the Muskingum River. This blockhouse became known as the Big Bottom station. After the erection of the blockhouse, an association was formed and the Waterford settlement began to grow near the Big Bottom. The dangers of such a settlement in Ohio at this time were clear; however, the settlers were impatient and unwilling to listen to advice. They stood on the belief their blockhouse would provide all the protection they needed to survive an Indian attack.

The whites at the Waterford settlement had become very comfortable and content. Their village cabins were arranged no differently than were those in a comparably small village in the east tucked far away from the dangers of an ongoing war. The village residents felt blissfully safe knowing they had the Big Bottom blockhouse close for their ultimate protection. It was under these conditions that the Wyandot took a great interest in the community as summer hunting parties began scouting and surveying the land and its development. The residents clearly seemed to be forsaking any kind of defense and were inviting disaster; a dangerous trip in the dead of winter was a risk worth taking on the defenseless community. The residents of Waterford, and their brash arrogance, needed a little readjustment. The attack came on January 2, 1791.

After crossing the frozen Muskingum River a little above the Big Bottom blockhouse, the twenty-five Wyandot and Delaware warriors divided into two parties. The larger party would attack the blockhouse while the smaller would concentrate on Waterford and quickly work their way through the village, killing its residents and taking prisoners without sounding an alarm. As the smaller party approached the first cabin, it was clear that its occupants, the Choates, were having supper and had no expectation of visitors. A few of the warriors boldly entered the cabin while the others remained outside. Speaking to the cabin's residents in English, the Choates did not suspect danger and offered the warriors food and shelter. As any traveler in the dead of winter would have done, the warriors accepted their offer and casually entered the cabin. While eating, the warriors obtained leather straps and bound the Choates as their prisoners without any resistance.

Think about it for a moment. What would you have done if you were a white settler and opened the front door of your cabin in the middle of winter after conversing with people on the outside in perfect English? With no signs of concern, you are now standing face-to-face with a few painted Wyandots. Surprise! Would you run? Where would you run? The only thing to do was act as though nothing was wrong. As your guests warmed at the fire and ate your food, their intentions would have been clear. After all, you were still alive. When they reached for the straps to tie your hands there was no choice but to comply and extend your hands. The only choice you have is to cooperate and hope for the best—resist and you will most certainly die a quick death.

As the larger party of warriors approached the Big Bottom blockhouse, the occupants' dogs remained oblivious to the warriors' approach and did not sound an alarm by barking. Even the dogs were comfortably lying inside the blockhouse next to the fire. Approaching, one warrior opened the door, stepped inside, and held the door against the wall as his fellow brothers stood outside and fired shot after shot killing or wounding most of the occupants. After the rifles were empty, they entered the blockhouse and finished each man with their tomahawks. No resistance was encountered, as the men had no knowledge of the presence of danger let alone the presence of Wyandot warriors. However, one woman described as a stout, resolute, backwoods Virginia woman survived the volleys and with an ax took a swing at one of the warriors. The warrior dodged the swing in a split second, and the ax just missed his head while slicing his cheek and finding rest in his shoulder. The woman was promptly killed with a much smaller tomahawk. The warrior lived and suffered the only injury during the raid; undoubtedly he suffered the ridicule of his brothers.

Two young men, John and Philip Stacey, initially survived the volley from the rifles. As soon as the first warrior burst through the door, John scurried up the ladder to the loft and out a hatch to the roof. Once he was outside and on the roof, posted guards who were tasked with making sure none of the occupants escaped killed John as he begged for his life. Philip initially hid and found shelter under bedding; however, he was discovered and his life spared. John, like the Choates, was taken prisoner. All twelve of the dead occupants in the Big Bottom blockhouse were piled in the middle of the single room and their bodies burned. Before the bodies and blockhouse were torched, all the food was removed and piled outside near adjacent stumps.

As John Stacey was begging for his life, occupants of a second cabin in the village of Waterford ran outside to see the commotion. Seeing that their village was under attack, they promptly ran back inside their cabin, grabbed their rifles, and disappeared in the woods outside their back door. For whatever reason as the warriors entered the cabin, knowing the two men had escaped through the back door, they did not give chase and stop their flight. The men fled about four miles to a hunting camp, where warning of the attack on Waterford was relayed. The two men and the occupants of the camp proceeded to Wolf Creek Mills, a distance of six miles, where they warned the community of the Indian attack on Big Bottom and Waterford. Knowing that the residents of Wolf Creek Mills and the small village of Millsburgh had been given ample warning to prepare for a possible attack, the warriors scouted the village leaving tracks hinting of their presence, but they did not attack. All thirty of the Millsburgh's residents took shelter in one small home.

From Millsburgh a runner was sent back to Waterford to warn the resident of the Indians' attack. The whole of the community extended for about two miles along the Muskingum River. One young man was recruited to assist in relaying the warning, and all the cabins were visited in about an hour, upon which sixty-seven residents fled the attack and assembled in their village's own blockhouse. Unlike what happened at the Big Bottom blockhouse, the dogs were kept outside to warn of the approaching Wyandot and Delaware warriors; however, the warriors did not directly approach and attack. With their raid spoiled the warriors collected their plunder and, along with at least five captives, returned to Sandusky and Detroit.[65] The residents of Millsburgh who took shelter in the one home were very, very lucky. For reasons unknown they were allowed to live. The Big Bottom Massacre would have been much worse if they had met the same fate as those who died in the more protective and secure blockhouse.

Massacre at Beaver Hat Town, ca. 1792

There are not many recorded accounts of Wyandots being ambushed and attacked with multiple casualties inflicted; however, I have no doubt many raiding parties were intercepted and many warriors killed, such as what happened with Big Foot and his party. As the war progressed, the Pennsylvanians and Virginians began to learn the Wyandot's tactics and even began to employ some of those same tactics against the Wyandot. In spite of the advantage the Wyandot initially possessed, the balance began to turn, which began to exact a terrible toll. As we will see in the next account, as some of the whites who had been captured and adopted as children returned to their homes, the knowledge they gained while living with their adopted families and learning Native languages was used against the tribes' warriors. Familiar faces and voices became treacherous and deadly.

Tradition states that during the border wars, not one *Huron*-Wyandot village was attacked by the whites with citizens killed in their homes; however, there is ample evidence to show that *Huron*-Wyandot men, women, and children were killed in their homes by their Indian enemies. As I searched for evidence to prove or disprove that Wyandot men, women, and children may or may not have been killed in their villages by the whites, I was pleased that I did not find one recorded account. I am sure that If there had been such an incident, the whites would have flaunted it to the greatest of their abilities just as they did the killing of Big Foot.

Oddly enough, as I was conducting my research, a request came through the Wyandotte Nation's website. Throughout the course of any given year the tribe receives hundreds of requests from people as they seek citizenship or ask for information on history or culturally related items. At times some people ask senseless random questions or make requests that are rather bizarre. Most of these requests are read with the delete button and quickly forgotten.

A lady, who appeared to be sincere and desperate, made one such bizarre request that seized my attention. She described some rather strange events in her city that were attributed to a massacre that had occurred in the late eighteenth century. Over the course of many generations since the massacre, she described the presence of apparitions, poverty, and an oppression that seemed to envelop her city. Her desperate plea was for the Wyandotte people to come and perform a ceremony to seek and achieve a sense of reconciliation. Her desire was for the murdered Wyandots in her city to find peace and rest and leave her city alone. I instantly began to research what she was saying, and sure enough I found that a massacre of Wyandots had taken place somewhere around 1792 in what was then known as Beaver Hat Town. I am unaware if the tribe ever responded or extended to her any assistance—the likelihood is doubtful.

During my research I found the following uniquely odd and rare event with little documentation outside one source and local tradition. The city of Wooster, Ohio, was surveyed in 1808; it was then home for a small encampment of Delaware who were still noted in the area. Chief Pappellelond called the area his apple chauquecake, translated as "apple orchard." It is believed the apple grove in his small village is one of the many planted by John Chapman, better known today as Johnny Appleseed.[66] The area of Chief Pappellelond's village sat at the intersection of the Cuyahoga War Trail, the Great Trail, and the Killbuck path. This intersection of paths served as an important center of trade, commerce, and travel during the days of the border wars and westward expansion. The village was then known as Beaver Hat Town, and after the survey the name was changed to Wooster, Ohio.[67]

The legend begins as a band of sixteen Wyandot warriors approached the Raccoon Creek settlement near Pittsburgh, Pennsylvania. The Wyandot's warriors attacked the town from within, burning several houses, and killing five of the town's residents in the process.[68] As they began the return trip to Sandusky, they crossed the Ohio River and were unknowingly pursued by at least thirty of the town's residents. What happened once the whites caught up with the Wyandot warriors is known today as the Massacre at Beaver Hat Town. It was indeed a massacre—not of women and children but of Wyandot warriors. The men died as noble warriors fighting a noble cause, and not as common criminals they were at the time made out to be. They died because of treachery and deception employed by someone who was once himself an Indian. Ben Douglass stated of the warriors, "They were distinguished for bloodthirstiness, stubborn antagonism to the Americans and the cause of national independence, and were, moreover, *particeps criminis* [an accomplice in a crime] to many of the atrocities that blacken the pages of our border history. Their fiendish cavorts, warring and plundering raids included vast areas, and to this hour fading, but unfaded, drops of human blood mark the line of their accursed marauds."[69]

Douglass told how a war party of sixteen Wyandots left the Sandusky for Raccoon Creek near Pittsburgh. Their intent was to look the part of friendly Indians and be welcomed by the residents with open hospitality. Once invited into the residents' homes, they would initiate their attack with calculated precision and deadly intent. Upon their arrival at the settlement their scheme went as planned; the friendly Indians were warmly received and then easily killed five residents. They then proceeded to burn seven cabins along with their occupants. The enraged residents promptly pursued the Wyandots with Captain George Fulkes in the lead of thirty men who were described by Douglass as "fearless of flints and fate."

Captain Fulkes had an advantage. At the age of three he was captured by an unknown Indian tribe and promptly adopted into that tribe. He remained a citizen until he became a young man. It was then that his birth father located, identified, and took him back from his captors. From his early days of captivity Fulkes knew a little of the Wyandot language; hence, he was the choice to lead the revenge party. Since his release from captivity Fulkes had rejected and shunned his childhood upbringing to become an avid Indian fighter. This garnered for Captain Fulkes the reputation of obtaining many Indian scalps.

After crossing the Ohio River, Fulkes and his men located the trail of the Wyandot warriors. Unaware if the Wyandot knew they were being pursued, Fulkes proceeded at a safe distance. Late one evening they overtook the war party outside present-day Wooster, Ohio, as the warriors settled in for a night's rest. Waiting until the full moon had risen, Fulkes positioned his men around the unsuspecting camp. At a given signal the whites fired upon the Wyandots as they slept on the ground or lazily lay around their camp. All but one of the warriors was instantly killed. The remaining survivor was alone checking traps on the river bottom when he heard the firing of the muskets. Rushing back to his camp, but before entering, the warrior called ahead asking, "What's the matter?" "Come on," shouted Fulkes in Wandat. "Nothing's the matter!"[70] As the warrior walked into his obliterated camp, one of Captain Fulkes's men "perforated his carcass with a bullet." A shallow grave was dug, and the sixteen Wyandot warriors were tossed inside and maybe covered with a sprinkling of dirt.

After being buried in shallow graves, the warriors were all but forgotten. Back at Sandusky the warriors who failed to return home were just more names added to the list of unknown fates. If not for the occasional tavern boast, murky legend, and apparitions that haunted the city of Wooster, the Massacre at Beaver Hat Town may have became lost in history. The ambushing militia may have disrespected the bodies of the Wyandot warriors—sons, brothers, fathers, and uncles—but the Wyandotte Nation will never forget their gallant sacrifice for the homeland. Their death on the frontier guaranteed that their people and families could live in relative peace knowing they would never have to endure the same fate. These sixteen men paid the ultimate price for their freedom.

Battle of Fallen Timbers, 1794

Today in contemporary literature the Delaware and Shawnee are often given so much attention, notoriety, and glory for making their stand in the Ohio

Country that at times it can look as though they fought alone. Many books, articles, and papers are noticeably silent and only on occasion mention the Wyandot as co-conspirators in the struggle. The personal journals, letters, and accounts of participants from the days of the Revolutionary War indicate that the Wyandot commanded much attention, fear, and respect. After all, Pomoacan was then the Half King, and throughout the border wars of the American Revolution, the Wyandot were then considered the leaders of the Indian alliance.

Why do history books often ignore or minimize the role the Wyandot played in the border wars? Remember what Colonel Edward Livingston Taylor said? At the time the white people wrote the history of the border wars, and many are doing the same today. When history is written it can often be distorted, embellished, or suppressed. Yes, I admit, from time-to-time I may do a little embellishing myself. It's just human nature to say, *"My dad is bigger than your dad!"* The worst way to portray history is to not only suppress an individual, people or event but also to strike them from the historical record as though he, she, they, or it never existed or happened. I do not believe this is the attempted fate of the Wyandot; however, I do believe there is such an exaggerated misunderstanding of what took place then that the Wyandot are too often overlooked or forgotten by contemporary histories.

What the Wyandot warriors did was phenomenal, brilliant, and mixed with much brutality. Allied with the Shawnee, Delaware, Mingo, and Miami, they resisted and withstood the advance of the Pennsylvanians and Virginians. The confederacy, as led by the Half King, successfully repelled the white invasion splashing across the northern bank of the Ohio River. The Wyandot warrior was an intelligent, noble, and brutal combatant who inflicted profound pain and destruction upon his enemies. The feats and accomplishments of the Wyandots were an embarrassment to the victor, who then defeated the greatest military power on the face of the earth—the British Empire. To have beaten the British and suffered heavily at the hands of the Wyandot Tribe was a blemish upon that victory. The best thing to do is to flaunt and promote the fact that you whipped the *redcoats* but ignore and minimize the fact the *redskins* whipped you. The Wyandot and all their many accomplishments had to be downplayed from the history of the border wars for the sake of saving the face and the honor of the victor.

On September 3, 1783, the Treaty of Paris was signed, bringing to a close the American Revolution. On January 14, 1784, the Continental Congress ratified the treaty. The United States was officially an independent nation, but

many challenges still lay ahead. One big challenge was those pesky, unrelenting Indians who could not have cared less that a treaty was signed officially
bringing the war to an end. The Indians' land was incorporated within the
new country and designated as the Northwest Territory in 1787.

> But the price had yet to be paid in blood; the old battle between civilization
> and barbarism had again to be fought. Boone, Kenton, the Poes, and others
> of like mould had broken the power of the savages on the dark and bloody
> ground. They had crossed the Ohio and taken their stand on the other side,
> boldly proclaiming that the line between themselves and the advancing whites
> should be drawn on the banks of the Beautiful River.[71]

The power of the savages had not been broken. The savages still had a
lot of power and a lot of fight left in their hearts. As for the white's stand
on the other side of the Ohio River, it was not much more than a toehold.
See how the victors write history? After the war with Great Britain came to a
close, the Americans presented the Treaty of 1785 to the chiefs and warriors of
the Wyandot, Delaware, Chippewa, and Ottawa nations, among others. This
treaty drew a proverbial invisible line in the forest and all but dared the tribes
to cross the line. The Treaty of 1785 stated, "The United States allot all the
lands contained within the said lines to the Wiandot and Delaware nations, to
live and to hunt on."[72]

The treaty bore the names of two Wyandot chiefs, Daunghquat and Abraham Kuhn, who presumably represented the Wyandot from Sandusky. "In 1785
Tarhe's name does not appear to the treaty of Ft. Mcintosh. Abraham Kuhn
signed it for Wyandots at Lower Sandusky. Half King's name is not attached
to same unless by the name, Daunghquat, which is probable."[73] There is no
doubt that if Pomoacan had signed the treaty, the great and powerful Half
King's mark would have been noted as such by the Americans. The three
most powerful and influential Wyandots at the time were Pomoacan, Tarhe,
and Kuhn.

The thirteen British colonies, now independent American states, barely
ratified the Constitution of the United States. With nine of the thirteen colonies needing to sign, New Hampshire became the ninth to ratify the document on June 21, 1788. Acting on the assumption that the constitution would
be ratified, the Northwest Territory was established and opened for settlement
in 1787. There was one minor problem: The land was still occupied by the
Indians. Pomoacan, the Half King, died in 1788. Tarhe would be his successor

as chief of the Wyandot Tribe; however, Tarhe did not have the same influence, as Pomoacan and he did not carry the title of Half King.

Many whites were now pouring across the Ohio River, many of whom were former soldiers of the Continental Army who were paid for their service with land grants. The Treaty of 1785 was worthless without Pomoacan's mark. The boundary as defined in the treaty was ignored, and the various tribes continued to define their land as bounded by the Ohio River—not by an imaginary line drawn by the Americans. "The attitude of the English and Canadians had much to do with the bold stand taken by the Indians. . . . Time had not yet reconciled the English to the loss of the Colonies, and the possessions which they had relinquished on paper were abandoned slowly, with reluctance and regret."[74]

Shortly after the close of the Revolutionary War, the Western Confederacy, or Miami Confederacy as it is also known, was organized with the influence of Joseph Brant, a Mohawk. The tribes gathered in November through December of 1786 in the small Wyandot town of Brownstown near Detroit. During the Revolutionary War, Joseph Brant was a staunch ally of Great Britain and carried a reputation for his brutality toward the white settlers and soldiers alike.

With the Wyandot being the leaders of the current confederacy, Joseph Brant had to come to the Wyandot with his proposal. Peter D. Clarke in *Traditional History of the Wyandotts* indicates that when Brant first presented himself to the Wyandot, it was at Brownstown and under extreme secrecy. Brant had anything but good intentions. Peter indicates that during his short stay at Brownstown, "Captain Brant and his party were kindly treated by the Wyandotts; they visited one another, and smoked the pipe of peace and friendship together; touched nothing of the past that would have a tendency to wake up or stir up any old grudge that might still lay hidden within each other's breast."[75] The potential for hostility still existed between the Wyandot and Mohawk that extended all the way back to the Huron and Iroquois War.

As Brant smoked the pipe of friendship, his emissaries made their way throughout the various tribes. Brant's messengers were carrying "a glass bead belt, of a dark green color, and having the figure of a beaver animal, made of white beads on it, emblematical of the *secret underground errand* that the messengers were entrusted with."[76] Upon reaching the Chippewa, the message in the belt was discovered and the messengers greeted with rebuke. Brandt was attempting to establish an alliance with the various tribes to attack and destroy the Wyandot. Brandt knew that the Wyandots were then the undisputed leaders of the Western tribes, and he wanted that position for his Mohawk. The Chippewa, longtime loyal allies of the Wyandot, confiscated the belt and presented it to the Wyandot at Brownstown, whereby the Wyandot learned of Brant's conspiracy.[77]

Brant's conspiracy failed after he understood that the Wyandot's friends and allies would not defy or forsake their friendships that extended back generations. There is a legend among the Wyandot that Joseph Brant, when he initially came to the Sandusky speaking of creating the new confederacy, was not initially welcomed into the villages. He was shunned because the old Wyandots considered him a traitor. At that time, it was known that the family of Joseph Brant descended from captives of the old Huron and Iroquois War who were adopted into the Mohawk. The relationship and the connection were strong enough that the old people knew Brant was a relative who swore loyalties to the Mohawk.

In spite of Joseph Brant's attempted coup, the Wyandot approved the new confederacy as many tribes, extending well beyond the Ohio Country, stepped forward to join the alliance. However, Brant was not well received by the various tribes of the Northwest Territory, nor was he considered the leader of the confederacy. In time Little Turtle, or Michikinikwa, a Miami war chief, emerged as the leading chief of the Western Confederacy. "As a warrior Little Turtle was fearless but not rash; shrewd to plan, bold and energetic to execute. No peril could daunt him, and no emergency could surprise him."[78] In essence, and in spirit, Little Turtle was the last Half King of the Ohio Country tribes.

The two principles agreed upon by tribes joining the Western Confederacy were (1) to defend the boundary line as established in the 1768 Treaty of Fort Stanwix and (2) that no tribe could cede land without consent of all the tribes. These terms were ably supported and promoted by Little Turtle. No whites were to be allowed north of the Ohio River. When the tribes of the Western Confederacy called upon Brant for aid after defeating General Harmar, Brant refused to send his Mohawk warriors to reinforce the confederacy. With these two tenets, and with the Americans taking the offensive, war resumed with no less ferocity than during the whole of the border war.

Battle of Kekionga, 1790

The following account of General Harmar's Defeat, or the Battle of Kekionga, is based upon William L. Stone's telling of the battle as found in *Life of Joseph*

Brant, Vol. II. The Battle of Kekionga was fought in a series of smaller battles and skirmishes from October 19 to 22, 1790. The battles of this expedition were the first fought by an army of the United States of America since gaining independence from Great Britain.

After the Revolutionary War came to a close, President George Washington's attempt to secure peaceful relations with the various tribes of the Northwest Territory failed. His next and only recourse was to mount a vigorous offensive against the hostile tribes. As for the hostile tribes, they too looked upon the United States as being equally combative. President Washington chose General Josiah Harmar to lead the expedition and bring the savages into submission. To effect this order an army of 1,450 soldiers was assembled. Within this fledgling army only three hundred twenty were regular troops with the remainder being Pennsylvania and Kentucky militia. Their objective was clear: destroy the Indian villages located in the general vicinity of the Maumee, St. Mary's, and St. Joseph rivers.

The expedition departed Fort Washington (Cincinnati) on September 30, 1790. Upon hearing of General Harmar's advance, the allied tribes initially abandoned Kekionga, the town in which they had assembled, and set it on fire. After the death of Pomoacan the center of the Western Confederacy shifted from Pomoacan's principal town of Sandusky to Little Turtle's principal town of Kekionga. After burning the town on October 19, the tribes assembled and attacked two hundred ten men under the command of Colonel John Harden at the Battle of Heller's Corner near the Eel River. Once the battle commenced and the first shots fired, all of Colonel Harden's militia fled the battlefield. The regular army stood their ground and sustained heavy casualties with only seven escaping with their lives.

Over the next few days a chess match ensued between General Harmar and Little Turtle. Upon learning that Little Turtle and his army were returning to Kekionga, on October 22 Colonel Harden was dispatched with a much larger force of three hundred sixty men to intercept and dispose of Little Turtle's army. In a twist of strategic fate Little Turtle ambushed Colonel Harden near the junction of the St. Joseph and St. Mary rivers. In this battle the militia stood their ground; however, Little Turtle's superior forces overpowered Harden's troops, and one hundred eighty-three men were killed along with thirteen officers. Little Turtle lost about one hundred warriors. The battle was intense and ended with the Americans abandoning the battlefield. "General Harmar thereupon returned to Fort Washington and claimed the victory with what propriety has never been ascertained."[79]

Battle of the Wabash, 1791

St. Clair's Defeat, or the Battle of the Wabash, is too often overlooked and likely purposefully forgotten in the history books. This one four-hour battle is still considered the single greatest defeat suffered by an army of the United States at the hands of the American Indians.[80] In comparison, one of the most infamous battles of the American West was the Battle of the Greasy Grass, better known as the Battle of Little Bighorn. This is where General George Armstrong Custer met his demise, and it pales in comparison to General Arthur St. Clair's disastrous defeat. "Thus Custer, his two brothers, nephew, brother-in-law, and his entire command of nearly 300 mounted officers and men, yield up their lives on the 25th of June, 1876."[81]

Richard M. Voorhees, Civil War veteran, attorney, and Ohio Circuit Judge in the early twentieth century, wrote a lengthy article for The Ohio State Archaeological and Historical Society—an all-encompassing biography of General Custer's military career. In his essay Voorhees compared General Custer's last stand to that of the Spartan General Leonidas and his fateful stand against the invading Persians. Voorhees continued by stating of General Custer, "He here found the one thing needed to complete his character as an ideal hero of romance, a glorious and terrible death on the field of battle."[82]

I am confident that it was not General Custer but Leonidas and Sitting Bull who were defending their homeland from an invading army. This alone makes them ideal heroes of romance—not that they were looking for heroism or any form of worship. General Custer and his American army were the invaders no different from Xerxes and his Persians. Earlier I compared Wyandot warriors to Sparta's warriors. As we will see, Wyandot chiefs and warriors died at the Battle of Fallen Timbers making a final stand as they tried to hold back the advance of the Americans. Their final stand bought time for their Indian friends and allies to escape the battlefield. They were honorable and noble in everything they did while defending their homeland from the invading army.

When compared to General St. Clair, the Sioux, Northern Cheyenne, and Arapaho's victory over General Custer was no less a decisive victory; however, the Western Confederacy achieved a resounding victory. "Of the 1,400 regulars, levies, and militia, 918 were killed and 276 wounded. Almost half of the entire U.S. Army was either dead or wounded in the aftermath of St. Clair's Defeat."[83] It's generally accepted that only about two hundred of General St. Clair's men survived the battle without being wounded or suffered only minor wounds; however, the men would have carried psychological wounds for the rest of their lives. The carnage was beyond brutal and indescribable. Camp workers, consisting of women and children, were even killed in the four-hour battle.

General Arthur St. Clair had a resume that preceded him by a mile. During the French and Indian War he served in the British Army. Upon the outbreak of the American Revolution he chose the side of the American Colonists and quickly rose to the rank of Major General in the Continental Army, but not without associated controversy. After the war ended, St. Clair served as President of the Continental Congress before being appointed Governor of the new Northwest Territory he helped to create. Once the section of the Northwest Territory that was destined to become the state of Ohio was organized, St. Clair became Provisional Governor of Ohio. It was he who suggested that another campaign be organized and fielded against the Western Confederacy in response to General Harmar's Defeat. In spite of General Harmar's denial of defeat everyone knew the campaign for what it was—a failure. Next to be added to St. Clair's impressive resume is one of the worst defeats suffered by an army of the United States. Maybe General St. Clair should not have been so critical of General Harmar.

General St. Clair insisted that the proposed chain of forts from Fort Washington (Cincinnati), deep into the heart of the Maumee Country, be built during his campaign. General Harmar was to have built the forts but did not. It was believed that it would be much easier to punish and control the various tribes from these forts. As General St. Clair departed on his little expedition, its true intent and purpose were still a little confusing: build forts, fight the Indians, make peace with the Indians—no one seemed to fully understand. The tribes of the Western Confederacy did not doubt St. Clair's intent, but the officers and soldiers found their cargo a little contradictory. "From the Government standpoint the expedition was not necessarily hostile, so that the pipe of peace was carried along in the same wagon as grape and the canister."[84]

In order to accomplish his task General St. Clair was given power not yet possessed by a general of the Continental or US Army. From recent experiences only one word of advice was extended to his command of the army: Be alert for a surprise attack by the enemy. Remember, unlike General Harmar's expedition, whose purpose was to destroy Kekionga and other Indian villages, General St. Clair was not embarking with the expressed purpose of fighting the Northwest Confederacy. Unfortunately, Little Turtle and his powerful army were unaware of General St. Clair's nonspecific intent. Any American army that ventured into their land was a threat, no matter the potential intent.

General St. Clair's Defeat was predicted before the campaign even started. As General St. Clair began hacking his way through the cold forest and building the overrated forts along the way, he did not heed the one bit of advice given. He was personally ill and his guard lax, and he was not prepared for any surprises thrown his way by a wise and wily enemy much at home in the cold and thickness—conditions that slowed St. Clair's advancing army's pace to five or six miles a day. By the time his exhausted army reached the eastern fork of the Wabash River, approximately a mile and half from the Ohio and Indiana state line, his men had dwindled to 1,400 soldiers. Upon departing Fort Washington two months earlier, General St. Clair had 2,300 soldiers, both regular army and militia, under his command.

In spite of omnipresent signs of the Indians, General St. Clair sent a detachment to search for their missing supplies, thereby weakening his army. With an army that was experiencing disquietude, and was decimated and demoralized, picket firing was heard throughout the night and early morning of November 3 to 4 as scouts reported movement in the front and along both flanks of their encampment. To make matters worse, a light snow had fallen and it was bitterly cold. It was then that Little Turtle first attacked the militia, three hundred to four hundred men who had been placed across a small stream in front of the main army, with brute force and strategic precision.

There was no time for General St. Clair's army to react to this surprise attack. The militia was routed with confusion and mayhem everywhere. "Only now and then could fearful figures, painted in red and black, with feathers braided in their long scalp-locks, be distinguished through the smoke." The warriors of the Western Confederacy found shelter behind trees and stumps, becoming invisible ghosts to the horrified soldiers who were indeed shooting at smoke wisps and vapors of warm breath. The soldiers were nothing less than targets in a turkey shoot or lumbering buffalo picked off one-by-one by huntsmen armed with Sharpe rifles never seen by their killers. The Indians were specific and deliberate in their attack, with the artillery first being silenced. The frantic soldiers turned, and like buffalo stampeding they razed their own camp. Mixed within the soldiers and fighting alongside the men for their lives were women, camp followers who met the same fate as the men they accompanied deep into the wilderness of frozen death.

As we have already seen, of the 1,400 soldiers, levies, and militia, 918 were killed and 276 wounded. At this time in the history of the United States military the losses accounted for nearly one-half of the entire US Army. "Oh!" said an old squaw many years afterwards, "my arm that night was weary scalping white men."[85] The tribes who fought in the four-hour carnage were Delaware, Shawnee, Wyandot, Miami, Ottawa, Chippewa, and Potawatomi—the principal tribes of the Western Confederacy.

For the United States of America the defeat was disastrous and spun scandals in the nation's capital. President George Washington came under intense criticism, and the legacy of his presidency was blemished; after all, he was commander in chief of the army. General Arthur St. Clair resigned his commission in spite of an investigation that exonerated him of any wrongdoing. Extreme damage was inflicted upon St. Clair's reputation. However, under scrutiny he retained the position of Governor of the Northwest Territory.

With the loss of so many lives the grief and anger were intense and almost insurmountable. Arthur St. Clair was looked upon with equal abomination as Little Turtle. For the Americans there could not be another defeat. If they were defeated once more, the likelihood of the United States being run out of the Northwest Territory was more than probable. If they were run out of the territory, it may have taken decades before the Americans could rebuild the army and gain popular support for another expedition. If such an event had occurred, it may have caused the British, sore losers as they were, to again retake control of their former colony. For the survivability of the United States and George Washington's presidency, another expedition into the Wabash and Maumee valleys must end with a resounding victory, not just a mediocre win.

Another devastating loss could have been insurmountable and fatal to the livelihood of the infant country. Another Indian victory would further inflame the Western Confederacy and fully inspire the boldness and radicalization of the tribes. The Western Confederacy's boldness and seemingly ease of victory over the Americans could have metastasized well beyond the tribes of the confederacy. The last thing the Americans needed was an escalation of Indian problems throughout their newly acquired territory and well beyond. The victories were inspiration for the Indians to strike deep and hard into the bowels of civilization, leaving death and destruction as yet to be seen upon the Great Island.

From the outcry of the settlers and the notion that the US government had to protect its citizens' right to the land, another expedition into the Maumee Country was planned. The fledgling army was reorganized as the Legion of the United States, and by an act of Congress its ranks and the number of troops were expanded. General Anthony Wayne was chosen as Major General of the new, improved, and expanded army. Upon his appointment on March 5, 1792, General Wayne would personally take charge of selecting his officers and new recruits. He too was consumed with their training, as well as the procurement of much-needed supplies, including a rifle for each man. Emphasis on the state's militia being the backbone of the standing army was minimized, and the militia was placed into a supportive role. In spite of the delays and obstacles General Wayne was successful in raising a 1,280 army; however, he did not immediately attack Little Turtle and the Western Confederacy. Instead, on President Washington's insistence, General Wayne vigorously trained his recruits for two years!

While General Wayne was collecting and training his army, the warriors of the Western Confederacy were striking deep into the frontier and even deeper into the bowels of civilization. The ranks of the confederacy were swelling, and the tribes were gathering along the bank of the Maumee River in frightful droves. The Miami were along the Maumee under the leadership of Little Turtle, the Delaware under Buckongehelas, the Shawnee under Blue Jacket, and the Wyandot under Tarhe. Although Little Turtle was the recognized leader of the confederacy, Tarhe still commanded great authority due to the *Huron*-Wyandot's position as Keepers of the Council Fire and their recognized role as leaders for well over one hundred years. These tribes were joined by bands of Ottawa, Potawatomi, Kickapoo, Chippewa, and other smaller tribes. They were a unified army that held various opinions of how diplomacy should be employed and various opinions of General Wayne's command.

In October of 1792 the Western Confederacy began to dictate terms of the engagement to the Americans. They at least took a first step toward acquiring a peaceful resolve to the issue at hand. The terms they presented were not bad, yet the Americans felt offended, as the Indians proposed that "they would lay the bloody tomahawk aside until they heard from the President of the United States."[86] This was a defiant sign of power and unity that expressed the Indians' desire for peace over war. From the conference at the Au Glaize River a truce was proposed until the following spring. It was a nice proposal, but it was not meant to be. Certain elements and factions of the Western Confederacy did not uphold the decree, and raids into the frontier resumed with unrelenting ferocity.

When spring arrived in 1793, General Wayne marched his men to Fort Washington. Stopping for a moment's rest he continued north near where General St. Clair met his defeat. It was then that General Wayne gave the men of General St. Clair's army a proper burial. Fort Greenville was established not far from the site of the disastrous battle, and General Wayne's army continued to drill and train there throughout the winter.[87] While at Fort Greenville

General Wayne sent forth his spies to begin collecting information as to the whereabouts and strength of his enemy. It was then that General Wayne came to learn what everyone else already knew of the Wyandots.

> When Gen. Wayne assumed the position of Greenville, in 1793, he sent for Captain Wells, who commanded a company of scouts, and told him that he wished him to go to Sandusky, and take a prisoner, for the purpose of obtaining information. Wells (who, having been taken from Kentucky when a boy, and brought up among the Indians, was perfectly acquainted with their character), said he could take a prisoner, but not from Sandusky. "And why not from Sandusky?" said the general. "Because," said the captain, "they are only Wyandots there." "Well, why will not Wyandots do?" "For the best of reasons," said Wells; "because Wyandots will not be taken alive."[88]

Once winter passed and the summer of 1794 arrived, General Wayne's Legion of the United States was complemented by the arrival of 1,600 mounted Kentuckians, at which point the army was marched into the stronghold of the Indians. "The move was a bold one, but there was in it nothing of *madness*."[89] Throughout the duration of the march General Wayne left nothing to chance. The mistakes of his predecessors were not going to be repeated. There had been plenty of time to study the mistakes of generals Harmar and St. Clair; in addition, General Wayne had studied the tactics of his enemy. Stopping at the junction of the Auglaize and Maumee rivers, General Wayne built yet another fort—Fort Defiance. The fort stood in defiance of danger and all but mocked the Western Confederacy. General Wayne now had his army strategically position in the heart of Indian country and his presence did not go unnoticed.

On August 13, 1794, General Anthony Wayne sent a message to the Indians on the Maumee River offering peace, and they came to council. From the appearance of General Wayne's army at Fort Defiance, the Indians did not believe he came looking for peace. Little Turtle recommended that the Western Confederacy accept the offer and seek terms of peace, but the other chiefs wholly rejected the offer. Little Turtle stated, "We have beaten the enemy every time and under separate commanders . . . but we cannot expect the same good fortune always to attend us. The Americans are now led by a chief who never sleeps. The night and the day are alike to him."[90]

On August 15, 1794, General Anthony Wayne led his army downriver toward the British fort located at the Rapids of the Maumee. Unlike previous commanders, General Wayne employed mounted troops far in advance of his main army to allow his foot soldiers time to prepare once the Indian army was contacted. The Indian army was located on the morning of August 20, 1794, lying in ambush amid fallen timber strewn through tall grass left from the aftermath of a tornado. The Indians had the advantage of surprise, and their strategy for the battle was a solid military maneuver; however, to their surprise General Wayne employed an even bolder military maneuver. He divided his cavalry into two detachments and directed each to strike the flanks. At the same time, his infantry formed and charged straight down the middle of the battlefield—they routed and tossed the Indian army no less than the tornado tossed the trees.

General Wayne's army attacked through the tall grass, weaving through and jumping over the fallen trees as the Indians were driven back at the point of bayonets. The Wyandot suffered horrible losses as they stood their ground refusing to turn their backs and run. Many of their Indian friends and allies were shot as General Wayne's soldiers poured volley after volley into their backs. The Wyandot, because of their courage and strength of character, would not turn their backs. Nine out of ten Wyandot chiefs on the battlefield were slain—dare I say with pointed bayonets and swords, not guns? How many warriors of the Indian army were killed has never been assessed.

After the battle General Wayne did not stop his army, and they proceeded to destroy villages and cornfields for miles on both sides of the Maumee River. The personal property of British agent Colonel Alexander McKee met the same fate as that of the Indians. It was clear that Colonel McKee furnished the Western Confederacy with materials and advice, yet when it came time to fight, he abandoned his allies to their fate by locking the gates of the British fort that commanded and guarded the battlefield where many dead Indians now lay.[91, 92]

Losing nine chiefs was a national disaster for the Wyandot! The confederacy and the power of the Indians had now been broken. The power and the influence of the *Huron*-Wyandots over the other tribes of the Northeast were severely weakened. Tecumseh and his brother would stand and now challenge the Americans with Roundhead, the great Wyandot war chief, at his side. Tarhe survived the battle but was severely wounded. Tradition states he was shot in the arm and sustained a terrible wound. How could such a disaster for the Wyandots have occurred? "Gen. [William Henry] Harrison yields the palm of superior bravery, among all the Western Indians, to the Wyandots. Flight is usually regarded by Indians as no disgrace, but rather as a matter of policy, if not of duty, when sorely pressed by superior numbers, or surprised by unwonted obstacles. Not so with the Wyandots"[93]

Almost a year after the battle, from June 15 through August 17, 1795, the tribes would again assemble, but this time at Fort Greenville. For over two months 1,130 chiefs and warriors were present or parties to this celebrated treaty.[94] The Treaty of Greenville was signed on August 3, 1795. With the signing of the treaty the tribes would cede 25,000 square miles to the Americans. Much of this ceded land would become the state of Ohio on March 1, 1803. In essence the Treaty of Greenville was a reaffirmation of the Treaty of 1785, the invisible line drawn by the Americans the Indians refused to acknowledge. This time the tribes honored the Treaty of Greenville. The treaty "saved defence-less [sic] settlements from the tomahawk and scalping-knife of the Indian, and supplanted the harsher tones of strife and bloodshed with the softer enactments of charity and love."[95] Awe, that was nice, but not all the Indians chose to embrace charity and love! A few did not attend the treaty signing and vowed to continue the fight. Henry Schoolcraft described the magnificent assemblage of the proud tribes at Greenville.

> Foremost among the tribes who turned their steps to his [General Wayne] camp, were the proud and influential Wyandots, who had so long been regarded as wise men and umpires among the tribes of the West. . . . They were astute, reflective, and capable of pursuing a steady line of policy, which had been, with some lapses, the stay of the western tribes, who were willing to tread in their footsteps. This tribe was the last to assent to the scheme of Pontiac; and when the confederation was broken up by the British, they adhered to that power with extraordinary devotion.
>
> In this train, also, followed the Delawares, who had been, since the time they first fled from Pennsylvania and crossed the Alleghanies, bitter enemies of the settlers in the West. There also came the Shawnees; the most vengeful and subtile [sic] of all the western tribes. Every day witnessed the arrival in the surrounding forests of delegates, decked off with all their peculiar ornaments, of feathers, paint, silver gorgets, trinkets, and medals. The Chippewas, Ottawas, Pottawatamies, Miamies, Weas, Kickapoos, Piankashaws, and Kaskaskias, were all present. The entire official power of the Algonquins was on the ground. Each delegation carried the pipe of peace, and expressed pacific desires. The whole camp presented a gorgeous display of wild and savage magnificence; and, for the number and variety of costumes, the scene has, probably, never since been equalled in America. All came bending to Wayne.[96]

Battle of River Raisin, 1813

President James Madison did not want war with Great Britain. The reality of Great Britain's aggression, and the fact that it ignored many of the terms of the Treaty of Paris, gave President Madison little he could ignore. The combination of both unresolved and lingering issues after the John Jay Treaty of 1795 and pressure from western states for more land to exploit meant that peace was no longer an option. In his message to Congress on June 1, 1812, President Madison gave his reasons for seeking a declaration of war. His three reasons were (1) illegal searching of American ships in American harbors and on the high seas, (2) forcing US citizens into British naval service, and (3) interfering with the neutrality of American merchants.[97] President Monroe mentioned briefly and in passing that British agents and traders were responsible for the Indian attacks on the frontier. Many historians have stated that the War of 1812 was America's second War of Independence from Great Britain's lingering control and interference; however, the war was essentially fought over the commercial rights of an infant country.

The strongest calls for war came from west of the Allegheny Mountains. The great Shawnee Chief Tecumseh and his Indian alliance were demanding that something be done quickly to ward off his threats of revolt. In spite of the powerful alliance representing most of the tribes throughout Ohio, Michigan, Indiana, and well beyond, Tecumseh did not command a unified loyalty from all the tribes. Tarhe openly opposed Tecumseh, as did his lifelong friend and ally Black Hoof, who was himself Shawnee. Both chiefs, as did Little Turtle after the Battle of Fallen Timbers, called for peaceful relations with the Americans. Tecumseh defied the wisdom of the old chiefs, declared them to be witches, and called for their executions. Both Tarhe and Black Hoof evaded Tecumseh's call for death and died as honorable, wise old men. Tecumseh died a disillusioned and defeated young man at forty-five years of age.

Before his death at the Battle of the Thames on October 5, 1813, Tecumseh began his military career in defeat, also, coincidentally, at the hands of General William Henry Harrison. It is actually a little deceiving to say Tecumseh was defeated when he was not present at the battle; however, it was his brother, Tenskwatawa the Prophet, and his Indian army who met defeat. Tecumseh had been amassing his alliance with no secretive pretenses. Unwilling to allow another Indian uprising, General Harrison marched to Prophetstown with a preemptive plan of destroying the alliance before it started. At the Battle of Tippecanoe on November 7, 1811, General Harrison's plan met success.

Although the number of casualties was essentially even, Tenskwatawa's forces were driven from the battlefield. Over the next two years Tecumseh's alliance would wreak havoc across the western states; however, without the assistance of the British and the Wyandot war chief Roundhead, Tecumseh's alliance may not have survived much past the Battle of Tippecanoe.

Long before war was declared on Great Britain, it was clear that war-makers in the United States were planning for the complete conquest of Canada. Henry Clay, a transplanted Virginian in Kentucky, was serving in the US House of Representatives and became a strong voice for war. His rhetoric inspired and motivated his followers with such declarations as "The conquest of Canada is in your power" and "I trust I shall not be deemed presumptuous when I state that I verily believe that the militia of Kentucky are alone competent to place Montreal and Upper Canada at your feet."[98] The naive United States was blissfully ignorant, prideful, and boastful of its recent independence. An aggressive campaign on the frontiers of the Northwest Territory and Canada had not been fully rationalized. In addition, the Indian allies of Great Britain, Tecumseh's alliance, were as always underestimated as a viable and respectful army. A three-pronged attack of Canada was devised and put into motion when war was declared on June 18, 1812.

General William Hull, governor of the Michigan Territory, was to command the far western prong of the attack on Canada and ensure Detroit's retention for the Americans. His army was primarily composed of Ohio militia. Reaching Detroit on July 12, 1812, General Hull quickly advanced into Canada and laid siege to Fort Malden. The logistics and complications of keeping his army supplied were underestimated and inadequately planned. To make matters worse, official documents that detailed his plan of attack were intercepted, and all elements of surprise were lost. The siege was short-lived and General Hull promptly retreated back to Detroit. There he learned on July 17 that the British had captured Mackinac and Detroit would be next. To make matters worse, Tecumseh's alliance was amassing warriors for an attack on Detroit. The Americans' ability to hold Detroit now looked untenable at best. All of this news seemed to paralyze General Hull instead of stirring him to action.[99] On August 15, 1812, General Hull surrendered Michigan and Detroit to the British without one shot fired in its defense. "On the same day that Hull surrendered at Detroit, the little garrison at Fort Dearborn (Chicago) yielded to an overwhelming Indian force. The fort was burned and the garrison massacred."[100] The stark reality of a war with Great Britain, which

the Americans so desired, was fully realized and underway in the most undesirable way.

History is clear: The Wyandot were divided and stood on opposite sides
of the battlefield during the War of 1812. It would not be until the Battle
of the Thames and the death of Tecumseh that his spell would be broken
from the minds and hearts of many Wyandots. Both an affinity for war and
the Prophet's overlying religious connotations proved mesmerizing for many
Wyandot. Roundhead, whose Wyandot name was Stayeghtha, translated as
Bark Carrier, was once the warpole of the Wyandot Tribe. Roundhead defied
the warning of Tarhe and sided with Tecumseh, essentially becoming his second in command.

Walk-In-The-Water was the recognized Wyandot chief at Detroit. Tarhe's
recognition as head chief of all the Wyandot was not as strong in Detroit as
it was in Sandusky. The Wyandots at Sandusky did not recognize Walk-In-
The-Water as their head chief. He and Roundhead initially stood on opposite
sides of the debate whether to support Tecumseh or not. Both Walk-In-The-
Water and Tarhe, head chiefs of the Wyandot, initially stood unified against
Tecumseh; however, Roundhead, Tarhe's warpole, and his brothers were sewing discord not only within the Wyandots but also within the other tribes.

The issue was severe and necessitated that drastic measures be taken to
keep the Wyandot at Sandusky and Detroit unified. Tarhe himself, along with
Shawnee Chief Black Hoof, made the trip in 1812 to Detroit to try to talk sense
into Roundhead. During this council the Potawatomi, Chippewa, and Ottawa
asked if the Wyandot were going to take hold of the British hatchet. Walk-
In-The-Water, who was then chief speaker for the Wyandot Tribe, answered,
"No, we will not take up the hatchet against our father the Long-knife."[101]

In a display of unity, Walk-In-The-Water stood with Tarhe and Black
Hoof in opposition to Tecumseh and his alliance. In Detroit, the word of
Walk-In-The-Water carried great influence with the Western and Lakes tribes.
Walk-In-The-Water's advice was to not fight the Americans. This advice did
not settle well with the British, who desperately needed the Indian alliance to
help defeat the Americans. Historically, as Keepers of the Council Fire, the
spoken word and advice of the Wyandot carried much weight and influence
over the surrounding tribes. If the Wyandot were not going to fight alongside
Tecumseh, the British could not risk the possibility that the other tribes
would abandon the alliance solely upon the spoken word of the Wyandots.

Charles Elliot was a Methodist missionary to the Wyandots at Upper Sandusky in 1822. The following account was written ten years after the event

occurred and illustrated the British response to Walk-In-The-Water's call for neutrality. What the British did was unprecedented and twisted the dynamics of the war in the west. While at Upper Sandusky, Reverend Elliot spent a lot of time with Between-The-Logs, who was Tarhe's ambassador to the Detroit Wyandots during this time of crisis. Between-The-Logs detailed the efforts of Tarhe to keep the Wyandots unified, which was successful until the British interceded.

At this council, the Potawatomies, the Chippewas, and Ottawas, solicited the Wyandots to take hold of the British hatchet. Walk-in-the-Water, who was at the head of the Wyandots on the American side at Detroit, and was the chief speaker of the nation at that time, answered:—"No, we will not take up the hatchet against our father the Long-Knife. . . . At a council convened at Maiden, Elliott, the British Indian agent, and the British commanding officer, demanded of the Wyandots whether they had advised the other tribes to remain neutral. To this, Walk-in-the Water answered:—"We have, and we believe it is best for us and for our brethren. We have no wish to be involved in a war with our father, the Long-Knife, for we know by experience that we have nothing to gain by it, and we beg our father, the British, not to force us to war. We remember, in the former war between our fathers, the British and the Long-Knife, we were both defeated, and we, the red men, lost our country; and you, our father, the British, made peace with the Long-Knife without our knowledge, and you gave our country to him. You still said to us, my children, you must fight for your country, for the Long-Knife will take it from you. We did as you advised us, and we were defeated with the loss of our best chiefs and warriors, and of our land. And we still remember your conduct toward us when we were defeated at the foot of the rapids of the Miami. We sought safety for our wounded in your fort. But what was your conduct? You closed your gates against us, and we had to retreat the best way we could."

This speech so enraged the British that they shortly after sent a strong detachment of armed men, surrounded and took prisoners the Brownstown Wyandots, compelled them to embark in their boats, and then carried them to Malden on the Canada side.[102]

In a letter dated August 4, 1812, American Brigadier General William Hull listed the reason for his retreat from Canada and the logic for surrendering Detroit to the British. One of the reasons given for his surrender is as follows: "Two days ago all the Indians were sent from Malden with a small body of British troops to Brownstown and Maguago, and made prisoners of the Wyandotts of these places. There are strong reasons to believe that it was by their own consent, notwithstanding the professions they had made."[103] With Walk-In-The-Water and the Brownstown Wyandots taken into custody and forced to fight alongside the British, Tarhe dispatched Between-The-Logs to again try to talk sense into Roundhead. After an rousing, stern, diplomatic, yet unconvincing message delivered by Between-The-Logs, Roundhead replied with a clear and defiant message: "Tell him it is our wish he would send more men against us, for all that has passed between us, I do not call fighting. We are not satisfied with the number of men he sends to contend against us. We want to fight in good earnest."[104, 105]

The loss of Detroit, after General Hull's surrender, was a major blow to the war effort of the Americans. The whole of Michigan, including Detroit, had to be retaken. After the Battle of Tippecanoe, General Harrison preserved and positioned his army to protect the Western frontier; however, with the loss of Forts Mackinac and Detroit the war effort was beginning to look bleak. General James Winchester commanded the American's first effort to recover Detroit. General Winchester's militia would be ranked among the tough and hearty Kentuckians when on January 18, 1813, he dispatched seven hundred men to rescue and protect the residents of Frenchtown from the Indians who had overrun their community. Frenchtown had earned its name from residents who were for the most part French, had stayed in North America, and had sworn allegiance to the United States. It was estimated there were between eighty and one hundred British soldiers and four hundred Indians represented by the Shawnee, Wyandot, Potawatomi, Chippewa, and Ottawa, among other tribes who had besieged Frenchtown. General Winchester's decision was a noble gesture; however, he did not seek the advice of his superior. General Harrison was located a few miles away at Lower Sandusky. The initial battle for Frenchtown on January 18 proved successful after a frigid battle lasting from mid-afternoon until sunset.

On January 19 the British commander at Detroit received word General Winchester had a division or brigade encamped at Frenchtown on the Raisin River. General Winchester's forces had successful driven a small detachment of British militia and Indians from the battlefield. British Colonel Henry Proctor decided to attack and repel General Winchester before reinforcements arrived from Lower Sandusky.

At daybreak on January 22 Colonel Proctor attacked General Winchester's position with 1,500 British soldiers and militia along with their allied Indians.

After five hours of intense battle around 11:00 Roundhead's forces captured General Winchester who promptly surrendered him to Colonel Proctor. In need of retreat, the Americans occupied the houses and buildings where they put up a desperate fight in fear of falling into the hands of the Indians. However, General Winchester sent his troops a white flag encouraging their surrender. The British promised protection from the Indians and preservation of their personal property. General Winchester's men reluctantly surrendered.

After the battle, the British promptly returned to Fort Malden taking with them all the American prisoners who could walk. The prisoners, who could not walk, estimated between 50 and 60, were left at Frenchtown to care and mend their wounds. The day after the battle on January 23rd, Britain's Indian allies including the Wyandots, massacred all the wounded American prisoners who remained at Frenchtown. Their bodies were left in the homes and buildings; whereas, the buildings were set aflame and burned. Other prisoners in the care of the Indians who were not wounded were also killed. These bodies were left to lie on the ground and were torn to pieces and eaten by hogs. After the Battle of River Raisin a letter was posted for the residents of the ill-fated community. The residents were already stressed from recent events and the letter compounded their anxiety—were they destined to meet the same fate as the American soldiers? The letter read as follows:

> The Hurons, and the other tribes of Indians, assembled at the Miami Rapids, to the inhabitants of the River Raisin.—Friends, listen! You have always told us you would give us any assistance in your power. We, therefore, as the enemy is approaching us, within 25 miles, call upon you all to rise up and come here immediately, bringing your arms along with you. Should you fail at this time, we will not consider you in future as friends, and the consequences may be very unpleasant. We are well convinced you have no writing forbidding you to assist us. We are your friends at present.
>
> Round-head # his mark.
> Walk-in-the-water @ his mark.[106]

First, Tecumseh's Indian alliance was formed upon the talents of three men—two brothers and a loyal, hopeful friend. Obviously, Tecumseh was head of the alliance, and his compelling personality, along with his flattering words, were a magnetic draw for a fragment of the various tribes. Second, Tenskwatawa's visions and challenge to return to the old Indian ways incited a religious revival. Such fervor would not be seen again until 1889 when a Northern Paiute medicine man named Wovoka inspired the Plains Indians with his own message. Last, Roundhead brought to the alliance his military genius, foxlike cunning, and unrestrained rage. For a man who was willing to assassinate his own brother—Leatherlips—upon the spoken word of Tenskwatawa, he would have no qualms about doing the same against the Americans or anyone else who stood in his way.

The British easily captured Detroit with the assistance of Tecumseh's Indian alliance. After the victory General Brock rewarded Tecumseh with his personal red sash. It was a high and noteworthy honor to have been given the general's red sash. Tecumseh in turn acknowledged the greatness of Roundhead by giving him the general's red sash.

> General Brock, as soon as the business was over, publicly took off his sash, and placed it round the body of the chief. Tecumseh received the honor with evident gratification, but was, the next day, seen without his sash. General Brock, fearing something had displeased the Indian, sent his interpreter for an explanation. The latter soon returned with an account that Tecumseh, not wishing to wear such a mark of distinction, when an older, and, as he said, abler, warrior than himself was present, had transferred the sash to the Wyandot chief Round-head [sic].[107]

With the death of Roundhead a long chapter in the history of the *Huron-Wyandot* people came to a close. In the next chapter I will look at the last few decades of the Wyandot's stay in Ohio and Michigan. With no more battles and wars to fight, the warriors became "debauched and worthless" as they turned to alcohol to mask the pain of idleness. Too often their idleness would turn into drunken brawls as they fought each other or killed their mates in intoxicated stupors. The observation and suggestion of British General Henry Gladwyn, reaching all the way back to the French and Indian War, could still be seen in full force as alcohol began to kill more Indians than bullets did. General Gladwyn observed in 1763 that alcohol would be the ruin of the nations when he stated, "They have lost between 80 and 90 of their best warriors; but if yr Excellency still intends to punish them further for their barbarities, it may easily be done without any expense to the Crown, by permitting a free sale of rum, which will destroy them more effectually than fire and sword."[108]

As the Methodist missionaries began to arrive on the Grand Reserve in the early nineteenth century, the Wyandot were still running naked, or half-naked, and very wild. They had been the scourge of the frontier and were still feared with the utmost admiration and disdain. They were phenomenal warriors, dreaded foes, noble and compassionate friends all rolled into one complex and very difficult to understand package. People then were asking the question, Who exactly are these Wyandot, also known as *Huron*? Today many people are still asking the same question. Believe it or not, alcohol is still a significant problem among the tribes. Not much has changed, yet everything has changed. The Methodist missionaries were successful in clothing the Wyandot and converting many to Christianity; however, alcohol could not be eradicated, nor could the many vices that spawned from the intoxicating liquors.

From the closing of this chapter to the beginning of the next, the story of the *Huron*-Wyandot people will change in many ways. I would like to close this chapter with an intimate look at Big Tree. Big Tree lived a hard life and fought in the wars to protect his homeland and way of life. He was a celebrated warrior of the *Huron*-Wyandot people. Accounts place him as being a leader, possibly a chief, in his younger days during American's War of Independence. Big Tree survived the Ohio Country wars and no doubt was a survivor of the Battle of Fallen Timbers. Big Tree was just an ordinary yet extraordinary Wyandot, and his description as provided by Reverend Finley in *History of the Wyandott Mission* is priceless. Big Tree, as his name implies, was an imposing and intimidating tree of a man. His name, like all *Huron*-Wyandot names, was perfect.

Reverend Elliott, in *Indian Missionary Reminiscences,* also spoke of Big Tree: "When I was at Sandusky, Big Tree was an old man, and much afflicted with rheumatic pains, so as to be compelled to use crutches."[109] Not long after the Methodist missionaries arrived to the Wyandot's Grand Reserve, it would have been hard for Big Tree to change along with the changes taking place around him, but he did. This honored and celebrated warrior of the *Huron*-Wyandot people accepted Christianity.

Big Tree's children would eventually move him into a palace: a comfortable, warm cabin, about fourteen feet square. Before moving to his warm, spacious cabin Reverend Finley described how and where Big Tree lived. I do not doubt that a good number of his contemporary Wyandot citizens lived much the same way. Yes, there were many citizens who had comfortable homes, and without question Big Tree's lodge was also comfortable for him. Big Tree made do with what he had and did not complain. I do not think Big Tree felt slighted when walking with his crutches down Fourth Street past the home of William Walker, Jr. I have seen Walker's home. It is a fine home and it must have looked like a king's mansion to Big Tree. The home is still standing in Upper Sandusky and is today a historic landmark. Big Tree's lodge and home are no longer standing.

It would have been a gross error to judge Big Tree solely on his outward appearance, for he undoubtedly had a heart of gold and countless stories to tell. Without hesitation he would have shared his last meal and lodge—with a stranger. How do you think your conversations would go over dinner if you were the stranger? What would you like to ask Big Tree? Would you even stay for dinner? His lodge was not fancy like William's home. In summer it was hot. In winter it was cold. There were bugs during both seasons and strange smells to tantalize your nose. If you stayed long enough for dinner, his menu would spare no expense. "On one occasion he gave brother Finley a noble treat. He broke fine the jerk, and put it in his old bark dish, mixed up with it also a good share of his best home-made sugar, and then poured on these a due proportion of his best bear's oil, and mixed up the whole by stirring the compound with his finger."[110]

For nightly entertainment the howl of dogs, inside and out, indicated another treed coon. The fiddling of crickets could easily lull Big Tree to sleep—and put you on edge. Ask yourself, Could you give up all you have today and be a Wyandot like Big Tree? Would this be too much to ask? Now in reverse: What if Big Tree came knocking on your door? Looking through the peephole, his appearance would be a shock. Would you invite him in or would you quietly sneak to a back room of the house and hide? If you opened the door, what would you fix for dinner? I doubt you would fix anything. You would order out pizza—meat lovers' with extra cheese, mushrooms, black olives, and jalapeños. Big Tree loved his vegetables and knew the value of a healthy diet.

Would you turn off the TV as you visited? Could you set the phone aside and get off Facebook long enough to show him you care? For Big Tree everything would be so clean and pristine. Your lap rat—*oh, sorry, "dog"*—would likely make him giggle. The modern conveniences would put him on edge. The lights are always on. The air is too cold in summer and too hot in winter. The smells are too tropical, and the smallest of small bugs have to die before the kids will go to bed. Would Big Tree want to stay? Most likely not. Big Tree's world had perfect imperfections. Our world also has perfect imperfections.

Along with the imperfections, Wyandottes share one thing in common with Big Tree—they are Wyandot.

Nowadays, many Wyandotte citizens would run and hide as Big Tree approached their homes or judge him as a weirdo. No. Big Tree is an icon; he is a Wyandot hero and legend. Big Tree died a happy man full of cherished memories and nightmarish regrets. Big Tree paid the price to be a Wyandot so that citizens can be Wyandotte today. Never let Big Tree's sacrifices die! Always honor his memory. Now meet Big Tree:

This Indian was of the Bear tribe [clan]. He was more than six feet high, and possessed great strength and activity. When I first knew him he was about eighty years of age. The rims of his ears were bent round; and by hanging weights of lead to them, they were so stretched that they hung down on his shoulders. The inner part of the ear was perforated with holes, for the purpose of wearing silver ear-bobs. There was a hole through the inner gristle of the nose, to which he hung his nose-jewel. His hair was cut off close, excepting a small portion on his crown. This was long and plaited, and drawn through a silver tube. His face was large, with aquiline nose, and high forehead and cheek bones. No person could look at this venerable man without feeling a reverence for him. His whole person was dignified, and his manners were friendly, open, and affable. He lived on the river bottom, in a small field, containing about one-third of an acre, which he had fenced with brush and tree-tops. He cultivated this in corn, beans, squashes, and some other vegetables.

In the middle of this patch he had a house, made of corn-stalks, set up on end like a shock, but larger; in the middle of which, and at the top, he had his chimney, made of bark, peeled from a tree. The chimney was set on a frame of poles, supported by four forks, which were set so as to brace against each other. Bark was wound round each of these forks, and extended from one to the other, so as to keep them in their right place, and to sustain the corn-stalks. The blades of the stalks were all carefully peeled off on the inside; and on the outside the tops were turned down. This was all done with so much exactness and regularity, that it was water-proof, and perfectly warm. The door was small, and was the only place to admit light or air. This was shut with a piece of bark drawn over it. The lire was in the middle. His bed was raised ten inches, by laying three sticks of wood, say three feet long, cross-ways, and then spreading his bark, peeled from the tree, then his skins, and last his blanket. His pillow was a small bundle of clothes, with his tobacco-pouch. He had a small kettle of brass; a gun, tomahawk, and a butcherknife; a wooden tray, and bark spoon. He had several horses, which got their living in the woods, summer and winter; an old saddle and bridle, with some bark kettles.

Such is a description of his house, property, and person.[111]

CHAPTER 4

"Farewell Ohio and Her Brave"

Why should they be driven from their homes, and the little residue of their
former extensive territory, to gratify the accursed cupidity of white men?
—The Reverend Charles Elliott, 1837[1]

"I Cannot Agree to Quit Painting My Face"

Ohio is a beautiful, rich, and bountiful country with land that was both cherished and coveted, land that was worth fighting to keep and to take. During
the last few years of the American Revolution popular sentiment regarding
removal of the Indians from Ohio and all states east of the Mississippi River
began to manifest throughout the British Colonies destined to win their freedom. Never forget that before gaining their independence, the Americans
were citizens of the British crown. Initially, many of the American policies
toward the Indians were essentially the same as those of the British. It was the
Americans who first wrote many of the British policies as Colonial Americans.
As the war came to a close, vocal and violent discourses wrapped in a frenzy
of hate eventually began to sway official Indian policies—as did the actions of
the Indians themselves. One of those fueling hatred was the American Hugh
Henry Brackenridge, who stated, "From hence they will see that the nature of
an Indian is fierce and cruel, and that an extirpation of them would be useful
to the world, and honourable to those who can effect it."[2]

The first time I read the words penned by Brackenridge, I was stunned and
angered. Brackenridge was writing about the *Huron*-Wyandot people. At the
time my grandparents six-times removed, Nunewaysa and Mononcue, would
have been toddlers or maybe a wee bit older. If Brackenridge had his way,
he would have killed them. Brackenridge was encouraging someone, anyone,
to go and exterminate my people as though they were nothing but a pesti-

lence. Hugh Henry Brackenridge was a student of divinity and served as an army chaplain during the Revolutionary War. In 1799 he was appointed to the Pennsylvania Supreme Court. Brackenridge felt he was a man of high moral standards with a responsibility to educate the ignorant and greedy as they too often "elected corrupt and hypocritical leaders."[3] It is unfathomable to think that a chaplain and Supreme Court judge, a man who regarded himself as having high moral standards, would incite genocide.

Why did Brackenridge want to kill the Wyandot people? He and many others believed that the Indians were something less than savage animals and that in all their savagery simply did not deserve to live. At the time all the Indians were doing was protecting their way of life, homes, and children from an attacking enemy. It's ironic: Many citizens of the Wyandot Tribe at this time in history were adopted white people. They chose to be *Huron*-Wyandot rather than return to the race of their birth. In his rant Brackenridge also implicated the Wyandot's good friends, the Delaware and the Shawnee. After the defeat of Colonel William Crawford on June 4, 1782, and his ensuing burning at the stake by the Delaware, all the various tribes' fates in the Ohio Country were sealed.

The essence of who or what someone is cannot truly be identified by their outward appearance. The true identity of a person is found deep inside their heart. Remember Adam Brown? Adam was born a white child; however, after being captured and adopted into the Wyandot Tribe, he chose to live, fight, and die as a Wyandot citizen. Today if you look at me, you will not see what society chooses to believe an Indian should look like. Like many of my ancestors who were adopted whites, back then they looked a lot like I do today. However, the British and the American governments knew that the identity of the adopted whites was not what they saw on the outside, but the ideology and way of life they embraced on the inside. The adopted whites were Indian; they were no longer white people. They were a threat. They were Wyandot. At the close of the Indian Wars in the east, the naturally born and adopted Wyandots alike had a choice to be peaceably removed or forcibly killed. Why? The Americans, no less than the British, believed, among other claims, that they had Christian rights to the land. It's funny, but most of the Wyandots, naturally born and adopted alike, were also devout Christians when the calls for their removal west of the Mississippi River began to resound loud and clear. A history of previous engagements superseded present confessions of faith and loyalty to the state and country that now surrounded them on all sides.

During the American Revolution the frontier of the Ohio Country was set ablaze by the various tribes' fearless, relentless, and intelligent warriors. They attacked not only frontier cabins and settlements but forts and towns deep behind enemy lines. Terror and dread became the lifestyle of many whites due to the way in which the attacks were carried out, with calculated precision and success. The number of warriors may have been small, but as we saw in the previous chapter, the heroic effort to defend their homelands was glorious.

After the Battle of Fallen Timbers the tribes essentially settled into their respective places and tried to survive the best they could. A few of the tribes began to move westward, even to lands west of the Mississippi River. Life was difficult, for white people were everywhere and continued to flood the land as though the Great Lakes had burst, gushing forth white people. Settlers were not just splashing across the Ohio River anymore; they were a deluge. The Wyandot were on the cutting edge of the ever-shrinking Ohio frontier when the state of Ohio was admitted to the United States in 1803. Actually, the frontier had all but dissolved, and the Wyandot Tribe was on the verge of becoming isolated. At this time in history the venerable Chief Tarhe had taken his Wyandot Tribe into a policy of isolationism—and then along came Tecumseh.

After the War of 1812 the Wyandot Tribe sank into a repressed state and a condition of waywardness. The Wyandot were a tribe of warriors, and for the first time in recent memory there was not a war to fight. Arthur A. Schomburg said upon the arrival of John Stewart that the Wyandot were "represented as the most abandoned and vicious tribe, having sunk in the most degrading vices such as drunkenness, lewdness and gambling, until many of them became the most debauched and worthless of their race."[4, 5] Worthless? Absolutely not, but as a people the Wyandot had lost their sense of hope and direction. All the Wyandots wanted was to stay in Ohio and Michigan and try to live in peace alongside the whites. Unfortunately, the Wyandots were having a difficult time living alongside themselves. The old *Huron*-Wyandot rules of community, as found in the clan laws, had been challenged and the order of society shaken to its very foundation. When the Wyandots did not have a war to fight and the fierce warriors who once brought dread to the frontier found themselves idle, there was only one place for them to release their aggressions.

In 1822 C. C. Trowbridge recorded that in the old days it was possible for a man to be nothing less than abusive toward his mate. How far back must one go to find the old days? Trowbridge stated, "It was customary for the husband to strike or otherwise punish his wife, if she disobeyed his orders or displeased him in any other way."[6] It is very likely that the white man's alcohol had a dominant role in this unfortunate custom. Men! Do this today and you are going to jail for a long, long time! Mutual respect was expected back in the day, no less than it is today, but unfortunately it was not always honored. There was a perceived balance in the relationship between a man and a woman. Both the man and the woman had the right to quit the relationship when it became desirable or when they feared for their well-being due to an overly dominating and oppressive mate. This was true for both male and female. Even in an abusive relationship all the woman had to do was set the man's belongings outside the home, and he had to leave. If he did not leave, he could have incited the wrath of his mate's family, and it would have been swift and potentially very painful or deadly.

While in a drunken stupor, Between-The-Logs confessed to The Reverend James Bradley Finley that he had killed his mate. After the fighting came to an end, Between-The-Logs, like so many other Wyandot, fell into a state of depression and decline. Turning to alcohol, his warrior passions were agitated, and he often succumbed to a drunken, uncontrolled rage. During one fit of rage Between-The-Logs killed his mate, insisting, "She was a bad woman, a witch."[7] This act of brutality would haunt him the rest of his life and would prove to be a key factor in his conversion to Christianity. The burden of guilt Between-The-Logs bore was lifted when the Lord God forgave his sin.

Murders, one Wyandot killing another within the Wyandot community, often met a very harsh punishment, but not in all cases as noted with Between-The-Logs. If an abusive man or woman killed their mate and was sentenced to death for the crime, their fate was a slow, brutal death. C. C. Trowbridge described the punishment within his narrative, and Reverend Finley recorded the same punishment in *History of the Wyandott Mission*.

> If a man should murder his wife, the body of the deceased would be placed on a scaffold some distance from the ground and the man would be taken by her relations and carried to the same place, when he would be laid upon his back, under the corpse. A gag would then be put in his mouth to stretch it wide open. Then he would be placed in such a position as to receive in his mouth the excrement coming from the woman, and he would be detained in this situation until he died, unless his relatives would intercede and with a large belt of wampum and many supplications, offered to the relatives of the deceased, save his life. And, if a woman should kill her husband she would be punished in the same way.[8]

If there were such punishments today, maybe, just maybe, there would be less abuse in our contemporary, so-called *civilized homes*. As we can see, in some cases the relationships between a man and a woman could be quite abusive. Men will be men and women will be women—we are only human and our deepest nature is not always good, kind, and noble. At times it is evil. This was true even of Wyandot women. You never want to upset a Wyandot woman; she can be a powerful force to reckon with. One moment she can be a mother bear lovingly playing with and cuddling her little cubs in a yellow-daisy field with pretty, little blue butterflies aimlessly fluttering on a sunny, warm spring morning. *Then,* in the blink of an eye, she can be enraged, snapping tall trees like matchsticks trying to tear the heart out of an antagonist bent on harming her snuggly little cubs. This can make for a very bad day for the very unlucky soul, which included her mate, if he stood in her way.

This was the condition of the *Huron*-Wyandot people when John Stewart came to the Grand Reserve. Many Wyandots were drunk, both men and women. Many were killing other Wyandots, both men and women. Many were trying to return to their old way of life, both men and women, but they could not remember what that way of life was.

John Stewart, a man described as a humble African,[9] colored man and a free mulatto,[10] whose parents claimed to be mixed with Indian blood,[11] arrived at the Grand Reserve in November of 1816. With his blind calling, he tried to bring social and religious changes which were initially rejected. Before being allowed to preach, John Stewart was intercepted and heavily interrogated by William Walker Sr. who was then serving as a subagent for the US government. There was a concern Stewart may have been a runaway slave, but he was not, nor had he ever been, a slave. However, William was a white man who had been adopted into the Wyandot Tribe as a slave by Adam Brown, who was also an adopted white man. The twists within the Wyandots were plentiful and aided in keeping the government quite confused.

Joseph Mitchell stated, "Mr. Walker being fully satisfied, gave him encouragement, and directed him to the house of Jonathan Pointer, a black man, who in his youth had been taken prisoner by the Wyandotts, and had learned to speak the tongue of the nation fluently."[12] Jonathan Pointer initially proved to be a thorn and hindrance to John Stewart as he began to preach. Jonathan lived among a relatively large population of free blacks in Negro Town on the Northeast corner of the Grand Reserve. The fact they both shared the same race was of no consequence to Jonathan.

The great Wyandot chief Tarhe died in 1816, the same year John Stewart began preaching. Tarhe's influence had been incredibly strong, as he stood in opposition to outsiders bringing a new way of life into the Wyandot Tribe. Tarhe was an isolationist. If not for the death of Tarhe it is doubtful that John Stewart would have been allowed to preach.

Isolated, seemingly lost and without purpose, the Wyandot people were hesitant to convert and conform to the preaching of John Stewart. They did not want to be deceived and again fall for an outside religion that served them no purpose and gave them no hope, only intolerable penitence and unbridled hatred. Many Wyandots began to rediscover and reclaim their traditional way of life. The Wyandot felt they had been deceived and led astray by the Catholics and more recently the Seneca and Shawnee prophet. They would not again follow anyone's religion but their own.

What was the difference between Handsome Lake, Tenskwatawa, and John Stewart? Stewart selflessly preached the name of Jesus Christ, along with love, acceptance, peace, forgiveness, and life. Charles Elliott said of Stewart, "Patience and fortitude were striking features of his character."[13] Handsome Lake and Tenskwatawa, on the other hands, preached hatred, defiance, war, vengeance, and death. Tarhe stood in opposition to such evil attitudes and philosophies. Stewart was different in spite of the message he preached requiring the Wyandots to change their way of life. The acceptance of Stewart's word was not instant or universal—nor was it guaranteed to have a lasting hold, but it did.

Early in the nineteenth century the Wyandot people struggled to fit John Stewart's form of Methodism into their conflicted lives. For many of the citizens, such as Mononcue, who were receptive to the Word being preached by Stewart, the conflict of old versus new was very troublesome and compromises were initially made. Those who were not receptive to the Word being preached also struggled as they watched and lamented the demise of their *traditional* way of life. The *Huron*-Wyandot people had a way of life which had remained untainted by any other Indian or European theology. No, this is untrue. A big part of the Wyandot's conflict is they had been bombarded with so many different theologies it was hard for them to know what was their time-honored traditions. It was heartbreaking and infuriating for Wyandot traditionalists to watch the conflicts play out and the inevitable transition to a whole new way of life.

Before the coming of John Stewart, the people were trying to recommit themselves to the old way of life. They were in the process of rejecting all external influences; the Wyandot's culture wasn't necessarily pure, but it was undeniably Wyandot. The clan mothers ruled with wisdom and a strong understanding of tradition. Deviation was not then tolerated. The shaman, defined as witches by the missionaries, would try to ensure oneness with Nature and seek spiritual guidance to fix life's big and small problems. Witches they were not; however, there were rogue practitioners of the healing arts that used the arts for unsavory purposes. These were the true witches, and they were exterminated by the Wyandots with a tomahawk to the head and a knife to the heart. The shamans were revered and practiced their healing arts well into the early twentieth century.

The Methodist missionaries recognized all the conflicts, stepped back, and let the Great Spirit do His work. All John Stewart wanted was to help tame the Wyandot's wild hearts, deliver them from alcohol, save their souls for Jesus, and help them move into a modern world. In helping he was also looking for a little self-redemption for his own soul as he, like all of us, was a man with issues that needed forgiving.

Upon his arrival to the Wyandot's little piece of Ohio, it would have been hard for Stewart to see the Wyandot as anything but civilized. The tribe was still "savage Indians" and because of their recent history of engagements remained an enormous threat to the United States and Stewart's own personal well-being. When Stewart came to Upper Sandusky, it was clear to him that the Wyandot were very intelligent, astute, and capable of debating theology. Mononcue was a very influential clan chief of the Little Turtle clan and chief speaker for the clan mothers. In one such debate a respectful yet very stern and convincing Mononcue debated the validity of the Holy Bible for the Indians.

This is a mistake; as He never intended that we should be instructed from a book which properly belongs only to those who made it, and can understand what it says. . . . The Son of God came among white people, and preached to them, and left his words written in a book, that when he was gone they might read and learn his will respecting them; but he left no book for Indians; and why should he, seeing we red people know nothing about books? If it had been the will of the Great Spirit that we should be instructed from this book, he would have provided some way for us to understand the art of making and reading the books that contain the words.[14]

For the Wyandot enough change had already come. In addition, why would they want to accept something that did not appear to be working for the people to whom it was originally given? The Indian could not read the Holy Bible, and evidently the white people were not reading the book either. The old way of life was good enough for the Wyandot, but what was it? Through Stewart's preaching the seed of Protestant Christianity was successfully planted, and Christianity took root. When Reverend Finley arrived at Upper Sandusky on November 4, 1821, the harvest produced by the labor of John Stewart was fully ripe.[15] Stewart had opened the door, wiggled a crack, and dropped a few seeds, and Reverend Finley gently and tenderly with increasing love kicked the door to the people's hearts right off its hinges and reaped the crop.

Initially when Stewart walked onto the Wyandot reservation, he did so on his own accord and terms. He was not affiliated with the Methodists or any other denomination. He felt a call and was led, although he did not know exactly where he was going or what he was supposed to be doing. He followed the call in spite of obvious danger. John Stewart was a missionary in the truest sense; he came to preach Jesus Christ regardless of the cost—even if it cost him his life.

Reverend Finley had different incentives when he first came to Upper Sandusky. He came with the sole purpose of being a preacher and teacher; he knew his mission and he knew his job. The Methodists sent Finley for two reasons: to obtain converts and to fulfill the requirements of a small, amended clause at the end of the Treaty of 1817. The US government paid and paved the way for the Methodist Church to come to the Wyandot Tribe. The government wanted the Indians civilized, educated, and Christianized. There was no concern about saving their souls. They hoped religion and a formal education would bring the savages into a civilized world, ultimately ending all hostilities.

The miraculous conversion of two Wyandot clan chiefs, Between-The-Logs and Mononcue, sent shock waves throughout the Wyandot Tribe. However, the Gospel still faced great opposition, but converts were steadily coming into the church. Once clan mothers themselves began accepting Christianity, time-honored traditions were destined to fall and fail. Finley indicated that Wah-Shu-Ta-Mah, or Queen of the Bear tribe, "was among the first who sought and found mercy."[16] Wah-Shu-Ta-Mah publicly renounced her clan religion and fully embraced the Gospel. Once other clan mothers began converting to Christianity, it was just a matter of time before the memory of the old ways would leave the tribe. Reverend Finley recorded the words of the clan mothers when on Wednesday, July 19, 1820, as they granted permission for him to bring Christianity to the Wyandot Tribe. Mononcue delivered the decision to Reverend Finley.

We thank the old father for coming to see us so often, and speaking the good word to us, and we want him to keep coming and never forsake us; and we let him know that we love this religion too well to give it up while we live; for we think it will go bad with our people if they quit this religion; and we want our good brother Stewart to stay always amongst us, and our brother Jonathan too, and to help us along as they have done. Next we let the old father know what our head chiefs and the others have to say. They are willing that the gospel word should be continued among them, and they will try to do good themselves and help others to do so too; but as for the other things that are mentioned, they say, we give it all over to our speakers; just what they say we agree to; they know better about these things than we do, and they may let the old father know their mind.[17]

A little over a year before this fateful meeting in July of 1820, Reverend Finley had been appointed missionary to the Wyandot Tribe at the Ohio Conference held in Cincinnati on August 7, 1819.[18] Finley was a new, yet seasoned, missionary appointed to officially take over the duties of John Stewart. Even though Finley was given permission and the blessing of the clan mothers to preach the Gospel to the tribe, he continued to have a difficult time and faced much opposition to the preaching of the Word.

Like John Stewart, James Finley initially supported his own ministry. Access to funds was minimal, and all the worldly items he possessed were packed into a wagon as he headed west. The facilities were not prepared; however, the Wyandot were prepared and anxiously waiting for him to arrive. Many Wyandots came to welcome his arrival and help unpack his belongings. Yet standing to the side were an equal number of Wyandots who did not come to welcome or help him with even the smallest amount of enthusiasm. Finley described his preparations, lack of resources, and the ensuing trip to Upper Sandusky: "There was no plan of operation furnished me, no provision made for the mission family, no house to shelter them, nor supplies for the winter; and there was only a small sum of money, amounting to two hundred dollars, appropriated for the benefit of the mission."[19]

Shortly after Finley's appointment and subsequent arrival at Upper Sandusky, the Wyandots began to change—and how quickly they changed. Many citizens freely converted to Methodism with and without compromises. Many, but not all, began to set the rum and whiskey bottles aside. The Wyandot also began to set aside their traditions, ceremonies, and clan religions. Did the plan of the US government work? No, it did not because it was not theirs to claim.

It was the Lord God's plan, and all the US government did was see that the missionaries were given a chance to preach the Gospel of Jesus Christ. Upon arriving at Upper Sandusky, Finley's first task was to organize the church. "In this mission there had not, as yet, been any regular formation of a Church. All was in a kind of national society; so that when any one did wrong, he left without any trial or censure; and any one came in and enjoyed the ordinances of the Church without any formal admission; and so they came and went at pleasure."[20]

A lackadaisical church was unacceptable to Reverend Finley. Gaining control and order, and establishing Methodist principles and discipline, were not merely top priorities but imperative. Between-The-Logs and Mononcue, along with other prominent Wyandot converts such as Big Tree, joined his crusade and pressed for order. The greatest obstacles to Reverend Finley's gain of control and order was Deunquot, head chief of the Wyandot Tribe, and Ron-Tun-Dee, his warpole. Deunquot thought the good reverend was trying to steal away his tribe and become head chief himself, and he often publicly confronted Reverend Finley. In addition, Deunquot and Ron-Tun-Dee were staunch supporters of the old Wyandot way of life and felt Christianity was a curse upon their tribe. The clan mothers did not agree. At this moment the clan mothers still retained enough authority and respect to enact monumental change on behalf of their citizens.

For Reverend Finley to try to publicly confront or embarrass Deunquot would have been just shy of a public tomahawking. To assist Reverend Finley in his very compromised position, Between-The-Logs stepped forward and became a powerful ally. Having no fear, but always restrained with reverent respect, Between-The-Logs became the oppositional voice keeping Deunquot at bay and focused away from Reverend Finley. With Mononcue also standing alongside and essentially becoming Reverend Finley's bodyguard, his safety was all but assured. William Walker Sr. and Robert Armstrong, two adopted white men, became Reverend Finley's armor bearers.[21] The arrangement appeared to be working until one intense public confrontation. Between-The-Logs then made the following suggestion to Deunquot:

> "I will make a bargain with you this day. You go on your own way, and take all that company with you; and if you are all lost, you shall bear the whole blame and punishment; and I will take these, . . . and if they will walk according to this Book, I will take the blame and punishment, if they are lost." Deunquot responded, "No—I am the head of the nation, and the head ought to be

believed. With these arms I can take hold of both parties, and try to keep you both steady."[22]

Reverend Finley indicated he was never again attacked in public. After obtaining a sense of freedom from their head chief's intimidation, many Wyandots joined the Church after only one service. Deunquot's stand against Reverend Finley and Christianity appeared to be a lost battle, and Deunquot stated, "This religion may go into all the houses on this reservation, but into mine it shall not come."[23] The Wyandot Mission Church was promptly built with US government money and is considered the only church built by the federal government. The building was erected in 1824 at the cost of $1,333.00 to the government. Within a year's time, in 1825, Deunquot died. The controversy that followed Deunquot's death as his nephew Sarahess and Ron-Tun-Dee vied for head chief of the tribe forever changed the Wyandot Tribe. The changes were just as great as, if not greater than, the advent of Christianity within the tribe.

How is it possible to tame wild, free hearts? A heart that is free and unencumbered cannot easily grasp order; a sense of time, a need for study, and words printed on paper contained in a book are useless nonsense to such peoples. Although formal education that teaches people to read, write, and learn the discipline of study was important, forcing the Wyandots to do anything would effectively cause the opposite to occur. Through suggestion and the proper demonstration of self-imposed discipline, Reverend Finley took a back-door approach that other missionaries had failed to recognize. Through gentle hands-off pressure, and the application of John Stewart's wisdom obtained from living with the Wyandot for six years, success was painfully slow, but clearly being achieved.

Between-The-Logs stated in August of 1822, "For our parts, we have no learning, and we are now getting old, and it is hardly worth our while to trouble ourselves about learning now; but we want our children learned, and we hope our school and mission will do great good for them."[24] The time had come to teach Wyandot children how to read and write. However, running around the reservations and corralling the kids was not going to happen, nor was it a wise thing to attempt.

After less than a year at the Wyandot Mission, Reverend Finley became ill and was called away to rest and recuperate. His temporary replacement was The Reverend Charles Elliott, who would be the Methodist missionary to effectively put into place the Wyandot Mission School. On October 5, 1822,

Reverend Elliott stepped foot for the first time upon the Wyandot reserve.[25] He was hoping and expecting to see Reverend Finley, but he had already left the mission. Disappointed and alone, Reverend Elliott and his wife put their trust in the Lord and left the result to him. The Elliotts immediately began to share their home, the little mission house, with the untamed Wyandot children. The children were untamed in the eyes of the missionaries; however, the children were very well disciplined with their clan laws and parents' careful guidance.

On December 20, Reverend Elliott indicated there were thirty-seven children in the small mission home which had few to no conveniences. The Elliotts undoubtedly had their hands full. Reverend Elliott indicated that it required the greatest attention to keep them in order. "These regulations I found necessary to make, for the purpose of preserving such order as that one part may not prevent the other from pursuing their several employs."[26] All it would take was one child, a wild and free Wyandot kid, to spoil the whole of the school. Reverend Elliott did not want this to happen, nor did Between-The-Logs and Mononcue, the two greatest proponents of the Wyandot Mission School.

The first day of planning for the mission school was a celebrated event, and all the chiefs were invited: Deunquot, Ron-Tun-Dee, clan chiefs, and several other respectable and influential persons in the nation. In an amazing display of neutrality, Deunquot neither sanctioned nor opposed the school. The thought of a formal education did not appear to be as much a threat as the introduction of Christianity to his people. Reverend Elliott, in an act of great wisdom, gave all the chiefs an active voice in the school's organization and the establishment of rules. Rather than have a premade, cookie-cutter list of rules to blanket and smother the children and their parents, Reverend Elliott allowed the chiefs to make the rules and take ownership of the rules. How mom and dad would accept the rules governing their children's behavior was a grave concern to Reverend Elliott. More important, how would the clans who had greater say-so in the lives of the children than their birth parents react to the rules? The best policy was to have as many of the clan chiefs as possible make the rules, and then enforce the rules, which is exactly what Reverend Elliott accomplished.

After discussing how the school should be organized and establishing base rules of operation, the doors and books were opened, and the educating of the Wyandot children commenced. It was clear: The world was changing and coming to the Grand Reserve. Now the children were being taught of this world and how to compete and succeed in it. The children followed the rules and learned how an established order in their lives proved both productive and good. Sure, there were children who did not receive an education due to opposition from their birth parents; therefore, some children did not receive a Christianized education and retained a stronger knowledge of old, traditional *Huron*-Wyandot ways. But order was established and rules were followed.

Just about everyone was in agreement that the Mission School would be good for the whole of the Wyandot people. Staying abreast of the changes that were coming to the Indian way of life meant they had to adapt. The Wyandot people embraced a formal education knowing that irreversible change could occur. While in Ohio, the future of the Wyandot Tribe—Wyandot children— were being taught to read and write, among a host of other things, by the Methodist missionaries. By the time the tribe left Ohio and Michigan in 1843 and arrived in Indian Territory, these same children had grown up and were in turn teaching more Wyandot children how to read and write. John McIntire and Lucy B. Armstrong served as the first teachers after the schoolhouse was built on the Wyandot Purchase. In addition, John McIntire Armstrong and John Wesley Greyeyes were members of the Ohio Bar at the time the tribe left for Indian Territory. These two men were attorneys, they were Wyandot citizens from prominent and influential families, and they were obviously well educated.

William Walker Jr., amid his many faults, was an absolute genius and capable of standing toe-to-toe with just about anyone from Harvard, Yale, William & Mary, or any other university then established in the United States. Why? William had sought and obtained a great education well beyond what was then being taught at the Wyandot Mission School. But wait: In 1822, when the Mission School was first established, William was at least twenty-two years old. Did William attend the Mission School as an adult? No, he had already obtained an education before the opening of the Mission School and likely participated in the establishment of the base rules of operation. William's attendance at the Mission School was not as a student but from time-to-time as a teacher. Where did William obtain his education? We know from William's 1874 obituary, printed in *The Wyandotte Herald,* that he received his education under the immediate instruction of Bishop Chase.

The small village of Worthington, Ohio, was established in 1803—the year Ohio became a state. An academy was established in 1808 and maintained by an Episcopal congregation.[27] In July of 1817 The Reverend Philander Chase and family arrived at Worthington, where he assumed the position of principal of the academy. Reverend Chase's wife described the appointment as nominal.[28] William received his formal and advanced education under the oversight of The Reverend Philander Chase at Worthington Academy in Worthington, Ohio, located just north of Columbus. Clearly, a good education was important to Wyandot citizens. Initially whites adopted into the tribe were more willing to send their children away from the reservations to attend school; however, by 1822 many citizens recognized the importance of an education and readily embraced the Mission School and Mission Church. Once this happened, the inevitability of conflict between tradition and progress was realized.

Does living a traditional lifestyle mean that all contemporary Wyandottes must give up their modern conveniences? No, not at all. William Walker Jr. was not a socialite, yet he loved the modern conveniences that existed in his day. Not all Wyandots lived like William or chose to pursue an advanced education and the modern conveniences society then had to give. William was Wyandot, but in many ways he was not like his fellow Wyandots. Did this make him or them more or less Wyandot? No, not at all. In addition to Wandat, William spoke and read English. William also read and spoke Greek, Latin, and French. If that were not enough, William also spoke the Delaware, Shawnee, Miami, and Potawatomi languages with fluency.[29] He was aware of his surroundings and kept abreast of events around the world. For William to go one week without his newspaper would be like your losing your phone for two minutes. Time comes to a standstill until you find that phone.

William took many modern conveniences to Indian Territory when he left Ohio. His newspapers were an absolute necessity. Give him an iPhone or Galaxy today, and he would be no different from you as you frantically search for your lost phone. William would be no different from the rest of us sitting around totally absorbed with news, tweets, games, Facebook, and hours upon hours of music and movies right at our fingertips. Maybe not the games—I just can't picture William playing Angry Birds or Candy Crush! I think he would be more of a chess kind of guy, or maybe Clash of Clans—who knows?

The Reverend J. S. Lemon, Episcopal Church, Diocese of Central New York, interviewed Seneca Chief Kettle in 1905. Reverend Lemon was confused as he witnessed Chief Kettle living in New York like a white man. Chief Kettle was a pagan preacher of the Seneca White Dog Feast, one of the last to serve as such. When asked how he could be a priest of the white dog feast, live among the whites, and use all their conveniences, Chief Kettle responded, "I may live and dress like a white man, but it was never paint or feathers, wampum or moccasins, that made our religion. Our religion is dressed only by the

FIGURE 4.1. Mononcue

heart."[30] Chief Kettle's revelation reigns true today among the Wyandottes, and all tribes for that matter. If the only thing you see in a Wyandotte is what's on the outside, yes, you may see a lot of white, but what truly counts is what is on the inside. It is the heart that makes the culture. It is the heart that makes the Indian. The blue eyes, blond hair, and even a freckle or two can never change the color of a true Wyandotte heart. This resounds true no matter where they may choose to live, the amount of education they obtain, and all the modern conveniences they choose to employ to make this lives better and more comfortable.

Today, the lips of the Wyandotte people may translate what comes from their hearts into English. Listen to what is being spoken, not merely the language. I am using an iPhone, iPad, and iMac to write this book. These are just modern tools, and shunning their convenience would be a contradiction to everything the old *Huron*-Wyandots achieved and the lives they lived. I do not believe Wyandottes should become reclusive, uncouth, and ignorant savages within the confines of this modern world in order to retain their *Huron*-Wyandot heritage. Moving to some isolated location, building palisades, not taking a bath, and trying to live as the ancestors once did will not make them more Wyandotte. It's what they have in their heart that makes them Wyandotte.

Many of the *Huron*-Wyandot clan mothers said yes to Christianity. Did this make them less Wyandot than the mothers who said no to Christianity? The mothers allowed Christianity into the Wyandot Tribe on July 19, 1820, through the vehement voice of Mononcue—my grandfather. Mononcue lived a powerful and influential life. I have no doubt that when he was born, he came out screaming; however, when he left this world, he left it in near silence. Mononcue's simple marker, his tombstone, is located in the Mission Church Cemetery in Upper Sandusky. Mononcue is buried alongside several prominent Wyandot converts and John Stewart. For a long time I did not feel or believe that Mononcue was buried in this small plot, because I could not find any documentation of his death. After years of searching, I finally found confirmation. "The Old Mission," written by Reverend N. B. C. Love, assures us that Mononcue died on July 28, 1838, and is indeed buried in the cemetery.

Stop for a moment and think what could have happened if Hugh Henry Brackenridge had been successful and convinced someone to go to Sandusky, or any of the other *Huron*-Wyandot villages in 1782, and kill Wyandots—men, women, and children. What if Mononcue had been killed as a toddler? His vehement voice, even present as a newborn, would have been silenced, and the clan mothers may not have given their blessing for Christianity to enter the tribe through another. Who knows? Mononcue's commanding presence and voice were the reason the clan mothers chose him as their speaker. When Mononcue spoke, everyone stopped and listened. Mononcue's presence of voice, knowledge, and wisdom was a tribal treasure.

Reverend Finley in *History of the Wyandott Mission* recorded one of my favorite quotes from Mononcue. The quote eloquently and simplistically defines the struggle all Wyandots had as they set aside their traditional way of life for John Stewart's Christianity. Mononcue stated shortly after accepting Christianity, "I have some notion of giving up some of my Indian customs; but I cannot agree to quit painting my face. This would be wrong, as it would jeopard [sic] my health."[31] The painting of one's face is a charm. Mononcue was convinced that if he stopped painting his face, he would lose his health. The painting of his face was rooted in his clan. Painting not only identified his clan, but through the power of his totem—his animal god, the Little Turtle—his health was assured.

In a letter dated May 21, 1838, The Reverend S. M. Allen wrote to Reverend Finley indicating that "his [Mononcue] lungs is [*sic*] so affected that it was with difficulty he could talk."[32] At this time Mononcue was reciting to Reverend Allen an account of his conversion and acceptance of Christianity. Clearly, Mononcue was on his deathbed and would die in about two months. The letter did not specifically say, but its sounds like my grandfather may have been battling pneumonia or the effects of tuberculosis. My other grandfather at the time, Robert Armstrong, died from tuberculosis on April 20, 1825.[33] Did Mononcue finally give up the painting of his face? If so, did it cost him his life? Mononcue was known for his vehement and overwhelming voice. How ironic that in his death, his voice had been weakened to a whisper. Yet Mononcue still testified to the saving grace of his God.

What are your charms? Do you paint your face? Do you wear a turtle amulet around your neck? What is in your medicine bag? Do you have a medicine bag? If you have a medicine bag, you need not say, for it's a private thing and not anyone else's concern. If you do not have a medicine bag, or a special charm that brings you your requests, that's OK too. Do you carry a thirty-pound Bible tucked under your arm wherever you go? If you do, be careful that it doesn't become your charm. Maybe your charm is your iPhone or Galaxy. Whatever brings you the most happiness, peace, and protection, this is your charm—in a way, it is your god.

Can you begin to see the dilemma that beset the old Wyandots? The dilemma is no less ours today as Wyandottes look back to try to understand a way of life they cannot truly comprehend. A weekend retreat where you are guided and compelled to contact your inner spirit by a shaman is not enough. A good old-fashioned Pentecostal revival is not going to fill the empty hole inside your heart and make everything better. Counting rosary, confessions, peyote, denial of everything, or trying to return to the old *Huron*-Wyandots' way of life, whatever that truly was, may prove difficult and full of *New Age* beliefs—not *old way* beliefs. If the Lord God, *the Great Spirit,* has to scream at you to get your attention, which He normally will not do—you are having a bad day! Something is desperately wrong in your life. The best thing you can do is to quietly listen, be aware there are competing voices, and *choose wisely* to whom or to what you listen. The Wyandots did not listen to the voice of Handsome Lake, Tenskwatawa, John Stewart, or even Reverend Finley. They listened to the voice of the Great Spirit and answered His call.

"Very Similar to That of the Cherokees"

The Wyandot's fight to remain in Ohio and Michigan was well fought and documented. It was a war fought with words on paper. Rhetoric and satirical humor exposed the ignorant and unwavering imposition of men twisted with hate and disdain. By the time the Wyandot had left Ohio in 1843, Ohio was one of the most industrious and prosperous states in the United States. Yet the barbarity displayed was inhumane and unjustified. Reverend Elliott was appalled when he first saw the petition sent to Congress calling for the removal of the Wyandot from Ohio. Reverend Elliott's reaction expresses the injustice.

> It seems a hard matter that this *small remnant* of a once powerful nation cannot be permitted to occupy their little reservation, without being compelled to sell it. Why should they be driven from their homes, and the little residue of their former extensive territory, to gratify the accursed cupidity of white men? . . . If they are driven away, their expulsion will bring a curse upon their oppressors. Such an outrage upon the principles of truth and righteousness is enough to endow the stupid with the gift of satire.[34]

There were many educated and righteous men, actually white men and women, who stood in support of the Wyandot Tribe staying in Ohio. From missionaries, judges, politicians, and famed visitors from foreign countries, their calls for justice were conveniently ignored. An extract from Judge John L. Leib's report to the Department of War gives an interesting account of his visit to Upper Sandusky on November 12, 1826. Judge Leib reported, "In short, they are the only Indians within the circle of my visits, whom I consider as entirely reclaimed, and whom I should consider it a cruelty to attempt to remove."[35]

I have always heard President George Washington was not a lover of Indians, and many Indians consider President Andrew Jackson the devil incarnate; however, in 1825 it was President James Monroe who, at the close of his second term, first proposed removal of the Indians as official US policy. It would take four years and the term of John Quincy Adams to pass before Andrew Jackson would successfully champion the Indian Removal Act of 1830. President Thomas Jefferson first presented the concept of removal in a letter to William Henry Harrison, then Governor of the Indiana Territory, in 1803.

Jefferson's letter, shortly after the Louisiana Purchase, set the tone for what would become official Indian removal policies in successive presidencies.

It was Thomas Jefferson who wrote, "We hold these truths to be self-evident, that all men are created equal, that they are endowed by their Creator with certain unalienable Rights, that among these are Life, Liberty and the pursuit of Happiness."[36] Classic, timeless words that make the heart of all humans, except ruthless tyrants, dictators, and Indian haters, swell with pride as tears form in the eyes. I initially did not want to believe that Thomas Jefferson was an instrumental player in Indian removal; however, his very words on the matter are self-evident and quite convicting.

Our system is to live in perpetual peace with the Indians, to cultivate an affectionate attachment from them, by everything just and liberal which we can do for them within the bounds of reason, and by giving them effectual protection against wrongs from our own people. The decrease of game rendering their subsistence by hunting insufficient, we wish to draw them to agriculture, to spinning and weaving. The latter branches they take up with great readiness, because they fall to the women, who gain by quitting the labors of the field for, those which are exercised within doors. When they withdraw themselves to the culture of a small piece of land, they will perceive how useless to them are their extensive forests, and will be willing to pare them off from time to time in exchange for necessaries for their farms and families. To promote this disposition to exchange lands, which they have to spare and we want, for necessaries, which we have to spare and they want, we shall push our trading uses, and be glad to see the good and influential individuals among them run in debt, because we observe that when these debts get beyond what the individuals can pay, they become willing to lop them off by a cession of lands. At our trading houses, too, we mean to sell so low as merely to repay us cost and charges, so as neither to lessen or enlarge our capital. This is what private traders cannot do, for they must gain; they will consequently retire from the competition, and we shall thus get clear of this pest without giving offence or umbrage to the Indians. In this way our settlements will gradually circumscribe and approach the Indians, and they will in time either incorporate with us as citizens or the United States, or remove beyond the Mississippi.[37]

Thomas Jefferson served two terms as president and was succeeded by James Madison. During Jefferson's presidency Madison served as Secretary of State throughout both terms. Jefferson's policies of dependent assimilation

or self-removal beyond the Mississippi River continued into Madison's presidency. It was under these policies that John Stewart became one of the first to
preach Protestant Christianity to the Wyandot Tribe.

The locations of the Huron River Reserve, Big Spring Reserve, and Grand
Reserve initiated a perpetual conflict of culture as the whites surrounded on
all sides. The *Huron*-Wyandot were never a large tribe with the luxury of
having an excess of warriors to expend toward the defense of the homeland,
now reduced to three reservations. In this new battle the loss of one citizen to
alcohol was no different from the loss of one to a bullet. It was no less a war
of minds and words. It was a war of resolve and attrition.

The writings of Reverend Finley present an appetizing, yet brief and near-
pristine, glimpse into the old *Huron*-Wyandot's traditional culture. They provide a rare look into the *Huron*-Wyandot's way of life and the ideologies they
once held. In 1823 the young Charles Christopher Trowbridge, a contemporary of Reverend Finley, was a private secretary to General Lewis Cass, then
Governor of Michigan Territory. General Cass asked Trowbridge to collect
the personal statements of the many Indian tribes in the territory he governed
around Detroit, one being the *Huron*-Wyandot. The promoted desire of General Cass in collecting this data was to better understand the tribes and their
personal interrelationships. When the works of these two men are combined,
along with the works of Reverend Elliott, they give us today a wealth of material to study and treasure.

I would now like to present a brief overview of the *Huron*-Wyandot's traditional government and how it changed shortly after the arrival of the Methodist missionaries. It was not the missionaries who effected the change, but
rather the inevitable culmination of an ancient system pushed to the point
of collapse. This was a transitional period when old and new traditions were
merging into something totally different. It was at this time that retaining tradition or adapting became a daily choice for every Wyandot citizen regardless
of his or her age. It was a slow and often painful process for *Huron*-Wyandot
traditions to change. The changes within the Wyandot's system of government did not happen overnight, but once an impasse occurred, the system of
selecting chiefs and councils changed rather quickly.

I have often wondered whether if this change had not occurred, how the
Wyandot Tribe would have responded to their call for removal west of the
Mississippi River. My heart tells me they would have eventually rebelled and
declared war, only to meet a terrible fate. As chiefs and chancellors chosen by
popular vote superseded chiefs who were once chosen and installed by the clan

mothers, new ideas backed by a formal education were now officially allowed into the Wyandot Tribe. This brought a new perspective on the Wyandot's relationship with the world that now surrounded them on all sides. These new ideas became representative of the tribe in whole and not limited to the perspective and desires of individual clans. New voices, many of which had previously not been given an opportunity to speak, could now be heard. And what they had to say was in need of being heard. Leading men such as William Walker Jr. could now serve his people, whereas under the clan-based system his influence would have likely been minimal. This was not a desirable change; however, at times change becomes necessary, and circumstances beyond our control initiate these changes.

Traditional *Huron*-Wyandot government was based within the clans, and without the clans government could not exist. Likewise, clans could not exist without government. Each of the clans had its own clan chief. Reverend Finley indicated that the clan chief was often a hereditary position.[38] Today when we think of hereditary claims, father to eldest son often comes to mind. This relationship was irrelevant in the clans. A father's son could not belong to his clan; therefore, his sons could never inherit his position of clan chief or any of his personal property. If heredity was involved in selecting a clan chief, it flowed through the clan chief's eldest nephew—one of his sister's sons. Trowbridge stated, "The title and honors do not descend from father to son but the descent is to the oldest nephew, by the sister of the deceased chief."[39]

The clan chiefs and head chief of the tribe were generally, but not necessarily, the oldest man of the clan or tribe. It has been assumed that the clan chief and the head chief could have been any age; however, there was a law applicable to both the tribe and the clans that established a minimum age: "If he possesses the requisite qualities and has arrived at the age of 30 years he is appointed."[40] Trowbridge continued by stating, "Among the Wyandots a man is never appointed to any place of trust or allowed to take part in the councils of the nation before he arrives at the age of 30 years. At this age he is considered a man."[41]

The clan chief was chosen and installed by his clan mother and her council of women. Even though the position of clan chief may have been a hereditary position, a full ceremony and presentation to the clan and tribal citizenry were done by the head chief of the tribe. Once the clan chief was installed, he usually held the position for life; however, he could be removed from office. If the expectations of the clan women were not achieved, or the chief proved to be incompetent, his position was short-lived.

The traditional way in which *Huron*-Wyandot chiefs were chosen was full of ceremony and tradition and was not easily changed. However, upon the death of Chief Deunquot in 1825, controversy swarmed and engulfed the Wyandot Tribe. Ron-Tun-Dee, more commonly known as Warpole, was Deunquot's warpole. Since Ron-Tun-Dee was the last warpole of the tribe, he assumed the name Warpole as his chosen name. Warpole was to temporarily serve as interim head chief until the Bear, Deer, and Big Turtle clans found time to nominate their candidates. These three clans produced nominations who were voted upon by the assembled clan chiefs.

Without delay, the Porcupine clan began promoting Sarahess, the nephew of Deunquot, for consideration by the tribal council. With all due formality, but not tradition, Sarahess was installed as head chief. Warpole, noticing the impropriety of the Porcupine clan's advancement of their candidate, refused to relinquish the position of head chief to Sarahess. Warpole was himself also from the Porcupine clan. The impasse required the tribal council to govern the tribe until a compromise could be obtained. It would take three years for an acceptable compromise to be found, and not without protest from the Pagan Party Wyandots who wanted tradition left alone. Tradition stated that Sarahess would be the next head chief. The Pagan Party Wyandots supported Sarahess, for he was also a pagan.

The impasse exposed a weakness in the clans, prompting a number of the clan chiefs—and, more importantly, appointed leading men—to seek a change in the old tradition of being obliged to choose their head chief from the Porcupine clan. This change also exposed the pending battle over ideologies between the Pagan and Christian factions within the tribe. The Pagans wanted the opportunity to choose a chief who would continue down the path of the old ways. The Christians also wanted to choose a chief who would bring the principles of Christianity into the tribe. Out of the ensuing debate and delay, a radical change in tradition would forever change Wyandot government.

After counseling took place with Reverend Finley (an adopted citizen of the Bear clan) and a few others, in 1828 an agreement was made to have a head chief and eight counselors, one from each clan, chosen by election annually on New Year's Day. The elected counselors would replace the clan chiefs on the tribal council. Thus, an ancient tradition changed, and the *Huron*-Wyandot form of government, initially based within the clans, changed to being an election based upon popular vote. According to the newly installed tradition, the Wyandot's first head chief, elected in 1828, was Warpole. With the election of Warpole as head chief, the office of war chief would never again be filled.

As the tradition of choosing chiefs from within the clans was being attacked and dismantled, I cannot help asking: Where were the clan mothers? Did they just sit back and let fate run its course? Where was their influence? If they indeed held so much influence and authority, why did they not intervene and stop the change? The answer is simple: It was beyond their ability and authority to do so. It also appears that some clan mothers supported the Christian Party's desire for change so that the Christians could have influence over the whole of the Wyandot Tribe.

Reverend Finley was intrigued and enamored by the *Huron*-Wyandot's traditional culture and did his best to include as much he could in his letters and books. He too was abhorred and was uncompromising in his desire to expose the dealings and appeasements of the US government and their use of trickery to effect the Wyandot's eviction from Ohio and Michigan. In both *History of the Wyandott Mission* and *Life Among the Indians,* Reverend Finley included many letters from government officials. It is a thrill to read the descriptions of the *Huron*-Wyandot's wonderful traditional culture; it makes you long for the blissful innocence of the past. It is enraging to read of the many contradictions and blatant lies the US government used to take it all away. It is hard to read what the government did, and many people choose to ignore and skip these sections of the classic books; however, what Reverend Finley included is very important, and no matter how difficult it may be to read—everyone should. The following is an excerpt from one such letter dated March 24, 1825. In a reply from the War Department John Quincy Adams, the newly elected President of the United States tried to comfort and convince his red children they would never be removed to the west.

> But be happy, and fear nothing from your Great Father. He is your friend, and will never permit you to be driven away from your lands. He never will fall upon a poor, helpless, red child, and kill it, because it is weak. His heart is not made of such cruelty. He would rather protect and defend it, and care the more for it, because of its helplessness.[42]

The exchange of words continued between the Wyandot Tribe and the War Department throughout Adams's presidency. It was a continuous circular dance of repetition—the same old blah, blah, blah. The Wyandot chiefs and leading men were aware of the appeasements being made, and in their desire for serious dialogue, they grew weary and leery of the ever-growing rhetoric. The hope of achieving a viable solution appeared fleeting. In another letter dated December 15, 1825, Reverend Finley wrote to General Lewis Cass, then Governor of Michigan Territory, and firmly defended the tribe's stance against removal with five key and very sound defenses.

1. As a conquered, subdued enemy, who were once a strong and powerful nation, to whom the pleasant homes we now enjoy once belonged, they have strong claims on our generosity. They contended for their country— as we would have done had we been in their places—as long as they could. But the overwhelming population of whites has well-nigh swallowed them up. They have given up their whole country, except a small reserve, on which the bones of their fathers sleep. This they would never have done willingly, but because they could not help themselves; and it would seem as though we were making a contract with them, but they must submit to our proposition in view of their helpless, forlorn, and dependent state. In view of what they have been, they possess some strong claims.

2. Since Wayne's treaty at Greenville, the Wyandotts have been faithful friends to our Government; and, in the last war, did their part in resisting, as agents, the combined power of Indian and British warfare. Many of their men fell in battle, or died with sickness, and left their families and friends destitute.

3. They have claims from this consideration, "Blessed are the merciful, for they shall obtain mercy." The Wyandotts, although not behind the first in battle, were more merciful than their neighbors. They saved more prisoners, and purchased many from other Indians, and adopted them into their families, till they are much mixed with white blood; and some of the best families in our country are allied to them; namely, the Browns, an old Virginia family; the Zanes, another well-known family; Walker, of Tennessee; Williams, Armstrong, M'Cullough, and Magee, of Pittsburg. This handful of Indians are mostly the descendants of our own people. Their fathers were citizens, and why not their children? Shall we not show mercy to our own?

4. Their present prospect for civilization is very promising; and little doubt can be entertained but, in a short time, these people will be well prepared to be admitted as citizens of the State of Ohio; and to remove them just at this time, contrary to their wishes, would be, in my judgment, a most cruel act. It would be undoing what has been done, and throwing them again into a savage state.

5. The promises made by the commissioners, in the name and faith of the President and Government, that if they would cede all their fertile lands but this spot, the Government would never ask them for a foot more, or to sell it and move; but that the Government would build a strong fence around their land, which should never be broken; and this promise was one strong inducement to them to sell their lands. Such strongly-plighted faith ought to be most sacredly observed.[43]

Reverend Finley's claims were strong but useless. Governor Cass was powerless and without motive to enact a defense of the Wyandot. Even if he were willing to help with whatever resources and influence he could muster, it was a futile cause. Removal was inevitable. Having been adopted into the Bear clan, Reverend Finley was a Wyandot citizen. He took the honor seriously and became an ardent defender and protector of the tribe as though he were a natural-born citizen. The reverend continued to fight against the tribe's removal until poor health forced him to leave the Grand Reserve in 1827. Afterwards, he kept a constant vigil, served as an advisor, and remained a loyal friend to the Wyandot Tribe until his death in 1857.[44]

Andrew Jackson was sworn in as the seventh President of the United States on March 4, 1829. President Jackson was from Tennessee and a hero of the War of 1812. He was an Indian fighter and self-professed protector of Indian culture. Andrew believed that the Indians had a choice and they could choose only one of three options. They could adopt the white man's ways and become assimilated; or they could move west and retain their culture far removed from white influence; or they could stay on their present lands east of the Mississippi River and die at the hands of the Americans. Without provocation, and reliant upon the fallacy of illegal policy, President Jackson has the auspicious disgrace and burden of removing thousands of American Indians, many to their death, upon his hands.

On December 6, 1830, President Jackson delivered his first State of the Union address. The whole of his speech can be quickly deduced with his first sentence: "It gives me pleasure to announce to Congress that the benevolent policy of the Government, steadily pursued for nearly thirty years, in relation to the removal of the Indians beyond the white settlements is approaching to a happy consummation."[45]

Unfortunately, the Wyandot Tribe was split on removal, and a compromise could not be achieved. The Pagan Party promoted a move to lands west of the

Mississippi River, and the Christian Party promoted their stay in Michigan and Ohio. The *Huron*-Wyandots who moved to Canada tried to ignore it all but found they could not. Yes, the tribe was divided, and the split appears to have been nearly in half. The Wyandot Tribe was at an impasse.

As soon as Congress approved the Indian Removal Act on May 28, 1830, the Wyandot's search for a new home officially began—although with no great earnest and sincerity. In defiance of an 1832 Supreme Court decision favoring the Cherokee, Jackson continued his objective by ignoring the Court's decision and forcibly removed the Cherokee to the west in 1838. James B. Gardiner in an 1832 letter to General Lewis Cass, Secretary of War, compared the Wyandot to the Cherokee. "I consider the situation of the Wyandotts, though on a smaller scale, very similar to that of the Cherokees."[46] After the Cherokee's forced removal, Wyandot chiefs and leading men worked to ensure that a forced removal did not happen to their tribe.

James B. Gardiner was a special agent of the United States employed with the task of removing the Wyandot from Ohio. Unbeknownst to him, he had met his match and would be bested and outcrafted by a Wyandot named William Walker Jr. In the fall of 1831 Walker was appointed, as were Silas Armstrong, James Washington, John Goulde, John Baptiste, and George Williams, as delegates to explore land being offered west of the Mississippi River as trade for the tribe's Ohio land. The Wyandot chiefs never formally approved George Williams for the expedition because he outwardly favored removal. The council desired an unbiased approach to the expedition and did not want it tainted before leaving for the west. In October of 1831 the delegation left Upper Sandusky for Cincinnati and their ultimate destination—Fort Leavenworth. The trip was not expected to take long, and, as expected, it did not.

After having explored the land and as the leading men were making their way home in January, Gardiner wrote General Cass and embarrassed himself with these words: "I flatter myself that I shall be able, in four or five weeks, to present you with a definitive treaty with this sagacious, intelligent and crafty tribe of Indians, which will be of the highest importance to a large section of this state, and greatly in aid of the benevolent policy of the Government."[47] During the less than twenty-four hours of writing the letter, Gardiner was told the land trade was rejected by the delegation. William Walker Jr. and the other delegates, with the exception of George Williams who was essentially a Gardiner handpicked spy, found the land totally unacceptable for habitation. Gardiner accused William Walker Jr. and Silas Armstrong of duplicity. Essentially, Gardiner believed that William and Silas had already made up their minds before going west and looking at the proposed land swap. Gardiner filed a formal excusatory and accusatory complaint with General Cass.[48] Gardiner tried to evade blame and cover his failure after losing his poker match to a bunch of Indians.

Shortly upon returning to Upper Sandusky from his expedition to the west, Walker wrote to The Reverend G. P. (Gabriel Pollion) Disosway, a prominent Methodist missionary, pastor, and banker who briefly served as a member of the New York State Assembly in 1849.[49] His letter to Reverend Disosway served a twofold purpose. First, he described the lands he and the committee were sent to explore. Second, he told of a meeting with two Flathead Indians, actually believed to be Nez Perce. Walker's description of the Flatheads and their plight was inspirational in the Methodists sending missionaries westward over the Rocky Mountains. Reverend Disosway published the letter from Walker on March 1, 1833, in the *Christian Advocate*.[50] Within a year's time, in March of 1834, money had been pledged and men assembled in Independence, Missouri.[51] The men would head west across the frontier—vast prairie and impeding mountains—on what would become known as the Oregon Trail.

In the letter to Disosway, Walker begins with a brief but intimate peek into his personal life and family. The complexities of William Walker—including his policies and the decisions he made—stand second to none when compared to those of other leading men and politicians of the time. Behind the tough, uncompromising, and reinvented Wyandot warrior, Walker was a family man who treasured his mate and children more than life itself. In his later years all his children, and two successive mates, would precede him in death. He was filled with grief, and photographs show him to be a miserable, heartbroken man.

Walker's assessment of the land was detailed and scholarly with a clear reflection of his personal feelings and education. There was no doubt that William took his assignment seriously and left no stone unturned. He stated, "The country we explore is truly a land of savages. It is wild and romantic; it is a champaign, but beautifully undulated country."[52] The report made by Walker and the committee to the Wyandot tribal council was expressly clear. The men listed many reasons why this offering of land would be the last place they would select for the purpose of removing the Wyandot Tribe. Items 8–14 on the committee's list illustrate that much research went into preparing the report. The following list contains the key points of the report, and each would be proved correct in coming years.

8. Politicians in the State of Missouri opposed to the settling of Indians on their frontier, as they were considered a "curse to the State;"

9. Attempts were already being made by Missouri to add the whole of the "Platte country" to the state;

10. Their neighbors on the eastern side bordering the State of Missouri were abandoned, dissolute and wicked people, essentially fugitives from justices from the States of Virginia, Kentucky, Tennessee and other southern states;

11. While on the western side their neighbors would be the Sacks & Iowas and they would view the Wyandots as intruders. With a bad history and unresolved state of war in place with the Sacks it would prove to be an unhealthy relationship for everyone involved;

12. Missouri was a slave holding state and slaveholders have proven to be unfriendly to Indians as in the recent case with Georgia and the Cherokee;

13. This little strip of land would inevitably become an asylum and sanctuary for runaway slaves and vagrant Negros, of which there was enough of that class already amongst us;

14. We shall have a more worthless and corrupt class of whites to deal and associate with than is to be found in this part of Ohio.[53]

Clearly, William and the committee were not impressed with the land offered by the United States. In both his report to the tribal council and his letter to Reverend Disosway, he reiterated his assessment of the proposed land swap. The rejection of the land by Walker and the appointed committee was not well received by James Gardiner. He was horribly embarrassed and his career placed in jeopardy. He held Gardiner in a state of checkmate. Gardiner had only one move he could make—he tipped his king and cried foul. However, his accusation would quickly prove to be invalidated. In a letter to General Cass, Gardiner made a ridiculous accusation. "The Delegation never saw the country which I had proffered to them in behalf of the Government! They spent but one night in the woods. They were but six days, in all, on the western line of the State of Missouri, and, . . . they occupied most of that time in the sport of bear-hunting, on horseback and with dogs!"[54]

For such an exhaustive list of negatives to have been compiled, and with the discovered knowledge of the state of Missouri's ongoing attempt to annex the strip of land, Gardiner's accusation was preposterous. Walker and the committee did not pursue a hunting safari with all expenses paid by the US government. The committee overturned every stone looking for anything positive to

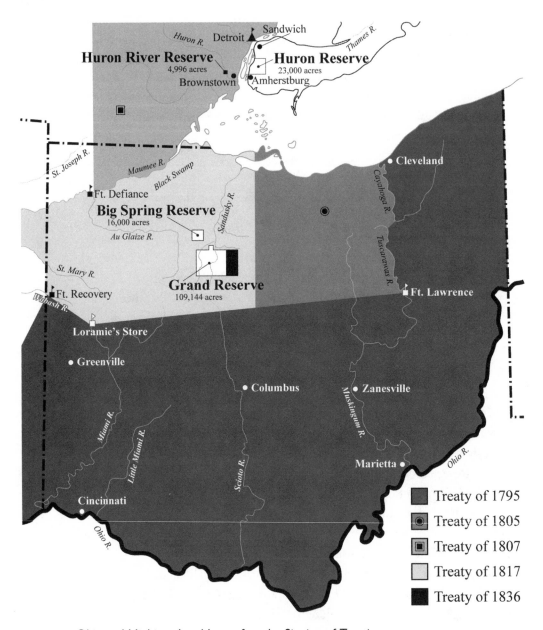

MAP 4.1. Ohio and Michigan Land Loss after the Signing of Treaties

justify a potential move. Unfortunately, no justification was found to endorse the trade of the Grand Reserve for land that was high, dry prairie and full of ravines. This offering of unacceptable land was contained within what would become the Platt Purchase for the state of Missouri in 1836. The committee's final recommendation to the chiefs and tribe: Cease all contention, bickering, and party strife, settle down, and maintain your position in the state of Ohio.[55]

Realizing that his goal of effecting a treaty of removal with the Christian Party was now impossible, Gardiner turned his fury upon the Wyandot's Pagan Party. The Pagans favored removal and appeared more than willing to conduct themselves in a land trade. In a spiteful fit of revenge and hopeful redemption, Gardiner was able to steal the Big Spring Reserve in the Treaty of 1832. The Pagans wanted to move to Indian Territory and begin life anew with the renewed old yet new *Huron*-Wyandot traditions. Unfortunately, and fortunately, their move would be no more than a mere ten to fifteen miles. The following quote, found in the Preamble of the Treaty of 1832, attempts to justify the Pagans' reason for the sell:

> WHEREAS the said band of Wyandots have become fully convinced that, whilst they remain in their present situation in the State of Ohio, in the vicinity of a white population, which is continually increasing and crowding around them, they cannot prosper and be happy, and the morals of many of their people will be daily becoming more and more vitiated.[56]

Is the statement correct? Yes, it most certainly is, but the key word found in the quote is band. Gardiner struck his deal with only the Pagan Party Wyandots and not the whole of the Wyandot Tribe.

This is an accurate description of the environment the Wyandot Tribe was now facing in Ohio. However, it was best to still stand firm, resist the whites, and remain united as the Wyandot Tribe. It did not matter; Pagan or Christian, everyone was still a Wyandot. The tribal council on the Grand Reserve sternly advised the Pagan Party not to sell, but the Pagans would not listen. The Pagan Party out of spite sold the Big Spring Reserve. Selling out was bad, but the government's attempt to split the tribe was unacceptable.

Prior to the Treaty of 1832 the tribe signed twelve treaties with the US government, and not one made an attempt to split the tribe and relocate a splintered group to lands removed. Article seven of the Treaty of 1832 states, "The band of Wyandots, herein treating, have separated themselves from the Wyandots at Upper Sandusky."[57] This was just short of a declaration of war against the Wyandot Tribe. The chiefs and tribal council at Upper Sandusky, even though they despised the actions of the Pagan Party, knew that keeping the tribe intact was supremely important. The Pagan Party was assigned its own subagent, Joseph McCutcheon. John McIntire Armstrong would refer to McCutcheon as a man with "as destitute of honourable principle as ever were permitted breathe."[58]

Citizens on the Big Spring Reserve were given the option to move to Michigan, Canada, "or to any place they may obtain a right or privilege from other Indians to go."[59] Essentially McCutcheon was saying, "I don't care where you go, just get out of Ohio!" Yet still the Pagan Party would refuse to leave Ohio. Without land on which to reside in Ohio, the Pagan Party Wyandot, and betrayed innocents who didn't consent to the sell, would now have to find a new home. Citizens of the Pagan Party were invited to move to the Grand Reserve. The homeless Wyandot accepted the invitation; however, the invitation would come with a price.

Shortly after the Treaty of 1832 was signed, it was determined that Gardiner and McCutcheon had employed some dishonest measures to obtain signatures to secure the land. Silas and John McIntire Armstrong, along with seventeen leading men who resided on the Big Spring Reserve, discovered that many who signed, opting for removal, were from the *Huron* Reserve in Canada.[60] Many of the Canadian Wyandots did not have a right to sign the treaty, as the land was technically not theirs to trade or sell. Matthew Greyeyes, Isaac Driver, Alexander Clarke, and John D. Brown signed the treaty as chancellors representing the Wyandot Tribe. Were they Wyandot? Yes, they were. Did they reside on the Big Spring Reserve? It's doubtful, as they are shown on the 1836 *Huron* Reserve allotment map as having land in Canada, which made them citizens of the Crown, or Canadian citizens.[61, 62]

It was then believed that the Canadian Wyandot were essentially hoping to obtain a little of the paid money and promptly return to Canada. After petitioning President Jackson directly, the chiefs and tribal council at Upper Sandusky persuaded the government to divert payment of the land from the Pagan Party to the Wyandot Tribal Council. Those from Canada were paid for their signatures, but the Pagan Party Wyandots lost their payments. Their money was used toward improvements on the Grand Reserve for the overall good of the tribe. This obviously infuriated the Pagan Party, for they felt that everyone involved had swindled them. The Pagan Party was permitted to move to the Grand Reserve and retain full rights as Wyandot citizens. The actions of the Canadian Wyandots rekindled some extreme resentment within many of the Ohio Wyandots.

The Pagan Party may have been the minority, and they may have suffered a terrible blow after the Treaty of 1832, but these were not deterrents to their efforts in trying to secure a treaty of removal. The attitudes and mindset of both parties had now been clearly exposed, and their ability to employ any means to secure their goals was quite evident. With unyielding differences and divided actions, bitterness and animosities had taken deep root within the Wyandot Tribe. For the next two years the parties were pushing and pulling on each other to try to obtain leverage and an advantage. The government agents were also perplexed and at a loss as to what they must do to remove the tribe from the state of Ohio. The white settlers were becoming very impatient as the Wyandots continued to reside on some of the best land in the state. All that stood between them and obtaining their prize were two warring factions within the Wyandot Tribe. Remember, the Wyandot are a tribe of warriors, and without a war to fight they could have turned upon themselves, as did the Cherokee; but they did not. The Wyandots differences were severely bitter, yet no lives were lost.

A second exploratory expedition was dispatched in 1834 to explore the lands south of the Kansas and Missouri rivers. This was the general area recommended by William Walker Jr. and the delegates from the 1831 expedition. If the tribe could move to this area, it would be a wonderful reunion of three old friends—Wyandot, Delaware, and Shawnee—or at least a partial reunion. Bands of the Delaware and Shawnee had chosen to move deeper into Indian Territory, splitting both tribes. Upon arriving at the Shawnee Agency, the task of exploring the area began with all due haste. Unfortunately, the land was found to be inferior to what the tribe already possessed in Ohio. A discouraging report of the area led the Wyandot Council to again refuse another proposed move.[63]

The Canadian Wyandot were not doing well in their dealings with the Canadian government. On February 2, 1836, the band signed a treaty effectively reducing the *Huron* Reserve by two-thirds.[64] As in Ohio on the Grand Reserve, they too became split over the subject of retaining ownership of the land. Some wanted to sell all the land and essentially become assimilated or seek shelter with their fellow Wyandots in Michigan or Ohio. Those who signed the treaty justified their actions by believing that if they had not sold off a part of the land, all of the *Huron* Reserve would be lost. As the Canadian Wyandot began dealing directly with the Canadian government, influence from Upper Sandusky began to weaken even more. The Canadian Wyandot had been doing what they wanted, independent of Upper Sandusky, for a long time. Both bands were equally Wyandot, but the geopolitical differences between both areas of influence were at times obviously and even blatantly evident.

In August of 1837, after additional efforts by McCutcheon to secure a treaty of removal, the Wyandot Tribal Council sought the assistance of Ohio Governor Joseph Vance and General Lewis Cass. Joseph McCutcheon was found to be unscrupulously enticing Wyandot citizens with the power of alcohol. The Wyandot Tribal Council and the Nation's Council did not want to leave Ohio. They repeatedly made this clear to McCutcheon. There had yet to be an acceptable offering of land in the west that could compare to the beloved Grand Reserve. William Walker Jr. in a letter to Reverend Finley wrote that he feared that if McCutcheon could secure a treaty of removal, he was going to try to break up the tribe[65]—essentially scattering the Wyandot, as had been done to the Delaware and Shawnee. Walker did not want this to happen. Pressure was mounting on the chiefs and tribal council to do something.

When dealing with the US government there was a no more prudent, shrewd, crude, and determined Wyandot than William Walker, Jr. He was an exceptional talent and exhibited the brashness and confidence to stand toe-to-toe with anyone Washington, DC, chose to send to Upper Sandusky. I have no doubt that Walker took pleasure in toying with McCutcheon as a cat does a mouse. He had one weakness: He was an alcoholic.[66] Like many other Wyandots, he had succumbed to the power of intoxicating drink. In 1836, upon the death of Tom Long, Walker became principal chief of the tribe and was appointed to serve the remainder of Long's term. Only once, in 1839, was Walker elected principal chief, yet his service to and mark upon the Wyandot Tribe are unparalleled as a leading man. The power and influence of the tribe's leading men were beginning to rival the authority of the elected principal chief. Unfortunately, intoxicating spirits often rendered Walker an unreliable consultant. In 1837 Principal Chief John Barnett sought the services of John McIntire Armstrong over William. The time had come for William to embrace sobriety, but unfortunately he never did.

John McIntire Armstrong, in a letter to Lucy Biglow, his fiancée and the daughter of Methodist Missionary Russell Biglow, described the tribe's ongoing resistance to removal. He also detailed many of the tactics used by McCutcheon to obtain removal. In April of 1839 Armstrong was admitted to the Ohio Bar;[67] his perception of the situation was enhanced by his education and gave him rare insight into the dealings of McCutcheon. As Armstrong gave his time and talents to the service of his people, it delayed his returning home to see Lucy. John apologetically, yet justifiably, wrote to Lucy who was living in Mansfield, Ohio, about forty miles east of Upper Sandusky.

As attempts to secure land in the west continued to fail, the Pagan Party became restless and decided to take matters into their own hands. This was nothing new; the Pagan Party had already done this on several occasions.

Three representatives, Warpole, James Washington (Peacock), and Porcupine, left for Washington, DC, in August of 1838 with the sole intent of effecting a treaty of removal.[68] Warpole was already a legendary chief among the Wyandot. He was a staunch traditionalist and ten years earlier was the first Wyandot to be elected principal chief of the tribe. Warpole, a celebrity, was old, influential, and fortunately unsuccessful in his attempt to secure a treaty. Upon his return to Upper Sandusky during a report to the tribal council, tempers flared and Warpole unsheathed a knife during a heated debate.[69] As a result of his actions, he and the others were thrown into jail, but only for a short time. This only served to further inspire Warpole's efforts, and within two months he sought yet another treaty. This time ten men from the Pagan Party would accompany him to Washington, DC. Noting his persistent sincerity, in October the US government proposed that yet another strip of land between the Verdigris and Neosho rivers be considered in exchange for the Ohio land.[70] This presented a problem for the Wyandot Tribe. The proposed strip of land currently belonged to the Cherokee; the Cherokee were the Wyandot's cousins, but over the years the relationship had been anything but friendly.

It would not be until May of 1839 that an agreement was made to send six men, three from the Christian Party and three from the Pagan Party, on a third exploratory expedition to survey the new proposed land. Only five would ultimately make the trip. William Walker Jr. led the last big expedition west; however, in 1839 he was Principal Chief of the Wyandot and this time could not go. Henry Jacques, Matthew R. Walker, John Sarahass Sr., Tall Charles, and Summundowat would undertake this expedition.[71] On June 10, 1839, the men made their way to Cincinnati and booked passage on a steamboat bound for New Orleans. Upon arrival at the junction of the Mississippi and Arkansas rivers, they disembarked and waited for another steamboat to take them into Indian Territory.

Upon reaching Fort Smith, Arkansas, the last stop before entering Indian Territory, the delegates learned that the Cherokee were in a very foul mood. They had been in Indian Territory now for about a year since their forced removal from Georgia, and their two parties, led by Major Ridge of the Treaty Party and John Ross of the National Party, were fighting. Both parties were comparable to the Wyandot's Pagan and Christian parties; the primary difference was that the Wyandot were not killing each other. For the Wyandot, the simple and inciting act of unsheathing a knife was unacceptable behavior when done so to a fellow citizen.

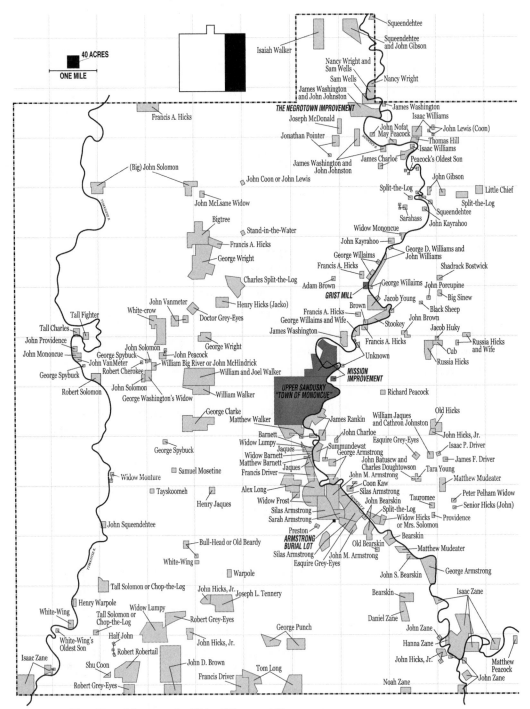

MAP 4.2. The Grand Reserve in Ohio, West and East

40 ACRES
ONE MILE

Isaiah Walker

THE NEGROTOWN IMPROVEMENT

Squeendehtee
Squeendehtee and John Gibson
Nancy Wright and Sam Wells
Sam Wells
Nancy Wright
James Washington and John Johnston
James Washington
Isaac Williams
Joseph McDonald
John Nofat
May Peacock
John Lewis (Coon)
Jonathan Pointer
Thomas Hill
Isaac Williams
James Washington and John Johnston
James Charloe
Peacock's Oldest Son
John Coon or John Lewis
John Gibson
Split-the-Log
Little Chief
Split-the-Log
Squeendehtee
Sarahass
John Kayrahoo
Widow Mononcue
John Kayrahoo
George D. Williams and John Williams
George Willaims
Francis A. Hicks
Shadrack Bostwick
Adam Brown
George Willaims
John Porcupine
Big Sinew
Jacob Young
Black Sheep
Brown
John Brown
Francis A. Hicks
Jacob Huky
George Willaims and Wife
Stookey
Russia Hicks and Wife
James Washington
Francis A. Hicks
Cub
Russia Hicks
Unknown
MISSION IMPROVEMENT
Richard Peacock
UPPER SANDUSKY "TOWN OF MONONCUE"
Old Hicks
James Rankin
William Jaques and Cathron Johnston
John Charloe
John Hicks, Jr.
Esquire Grey-Eyes
Isaac P. Driver
Summundewat
George Armstrong
James F. Driver
John Batuscw and Charles Doughtowson
Tara Young
John M. Armstrong
Matthew Mudeater
Coon Kaw
Silas Armstrong
Peter Pelham Widow
Tauromee
John Bearskin
Senior Hicks (John)
Split-the-Log
Providence
Widow Hicks or Mrs. Solomon
Bearskin
Old Bearskin
Matthew Mudeater

(Big) John Solomon
Francis A. Hicks
John McLsane Widow
Bigtree
Stand-in-the-Water
Francis A. Hicks
George Wright
Charles Split-the-Log
Henry Hicks (Jacko)
John Vanmeter
White-crow
Doctor Grey-Eyes
Tall Fighter
Tall Charles
John Providence
George Wright
John Mononcue
John Solomon
George Spybuck
John Peacock
John VanMeter
William Big River or John McHindrick
Robert Cherokee
William and Joel Walker
George Spybuck
John Solomon
George Washington's Widow
William Walker
Robert Solomon
George Clarke
Matthew Walker
Barnett
Widow Lumpy
Jaques
Widow Barnett
Matthew Barnett
Jaques
Francis Driver
George Spybuck
Samuel Mosetine
Alex Long
Widow Monture
Widow Frost
Silas Armstrong
Tayskoomeh
Sarah Armstrong
Henry Jaques
Preston
John Squeendehtee
ARMSTRONG BURIAL LOT
Silas Armstrong
John M. Armstrong
Bull-Head or Old Beardy
Esquire Grey-Eyes
White-Wing
George Armstrong
Warpole
John S. Bearskin
Tall Solomon or Chop-the-Log
John Hicks, Jr.
Joseph L. Tennery
Bearskin
Isaac Zane
Henry Warpole
Widow Lumpy
White-Wing
Tall Solomon or Chop-the-Log
Robert Grey-Eyes
Daniel Zane
Half John
John Zane
White-Wing's Oldest Son
Robert Robertail
John Hicks, Jr.
George Punch
Hanna Zane
Isaac Zane
Shu Coon
John D. Brown
John Hicks, Jr.
Matthew Peacock
Robert Grey-Eyes
Francis Driver
Tom Long
Noah Zane
John Zane

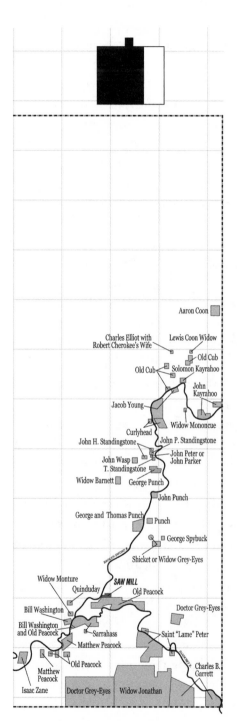

Aaron Coon

Charles Elliot with
Robert Cherokee's Wife

Lewis Coon Widow

Old Cub

Old Cub

Solomon Kayrahoo

John
Kayrahoo

Jacob Young

Widow Mononcue

Curlyhead

John H. Standingstone

John P. Standingstone

John Peter or
John Parker

John Wasp

T. Standingstone

Widow Barnett

George Punch

John Punch

George and Thomas Punch

Punch

George Spybuck

Shicket or Widow Grey-Eyes

Widow Monture

Quinduday

SAW MILL

Old Peacock

Bill Washington

Doctor Grey-Eyes

Bill Washington
and Old Peacock

Sarrahass

Saint "Lame" Peter

Matthew Peacock

Old Peacock

Charles B.
Garrett

Matthew
Peacock

Isaac Zane

Doctor Grey-Eyes

Widow Jonathan

Shortly after leaving Fort Smith, the steamboat stopped long enough to pick up John Brown, a chief of the Treaty Party Cherokee.[72] After visiting with Chief Brown and hearing of the dissension, the delegates determined it was useless to try to negotiate let alone meet with the Cherokee. To fulfill their mission the delegates continued with their exploration of the Cherokee Neutral Land. The delegates also decided to explore land that was then reserved for the New York Indians. This land lay a little further north and ran westward from the Missouri state line near where Fort Scott would eventually be established.

The Cherokee Neutral Land was an expanse of land in the southeast corner of the present-day state of Kansas. Back then it was all Indian Territory, and neither Kansas nor Oklahoma existed. The Neutral Land comprised the majority of present-day Cherokee and Crawford counties in Southeast Kansas. After the Cherokee Neutral Land was explored in the middle of July, it was determined the climate was unacceptably hot. I have no doubt that ticks and chiggers, the irritating bloodsuckers they are, also played an influential role in their decision. Continuing on, the delegates explored the land reserved for the New York Indians. The delegation agreed that this strip of land would better meet the needs of the tribe due to a better supply of water.[73] The land presumably reserved for the New York Indians was a strip that extended westward from the state of Missouri near Fort Scott.

Since the exploring committee was so close, the delegates decided to stop and visit the Mixed Seneca and Shawnee on the Cowskin River. Upon their arrival at the reservation, wampum was exchanged and traditional ceremonies of friendship were celebrated as in the old days of Ohio. It was a great reunion of old friends, and the committee should have paid much closer attention. The heat, ticks, and chiggers would have been a lot less irritating to the Wyandot Tribe as forthcoming events and unscrupulous characters would prove to be.

In just a few short years the Wyandot were betrayed by the Shawnee, and the Delaware expected them to pay a premium price for land. On the other hand, the Mixed Seneca and Shawnee extended unmerited and unconditional favor to them. If the Wyandot leading men had noticed the sincere friendship that was extended to them in the summer of 1839, a lot of hardship could have likely been avoided. They did not take advantage of the hospitality and ask for sharing of the land. Why? The climate was too hot and the tick and chiggers too irritating. I doubt that if the men had asked, they would have been declined, and the Wyandot Tribe's history would have been totally different.

After a wonderful time with the Mixed Seneca and Shawnee, the delegates proceeded to Westport, Missouri. From there they crossed back over into Indian Territory and proceeded to inspect the reserves of both the Delaware and Shawnee. They were favorably impressed. Strangely enough, the second expedition of 1834 was also sent to this general area, and the land was then found unfavorable. Upon returning to Upper Sandusky and giving a report to the Tribal Council, a fourth expedition was promptly dispatched back to the Shawnee Reserve with the intent to negotiate a treaty to purchase a portion of Shawnee land. Principal Chief Francis A. Hicks and Special Commissioner William H. Hunter would formally conduct this expedition in November of 1839.[74] In an ironic twist, earlier on February 13, 1839, Indian agent Richard W. Cummins, stationed in Fort Leavenworth, sent the following memo to T. Hartley Crawford. Crawford was Commander of Indian Affairs in Washington City.

Sir, The Shawnees state that they have understood that their old friends the Wyandots have stated that they would be willing to move to this country if they could get a tract of land as good as that which the Shawnees now reside on; and that they the Shawnees have a great desire to have their old friends the Wyandots for neighbors once more.[75]

The tribes prepared a draft treaty for the purchase of the Shawnee's land; however, the treaty was contingent upon ratification by the US Senate. After much promotion and debate, on June 8, 1840, the US Senate rejected the proposed treaty. Rather than continue to pursue the sale of land, the Shawnee withdrew their offer, betraying that which they had been previously committed to doing. Evidently their desire to have the Wyandot again as neighbors was not that great. Again the Wyandot were left with no viable option for removal west. As a result, special agent Hunter retired from active service. Veteran and retired agent John Johnston would be called back into service to replace him.[76] It was beginning to appear as though the US government was doing everything in its power to ensure that the Wyandot Tribe would be shattered into indiscernible pieces.

"Like Sheep among Wolves"

The horrific and tragic death of the Wyandot's beloved Chief Summundowat, along with his niece and nephew, in December of 1840 was a hard blow for the tribe. His death emphasized the urgency with which the tribe must accept and prepare for their removal from Ohio and Michigan. At the time of Summundowat's murder, he was the Principal Chief of the Wyandot Tribe. He was also a licensed exhorter and preacher of the Methodist Episcopal Church. Wyandots and whites alike held the man in high regard. In *Life Among the Indians* Reverend Finley gives an account of Summundowat's murder and noted the date of his death to be about 1841 or 1842. The Charles W. Evers's account in *Many Incidents and Reminiscences of the Early History of Wood County* gives the year of Summundowat's murder as 1845.[77] This date is clearly inaccurate as the Wyandot Tribe left Ohio in July of 1843; however, Evers's account of Summundowat's murder is rather fanciful and detailed, thus making it a legend of Ohio. Charles Buser indicated the date of Summundowat's death to be December 1840.[78] Unfortunately, as was the case with much of Buser's work, his source of the date was not documented; however, due to the influence of his work, most Wyandottes readily accept this date. Therefore, December 1840, has become the traditional date of Summundowat's death.

It is believed that Summundowat was murdered in Henry County while on a seasonal raccoon hunt in an area known as the Black Swamp. Henry County is located in Northwest Ohio about fifty miles from the Grand Reserve. With Wyandots in the Detroit area, as well as Canada, many traveled back and forth from the Grand Reserve as family members often resided on the two reserves. Many Wyandots still roamed throughout Ohio as in the old days, hunting and visiting areas that were considered sacred or held special sentimental value. They were discouraged from doing this, but who could stop them? One of the trails to Detroit passed through Henry County; therefore, the Black Swamp was a well-traveled and familiar place for both Summundowat and Reverend Finley. They often traveled together to Detroit in the early days of Methodism coming into the tribe.

In December of 1840, after a very successful hunt, Summundowat decided to leave for home early with several horse loads of raccoon pelts. While he was slowly making his way back home, one evening two men entered Summundowat's camp and appeared to be lost and hungry. They asked to stay the night, and permission was promptly extended. The men were provided food and a place to sleep was prepared. Summundowat, being a Methodist preacher, had prayer before they retired for the evening's rest. While Summundowat and his family were sleeping, the two men arose and simultaneously struck both Summundowat and his nephew in the head with camp axes. Nancy, Summundowat's niece, was awakened and horrified with the nightmare she awoke to see. Fleeing for her life, she was caught and delivered the same fate. Additional descriptions of the grisly scene indicate that all three were repeatedly chopped with the axes. All three bodies and their severed pieces were collected and covered with logs and brush. They were left for the wild animals of the swamp to consume and destroy all evidence of the odious crime. For what purpose were Summundowat and his nephew and niece hacked into countless, bloody pieces? The men eventually captured for the crime indicated they killed them for the raccoon pelts and Summundowat's hunting dogs.

The following day, the remaining hunters in Summundowat's party were following his trail back home and discovered the grisly scene. The murderers failed to cover their trail, or felt it unnecessary; therefore, Summundowat's friends, who consisted of both Wyandots and whites alike, easily overtook the murderers. They were captured and promptly put into jail to stand trial. Yet they escaped. It is assumed they escaped jail with the help of friends or an additional accomplice. The murderers never stood trial or paid for their heinous crime.[79] It is believed that the names of the two murderers are John Anderson and James Lyons.[80] Before the Wyandot Tribe left Ohio, the pieces of Summundowat's body were exhumed from where they lay in the Black Swamp. This was likely a variation of the ancient feast of the dead still practiced in the

FIGURE 4.2. Summundowat

mid-nineteenth century. Summundowat was reburied at the Wyandot Mission Church Cemetery at Upper Sandusky.

The Reverend James Wheeler was assigned to Upper Sandusky in September of 1839. Before leaving Ohio he wrote to Reverend Charles Elliott and briefed him on recent events, including the death of Chief Summundowat. Coincidentally, at that time Reverend Elliott was publisher of the *Western Christian Advocate,* a very popular magazine in the mid-nineteenth century.[81] Reverend Wheeler's letter was subsequently published in the *Western Christian Advocate,* along with a portion of his remembrances of Chief Summundowat.[82]

Resistance to all removal efforts had been the majority sentiment within the tribe for a long time. It was a custom that majority rules even when there is opposition to an issue. This custom remains true even when a chief or leading man does not support the issue; what the majority people of the tribe want is honored. The Pagan Party pushed this tradition to the edge of insubordination and treason with their defiant efforts to secure a treaty of removal against the wishes of the tribal council. The Pagan Party's saving grace is that they could not secure a treaty that affected the whole tribe.

As Reverend Wheeler reflected upon the life of Summundowat, he noted that Summundowat was principal chief in 1835. At this time negotiations were being made on what was a final draft of the Treaty of 1836. The issue of annuity payments became a point of contention, and Summundowat is said to have broken tradition. Article Six of the treaty called for the selling of a five-mile-wide strip on the eastern side of the Grand Reserve and stated that "the funds for the tribe shall be distributed by the Register and Receiver to each person entitled thereto."[83] Although the majority of the tribe favored receiving the payments, Summundowat was sternly opposed to the payments and brought upon himself the charge of obstinacy. Summundowat told his fellow citizens he knew enough about annuity payments that traders would be always present, whiskey peddlers swarming, and many citizens drunk. It would also be impossible to keep the Mission Church and graveyard from being desecrated.

Reverend Wheeler continued his remembrances by stating that the citizens favoring the payments reminded Summundowat that a majority had approved the terms. Summundowat was then noted as saying, "Well, I don't care; you cannot have the money": hence the accusation of being stubborn, which, by the way, is a normal Wyandot character trait. A government official overheard Summundowat's appeal to the citizens and rebutted him by saying that his concerns were unfounded and all efforts would be made to ensure that never happened. Ultimately Summundowat lost the debate when in 1836 Tom Long was elected principal chief. Shortly thereafter Chief Long died in office. William Walker Jr. was selected to complete his term, and as tribal leader he signed the Treaty of 1836. Upon the signing of the treaty and the ensuing selling of the land, payments to citizens were scheduled.

As the time came for the first payments to be made, everything Summundowat predicted came true. Monday, following a Sunday service in the church, the holy sanctuary was to be used as the place of distribution and, as a result, was going to be desecrated. Traders had also erected their tents and tables waiting like a flock of vultures for the rich Indians to come buy their whiskey and goods. Chief Summundowat attempted to block the distribution of payments by barricading himself inside the church. His protest lasted three days until the government officials decided to find another location. Chief Summundowat was overheard saying that if they entered the church, "they would have to enter over his dead body, and the blood of Summundowat would stain the sacred place."[84]

Again in 1840 we find Summundowat Principal Chief of the Wyandot Tribe. Can we believe that his immovable, stubborn stance on issues he did not agree with would have changed over the last five years? No, it's likely he would have developed an even stronger resolve. Summundowat again stood as an impenetrable barrier to the signing of a treaty securing removal of the Wyandot Tribe. Should we accept the story that Chief Summundowat was randomly and brutally murdered over raccoon skins and coon dogs? Given the questionable circumstances befalling the escape and elusion of his killers, should we more readily accept his death as an assassination? Regardless of whether his death was an assassination or a random act of murder, it was successful in obtaining a majority consensus of the tribe—the time for removal west had finally arrived. No one was safe in Ohio, not even the Christians, let alone a principal chief and Methodist preacher.

In 1842 famous English author Charles Dickens and his wife were taking a stagecoach from Columbus to Sandusky City. An overnight stop landed them in Upper Sandusky and a night spent at the old log cabin tavern. Since alcohol was illegal on the reservation, let's call the tavern an inn. They arrived at the inn between 10:00 PM and 11:00 PM, and everyone had retired for the night. They knocked at the door, it was was opened, and they were served complimentary tea before bed. The next morning they were entertained when a traveling companion scratched and danced what looked to be an old Wessex jig. The traveling companion had spent the night in the stagecoach with bed bugs and could not ease his discomfort without a glass of fine brandy. Unfortunately, the inn's proprietor could only serve him a cup of tea. Charles wrote, "for in Indian villages the legislature, with very good and wise intention, forbids the sale of spirits by tavern-keepers. The precaution, however is quite inefficacious, for the Indian never fails to procure liquor of a worse kind at a dearer price from travelling peddlers."[85] Charles continued in *American Notes for General Circulation,* Vol. II, by detailing a conversation held with Colonel John Johnston over breakfast:

It is a settlement of Wyandot Indians who inhabit this place. Among the company was a mild old gentleman, who for many years employed by the United States government in conducting negotiations with the Indians, and who had just completed a treaty with these people by which they bound themselves, in consideration of a certain annual sum, to remove next year to some land provided for them west of the Mississippi and a little way beyond St. Louis. He gave me a moving account of their strong attachment to the familiar scenes of their infancy, and in particular to their burial places of their kindred, and of their great reluctance to leave them. He had witnessed many such removals, and always with pain, though he knew that they departed for their own good. The question whether this tribe should go or stay had been discussed among them a day or two before in a hut erected for the purpose, the logs of which still lay upon the ground before the inn. When the speaking was done the ayes and noes were ranged on opposite sides, and every male adult voted on his turn. The moment the result was known the minority (a large one) cheerfully yielded to the rest, and withdrew all kind of opposition.[86]

After years of resisting removal, it was now time to leave. On March 17, 1842, the Wyandot Tribe signed a treaty of removal *without* a designated place to move. After defiantly standing so long and firm against removal, this is absolutely amazing! I don't think we can fully understand or appreciate the effect Chief Summundowat's assassination had upon the people. His death was a horrific and violent murder perpetrated by white men for no apparent reason other than random greed—at least this is what the Wyandot people were led to believe. One day Summundowat was with his tribe and the next day he was gone—and no one could look upon his face and say their fond farewells. It was a harsh blow for the Wyandot Tribe and it so demoralized their fight against removal that tribal leaders succumbed to emotions and the majority consensus to finally move west.

The US government did grant the Wyandot Tribe 148,000 acres in exchange for their 4,996 acres in Michigan and 109,144 acres in Ohio. In what appears to be an obvious case of bribery, certain chiefs and leading men within the tribe were given special land grants on unclaimed Indian land west of the Mississippi River. These grants, now called floats, were assigned to thirty-five men.[87] The floats initially looked very appealing for the tribe, or more appropriately the individual recipients to whom they were assigned; however, the floats actually turn out to be a curse for the Wyandot Tribe. The floats became enticements for white land speculators to fight over—as did tribal citizens.

A few of the leading men in the tribe were successful businessmen. This created an imbalance and division of classes never before seen among the *Huron*-Wyandot people. The Armstrong and Walker brothers were men of extreme persuasion both inside and outside the tribe. Rum and whiskey had become a scourge, and many traditions were on the verge of collapse. The Pagan Party wanted to buffer citizens from the whites and remain Indian. They had now been granted their heart's desire. Again, the big question was

Where were they going to move? The Grand Reserve was well developed with many improvements such as a sawmill and a gristmill. It was indeed an enticing little piece of Ohio that drew white settlers like blood-sucking mosquitoes and they came in a black swarm.

Article Seven of the Treaty of 1842 gave the tribe use and occupancy of the Huron River and Grand Reserve until April 1, 1844. This right did not prevent the US government from surveying and selling the land at any time prior to their eviction. Promises were made in the past and broken; this was another promise clearly wrapped in a bitter pill of intent. It was time to go. On June 1, 1843, subagent Purdy McElvain reported that the tribe was busy making preparations to move. Property such as cattle, hogs, furniture, and farm implements were sold.[88] McElvain indicated that the tribe should be ready to leave by the first of June. Unfortunately, the departure was delayed until July, as property deemed too valuable to surrender to the whites still needed to be sold.

On June 2, 1843, George Ironside Clarke, a Canadian Wyandot who chose to move west with the tribe, and Silas Armstrong, an Ohio Wyandot, arrived in Indian Territory to make preparations for the arrival of the tribe. Both Clarke and Armstrong were considered wealthy Wyandots. Clarke would serve the tribe on a number of occasions as principal chief and also as a Methodist preacher. Armstrong was the owner of the trading store at Upper Sandusky that was closed not long before the Wyandots departed town. Upon arriving in the west, Armstrong reopened his trading store in a rented building in Westport, Missouri.[89] Westport lay about two miles south from where the tribe would initially settle into hardship and misery.

On Sunday, July 9, 1843, the entire Wyandot Tribe, at least the six hundred sixty-four souls who intended to move west, assembled at Upper Sandusky. One last service was held on the grounds of the Mission Church. Reverend Wheeler presided over the service and preached the last farewell sermon. Squire Greyeyes, also an ordained Methodist minister, delivered to those assembled a rousing farewell speech in Wandat. Squire Greyeyes eulogized the Wyandot Tribe's departure from Ohio.

> My people, the time for our departure is at hand. A few words remain only to be said. Our entire nation has gathered here for farewell. We have this morning met together for the last time in our Love Feast. More than two hundred have testified to the great power of God. Brother Wheeler has preached the funeral for our dead—our John Stewart, our beloved Mononcue, our recently

murdered Summundewat, our eloquent Between-The-Logs. They sleep the sleep of death, but the hope of immortality is strong within our breasts. Our chiefs have committed to the care our White Brothers, our temple; to the Great Spirit, the grave of the Wyandots. The Indian does not forget the pale-faced brother who came to him with the message from the Great Spirit, and who loved him well and served him well.

The White Man's God has become the Indian's God, and with us go ever to our new home, our beloved shepherd, Brother Wheeler, and sister Lucy Armstrong, the Wyandot bride. Surely like the white-faced truth of all that she says: "Whither thou goest, I will go and where thou lodgest [*sic*], I will lodge; thy people shall be my people, and thy God my God; where thy diest [*sic*] I will die, and there will I be buried."

It remains only for me to say farewell. Yes, it is indeed farewell. No more shall we engage in the solemn feast, or the feast of rejoicing. No more shall Sandusky's Plains and forests echo to the voice of song and praise. No more shall we assemble in our Temple to sing the sacred songs and hear the story of the Cross. Here our dead are buried. We have placed fresh flowers upon their graves for the last time. No longer shall we visit them. Soon they shall be forgotten, for the onward march of the strong White Man will not turn aside for the Indian graves. Farewell—Farewell Sandusky River. Farewell—Farewell our hunting grounds and homes. Farewell to the stately trees and forests. Farewell to the Temple of the Great Spirit. Farewell to our White Brothers, and friends, and neighbors. It is but a little time for us till we leave our earthly home; for here we are no continuing city, but we seek one that is to come, whose builder and maker is God. Let us remember the dying words of Brother Stewart: Be Faithful.[90]

Reverend Wheeler was encouraged by Bishop Roberts to make the trip west with his congregation in spite of the recent loss of a child. Initially, both he and his wife Caroline were reluctant, but they understood that if they abandoned the tribe, all could be lost and the work of the Church undone in very short order. Through trials and hardship equally suffered alongside his Church, they would both serve the tribe with compassion and loyalty until May of 1846.[91] As the majority of the tribe left Upper Sandusky on Wednesday, July 12, Reverend Wheeler began a journal account of the trip, and he documented the events as the tribe passed through Bellefontaine, Urbana, Springfield, Xenia, Lebanon, and the final destination of Cincinnati on Wednesday, July 19.

There were six hundred nine Wyandot from Ohio, twenty-five from Michigan, and thirty from Canada. In one of Reverend Wheeler's first journal accounts, he observed that many Wyandot citizens were leaving with a solemn countenance as if they were attending the funeral of a departed friend. It is easy to envision white families immediately occupying many of their homes the next morning or in the next few days. These white families stepped into fields already plowed, drew water from wells that were deep and wet, and indulged in the sweet sap of many maple trees. Undoubtedly, many of the same families the next Sunday morning attended church and held hands while singing hymns of praise to their Lord and God just as the Wyandots did days before— to the very same God.

I can also imagine many of these same white families holding a church social, a picnic basket lunch, near the cemetery in the same field earlier occupied by the departing Wyandots. They celebrated the final and glorious removal of those savage Indians from *their* land. In contrast many white families lamented over the loss of some of their dearest friends and most loyal neighbors—the Wyandot Indians. The injustice of it all was the first obstacle the Wyandot people had to overcome. As the familiar sites of Upper Sandusky faded below the horizon, that injustice would be hard to overcome.

When passing through the outskirts of Bellefontaine, a local reporter with the *Logan Gazette* praised the Wyandots: "The tribe move themselves, and deserve credit for the order and decorum they observe. During the greater part of two days they were passing our village, we noticed but one drunken man. They were sober in conduct, as well as countenance."[92] A prideful people, prepared and persistent, yet plagued with whiskey peddlers along the whole of the route to Cincinnati. The one drunken man seen at Bellefontaine was not representative of the tribe—many were drunk! Reverend Wheeler observed that whiskey peddlers, at least most of them, were very much like the devil: The more mischief they create, the more they were pleased. They snuck into the camps at night and stood in the bright light of day ready to indulge those who could not cope with the loss of their homes. Throughout the trip there was no protection for the tribe as provided in the treaty. The US government abandoned the Wyandot Tribe. Sentries were posted at night, and a defensive force was organized to protect citizens along the way; however, the whites stole horses, wagon harnesses, food, personal belongings, and even linchpins out of the wagons. It was madness, a free-for-all, and any possession of the Wyandots was a grand prize. The Wyandot Indians were a once-in-a-lifetime grand spectacle being paraded across the state of Ohio, yet they never relinquished their dignity and pride.

Just fifty years earlier most of Ohio belonged to the Indians, and much of it was Wyandot land. As the tribe made its way south from town to town, many of the whites had never seen an Indian, let alone a Wyandot. There were such high expectations and great eagerness to see the Indians; it was as if a circus was coming to town and people were lined up to see the exotic animals. Even though the town residents meant no harm, they surrounded and often crowded the wagons in hope of a closer look or to claim a memento of the once-in-a-lifetime occasion. Reverend Wheeler indicated that many citizens thought the whites were in need of being taught some manners.

Upon reaching Urbana, Principal Chief Henry Jacquis and many leading men left the tribe for an official visit to Columbus, the state capital of Ohio. There Chief Jacquis bid Governor Wilson Shannon an official farewell. Chief Jacquis expressed the tribe's kind and warm feelings for the people of Ohio and reiterated the long-standing peace and friendship enjoyed by both. Governor Wilson Shannon is said to have replied in like manner.[93]

A few days before arriving in Cincinnati a delegation of leading men were sent ahead to make way and prepare for the arrival. A bidding war ensued as captains fought over the opportunity to transport citizens west. The captains of the steamboats Nodaway and Republic won the contest and were contracted to take the Wyandots to the western border of Missouri. This would cost the tribe $4,500, almost half of what the government allocated for the entire trip west.[94]

Before entering Cincinnati on July 19, the wagon teams were first to arrive and unload the citizens' personal possessions and cargo. Armed guards had to be placed on the docks to prevent the personal possessions, what little remained, from being stolen. As tribal citizens began entering the waterfront, Reverend Wheeler described the scene. He lamented, "We are in the midst of danger, toil and death." He continued by describing a horse taking fright and the driver of its wagon being thrown and run over, breaking bones amid the busy, bustling crowd. Across the way a body was seen hanging by the arm still in the water after falling from a boat and drowning. The cry of fire onboard one of the boats bobbing on the river caused an alarm, but the fire was promptly extinguished. In the middle of the chaos a sick Wyandot child belonging to the widow Half-John died. If not for Reverend Wheeler, the death of this child would have gone unnoticed. Another team of horses took fright and stampeded. Residents of Cincinnati, as in the smaller towns, tried

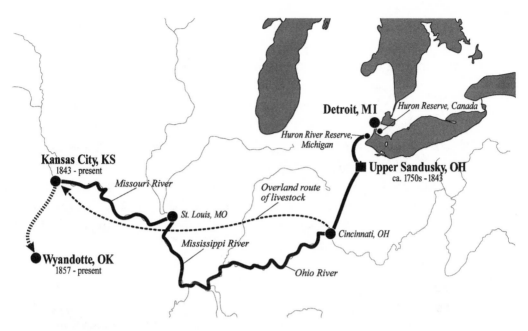

MAP 4.3. The Route to Indian Territory

their hardest to press in close and get a glimpse of the Indians. The whiskey peddlers, yes, they were also on the docks, like blood- and life-sucking leaches.

Throughout the day whites entered the two steamboats, and the captains forcibly removed them from the decks; however, one overzealous and curious white brought measles on board. This pestilence could not be as easily removed.[95] Once tribal citizens were on board, the planks of the two ships were withdrawn to impede further incursions from the crowd. As the steamboats were secured, they provided the first sense of safety since leaving Upper Sandusky. One of Reverend Wheeler's last entries for Wednesday, July 19, indicated, "Another donation in Bibles has been received from the friends in this place, which will be disposed of according to the design of the donors." Matthew Walker was dispatched to the west with a select and reliable group of young men. Their task was to drive over land all the horses and livestock yet retained by the tribe.

An elderly Wyandot, Mrs. Bull-head, was ill upon leaving Upper Sandusky. Near the small town of Xenia, a doctor was brought to her, but due to her age and poor condition his interventions were of no use. Mrs. Bull-head died within moments of being placed upon one of the steamboats. Her body, and that of the widow Half-John's young child, were given to Cincinnati's coroner for a proper burial. The body of James B. F. Driver was never recovered from the Ohio River. He, being drunk, fell from one of the steamships and his body was never recovered. The tribe was fortunate and suffered just three deaths before leaving Ohio. If only the tribe's fate had been so auspicious upon arriving in Indian Territory. Unfortunately, it was not!

The newspapermen were also in Cincinnati. After observing the chaos on the dock, an editor wrote the next morning, "Perhaps they are indifferent and we hope they are. . . . Just civilized enough to have lost their savage courage they go forth on the broad prairies of the west, like sheep among wolfs [sic]."[96] The Wyandot Tribe had lost nothing; their courage was intact. How could a cowardly people have done what the Wyandot did? The tribe withstood the relentless pressure of the United States longer than any other tribe in Ohio. Along the journey the tribe lost three citizens to death: a young child, an old lady, and a young man in the prime of his life.

On July 21, 1843, the Nodaway and the Republic left Cincinnati. Within an hour, Principal Chief Henry Jacquis requested Captain Cleghorn of the Nodaway to immediately stop the steamboat.[97] The tomb of former President William Henry Harrison lay just ahead overlooking the Ohio River at North Bend. While silently drifting with the strong, swift current, Chief Jacquis stood with his chancellors and leading men facing the shore and tomb of General Harrison. The Wyandot Tribe's proud warriors lined the hurricane deck of both ships. The silence was deafening as the dark and formerly bloody water could be heard lapping against the hulls. Many older warriors on the ships fought alongside General Harrison during the War of 1812. The memories of those last battles were both very bitter and very sweet. As the ships silently floated past the sacred tomb of a respected and beloved warrior from the old days, a volley was fired from the big gun aboard the Nodaway.

The cannon boom broke the silence with a disruptive roar. All hats were removed and waved with respect. With a voice of thunder comparable only to Henǫ's, Chief Jacquis exclaimed, *"Farewell Ohio and her brave!"*[98] Chief Jacquis's voice overcame and silenced the cannon's boom. After a momentary pause, the paddle wheels began to again grip and tear the water's surface as the Wyandot people now looked west toward the unknown.

I want to close this chapter with a very obscure quote from The Reverend Nathaniel Barrett Coulson (N. B. C.) Love. The following quote is the closing to a very short article titled "The Old Mission." All the missionaries from the Methodist Episcopal Church who labored among the Wyandots did everything they could to help prepare the Wyandots to live alongside the whites as productive citizens of Ohio and Michigan. In spite of not being citizens of the United States of America, in 1843 citizens of the Wyandot Tribe were in many cases more civilized and loyal to the United States than many of the white Americans who surrounded them on all sides. Not willing to give up their heritage, the Wyandots did everything asked of them by the US government, even to the extent of moving west and surrendering their lands. *"Farewell Ohio and her brave!"* were the last words spoken in this chapter of the Wyandot Tribe's history.

The following, written by Reverend Love in 1869, speaks for all the various tribes then living upon the Great Island on land governed by the United States of America. It stands as an epitaph to the closing of the Indian Wars in the east and a prophecy to the doctrines of total and forced assimilation yet to be experienced.

> The footprints of the Indian are disappearing, and if half the money expended by the Government in their extermination were employed in their civilization, better results would follow. Let the old church [in Upper Sandusky] long stand as a monument of successful missionary labor.[99]

"Strangers in a Strange Land"

Since our arrival here we have had much sickness. . . . Deaths since we left there is 49: this bill of mortality was confined principally to young children diseases I think contracted on the boat including the unhealthy situation of their encampment it being on a low bottom.[1]
—Matthew Walker, 1843

The Decisions We Make

While doing research for this book, I was thumbing through files within the Wyandotte Nation historical archives when I found a tribal letterhead that was surprisingly and unexpectedly different. The letterhead was dated April 19, 1976, and it stopped my research for the day. The letterhead was imprinted with the name "Wyandot Tribe of Oklahoma." In addition, the letterhead carried a willow tree emblem very similar to the one used today by the Wyandot Nation of Kansas. At first glance I though the letter was correspondence from Kansas, but there is no way that was possible since the tribal name included Oklahoma.

A few file folders earlier I had passed another letterhead that did not command my attention; however, I promptly went back and relocated the letter. This letterhead was dated April 1, 1977, and the tribal name was "Wyandotte Tribe of Oklahoma." Unlike the first letterhead, this one carried our glorious turtle, the original traditional version, designed by the late Edward "Ed" Faber, a good friend of the Wyandottes from Upper Sandusky. Today our tribal emblem is a modernized version of Faber's classic turtle I redesigned in May of 1991 at the request of then Chief Leaford Bearskin.

I remember questioning Sherri Clemons, the Wyandotte Nation Tribal Heritage Department Director, why the letterhead from 1976 was using the

FIGURE 5.1. Leonard Nicholas Cotter Sr.

name "Wyandot" Tribe of Oklahoma. Sherri had no idea why. The Wyandotte's 1937 tribal constitution established the spelling of the tribal name as Wyandotte. The only logical explanations I could gather were that Chief Leonard Cotter used "Wyandot" as a matter of personal preference; or it was a typographic error; or, because of the presence of the willow tree, we have ourselves a conspiracy. I have no doubt that Cotter would have shunned all resemblances of anything deemed questionable; therefore, a conspiracy is highly improbable.

Like many of his contemporaries, Cotter undoubtedly held a limited knowledge of *Huron*-Wyandot tribal history and traditional culture. However, being the grandson of Chief Nicholas Cotter, and having a close personal relationship with then–tribal historian Charles Aubrey Buser, Leonard Cotter likely possessed knowledge of the tribe's history then unknown by most citizens. Chief Leonard Cotter died in office on November 18, 1976, and it was Chief Mont Cotter who changed the willow tree to Faber's turtle and corrected the spelling of the tribe's name.

Chief Leonard Cotter served his people as chief during three separate periods: 1936–42, 1948–54, and 1963–76, for a total of twenty-five years. Only Chief Leaford Bearskin served his people as head chief longer: twenty-eight years, since the Wyandotte Tribe was reorganized in Indian Territory in 1867. If Chief Cotter had not died in office, he would have undoubtedly served his people even longer. Unlike Chief Bearskin, Chief Cotter also served his people as second chief during the years of 1932–36 and 1954–63. This gives Chief Leonard Cotter the unrivaled distinction of serving his people longer than any other contemporary chief—an amazing thirty-seven years!

Like his grandfather who traveled to Washington, DC, one hundred years earlier in 1877, Chief Cotter traveled to Washington, DC, in 1976. While there representing the Wyandotte people, Chief Cotter met President Gerald R. Ford. It was during this time that Chief Cotter championed an all-out effort for the reform of many social issues and focused on obtaining the Wyandotte Tribe's reinstatement as a federally recognized tribe. I would have loved visiting with Chief Cotter. One question I would have asked is Why did you use the name "Wyandot Tribe of Oklahoma?"

Recently many questions have arisen regarding the possible reunification of the three bands of Wyandot people. Tribal members from the Wyandot of Anderdon Nation and the Wyandot Nation of Kansas have been unable to seek citizenship within the Wyandotte Nation. Some feel that this rule is unfair and appears as if Oklahoma is denying the Wyandot their heritage. Some have even stated that the name "Wyandotte Nation" invokes division as it mocks and insults the other two bands simply because Oklahoma no longer appears as part of the name. The other two bands use a geographical reference. The Wyandotte Nation officially dropped all references to Oklahoma in 1999; therefore, some say the tribe is purposefully presenting itself as being superior to and dominant over the other two bands. This is untrue, but then again the Wyandotte Nation is the only federally recognized tribe of the three bands. The name was changed to better represent the tribe and better position its legal relationship not only with the United States of America and the state of Oklahoma, but with all state and corporate entities. In addition, with citizens spread across the United States and the world, the geographic location—of Oklahoma—is no longer exclusively valid. The name Wyandotte Nation is a better representation of the tribal or national status both politically and socially.

I have always said that we are the same people, Wyandot or Wyandotte, that the spelling of the name doesn't really matter—or does it? Why the difference? Why are there three bands of Wyandots? It is within the time frame of this chapter that the split between Wyandot and Wyandotte occurred. During the one hundred fifty years since the split occurred, the histories, traditions, and ideologies of the three bands have progressed separately from a common cultural heritage. Chief Cotter must have known of the historical implications of spelling the tribal name as Wyandot Tribe of Oklahoma. The 1937 tribal constitution, the one under which Chief Cotter served and was instrumental in writing, declared the name to be the Wyandotte Tribe of Oklahoma. The correct and legal spelling of the name is very important; however, I admit, for historical purposes I would prefer the spelling of the tribal name as Wiandót or Wyandot.

The issues regarding the spelling of the names and potential reunification of the three bands are a social and political nightmare. Many people quickly become confused, others combative, and some sympathetic to a cause they truly do not understand. Many generations have passed since the Wyandots split into three bands, and it's hard for many to accept the reality of the fate as still being binding. Others seem to carry a grudge for reasons they cannot remember. If it's of any comfort, the Wyandots are not the only Indian people dealing with this issue. Other tribes have very similar circumstances in their histories. The big difference in comparison to many of the other tribes is that only one of three, the Wyandotte Nation, is federally recognized, and for good reasons.

In the early nineteenth century the Detroit Wyandot who moved to Canada after the War of 1812 were considered citizens of the Crown, or Canadian citizens. Here in the United States, after the Treaty of 1855 most, but not all, Wyandots willingly forfeited their right to be citizens of the Wyandot Tribe in exchange for US citizenship. Afterwards, the relationship between the Citizen and Indian Party Wyandots became highly contested and divisive.

The United States of America did not divide the Wyandot people, nor is it the current leadership of the Wyandotte Nation who keeps the Wyandot people separated. The United States and chiefs of the Indian Party Wyandots provided a way for the complete reunification of all Wyandots in 1867 after the short, yet difficult, twelve years of dissolution following the Treaty of 1855. Not many people took advantage of the invitation to seek adoption into the Wyandotte Tribe, as it was being reorganized in Indian Territory, for many no longer desired to be Wyandotte. Yes, I have no doubt there were some who missed out on the opportunity to again be Wyandotte due to misguided fate; however, knowing who purposefully chose to deny their heritage, and who fell to fate, is not today easily proved. The fact that many who once identified themselves as Wyandot no longer wanted to be identified as Wyandotte did not mean they were no longer Indians. These people were then US citizens of American Indian descent—they just could not identify themselves as being Wyandotte citizens.

This chapter is not intended to demote the tribal members of the Wyandot of Anderdon Nation or the Wyandot Nation of Kansas. It is my hope to explain what happened so long ago—nothing more. Much groundwork will have to be laid until we can fully understand how the Wyandot people became divided and why reunification is not yet a viable proposal. At times it may appear I am taking a critical stance, but I can assure everyone this is not the case. I am a realist and have a hard time painting fuzzy feel-good notions when at times things are simply black and white. I have formed some wonderful and cherished relationships with many tribal members from Anderdon and Kansas, and the thought of losing these friendships is troubling; however, questions have been raised and answers need to be provided.

The Wyandot people became divided through the culmination of the passing of time, inevitability, selfish decisions, and terrible fate. What happened long ago seems so distant, benign, and irrelevant to today's generation of Wyandots. When living in a sense of today's reality, and the immediacy it commands, we too often forget that the decisions we make can and will affect future generations. Semi-isolation of the Wyandots in the Ohio, Michigan, and Kansas wilderness in the late eighteenth and early nineteenth centuries seems to indemnify them for the decisions they would make. No, the Wyandot were intelligent, cunning, well educated, and wise to the ways in which the world was changing.

The Wyandot people would not be here today if their ancestors had been anything less. In *A History of Northwest Ohio,* Nevin Winter stated, "At the time of the settlement of Northwest Ohio, the Wyandots were admitted to be the leading nation among the Indian tribes of the Northwest. This was not because of numbers, but for the reason that they were more intelligent and more civilized in their manner of life."[2] After the Wyandots moved west of the Mississippi River, and as things began to unravel in Kansas Territory, many hard decisions needed to be made. The Wyandot's chiefs and leading men would again unite the various tribes and devise a magnificent plan to preserve their way of life the best they could. As we will see, this plan was so complex and brilliant that it still confuses many historians to this very day. William E. Connelley explains, "It was plain to the intelligent Indians that the tribes would soon be compelled to move. If they must sell their lands, they wanted as good a price as could be obtained. To enhance the value of their lands it was necessary that white men should have liberty to settle in their vicinity, in numbers, and for the purpose of allowing them to do so the Indian tribes themselves moved for the organization of Nebraska Territory."[3] The Wyandots knew what they were doing; I just don't think they comprehended the generational consequences their decisions could carry.

Conquer or Be Conquered

The Wyandot Tribe was the last Indian tribe to leave Ohio in July of 1843. Upon heading west on the steamboats *Republic* and *Nodaway,* they hoped things would be different from and better than what they were leaving behind. It is believed Silas Armstrong was the chief planner and organizer of the removal efforts once the Wyandot's fate in Ohio was sealed. Armstrong's efficiency and attention to even the minor details are most impressive; however, he overlooked one massive detail. This detail, regardless of its ominous and critical omission, cannot be attributed to Silas as being his fault. Where was the tribe moving? Yes, the tribe was moving to Indian Territory, but an exact location with land set aside and waiting had not been established. It would take about six months after arriving at the confluence of the Missouri and Kansas rivers before land would be purchased as their own. Even then its security would remain in doubt.

The Wyandot elected to make their trip west as comfortable and speedy as possible by hiring the services of two steamboats to transport their citizens by way of the Ohio and Missouri rivers. The steamboat *Nodaway* was the larger of the two vessels and carried the majority of citizens. During the trip, events on the steamboat were not respectful of the people who had contracted its services. Lucy Bigelow Armstrong, wife of John McIntire Armstrong, was a passenger onboard the *Nodaway.* Lucy later reminisced of the ordeal:

It had been agreed between [us and] the captain that the first payments of fare should be paid at Louisville Falls, the second at St. Louis, and the third at Lexington, Missouri. All went smoothly until the boat passed Louisville, and the first payment had been made. The boat was nicely furnished, and the voyagers were well treated up to that point. The captain then seemed to become possessed with the apprehension that the Wyandots would ruin his furnishings. He, therefore, ripped up the carpets and packed them away, put his patrons on short allowance, and otherwise imposed upon them, and made them uncomfortable. The worst of it, however, was yet to come.

When the Nodaway finally arrived at the intersection of the West line of the state of Missouri with the Missouri River, the sun was down and a heavy dew was on the grass. There was only one small house which could be occupied, and the captain was requested to allow his passengers to remain on the boat over night. He replied that he must go to St. Joe that night, and the Wyandots were turned out like sheep by a heartless shepherd. There was only a small spot which was treeless, and here the men, women, and children huddled together over night. . . . Early in the morning the boat was still at the landing, the "hands" having spent much of the night in putting down the carpets again, and "putting things to rights." It is little wonder that when the tired and faint and sick band of travelers perceived this additional harsh treatment, the Captain and his boat were privately and publicly anathematized [cursed].[4]

The steamboat *Republic* arrived at its destination on July 28, 1843, followed by the *Nodaway* three days later on July 31. Without any land assigned for their arrival, the Wyandot Tribe would temporarily claim an undeveloped strip of land lying between the state of Missouri and the Kansas River called the French Bottoms. The French Bottoms, known today as the West Bottoms, received its name as being the place where French traders and trappers conducted trade with the Kansas (Kaw) Indians.[5]

The western boundary of Missouri ran south from the confluence of the Kansas and Missouri rivers. This invisible line essentially divided the French Bottoms so that approximately four hundred acres of land lay in Indian Territory and six hundred acres lay in the state of Missouri. Since the French Bottoms was essentially abandoned land, it would be safe to assume the six hundred fifty Wyandots, or thereabout, set up camp throughout the whole of the French Bottoms. It would be unlikely they confined themselves west of the invisible line that divided the swampy land. Try and imagine six hundred fifty people with all of their personal belongings and livestock living on maybe at best one thousand acres. The living conditions would have been appalling and demoralizing, especially knowing you just gave up some of the best land in the state of Ohio.

After being obtained by the United States as a part of the Louisiana Purchase, the French Bottoms had initially been designated as the place for a new military fort. The fort was never built, and the land essentially became unallocated federal land. The land was prone to flooding, a swampy floodplain, and thus considered unsuitable for human habitation. This little worthless and uninhabitable piece of land was now the home of the Wyandot Tribe.

Fortunately, a few wealthy Wyandot citizens were able to rent homes in nearby Westport, Missouri. A vast majority of the tribe would be exposed to the elements and camped on the swampy, muggy land. Just a few weeks earlier they were comfortably yet nervously huddled in their homes contemplating the move. I can't help imagining that they expected difficult times; however, what awaited them is the thing of nightmares. They were not fully prepared for the worst that was yet to come. Makeshift camps, tents, and soggy blankets spread on the bare, wet ground were primitive and barbaric. The conditions were inhumane, and many citizens would pay the ultimate price for being Indian. Upon his arrival, William Walker Jr. secured a comfortable location for his family in Westport and then wrote to a friend back home in Columbus, Ohio.

> We have landed near to our future home. . . . I have been employed busily since we landed in collecting and getting under shelter my household goods and in getting a house to live in temporarily. . . . My company are all about two miles above this place, some in tents, some in houses, and some under the expanded branches of the tall cotton wood trees. You cannot imagine my feelings on landing . . . and hunting a shelter for the family—faces all strange—we feel truly like strangers in a strange land.[6]

Walker's company, his people, were hurting in ways he at the moment could not begin to imagine and feel for himself. It was a slow and invisible hurt. It was indeed a strange land, and for the first time in a long time the people felt alone and totally abandoned. Where were their friends? The Wyandot people were homeless and hurting, yet no one complained. Everyone pitched in, stepped up, and went to work. This is what Wyandots do. Remember, they do not turn their back to an enemy, no matter what shape or form the enemy may present.

The Wyandot's old friends the Shawnee were across the river, as were the Delaware. It would be the Delaware who remembered their kindness and hospitality in Ohio when they too were once homeless. Back in the mid-eighteenth century the Wyandot laid claim to the majority of the state of Ohio and gave the Delaware, as they did the Shawnee, a significant piece of land to live on. The Delaware would return the token of hospitality. The Shawnee would betray their original intent to sell land and snub the Wyandot's Ohio hospitality.

When the Wyandot Tribe departed Upper Sandusky in July of 1843, there were families and individuals who chose to remain behind in both Ohio and Canada. As the main body of Wyandots reconciled and settled into a new life in Indian Territory, those who had remained in Canada continued to elect their own chiefs and formed their own tribal government. They did not have a desire to leave their homes and move west. The Wyandot on the *Huron* Reserve in Canada were capable of continuing outside the main body of Wyandots. Land in Canada was first set aside for the Canadian Wyandot in 1791.[7] Chief Francis Joseph Warrow was the first to permanently make the move to Canada from the United States in 1798.[8]

After the War of 1812 all Canadian Wyandot were considered subjects of the Crown, or Canadian citizens, regardless of whether they were born in Canada or the United States. There was a committed Wyandot presence in Canada until the last of the *Huron* Reserve was sold in 1892; it became the township of Anderdon. Then all Canadian Wyandots essentially became assimilated. Some individuals and families moved back to the United States beginning in 1895.[9] With no official tribal government recognized by either the Americans or the Canadians, the Canadian Wyandot integrated into local society. They have never forgotten who they are and have since resumed their own election of chiefs and a tribal council. Active membership in the tribe is obtained through the payment of annual dues. Without access to federal funding or tribal economic developmental initiatives, the tribe's ability to provide services to tribal members is unfortunately very limited.

Even before a large number of the Wyandots living on the *Huron* River Reserve moved to Canada in the early nineteenth century, they had been keeping their own chiefs alongside those from Upper Sandusky. These chiefs often took a different geopolitical stance against Upper Sandusky. The Wyandot of Anderdon Nation is Wyandot in the boldest sense. They are strong, independent, defiant, and resourceful survivors even under the most adverse and seemingly insurmountable conditions.

Both bands quickly ventured down different paths and focused on the specific needs of their people. Each had to deal with the American or Canadian governments in similar fashion, as land rights, assimilation, and cultural preservation were common issues facing both bands. Today the Wyandot in Michigan are the Wyandot of Anderdon Nation. They have sought, but have yet to claim, recognition from either the United States or the Canadian governments. The tribal members of Anderdon have not been on Wyandot tribal rolls since choosing to stay in Canada when the main body of the tribe moved west in 1843.

A few individuals, Peter D. Clarke being the most celebrated, did at times move back and forth between the two bands, holding dual citizenship. The tribal councils of both bands often found this a conflict of interest and established precedence stating that it's in the best interest of both the tribe and the citizens that only one band be chosen and given allegiance with citizenship. Both bands are undeniably Wyandot, but each had different accountabilities that needed to be upheld. Clearly both the Canadian and the American Wyandots were functioning as two independent and sovereign tribes. The Wyandot who remained in Ohio or returned back to Ohio from Indian Territory did not form any governmental base. They were quickly absorbed into the surrounding communities and over time denied or forgot their heritage.

In the mid-nineteenth century things were very fluid between Indian Territory, Ohio, and Canada. It was a very confusing and unsettling time. For years after moving to Indian Territory, the Wyandot tribal council debated the status of Wyandots who would show up late. Most were added to the rolls; however, a few were not given full tribal status or access to tribal funds and resources.

Back at the French Bottoms the Shawnee defiantly refused to sell a portion of their land as promised in the unratified treaty of 1839. The Shawnee never sold or gave the Wyandots one acre of land. They apparently did not want to incite the Americans by honoring their promise after the US Congress invalidated the treaty. In stark contrast to the Shawnee's inaction, the Delaware, in a move of bold defiance, friendship, loyalty, and sympathetic compassion, gave the Wyandot a small plot of land on their reservation, "a beautiful spot of ground on a high ridge, in a shady grove, as a burial place for dead."[10]

The plot was located on the top of a hill about a half-mile west of where the Wyandots were encamped. Many were buried in unmarked graves, and their locations are still unknown to this day. In a sad, ironic twist of fate, one of the earliest confirmed burials is that of Warpole on November 17, 1843.[11] Warpole was determined to get his people out of Ohio so that they could remain Indians unscathed by white influence. Warpole lived to see his desire fulfilled, but he never saw the new homeland. Due to old age—it's believed he was sixty-eight—and exposure to the new climate, Warpole succumbed to death.[12]

Throughout the latter half of 1843 tribal leaders frantically yet futilely searched for 148,000 acres they could rightfully and legally claim according to the Treaty of 1842. Of all the vast amount of land available in Indian Territory, according to the US government, very little was left unclaimed. On the Josiah Gregg map of 1844 showing Indian Territory, the strip of land along the Missouri border just above the Cherokee Outlet was designated as belonging to the Wyandot. This would be a swath of land running from the Missouri state line west and encompassing the present-day city of Fort Scott, Kansas. Unfortunately, the tribal council rejected the land in 1839, and it was then promised to the New York Indians—but the New York Indians never laid claim to the land. This was the land the Wyandot Tribe again wanted; however, the government said they could not have it, not now, not ever. During this period there were many other maps that show the Wyandot name inked-in various places throughout Indian Territory. It was a very confusing time.

The Munson map of 1845 indicated that the Wyandot's new home was located on the Kansas and Nebraska state line, or thereabout. Unfortunately, if the Wyandot had chosen this location as their home, one of their closest neighbors would have been the Sauk and Fox. Going back to the early eighteenth century, peace had nominally been established between the two nations, and renewed hostilities would have been all but assured. Wyandot tribal leaders did not fear the Sauk and Fox; however, they did not want a war. It was already early summer, the tribe was living in a swamp, and they did not have any crops planted for the coming winter. A move to this parcel of land so close to the Sauk and Fox, without ample preparation and resources, would have strategically compromised the tribe. The tribe barely had enough resources to feed the people, let alone sustain the shortest skirmish or a protracted war. It was also clear that the Sauk and Fox did not want a war with the Wyandot—in the past, the Fox never fared well in those wars.

Four years after arriving in Indian Territory, Peter D. Clarke was in attendance during an intertribal council held in October of 1848. The Wyandot's position in the territory was now firmly established, yet the tribe's susceptibility to hard times had not been fully eliminated. The Wyandot were still the newcomers, but they brought with them from Ohio and Michigan strength, resilience, respect, a reputation, and history no other tribe was willing to outwardly contest. At this council all the tribes from the old Northwest Indian Confederacy reinstated the Wyandot as Keepers of the Council Fire. The Fox were invited and initially attended the council with much wariness.

A group of Fox Indians were noticed to be rather reserved and distant at this general Council, and who knew of a certain dark bead belt then in the hands of the Wyandotts, with the shape of a tomahawk of a red colour on it, indicating some contemplated warfare whenever it was exhibited in a general Council. They knew, too, of the hostile incursions their forefathers used to make against the Wyandotts and other tribes about Detroit, over a century ago; how they were chastised by them at different times, and that they never made peace with each other.

The group of Fox Indians watched the Wyandotts with an eagle eye, and no sooner than they observed the crimson tomahawk exhibited, than they were off to their homes on their ponies, followed by wolfish-looking dogs.[13]

With the Wyandot unable to find suitable land, negotiations commenced in October of 1843 with the Delaware to sell a small portion of their reservation. As the negotiations were underway, the Delaware allowed the Wyandots to move their encampments onto their land. The Delaware were not afraid to do what was right. The area of the reservation they allowed the Wyandot to move was essentially uninhabited and a distance from the Sauk and Fox so as not to entice an unwanted war.

On December 14, 1843, an agreement was made between the Wyandot and Delaware that would allow the purchase of 23,040 acres, or thirty-six sections of land for $46,080. For the day this was a highly inflated price of $2.00 per acre. What else could the Wyandot chiefs and leading men do but accept their offer? There were no other choices to be had. Could the $2.00 an acre be the first documented case of land speculation and price inflation that would soon consume Kansas? The agreed terms were to be paid out over a period of ten years. The Delaware in respect and honor gave the Wyandot Tribe an additional three sections, or 1,920 acres of land, in remembrance of the Wyandot's gift to them while in Ohio. The agreement, and the land purchased by the Wyandot from the Delaware, is known as the Wyandot Purchase.

The spring of 1844 in Indian Territory had been warm and very dry. Then it started to rain in May and did not stop for six weeks. Nothing short of a deluge reminiscent of the Good Twin's piercing the bag of water after being taken captive by his Bad Twin ensued. The tributaries of the Missouri and Kansas rivers, extending all the way back into central Kansas, were well above flood stage. The Flood of 1844 was of historic proportions and was one of the greatest floods ever recorded in the United States. Driftwood and the carcasses of dead animals littered trees like Christmas ornaments many feet above the ground. There the dead animals began to rot, and their putrid droppings began to drip like rain—toxic rain of death. Along the creeks, streams, and rivers it looked and smelled like a war zone. This surrounded Wyandot citizens who were busy settling in and rebuilding their lives and homes on the new Wyandot Purchase.

Frenchmen, known as Papans, were living among the Kansas Indians near present-day Topeka over sixty miles from the confluence of the Kansas and Missouri rivers. The Papans noted that the Kansas River had swollen to eight or ten feet above flood stage.[14] The French Bottoms at the confluence of the Kansas and Missouri rivers in June of 1844 was covered with fourteen feet of water.[15] Six months earlier the Wyandots had arrived and were camping on these very grounds that now lay submerged. What would have happened if the rains came upon their arrival to this desolate and God-forsaken strip of land?

In early July as the waters began to subside, the mosquitoes swarmed in famished blood-seeking clouds. The humidity and heat hung in the air as a fog and would have been suffocating. A stench from the putrefying, rotting flesh and vegetation swept over the entire area. The ground along the rivers sloshed and sucked each foot that stepped into its swampy, infectious stew like quicksand. Flies swarmed below, vultures circled above, and no vegetation grew, as the ground was nothing less than a soaked and rotting sponge. Sickness quickly followed, but death would not be as quick. Death was an enduring occurrence that lasted for days, weeks, and months. The young and old alike fell to its fate, and the sight of the dead bodies did not extend any confidence that the move west had been the right choice for the Wyandot people. "Disease was also busy in the midst of the nation, the cause of it being the great flood of 1844. . . . The species of sickness, which prevailed the most and made the most havoc in the nation, were chills and fever and bloody flux. It [is] stated that there was not a single well person in the nation by the latter part of the fall of 1844."[16]

It's estimated that no fewer than one hundred tribal citizens eventually died from the diseases and their side effects: cholera, diarrhea, malaria, pneumonia, skin infections, oozing lesions, and fungal infections, all brought on by the flood of 1844. The mental stress of having to endure and watch so many people die was traumatic. In total, nearly one in six tribal citizens would die in six short months. The new land had already proven to be hard and unforgiving. Difficult times meant desperate measures, and one of two choices was presented: Conquer or be conquered. The Wyandot Tribe conquered and then thrived.

The Great Flood of 1844 and the fate of the Wyandots are given little attention by most historians. What do command great attention are the political and social events just before and after the Treaty of 1855. Many historians look back and say the Wyandot eventually sold and discarded this tiny piece of land for nothing less than the almighty dollar. That is an absolutely preposterous assumption; however, a few leading men did sell their souls to progress, riches, and fame. The price the Wyandot Tribe paid for the land far exceeded both the money paid to the Delaware Tribe and the value the whites eventually placed on its dirt they quickly covered with a bustling city. The dirt that was still damp with Wyandot blood, sweat, and tears when stamped with progress. Why would a people who truly cherished their land, and paid such an extraordinarily high price, just throw it all away? They would not! The plan devised by the Wyandot chief and leading men, with an intent to keep the land, was then, and remains today, too grand and complex for most historians to appreciate. Likewise, very few want to believe that a bunch of Indians were capable of devising and organizing a grand scheme to perpetually protect the land they had been assigned or purchased west of the Mississippi River.

The Richest and Most Valuable Territory

By the time the Wyandot Tribe left Ohio and Michigan, many, but not all, within the tribe had adopted cultural traits of the surrounding white population. Yes, by all standards then and now the Wyandot Tribe was civilized, but still very much Indian. The Wyandots lived traditional culture; however, it was compromised and no longer served a vital role in the daily lives of citizens as in the old days. The Wyandots did not possess US citizenship, whereas their Canadian brothers and sisters had already been deemed Canadian citizens. The tribe now occupied land in Indian Territory that was considered outside the boundaries of the United States. This land, as in Ohio, was held in common by citizens and could not be sold.

Wyandot citizens did not have any rights to conduct business equally with the nearby white population. This did not stop many leading men from becoming successful, and some individually wealthy. The one thing the Wyandot chiefs and leading men became suspiciously aware of was their lack of political representation. There was an Indian Agent who was supposed to be representing the tribe's interest and needs, but this did not mean the tribe had any say in determining their future. The pending and obvious crisis that loomed over their new home demanded they have more direct representation.

Since the tribe was now located outside the boundary of the United States, how could this happen?

The US Senate did not officially approve the sale of the Wyandot Purchase until July of 1848. Why did it take so long? Government officials were irritated and resentful over the tribe's rejection of their misguided proposal of land next to the Sauk and Fox. Furthermore, the government felt that the tribe overstepped its authority by directly contacting and making treaties with the Delaware. What else was the tribe to do? President Tyler and his government agents were being irresponsible by not honoring the stipulated 148,000 acres as guaranteed in the Treaty of 1842. They were not presenting any acceptable proposals or compromises. President Tyler was also uncertain of his legal rights outside those of the US Senate. After the Wyandot's rejection of land next to the Sauk and Fox, the government all but ignored tribal rights as found in the Treaty of 1842 and the Wyandot's proposed treaty with the Delaware Tribe. The government dangled the Wyandot Tribe on a string for over four and a half years, not knowing what their ultimate decision would be regarding the arrangement with the Delaware.

What if the treaty had not been ratified in 1848 or indeed had never been ratified? Before the proposed treaty had been ratified, and even continuing after it had been ratified, some in the tribe were proposing a move to Minnesota Territory. Why Minnesota Territory? It was close to Wisconsin. Do you remember the Wyandot's connection to Wisconsin? The Minnesota Territory was opened for settlement in 1849. The proponents of the move lost faith in the tribe's ability to stay in Indian Territory and remain a sovereign tribe. They felt the only way the tribe could remain sovereign was to move again. The notion of moving again was soundly defeated by a vote of the Nations Council, 72 to 5, on January 29, 1850.[17]

During the time it took the US Senate to ratify the treaty, the Wyandot turned what was virgin timber and prairie into a bountiful and very desirable little piece of land. The people did not sit back and do only as needed while waiting for a decision to be made by the US Senate. In true Wyandot fashion they went to work. The purchased land would be taken through a metamorphosis that was miraculous.

In October of 1848, upon receiving confirmation and gaining confidence that the Wyandot Purchase belonged to the Wyandot Tribe, the chief and leading men called upon their right to assemble the various tribes for council. The intent of the council was necessary and noble. It also was right in line with the logic being proposed by citizens who were saying that the tribe should move to Minnesota Territory. It was clear that the new, little piece of land would not remain in the possession of the Wyandots very long. Pearl W. Morgan, in *History of Wyandotte County Kansas and Its People,* eloquently relays what happened better than anyone else.

> The Indians of the northwestern confederacy, with the Wyandots at the head, were first to make a move to establish government for their hunting grounds. The Wyandots had brought with them then from Ohio a constitution and a form of civil government under which the tribes of that nation had been ruled wisely and well. Soon after they came to Kansas, efforts were made in congress to organize the Nebraska territory, which embraced in its limits the present state of Kansas and Nebraska. Stephen A. Douglas introduced bills for this purpose at different times; but they were referred to the committee on territories, without further action being taken. These different movements aroused great interest among the Indian tribes whose lands were within the boundaries of the proposed territory. It was evident to them that they must surrender their lands very soon if the territory was established, although the government in the treaties with them had promised that the land should be theirs as long as grass grew and water ran, and should never be a part of any territory or state. So, realizing the great importance of such an organization, these Indians desired to become citizens and to have a share in the shaping of affairs, that just and equitable laws might be made for the government of their beloved territory. The leading men of the different tribes called a convention for the purpose of discussing the matter. This congress met at or near Fort Leavenworth in October, 1848, with the following tribes represented, which had belonged to the ancient northwestern confederacy of Indian tribes: Wyandot, Delaware, Chippewa, Ottawa, Pottawatomie, Shawnee and Miami. Two other tribes were admitted to the confederacy at this time—the Kickapoo and the Kansas. The Sac and Fox were represented, but, as they were ancient enemies of the Wyandots and peace had not been declared between them, they were frightened by a speech made by one of the Wyandot representatives and fled from the convention. This convention continued in session for several days, and the old confederacy was organized, and the Wyandots were reappointed as its head and made keepers of the council-fire.[18]

Long before Morgan gave such an eloquent explanation of the Wyandot's intent, William Walker Jr. in an unsigned, but confirmed, manuscript indicated it was the Wyandot who took the first step toward formal representation in the US Congress. It may have been the Wyandot who took the lead and did much of the planning; however, it was not the Wyandot alone. All the emigrant tribes west of the Missouri state line were engaged in the planning and sought the same mutual goal. The following is about as simple as it gets. This is the reason Wyandot tribal leaders would initially seek dissolution, citizenship, and division of the land in severalty. They wanted a territory for the Indians governed by the Indians. Walker stated:

> It turned out that it was the Indians, not the indigenous, but the Emigrant Indians themselves especially the Wyandotts that warmly favored the occupation by white people of the vacant lands and ultimate organization of the territory. They foresaw that the pressure Westward and from the Pacific slope Eastward of emigration would ere long force the government to abandon its restrictive policy. The Wyandotts and such whites as were within their [tribe] took the initiatory step, by holding an election for a Delegate to Congress in the fall of 1852.[19]

> It is here worthy of remark that in each of the emigrant tribes of Indians elections were held and they voluntarily and freely participated in them; showing clearly that they anticipated and were prepared for the change in their political condition which they saw would soon be wrought out.[20]

Wyandot chiefs, councilors, and leading men saw no other choice in the matter and wanted to proactively exert a little self-destiny, self-governance, and self-control. They had hoped to establish a territory and eventually a state within the United States of America for the Indians—self-governed by the Indians. The only way they could do this was to become US citizens and residents of a territory or state within the union. Indian Territory, despite its name "Territory," was then considered outside the boundaries of the United States. With a few noted exceptions, the only people who should have been living in Indian Territory were the Indians, and they were not citizens of the United States. In reality, at the time they were considered savages and something a little less than human—they were not citizens of the United States of America!

To become an organized and recognized territory of the United States, the Indians had to reside within the United States. The only way they could get their new territory recognized was to become US citizens. It was a grand, sensitive, and very complex scheme. If it had not been for the issue of slavery, their plan might have succeeded. From the first council meeting of the revived confederacy until the establishment of Kansas Territory on May 30, 1854, much happened, and the Wyandot were the instigators and stuck smack-dab in the middle of it all. If anyone in Washington had been paying attention, and if the government agents in Indian Territory had been aware of their surroundings, they should have caught on to the Indians' intent. Yet they apparently did not think or incorrectly thought that the plan would just fizzle out. The agents may have also thought the Wyandot were incapable of making such a grand scheme work.

Wyandot chiefs and leading men did not make a public service announcement, nor was a press conference held and the media briefed from the council house. In spite of the absence of billboards, flashing neon signs, email blasts, and full-page newspaper ads, it was expressly clear that the Wyandot Tribe was opposed to slavery in the new territory. Well, most of the Wyandots were opposed. As we will see, some men took a hypocritical stance and denounced slavery while at the same time keeping slaves in their homes. Instead of making a big commotion, nineteen tribal citizens wrote and signed a short letter and sent it to the US Congress. Each man put his convictions into action and knowingly took a risk by doing what they knew was right.

The letter was brief yet expressly clear in its wording. The letter may have been read and then tossed aside, as the red children who signed were in no position of authority. They were just ordinary Wyandot men, yet still they were no less brilliant than the big names within the tribe. These men were concerned citizens, and not one was serving on the Wyandot tribal council. Oddly enough, William Walker Jr., who was serving on the tribal council in 1848, was a slave owner. William's brothers, Joel and Matthew, were also slave owners, as were Francis A. Hicks, the Garrett brothers, and a few other Wyandots.

When you read the men's letter to Congress, think about this: If these common, ordinary Wyandot men were so well versed on the political climate of the United States and knew the country's laws, what does this say for the not-so-ordinary Wyandot men who were always playing the political game? Do you think they knew what they were doing and were capable of seeing their plan for a territory through to fruition? You can bet they did. The letter sent to Congress by the concerned, non-slave-owning citizens of the Wyandot Tribe stated:

Indian Territory Oct. 27th 1848
To the American Congress.

Your red children of the Wyandott Nation would respectfully inform your
noble Council that negro slavery has been introduced into our Territory West
of the State of Missouri contrary to the law which you have heretofore made.
The Missouri compromise act expressly forbids and forever excludes involun-
tary servitude in this Territory North of 36 degrees and thirty minutes latitude
Your humble petitioners ask that some measure be taken to carry into effect
this law. We are not abolitionists nor have we any sympathy with them but we
believe that territory already free ought to remain free.

With great respect &c

James Whitewing	John Mononcue	Big Town
John Solomon	Squire Gray Eyes	Thomas Coonhawk
John Bigarms	John VanMeter	Geo. Steel
Geo. Spybuck	John Arms	Peter Buck
W. Johnston	James Bigtree	Lewis Clark
John Spybuck, Jr	John Curleyhead	White Crow
John Chop the Logs[21]		

A beehive of activity swarmed from Parkville, Missouri. The town outwardly identified itself with an aggressive stance in favor of slavery. Although
a significant majority of citizens within the Wyandot Tribe rejected slavery,
a few citizens continued with their hypocrisy. Runaway slaves were welcome
on Wyandot land. Slaves were given sanctuary and ultimately safe passage to
northern states through the Underground Railroad. In 1855, after Quindaro
was established as an abolitionist town to contest Parkville, many slaves from
Missouri were channeled through the town and ultimately gained their freedom. Quindaro also served as the gateway for many abolitionists entering
Kansas. The booming town was an opposing beehive with no less fervor in
support of freedom. How many slaves gained their freedom through Quindaro
is unknown. Obviously, secrecy was a necessity, and official records do not
exist. If only one slave found freedom, he or she was worth all the risks taken.
Wyandots were not going to be intimidated by slave-owning whites, and they
were definitely not going to be intimidated by slave-holding Wyandots.

"Strangers in a Strange Land"

Walker's hypocritical stance on slavery was likely a major contributing factor to his political downfall. How could the provisional governor of Nebraska Territory, with a platform of freedom and antislavery, garner any respect or cooperation when Walker himself was a slave owner? Joseph Pomeroy Root was a physician, politician, and leader of the Kansas Free Staters. In a letter to William Hutchinson dated November 17, 1857, Root speculated that Walker's administration was in jeopardy. Root also commented on the negative view of Free State party members toward proslavery Democrats in Kansas.

> I think it would be well to press Sec Stanton to call the extra session—a great many things may be brought to bear upon him, the fact is, if Walker has left without doing this, he will be in very bad odor with the people, and this fact together with the Kickapo [sic] revelations will probably annihilate his bright prospects, for his own disaffected brethren will use some of these tools to his injury, and between all the fires, he stands a very poor show.[22]

In addition to his hypocrisy, Walker had another underlying issue, notwithstanding the fact he was an alcoholic: He was an elitist. His sense of dominance and self-flattery was often displayed to his own people. His disdain for the common person was often masked in public, but in private his feelings were too often fully exposed. He made the following statement in his personal journal: "Lame and decrepit as I am, I am compelled to do my own work—cut wood, make fires, and feed my stock. I cannot get one of our vagabonds to work for me, no difference how extravagant may be the wages I offer."[23]

Maybe this is why Walker bought a slave. His own people—you know, those common everyday Wyandots we mentioned earlier—wanted little to do with him. In his younger days he loved to entertain and socialize with those common, everyday Wyandots, both family and friends. His mate and children were the center of his life, and he was a good father, but as he grew older, bitterness began to consume his life, and health issues often banished him to his home. He changed and often became disagreeable, but he never ceased to help when his people came calling with a need.

Where did the loyalty of William Walker Jr. reside? I believe that long before he accepted US citizenship as granted by the Treaty of 1855, he already looked upon himself as a citizen of the United States. If he did not, then through his own acts of admission, the torment of a previous oath rendered him incapable of swearing loyalty to his own people. He had three contradictory conflicts that disallowed him to invest his enormous talents into one arena.

Walker was obviously born a Wyandot and by birth should have automatically given his unquestioned loyalty to his people for life. As a young man he had swore an oath of loyalty to the United States as postmaster at Upper Sandusky. Upon swearing this oath, did he rescind his loyalty to his own people? Who was his master? He was his own master and served himself, but, as mentioned above, he had three conflicting loyalties: The Wyandot Tribe, the United States of America, and the Provisional Territory of Nebraska. Which one of the three took precedence in the decisions Walker made? In his younger days clearly the Wyandot Tribe was first priority; however, it looks like the United States of America commanded his loyalty in his old age. Prior to his own death on February 13, 1874, his health was a constant struggle and alcohol his committed friend.

> The Council sent for me and notified me of my election to [the] office of Clerk of the Council. I informed that Honorable body that I duly appreciated the honor done me by the voters of the Wyandott nation, but unfortunately I was ineligible. I held an appointment under the U.S. in the Indian department, that of U.S. Interpreter for the Wyandott nation, and had been sworn into office and also to support the Constitution of the U.S.; and the law of the Wyandott nation required the Clerk, before entering upon his duties, to take an oath of fealty to the Wyandott nation, thus requiring the same individual to serve two governments.[24]

In the years 1849–50 it is estimated that more than 100,000 white emigrants passed through Indian Territory.[25] At the time, Indian Territory predominately covered the land area that eventually became the states of Kansas, Nebraska, and Oklahoma. The emigrants were traveling to California, Utah, New Mexico, and the Oregon Country. Many of the California emigrants found the trip more difficult than expected and were now in Indian Territory and had no intention of leaving.[26] Also, with many of the wagon trains originating out of Independence, Missouri, it is likely that more than a handful, who actually continued with their migration, would have stepped foot on the Wyandot Purchase either before or during their trek west. The small reservation must have been like an old five-and-dime store, and the whites were no better than shoplifters. Many whites who initially had aspirations to go west changed their minds, ran out of resources, or succumbed to weariness; there-fore, their population began to swell along the Missouri border.

A public meeting was held in the spring of 1852 in Uniontown, a trad-ing post on Shawnee land, to draft resolutions for the Provisional Territorial Government. It was then noted that there were hundreds of white families nearby who were bona fide settlers and were in suffering and need of civil government.[27] The whites were already, and illegally, across the border into Indian Territory, with most of them on the vast and sparsely populated Shaw-nee and Delaware reservations; however, the Wyandot's tiny reservation even-tually became the epicenter of expansion into Kansas Territory. What had been nearly uninhabited land just a few years earlier was destined to become a metropolis and major cultural center west of the Mississippi River.

Noticing the looming crisis, the Wyandot chiefs and leading men took the initiative and began the process of preparing for a provisional government. The Wyandot had aspirations to proactively organize the Indian Territory into the Provisional Government of Nebraska Territory. Russell Garrett, a Wyandot citizen, prepared the notice that was sent both to all the tribes and to the whites who were then legally living in Indian Territory. Russell invited only the whites who were in service of the government in the capacity of agents, missionaries, agency-farmers, agency-blacksmiths, agency-carpenters, and licensed Indian traders who were permitted to live in the territory.[28] These legal white residents were but a minor representation of the true white popu-lation. The white population would prove to play a minor or no role in the formation of the government they so desperately desired and needed.

Wyandot citizens had wonderful and well-equipped little farms; however, they were thinly and indefensibly spread across the whole of the Wyandot Purchase. Eventually the land would be allotted after the Treaty of 1855, and heads of households would receive at least forty acres—some received a lot more. Land was supposed to be allotted according to the assessed value of the land. One citizen may have received only forty acres of prime farmland while another, an adjoining neighbor, received one hundred twenty acres. Why the discrepancy? The adjoining neighbor may have been allotted floodplain and river bottom. It took more land in acreage to equal the value of the one forty-acre plot that the adjoining neighbor received. The policy of awarding land according to its value would follow when the Wyandotte Reservation in Indian Territory was allotted in 1888.

Protecting and defending each farm was proving to be impossible. The plight of Mary Muntum is representative of many Wyandots spanning the late 1840s through the early 1860s. The Shawnee and Wyandot Agency court records are full of pleas to compensate citizens for losses. Many Wyandot citizens desperately sought to have their property recovered or replaced. With so many whites living on the reservations in a destitute condition, if something was not tied down, it was considered fair game to freely take. In all reality, if a cow was tied to a post in a barnyard, it was still considered fair game and too often came up missing. The whites were generally thought to be guilty of stealing much of what was missing. Proof of any accusation was always hard found; consequently, the thieves would normally go unpunished. The reservation was being picked out from under the tribe stone by stone, cow by cow, and it had to end, but how? Wyandot tribal leaders could plainly see what they believed to be the answer and began organizing the government that could have saved it all. It was incredibly unconventional. If it were not for their reasonable logic, today it could easily be looked up as something just short of treason. In the Wyandot's defense, it cannot be regarded as treason, just absolute brilliance!

Let's take one last look at the report William Walker Jr. gave to the Wyandot tribal council in 1831. Walker had nothing good to say about Missouri. He called the state's citizens an abandoned, dissolute, and wicked people. He also noted that Missouri was a slave-holding state and slaveholders had proven to be anything but friendly to the Indians. His observations were almost prophetic, for it would be the slaveholders from the state of Missouri that rallied and ultimately upset the Wyandot's plans. Throw into the mix with the slaveholders two ardent Missouri Democrats, Thomas Hart Benton (antislavery) and David Rice Atchison (proslavery), bitter enemies bent on the vengeful invalidation of each other, and war was imminent.

As the Provisional Government of Nebraska Territory was slowly, methodically, and carefully being organized by the Indians, citizens of the Wyandot Tribe continued to pursue personal interests. One of the most daring and adventurous expeditions occurred in April of 1849 as the Wyandott Mining Company started making preparations for their long, perilous journey to California and the gold fields. As whites were making their way west, gold fever infected the Wyandot Purchase. On May 31, 1849, the Wyandott Mining Company set out for California. William Walker Jr. identified the following as being members of the company: Irvin P. Long, Theodore F. Garrett (elected captain of the expedition), William Bowers, William Lynville, Ira Hunter (blacksmith), Matthew Brown, Charles B. Garrett, Philip Brown, Adam Hunt, R. Palmer, and Russell B. Garrett. E. B. Hand went as physician.[29]

On June 20 the expedition arrived at Fort Laramie. The Lakota are said to have stolen several of the Wyandott Mining Company's horses promptly upon their arrival. This was not an unusual occurrence, and for many the loss of a few, fine horses was an acceptable loss. Losing a horse was much better than losing your life when directly confronting the Lakota in an attempt to recover stolen property. Losing a horse was not an acceptable loss for the Wyandots. How dare the Lakota steal their horses! There was no love lost between the Wyandots and the Lakota. The memories of what had happened in Wisconsin back in the latter part of the seventeenth century were still fresh, and peace between the two had not been realized. Four Wyandot men, whose names are not recorded, promptly tracked and located the party of Lakota. I have no doubt that one of the men was Irvin Patton Long.

Long was a Wyandot warrior chipped from the flint of *Huron*-Wyandot legend, and he was destined to be Principal Chief of the Wyandot Tribe. He served in the Mexican-American War, and his commanding officer, Major W. P. Overton, was quoted as saying that Long was the bravest soldier he ever saw. He continued by describing Long's participation in a charge upon a battery. He stated that every man in the charge either was killed or retreated, but Long rode his horse amongst the gunners and killed every one of them with his sword. "This," he said, "I have seen him do more than once; and in battle he constantly yelled the Wyandot war-whoop, a peculiar sound that almost curdled my blood and made my flesh creep."[30]

Long also served as sheriff of the Wyandot Tribe for many years. His grit would have been clearly noble yet, when needed, quite abrasive. He did not take any disrespect from anyone, especially the Lakota, who had given the Wyandot much grief in the not-so-distant past. Upon locating the stolen horses, the four Wyandot warriors promptly and boldly walked into the Lakota camp, announced who they were and what their intended business was, reclaimed the stolen horses, and left unharmed. I dare anyone to try that in 1849 and walk away with their scalp intact! The Wyandot's savage courage had not been conquered, and it was incapable of succumbing to fear.

It would take another four months for the Wyandott Mining Company to reach their destination. Upon arrival they began their mining operations near Lake Lassen on the North Fork of the Feather River in the Shasta Cascades of Northern California, where they reportedly mined much gold.[31] The Wyandott Mining Company introduced many Wyandots to California and the west coast. In the ensuing years a handful of Wyandot citizens would move to California, never to return to Nebraska. Today for various reasons there is a large population of Wyandottes that resides on the west coast from California to Washington State.

Not long after the Wyandott Mining Company arrived in California, the Wyandot Tribal Council sent Principal Chief Francis A. Hicks, George I. Clarke, and Joel Walker to Washington, DC, in November of 1849. At this point the Wyandot Tribe literally had citizens from coast to coast. The delegates were sent to find closure in the matter of the delinquent 148,000 acres promised the tribe in the Treaty of 1842. While there, without the permission or knowledge of the tribal council, they asked for a new treaty containing citizenship status for the tribe and also for the Wyandot Purchase be divided in severalty. The Commissioner of Indian Affairs promptly and soundly rejected their request, indicating it was not in the best interest of the United States to engage in such a treaty. Obviously, they needed the Wyandot right where they were in order to provide a buffer zone that would prevent slavery from entering the territory west of Missouri. The delegation returned home, and the ensuing Treaty of 1850 provided for a cash payment of $185,000 in lieu of the 148,000 acres. From this cash payment the tribe's remaining debt with the Delaware Tribe was paid in full.

If the tribal council had known of the delegates' intent to ask for a new treaty, would they have objected? The answer is both yes and no. They would have objected and said no to the proposal because it was not the proper time to make such a request. Then again, they would have said yes because the tribal council agreed that such a request needed to eventually be made. The convened council of the various tribes had not been given ample time to design and implement a provisional government, and therefore the request of the delegates was premature and ill advised. It would take another two years before the provisional government could be established and a delegate be elected and sent to Washington, DC. This delegate to Congress would have one purpose. He alone would go to Washington, DC, and represent the interests of the Indian tribes living in Indian Territory. Representation would no longer be needed or accepted from the designated Indian agent sent to Indian Territory from Washington, DC.

After much planning, on October 12, 1852, a convention was held to elect a delegate to Congress. The convention was hosted in the council house of the Wyandot Tribe. William Walker Jr. indicated in his journal, "A. Guthrie received the entire vote polled."[32] Abelard Guthrie had recently returned to the reservation from an expedition to the California gold mines. In May of 1850, upon hearing of the Wyandott Mining Company's successes in California, Guthrie led a second expedition of Wyandots to the gold mines. In true fashion, he would return to the reservation without finding his fortune. Upon returning he would focus all of his efforts into organizing the territorial government. Before being elected the first delegate to Congress, he had issues with Adam Brown Jr., his father-in-law, in what Walker described as a bloody quarrel.[33] They were both arrested after Brown fired his rifle at Guthrie with intent to inflict mortal harm. Adam would leave for Canada where he stayed until the friendship could be restored between the embattled father and his son-in-law.

Abelard Guthrie is an interesting and frustrating fellow. He first became familiar with the Wyandot when he was serving as chief clerk for Indian agent John Johnston while the tribe still lived in Ohio.[34] Following the tribe to Indian Territory in January of 1844, he promptly married Quindaro Nancy Brown, Adam Brown's daughter, in what was possibly the first marriage performed on the Wyandot Purchase. Adam did not approve of the marriage. As was tradition, upon marriage Guthrie was adopted into a Wyandot clan—the Bear clan. He was immediately extended full rights to everything as though he were a natural-born citizen. He quickly laid claim to those rights, settled in, and became a productive citizen for the tribe. Unfortunately, he at times had difficulty understanding and fitting into the Wyandot community. In addition, he was always seeking his fortune, thereby keeping him at odds with just about everyone he met.

Prior to Guthrie's election as the first delegate to Congress, there was much opposition from government officials in the Indian Territory. The United States was finally catching on to what the Indians were attempting to accomplish. The officials and agents demanded that the election of a delegate cease. If the Indian Territory were indeed organized into Nebraska Territory, whites could legally settle the new open land, and with them would likely come slavery. The issue of whether the new Nebraska Territory would be a free state or a slave state would then become a national issue. Washington, DC, was opposed to this proposition, as the Missouri Compromise disallowed slavery in any new territories founded within the area obtained in the Louisiana Purchase—Missouri excluded. The issue of slavery in the states had been resolved with the Missouri Compromise, and the debate was not going to be reopened—hence the reason any previous attempts to territorial expansion had failed. The discussion of white settlements again became a heated topic resulting in action opposite and contradictory to its original intent.

According to law, the government could use the US Army to physically remove white settlers who illegally encroached upon the land found within Indian Territory.[35] If the government was willing to use military force and remove any illegally settled whites from the land, doing so would prove to be a most difficult job. Obviously, military force was never employed to remove the whites; however, military force was eventually used to remove the Indians from Indian Territory.

Shortly after Guthrie was elected, he promptly departed for Washington, DC, to occupy his seat in Congress. He was severely disappointed when he was not recognized as being from a legitimate territory and was banned from the floor and required to sit in the balcony. His presence in Washington, DC, received much opposition. In addition, from that moment forward, much attention was given to what the Indians were doing out west. The thought that the Wyandot Tribe was forming the Provisional Government for the Nebraska Territory was terrifying! The Indians successfully elected a delegate to Washington, DC, but what would happen if they were successful in electing a governor?

The government's fears were realized when on Tuesday, July 26, 1853, William Walker Jr. was elected Provisional Governor of Nebraska Territory. In his journal he confirmed the election by stating, "In accordance with the resolutions adopted, the following officers were elected as a provisional government for the Territory: For provisional Governor, Wm. Walker; Sec'y of the Territory, G. I. Clark; Councilmen, R. C. Miller, Isaac Mundy, and M. R. Walker."[36] Walker did not want the job; he hoped that one of his two younger brothers would be elected Provisional Governor instead. It did not take long for Washington, DC, to invest their interest into the new Provisional Government. On October 7 Walker again wrote, "Attended a Council called by the Com. of Indian Affairs. Speeches were passed between the parties on the subject of the Territorial organization, [and] selling out to the gov't."

On September 6, 1853, The Reverend Thomas Johnson, a Methodist missionary to the Shawnee and a slaveholder, along with George W. Manypenny, Commissioner of Indian Affairs, sat in on a Wyandot tribal council meeting. It was at this meeting that they witnessed and overheard discussions revealing the true intent regarding the organization of the territory.[37] The new territory was going to be a free state. This news was promptly carried across the border to Missouri. Within days another election was to be held for the purpose of electing the delegate to Washington for a second term. Reverend Johnson would run against incumbent Abelard Guthrie and defeat him with an overwhelming majority. The previous year Guthrie had won the nomination with a unanimous majority. This change of results in less than a year would clearly show the persuasive power Missouri would claim over all elections in the territory. Reverend Johnson was backed and supported by his good friend Senator David Rice Atchison. Guthrie was known to be a Benton Democrat and stood against slavery in the territory.

The Kansas-Nebraska Act of 1854 abolished the Missouri Compromise and so allowed the territorial citizens the right to determine through popular sovereignty whether slavery or freedom would prevail. The whites came in and literally took everything over, pushing the Wyandot and all the other Indians aside. This action immediately nullified the Provisional Government of Nebraska Territory that the Wyandot so diligently and marvelously established.

After the Kansas-Nebraska Act opened Kansas Territory for settlement, antislavery settlers backed by the New England Emigrant Aid Company founded Lawrence, Kansas, in the fall of 1854. In an attempt to prove their resolve and make Kansas a slave state, proslavery forces attacked and burned Lawrence on May 21, 1856. Samuel J. Jones, proslavery sheriff of Douglas County, instigated the attack under the guise of a posse authorized by a grand jury to rid Lawrence of its nuisances. Those nuisances were the Free-state Hotel and the *Herald of Freedom* and *Kansas Free-State* newspapers.[38]

The border war would promptly erupt with an unbridled vengeance. Excursions and all-out invasions by the slave state backing Missouri Bushwhackers would keep the free-state Kansas settlers prone to and expectant of attack. Kansas Jayhawkers would return the favor with their own incursions across the border into Missouri. Murder, pillage, and plunder quickly masked the reason for many who were involved in the raids. Justification for the attacks was soon lost, and both sides succumbed to the resident darkness found in the hearts of men. Both sides stood on the precipice of no return as lawlessness prevailed. On January 29, 1861, Kansas was admitted to the Union as a free state. Open hostilities began on April 12, 1861, when Southern Confederate forces fired upon Union Fort Sumter in South Carolina. The US Civil War had begun. What had initially erupted in Kansas now spread as an apocalyptic plague across the whole of the United States of America—both Union and Confederate.

Once the Civil War started, warfare along the Kansas-Missouri border intensified. The complexion of the war changed with organized military units leading the attacks—both Union and Confederate. From this era of conflict, a notorious name, William Clarke Quantrill, would emerge. Quantrill would ascend and take his place in the infamous pages of American history and folklore. There is a fascinating Wyandot connection to Quantrill that is compelling and worthy of study.

At twenty-two years of age Quantrill began forming his political views, which quickly began to lean toward proslavery. When his chosen career as a schoolteacher came to an abrupt halt, he became a runaway-slave hunter and in his new career achieved financial stability. To keep his newfound career vibrant, Quantrill needed slaves to remain in abundance. Slave owners in Missouri employed his services, and his reputation soared in spite of tactics that were considered brutal and eccentric.

In the spring of 1861, as the Civil War erupted, Quantrill moved to Texas after coming to believe Missourians to be unappreciative of his slave-hunting talents. Texas would prove to be unappealing, and he would again move to the Cherokee Nation where he befriended Joel Mayes.[39] The "irresponsible life" of the Indian was found to be appealing to Quantrill.[40] Only part Cherokee, Mayes had Confederate sympathies and was a captain serving in General Ben McCulloch's Confederate Indian Army. Quantrill accompanied Mayes to Missouri where he fought at the Battle of Wilson's Creek about ten miles southwest of Springfield. A Confederate victory, it proved to be an inspiring adventure for the young Quantrill. After the battle he left McCulloch's army and returned to Northern Missouri where he formed his own small guerrilla army. While in the company of Joel Mayes, he learned the Indian mode of warfare and became a competent guerrilla fighter. The taking of scalps became a custom and signature trademark of Quantrill.[41] Until then there was nothing that set Quantrill apart from the rest of the young men who chose to take up arms and fight for either the Confederate or the Union armies—but the taking of scalps by a white man changed everything.

Settling in Blue Springs, Missouri, Quantrill formed a small, loyal, and pro-Confederate guerrilla band. In 1862 a few of his recruits added a high level of familiarity to the band: the Younger Brothers, William "Bloody Bill" Anderson, and Frank and Jesse James. Also somewhere around this time Nicholas Cotter and Frank Whitewing joined the ranks of Quantrill's guerrillas.[42] What was so important about Cotter and Whitewing? They were Wyandot citizens. They and two additional unnamed Wyandots were members of Quantrill's guerrillas.

In his 1937 Indian-Pioneer Papers interview with Nannie Lee Burns, William Long mentions the Battle of Baxter Springs. This battle was fought on

October 6, 1863, and both Cotter and Whitewing are believed to have been there. The Battle of Baxter Springs was fought as Quantrill was taking his army south to Texas for the winter after the massacre at Lawrence occurred. Were Cotter and Whitewing direct combatants? Or were they scouts who guarded the perimeter and warned Quantrill of the advancing Delaware warriors coming to the aid of the town? We can never know, and, after so many years, does it really matter? At Baxter Springs ninety-eight Union soldiers were killed in retaliation to General Order No. 11.[43] The order, issued in response to the Lawrence massacre, demanded the evacuation and depopulation of Bates, Cass, Jackson, and Vernon counties in Western Missouri. These counties were believed to be ardent supporters of Quantrill's army.

Long also discusses other battles and skirmishes that occurred between Quantrill's guerrillas and Union forces. In one skirmish at Hudson Bottom, five Union soldiers were killed. Contemporary maps show that Hudson Creek can be found west of the Neosho River located in a bend of the river that became known as Mudeater Bend. It can easily be assumed that the skirmish took place in the river bottom at the junction of the Neosho River and Hudson Creek. The soldiers were buried in what became Bland Cemetery. From Hudson Bottom to Bland Cemetery is just about a mile and a half due east.

The Wyandots in Quantrill's service must have left an indelible impression upon their fellow guerrilla fighters. Years after the Civil War ended and the James and Younger brothers were deep into their careers as bank and train robbers, they showed up on the Wyandotte Reservation in Indian Territory. In his 1937 Indian-Pioneer Papers interview with Nannie Lee Burns, Jared Silas Dawson described unexpected dinner guests in 1876.[44] I wonder if Jesse took the time to look up his old colleague Nicholas Cotter.

Nicholas Cotter would become Principal Chief of the Wyandot Tribe in 1880. Cotter's feelings for the Confederacy were indeed strong; he named his son Jefferson Davis Cotter. Nicholas, along with Matthew Mudeater and Irvin Patton Long, all Principal Chiefs of the Wyandot Tribe, are buried at Bland Cemetery. Also buried in the cemetery are five Union soldiers and many Wyandotte citizens—including my immediate family.

In 1856 William Phillips published *The Conquest of Kansas By Missouri and Her Allies*. In one paragraph he theorized why the tribes had been moved to Indian Territory and why the Kansas-Missouri border war persisted. Phillips's theory explains why once Reverend Johnson and Commissioner Manypenny learned of the Wyandot's intention, they reacted so unfavorably and quickly. Johnson, representing the Missouri slave owners, wanted slavery for Kansas, but the Wyandot did not. Manypenny, representing the United States, wanted the tribe to remain Indian and not seek US citizenship. He, following policy, wanted the Wyandot to remain part of the buffer that inhibited the expansion of slavery into the territory. A few within the Wyandot Tribe no longer wanted to remain Indian, and most no longer wanted to be part of the government's buffer zone. Manypenny also knew that the Wyandot were very influential with the other tribes. If the Wyandot's plan succeeded, both men would lose, and this could not be permitted. Phillips summarized by stating:

> Western Missouri looked with envious eye upon Kansas. It acted as if Kansas really belonged to it. Years before the American people heard a syllable about the repeal of the Missouri Compromise, it was contemplated and discussed in Western Missouri. The propagandists, who, acted under the conviction that Kansas was lost to slavery, had tied it up with Indian treaties that would effectually prevent any attempted settlement, began to plan a double villany, a breach of faith with the aborigines, and a breach of the sacred compromise by which it had been hoped the vexed question was amicably settled.[45]

The number of Indians along the border was not that great, but they were relatively civilized. The Indians had mostly good farms and good houses considering how far west they were. Many were living intermarried with the whites.[46] Phillips preceded his description of the Wyandot Reserve with an exhaustive painting of the land and its inhabitants. His writing revealed how it was nearly impossible to separate the land from the people—the Indians who now called the land home. The land and the people were one. Phillips stated, "The remnants of numerous and powerful tribes were scattered over the eastern portion of the territory. . . . These reserves embraced a considerable portion of the country adjacent to the Missouri river, and one hundred and fifty miles west of it. This is the richest and most valuable portion of the territory."[47]

As the whites came pouring in, many Wyandot citizens were forced out. In 1857 Matthew Mudeater was the first to lead a small band of distraught and demoralized Wyandot to the Mixed Seneca and Shawnee Reservation in Indian Territory. Kansas had been the Wyandot's home for a meager fourteen years. During this period the tribe was afforded no time to rest and enjoy the favors of the land. In Indian Territory the Seneca's hospitality was impeccable, but still hardship would follow the Wyandot.

The difficulties met by the Wyandot people who wanted to escape the hard times in Kansas would only worsen. Upon their arrival to the Mixed Seneca and Shawnee reservation, their crops would fail as drought prevailed and starvation became an imminent danger. The Mixed Seneca and Shawnee Reservation was located in the far northeast corner of what became the state of Oklahoma. The weather is ever changing and at times harsh: cold winters; spring thunderstorms and tornados; and floods along the Neosho, Spring, and Grand rivers which spawned mosquitoes the size of small birds. Never minimize the chiggers and ticks during the unbearable heat of August and September. One could easily think that the Bad Twin made Oklahoma. As the famous movie line says, "We're not in Kansas anymore," nor Ohio for that matter. Dealing with the harsh land was a challenge, and then came the secessionist Indians—the Wyandot's cousins, the Cherokee.

The Wyandot citizens led to Indian Territory by Matthew Mudeater were taken into captivity by the secessionist Indians. After escaping from the secessionist Indians, these Wyandots would be classified as Refugee Indians.[48] This classification is one of the factors leading to the Wyandot's reinstatement in 1867 as a recognized tribe. If Mudeater had not taken the Wyandot to Indian Territory before the outbreak of the Civil War, it's doubtful that the Wyandotte Tribe would have been reinstated.

Almost immediately upon the outbreak of the Civil War, the Cherokee, and what's described as rebel portions of the Seneca, invaded the Mixed Seneca and Shawnee lands where the Wyandot were eking out a meager living.[49] All the Wyandots were forcefully demanded to submit allegiance to Confederate forces and take up arms against the Union. *The Wyandot refused!* Upon their refusal all the Wyandots in Indian Territory were taken hostage, placed in guarded captivity, and denied the right to leave the land and return to Kansas. All their property, including the valuable horses, was seized as contraband.

During this time the Wyandots remaining in Kansas attempted to organize and send a rescue party. A force large enough could not be mustered; plus Union troops necessary to protect the expedition and ensure its success were not available. A few citizens who were already serving in regular Union companies requested to be transferred into a special company for the purpose of rescuing their brothers and sisters. The transfers were denied. After the Wyandots had lived for several months in insufferable conditions, the Confederate guard was relaxed, and those held hostage managed to make their escape back to Wyandott City in the spring of 1862.[50] They returned destitute, yet in their suffering they enriched the lives of countless generations to come. A down payment had been placed upon the land that was destined to become their home.

For many years the Wyandotte people questioned the whereabouts of their wampum belts. It was about this time, as the refugee Wyandots were making their way back to Wyandott City, the wampum belts had disappeared. The belts were known to be culturally valuable not only for the Wyandot Tribe but also for the Ottawa, Chippewa, and Potawatomi Tribes. The Wyandots were Keepers of the Council Fire and entrusted with the care and keep of the wampum belts and various documents such as treaties. Emma Blair explains:

> Early in the eighteenth century an alliance was formed by the Wyandotts, Chippewa, Ottawas, and Potawatamies for their mutual protection against the incursions of hostile western tribes; the French made a fifth party to this alliance—which before many years fell through. About 1720 those four tribes made an arrangement as to the respective territories which they were to occupy—each tribe; however, to have the privilege of hunting in the territory of the others. The Wyandotts were made the keepers of the international council-fire (a figurative expression, meaning their international archives), and arbiters, in their general council, of important questions that concerned the welfare of all the four tribes. "From that period might be dated the first introduction of the wampum belt system, representing and agreement among the four nations. The belt was left with the keepers of the council-fire. From that time forward until the year 1812 (when the council-fire was moved from Michigan to Canada) every wampum belt representing some international compact was placed in the archives of the Wyandott nation. Each belt bore some mark, denoting the nature of a covenant or contract entered into between the parties, and the hidden contents of which was kept in the memory of the chiefs." About 1842 part of the Wyandotts left Canada, to join their tribesmen in Ohio, and with them remove to Kansas, to which territory they sent (1843) their archives; but when those were desired (about 1864) by the eastern Wyandotts it was found that most of the belts and documents were dispersed and lost. The last general council of those tribes, at which the belts were displayed and their contents recited, was held in Kansas in 1846.[51]

Percy Ladd Walker, son of Matthew Walker, in his 1937 WPA interview gives a brief yet insightful glimpse to the events just before the Wyandot's escape from Indian Territory and return to Wyandott City. Tauromee, also known as John Hatt, lived in a quaint little cabin along the Lost Creek Valley east of present-day Wyandotte, Oklahoma. Tauromee, who was then the recognized chief of the Wyandots in Indian Territory and brother-in-law to

Matthew Mudeater, had been entrusted with a number of wampum belts. In his haste to leave for Wyandott City, he neglected to retrieve the trunk of wampum belts entrusted to his care.[52] Percy indicated that Tauromee sealed his cabin the old Indian way, that is, he set a heavy stick upright by the door, and while the stick remained, the house was considered locked and no Indian would enter. Maybe an Indian would not enter Tauromee's cabin, but a white man would have no knowledge of the stick and its purpose. Even if a white man had knowledge of the stick, it's unlikely that he would respect the stick and would still enter. Percy identified a man named Hopkins as being the leader of the Bushwackers who desecrated the Wyandot's trunk of wampum belts.[53]

After a lot of research, I learned that Captain Henry Hopkins attached to Union forces from Kansas, Company B, 3rd Kansas Battery; he appears to be the officer who entered Tauromee's cabin. Captain Hopkins was noted as participating in the Battles of Cabin Creek, Prairie Grove, and Honey Springs. This knowledge acknowledges Captain Hopkins's presence in the Indian Territory in 1862 and 1863. He is directly referenced in *History of the State of Kansas* as a Union officer at the Battle of Cabin Creek.

> Capt. Hopkins had an encounter with the forces of Gen. Gano, at Cabin Creek. Capt. Hopkins had under his command about 600 men, nearly two-thirds being Cherokees. He was attacked in the night by 3,000 rebels, with artillery, two pieces of which were posted in his front, and two opposite his right flank. Guarding his train as well as he was able, Capt. Hopkins defended his position six hours, when the enemy made an advance, and planting their artillery within one hundred yards of his lines, forced him to abandon his train, and fall back to Grand River.[54]

If Captain Hopkins fell back to the Grand River, guess where his retreat could have easily taken him. That's right: He would have been in the general vicinity of Tauromee's abandoned cabin. Can't you see a very upset, defeated, and ill-tempered Captain Hopkins kicking down the big stick that locked Tauromee's cabin door only to find the chest of wampum belts? Out of anger and disrespect, he slung the belts with all his might, and the priceless beads went flying and bouncing everywhere. If not Hopkins personally, it could have been one of his scouts who came across the cabin and destroyed the belts. It does not matter if Hopkins or one of his men destroyed the belts. Hopkins was in command, and he will always bear the blame.

The Wyandot's wampum belts were broken and scattered around the area of Tauromee's cabin. Only remnants could be retrieved upon his return after the Civil War ended. The trunk in Tauromee's possession did not contain all of the Wyandot's wampum belts. Bertrand Nicholas Oliver (BNO) Walker indicated there were several belts in the possession of other leading men. I cannot imagine the heartbreak Tauromee must have felt as he paused to gaze upon the bits and pieces of belts scattered across the ground. The pain of knowing he was the last to hold and possess the belts, which had been revered as a sacred honor, must have been horribly demoralizing. This, too, knowing a little of Tauromee's personality, must have been a flashpoint propelling him to again pursue tribal reinstatement and the acquisition of land for the Wyandot to again call and claim as their own.

According to Peter D. Clarke, his grandfather, Adam Brown, was in charge of the Wyandot tribal archives. As Clarke was known to exaggerate, this claim may have been somewhat dubious. The archives, supposedly in Brown's care, would have included the wampum belts, which were initially archived in the village of Brownstown. In one of his personal journals BNO indicated that an elderly Wyandot man named Boyer was custodian and reader of the belts. It just so happened that Brown had made the chest that safely protected the wampum belts. According to Clarke, since Adam Brown made the chest, this also made him the caretaker of the belts.

BNO continued by stating that Boyer was of the Michigan Band Wyandots living at or near Gibraltar on the Canadian side of the Detroit River. When the Wyandot Tribe prepared to move to Indian Territory, Boyer had no intention of moving. Boyer was old and content to die in Canada with or without his tribe. Being the true, only, and rightful keeper of the tribal archives, Boyer had to keep the wampum belts where he resided. This did not sit well with the Wyandots from Upper Sandusky, and they decided to take matters into their own hands. Just before the move west was to transpire, a group from Upper Sandusky traveled to Canada, where they forcibly removed Boyer and his chest of tribal records. Boyer and the belts were taken to Upper Sandusky and then on to Indian Territory. Kidnapping a man against his will was excusable, but taking a chest of tribal records without their caretaker was not acceptable.

Sadly enough, Boyer was likely one of the first Wyandots to die in Indian Territory. BNO Walker indicates Boyer was buried in the swampy land near the eastern bluffs that framed the French Bottoms to the Kansas River. BNO continued by stating that his grave likely resided near where the old Kansas City Union Station once stood. If this is true, Boyer would have been buried

FIGURE 5.2. Bertrand Nicholas Oliver Walker as Hiawatha

on the Missouri side of the line. Boyer did not have the comfort of resting in Canada or even in the *Huron* Indian Cemetery with his fellow citizens.

After Boyer's death the wampum belts were divided among a few of the breechcloth chiefs, one being Tauromee. BNO continued by stating that his uncle, William Walker Jr., eventually came to possess three intact belts and several that were broken beyond repair. Maybe these were the remnants of the belts Tauromee abandoned in the Lost Creek Valley in 1862. In 1871 or 1872 William traveled to Indian Territory and gave the intact belts to Irvin Patton Long, and the broken belts to John Wesley Greyeyes. The broken belts and beads were said to nearly fill a flour sack. In the mid- to late nineteenth century, the average-sized flour sack held just shy of one hundred pounds of flour. If BNO was referencing flour sacks of his day, the early twentieth century, they averaged around fifty pounds of flour. Regardless of the size of flour sack—that's a lot of wampum beads!

John Wesley Greyeyes, in turn, gave the broken beads to Mary Williams Walker, his sister-in-law and BNO's mother. Mary was instructed to string the beads for each of her children. BNO indicated that there were several strands of the wampum beads in his possession. The 1909 photo of BNO dressed for the lead role in the Haskell Indian School's production of "Hiawatha Indian Play" gives us a rare and personal look at the wampum beads strung by BNO's mother. The wampum beads hang around BNO's neck behind the bear-claw necklace. In 1924, a few years before his death, BNO gave one of the priceless relics, a string of wampum beads, to the Oklahoma State Historical Society. When giving the beads to the Historical Society, BNO stated, "May the wampum never again be removed, but forever remain in Oklahoma the home of the Redman." There were other strands of beads, which stayed in the Walker family, and some are now in the possession of BNO's great-nephew.

After the death of Irvin Patton Long, two of the three belts were sold to the Smithsonian and the Field Museum of Chicago. BNO indicated he had the privilege of seeing one of the three intact belts and described it as the Treaty of Greenville belt. BNO never indicated who was in possession of the belt at the time; however, he indicated that it was sold around 1909 or 1910 to the Penn (Pennsylvania) Historical Society.

Until recently, the existence of a fourth intact Wyandot wampum belt remained unknown. In 2005 a wampum belt surfaced in Santa Fe, New Mexico, to be auctioned to the highest bidder. Unfortunately, the belt was sold to a private party and believed to have been shipped overseas. The wampum belt was remarkable and accompanied with documentation to prove its authenticity. Unbeknownst to just about everyone William Walker Jr. had given a fourth belt in his possession to Silas Armstrong Jr., undoubtedly at the same time he gave the three belts to Irvin Patton Long.

The belt in the possession of Silas has a solid field of white glass beads signifying friendship, harmony, and peace. In the center of the belt lies a symmetrical dark purple cross of wampum containing a single white bead center. Given the origin and purpose of the belt, we know that the cross represents Christianity, or Catholicism. A handwritten letter from Silas Armstrong Jr. to his wife dated July 31, 1898, identifies the belt as the one given the *Huron* Tribe by the Catholic priests when the new corn feast was first established on August 15 to coincide with the natal, or birthday, of the Virgin Mary. The belt is one of only two made, with the second somewhere in the archives of the Catholic Church. The wampum belt could easily be somewhere around three hundred to three hundred ten years old—absolutely amazing!

When the wampum belt was first sold and shipped overseas, there was such a sense of disappointment that words cannot express the feelings of loss. As quickly as the belt first appeared, it again was listed for sale on a Santa Fe broker's website in April of 2017. This time, the Wyandotte Nation purchased the Catholic's new corn belt. It's not important to say how much the wampum belt cost, but it's fair to say it was very expensive and worth every penny. After nearly one hundred twenty years of traveling around the world, the wampum belt returned home to Wyandotte, Oklahoma, and will never again leave the tribal museum. It is amazing to see the wampum belt in person. The awe it inspires and the feelings evoked by knowing that many Wyandots touched the belt, *as did I,* under the watchful eye of the women, *in my case Sherri Clemons,* send goose bumps all over my body.

Land Bribes and Floats to Nowhere

In one of Abelard Guthrie's many quests for fortune, in November of 1855, he and Joel Walker formed the Quindaro Town Company. Guthrie was approached by Charles Robinson, one of the founders of Lawrence, Kansas, with hopes of establishing a town on the Missouri River to serve as a free-state port.[55] Now that the Wyandot's reservation had been allotted and individual citizens owned the land, Robinson needed permission to establish a town. Permission was now needed from an individual landowner, not the tribe in whole. Guthrie was adventurous, at times took unnecessary risks, and had an affinity for money. Walker would serve as the company's president; Guthrie as vice president; and Robinson, along with S. N. Simpson, as treasurer. With them came investors from the east coast, and overnight Quindaro became an instant boomtown. The new town also became competition for Wyandott City, which lay just a few miles to the south. In December of 1856, the new town was surveyed, platted, and named Quindaro, after Guthrie's wife.[56] The town was established during an economic boom unlike that in any other time in the history of the United States.

No expense was spared in the attempt to make Quindaro appealing and successful to investors and hopeful residents alike. A ferry was first established between Quindaro and Parkville. Next, a stage line was established between Quindaro and Lawrence. In one of the most elaborate and successful endeavors, the town bought the light draft steamboat *Lightfoot* from the dockyards at Cincinnati. The *Lightfoot* would run up the Kansas River all the way to Lawrence. In spite of the investments made into the town, progress was not sustainable, and the town began to falter. In one of the last attempts to save the town, a most improbable yet hopeful enterprise was established: The *Quindaro, Parkville and Burlington Railroad Company* was financed with the hope of bringing the elusive and needful town-saving railroad to Quindaro.

After many exhaustive years of trying to entice the railroad to Quindaro, hopes were dashed when the railroad went through Wyandott City. In light of the town's failure it cannot be said that the founding fathers did not try to ensure the success of the town at all cost. What would it cost Guthrie? Everything. Bankruptcy. He went to his grave a bankrupt and broken man. His widow, Nancy Quindaro Brown Guthrie, in a letter dated December 29, 1875, to the Canadian Wyandots pleaded for their permission to return to Canada and the home of her grandfather Adam Brown. She continued by stating that she was in straitened circumstances, not having enough money to pay for life's barest necessities.[57]

Joel Walker invested in Quindaro and Wyandott City. Joel was wise and spread his money in spite of potential conflicts of interest. Quindaro was established as a free-state town and was advertised and openly promoted as such. Walker was a slave owner and president of a company backing a free-state town. This had to be a rather delicate arrangement, especially when dealing with east coast investors. Somehow he was able to keep his personal interests separate from his professional, and they appear to have

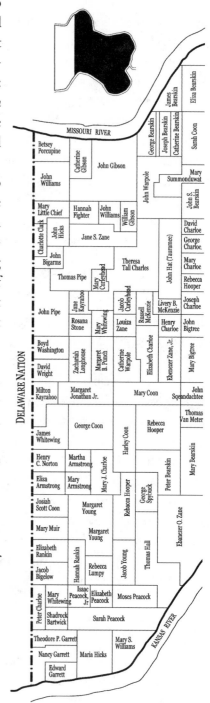

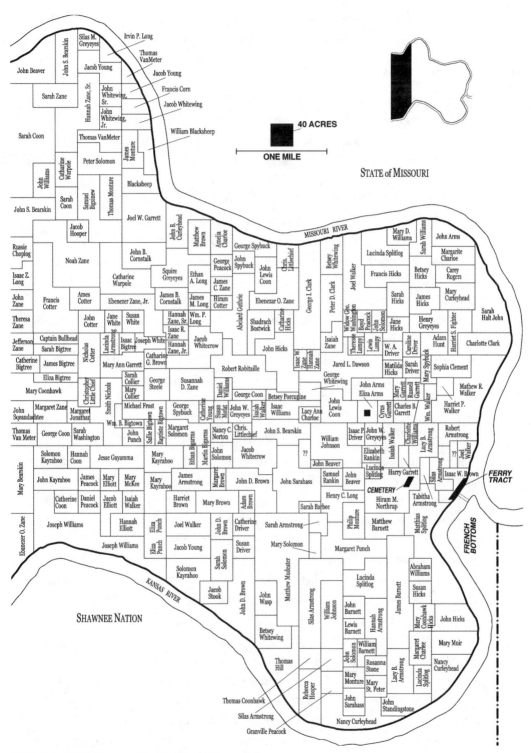

MAP 5.1. 1855 Kansas Allotments, West and East

never conflicted. Guthrie was known to oppose slavery and, unlike Walker, wore his personal ideologies on his sleeve. Wyandott City was not a free-state town, nor was it an openly proslavery town. Wyandott City claimed a neutral stance.

The Panic of 1857 was caused by a declining international economy and overexpansion of the domestic economy. This imbalance caused stock prices to plummet, banks to fail, and bankruptcies to soar in the east.[58] Yet amid the obvious financial turmoil besetting the nation, Quindaro still pressed forward with growth that peaked in early 1858. Then the money stopped flowing, the people stopped coming, and the town failed.

The Wyandott Town Company was incorporated on February 11, 1858. Three of the seven investors were Wyandot: Isaiah Walker, Joel Walker, and Silas Armstrong. The city was plotted on land secured by Armstrong almost immediately upon his arrival to the west in 1843 to 1844. He became a very rich and powerful man. Wyandott County was organized in 1859, and Wyandott City, not Quindaro, became the county seat. Free-state factions had secured the state of Kansas, and slavery was no longer an issue when it was admitted as a free state in 1861. Quindaro no longer had a purpose or a need to exist. By 1860 Quindaro was just another Kansas ghost town, but Wyandott City would grow into a mega-metropolis.

Guthrie hoped the town would provide his fortune. In his quest to secure financial stability and wealth, he had many ill-fated projects and investments that would go bankrupt. Seeing an opportunity that proved irresistible and an immediate solution to his debts, he made a bad choice and began to wrongfully use Wyandot tribal funds. As the tribe was reforming in Indian Territory, he served as tribal attorney for the Indian Party Wyandots and was known to divert funds to personal interests. John Wesley Greyeyes would eventually discover his crime, and, with the assistance of William Walker Jr., he had tribal funds diverted far from Guthrie's reach. Guthrie would die of heart failure in Washington, DC, on January 13, 1873, in financial ruin.[59]

The Wyandot floats were essentially bribes and incentives for chiefs and leading men of the Wyandot Tribe to accept and sign the Treaty of 1842. I doubt that the US government fully intended to honor the floats—maybe a few, but certainly not all. I also think the floats can be considered much like a manufacturer's rebate coupon. A $50.00 rebate looks really enticing and is often the determining factor in buying one product over another, but how many rebate coupons ever actually get redeemed? Very few. The coupons get lost or are forgotten, are technically too difficult to redeem, or, out of frustration, are discarded. In essence very few rebates are used, and manufacturers get to keep the full price of the sale. This is capitalism working at its finest.

The US government thought the same with the Wyandot floats, but they were wrong. Promise an Indian land and guess what—he's going to take the land! Unfortunately, the land in most cases was not retained by the original grantee. Most of the floats were sold to white farmers and land speculators, who in turn were the ones to profit from the sale of the land. The floats were of no value to the overall citizenry of the Wyandot Tribe. Instead, thirty-five leading men, chiefs, and councilors were to become landowners. They each were to receive six hundred forty acres at the government's expense for a total of 22,400 acres. Cumulatively, the floats were less acreage than the Wyandot purchase—23,040 acres, not that much difference. All land was supposed to be held in common by the tribe, with the floats being an exception.

Precedents for the Wyandot floats in Indian Territory west of the Mississippi River had been established in previous treaties with the various tribes. For example, in the Wyandot Treaty of 1817, Article Eight stated that various amounts of acreage were reserved for persons "connected with the said Indians, by blood or adoption." Six nations were included and signed the treaty: Seneca, Delaware, Shawnee, Pottawatomi, Ottawa, and Chippewa. Not only did a few citizens of the Wyandot Tribe receive special land grants, but citizens from the Shawnee, Ottawa, and Pottawatomi also received them.

The allocation of special land grants was not a new idea reserved specifically for the Wyandot Tribe, nor was it first or last seen in the Treaty of 1842. The land grants were unique in that each parcel of land could be chosen by the grantee from any lands that were west of the Missouri River set apart for Indian use and were not already claimed or occupied by a person or a tribe.[60] Once claimed, the title to the land could not be conveyed without special permission from the President of the United States. Thus, the owner of a title could not pass ownership even to their direct heir without permission. Who truly owned the land? The US government owned the land.

Peter D. Clarke first tried to sell his float in 1851 but could not.[61] The Bureau of Indian Affairs and the General Land Office ignored all claims for floats. Remember, it would take presidential approval before any float could be sold or transferred. In essence the President of the United States did nothing, nor did the Bureau of Indian Affairs, nor did the General Land Office. The floats became unredeemable rebates that proved nearly impossible to claim. Homer E. Socolofsky in "Wyandot Floats" stated, "The Wyandots, recognizing that their opportunity to engage in a real estate venture of their own was

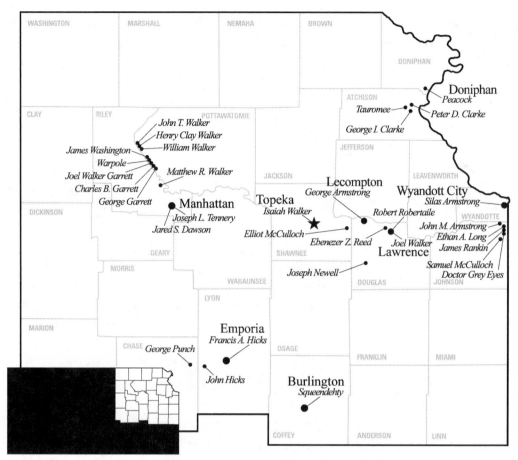

MAP 5.2. General Location of Wyandot Floats throughout Kansas

fast fading, initiated a new treaty with the United States government."[62] As we have already determined, the speculation and selling of tribal or float lands were not the reasons the tribe sought citizenship; however, it would take the Treaty of 1855 before any of the grantees could claim their floats. Article Nine stated, "It is stipulated and agreed, that each of the individuals, to whom reservations were granted by the fourteenth article of the treaty of March seventeenth, one thousand eight hundred and forty-two, or their heirs or legal representatives, shall be permitted to select and locate said reservations, on any Government lands west of the States of Missouri and Iowa."[63]

That all sounds wonderful, but if you are a white man looking for land in the newly opened territories of Kansas and Nebraska, are you going to respect the treaty rights of the Indians? No way! The Indians did not have any rights. Well, hold on: yes, now they did! Citizens of the Wyandot Tribe now had rights, for they, at least those who so desired, were now citizens of the United States of America according to the Treaty of 1855. The Wyandots were now US citizens? Sure enough, but the whites still did not respect those rights until they ended up in court and stood before a judge alongside a Wyandot Indian. The idea that Wyandot tribal citizens were now US citizens was so foreign that it could not be understood or accepted by many of the white settlers, farmers, ranchers, or town founders. Benjamin F. Stringfellow, a white man who purchased a Wyandot float, stated in a letter to Commissioner Manypenny, "I speak of these persons as Indians. This is a misnomer, for by the Treaty of 1855 under which these rights were perfected, they are made citizens entitled to all the rights of citizens."[64]

Indian land had always been free for the taking, but the Indian first had to be run off the land or killed. Now they had to be equally respected as rightful landowners. Once the Wyandot Reserve was allotted to tribal citizens, it was relatively easy for the whites to gain ownership of the land. The floats, however, were nearly impossible to explain, let alone begin to legally defend. As we have seen in earlier parts of this chapter, the lawlessness that prevailed in what was Kansas Territory was profoundly anti-Indian. The Treaty of 1855 was between the Wyandot Tribe and the United States of America. Then, in Kansas Territory, the Treaty of 1855 may have been a legal, binding agreement, but in the eyes and opinions of most Kansans, it really wasn't worth the paper it was written on.

Litigation encompassing the Wyandot floats was both time-consuming and costly. At times both the Wyandot seller and the buyer were caught in a tangled web of legal issues. Most of the floats were sold to farmers or land speculators and were some of the finest and most valuable land in Kansas. Only the floats owned or managed by Charles B. Garrett truly stayed within Wyandot ownership for an extended amount of time. The Treaty of 1855 was ratified on February 20, 1855. Garrett was the first Wyandot to file for a patent on July 19, 1855. Lucy B. Armstrong was the last to be issued her patent, on March 12, 1858, on behalf of her late husband, John McIntire Armstrong.

One of the strengths of the American Indian is found in his or her selflessness and oneness with his or her people and their land. This is called community, and this is what many Wyandots lost as they began to think and act like white people. In actuality, it was many of the white people who were adopted into the Wyandot Tribe who could not fully understand the Indians' way of life. Their lack of oneness with the people and land brought irreparable change. The tribe would ultimately split in the mid-1860s over this very issue among others. In the ensuing years the tribe was painfully purged of those who chose to be white or remain white over being an Indian. Those who chose US citizenship were not initially banned or excluded from the Wyandotte Tribe. The opposite occurred: They were encouraged to move to Indian Territory and be adopted into the tribe. Many ignored the invitation. Many who refused adoption did so out of greed and pride. Families were split as siblings and cousins chose different paths. Some stayed in Kansas, some went to Indian Territory and were adopted into the Wyandotte Tribe, and some just went elsewhere.

Citizen versus Indian

The Treaty of 1855 called for the complete termination of the historic Wyandot Tribe. However, it would take many years for the termination process to conclude. It was to be a slow and painful demise. Nothing in the Treaty of 1855 allowed for the continuation of the Wyandot Tribe. The only hope of those who deferred citizenship and wanted to remain Indian was to seek adoption into another tribe. Although most Wyandot citizens accepted US citizenship, many did not understand the proposal or quickly attempted to rescind their decision. Unfortunately, rescindment could not be done.

Once the Treaty of 1855 was ratified, circumstances began to quickly unravel, and most of the common everyday citizens found themselves in dire straits. The floats commanded much attention and became a distraction for the leading men. When the men were not dealing with their floats or other business interests, they were consumed with managing the money and affairs of the Incompetents and Orphans. Rather than protecting the Wyandot Reserve as a whole, family units now had to protect their own allotments, their own little piece of land. The dark days of Bleeding Kansas forced most citizens indoors, *figuratively speaking,* and then the Civil War erupted with a vengeance. There looked to be little hope, and even fewer options, for the once proud and mighty *Huron*-Wyandot people.

The Wyandot Tribal Council had settled into managing the tribe's affairs no less than a civil court would. Since by treaty the tribal council no longer existed as a sovereign, legal, and administrative body, they had nothing better to do when managing the affairs of former citizens of the tribe. The historic Wyandot Tribe and tribal council closed their books on July 9, 1862. The last entry in the tribal council minutes was a tear-jerking moment. Why? Technically, upon the closing of the minutes book, the historic Wyandot Tribe ceased to exist. The last entry of the council clerk read as such. *Wait!* Before you read, go get a Kleenex. It is quite the tearjerker. *OK. OK.* Go ahead and read it now, but don't say I didn't warn you!

Wyandott Council Room July 9, 1862

Jane Barnett widow of the late James Barnett dec, came and presented one order which was given by the Council on the 9th day of August 1860, to Catherine Young one of the heirs of the Estate of Jacob Young Died amounting to one hundred dollars the same having been paid by the said James Barnett in full. A receipt is hereby given to the said Jane Barnett, the order being left with the clerk of the Council.[65]

Seriously? That's it? That was the last official record of the Wyandot Tribe? Yes, it was, and it was definitely business as usual. It's nothing less than a receipt for $100 paid to Catherine Young by Jane Barnett, the widow of James Barnett. The book was then closed on the historic Wyandot Tribe. But wait! On December 22, 1862, a group of Wyandots met at Abelard Guthrie's home in the small struggling town of Quindaro. On that day they formed the Indian Party Wyandot. The party was a loose federation of men who were determined to seek reinstatement of the historic Wyandot Tribe in Indian Territory. The men did not have a constitution, and apparently no elections were held; however, Tauromee would emerge as the leader or chief of the Indian Party Wyandots.

The men who served as the last elected leaders of the Wyandot Tribe held their own elections in May of 1863. These men reemerged as the Citizen Party Wyandots. Their leader was Matthew Mudeater, the brother-in-law of Tauromee. Two rivalries now existed—one among men, brothers-in-laws nonetheless, and the other competing for the right to again call itself a tribe of people known as Wyandot.

In 1863 William Walker Jr. declared his support for the Indian Party Wyandots, saying the Citizen Party Wyandots were no longer part of the tribe. By supporting the Indian Party Wyandots, Walker, essentially at the same time, declared he was also no longer part of the Wyandot Tribe. He chose to retain his US citizenship. Legally and technically, everything that was happening was a moot argument, for, according to the US government, the Wyandot Tribe no longer existed as an organized and recognized body of American Indians. Yet the government continued to engage the Wyandots in dialogue. Walker would reverse his decision in support of the Indian Party Wyandots when in 1866 Tauromee moved to Indian Territory, leaving the Indian Party Wyandots in the care of acting chief John Wesley Greyeyes. Walker's flip-flopping support and the governments' continued dialogue are powerful testaments to the temperament that must have confused all Wyandots at the time.

The historic Wyandot Tribe officially no longer existed, yet the government was still communicating and doing business with both the Citizen Party and the Indian Party Wyandots just as though nothing had changed. The fact that a minority of the Wyandots escaped as hostages from the Secessionist Indians in 1862 and were then classified as Refugee Indians is a major factor of this continued relationship. In addition, recall that in 1850, when the Wyandot Tribe first requested a treaty to dissolve the tribe, take their land into severalty, and obtain US citizenship, the US government refused. It's possible that the continuation of dialogue between the United States and Citizen Party Wyandot was in part a meager attempt by the US government to reconcile some of their mistakes. One of the government's biggest mistakes was allowing the Treaty of 1855 to be formally ratified by the US Senate.

The Civil War ended on May 9, 1865. Peace had been nominally achieved, yet before a sense of normalcy returned, reconstructing the embattled states and knitting the broken pieces back together would take several years. Peace had to be secured, and part of that security meant a new treaty with the Secessionist Indians. A peace conference was called, and all the Indians were to attend—including the Wyandot. A Wyandot delegation attended the peace conference scheduled for September 8–21, 1865, in Fort Smith, Arkansas. Principal Chief Silas Armstrong and Matthew Mudeater represented the Wyandot people.[66]

Armstrong and Mudeater attended the council representing the Wyandot—not as Citizen Party Wyandot or Indian Party Wyandot, but simply Wyandot. They were received and seated, and Armstrong was given an opportunity to speak. Much of the discussions at the conference were not applicable to the Wyandot, as the tribe was never considered to be one of the secessionist tribes. Quite the contrary: The Wyandot were considered loyal to the United States. Seven stipulations were submitted to the Secessionist Indians as necessary elements to be contained in the new treaties. Point number five opened the door for the Wyandot Tribe to be reinstated as the Wyandotte Tribe in Indian Territory.

After being taken hostage by Secessionist Indians and adamantly refusing to sign a treaty of alliance supporting the Confederate cause, the Wyandot's good friends and hosts did sign the treaty supporting the Confederates. The Mixed Seneca and Shawnee protested being classified as Secessionist Indians: "They had signed a treaty under duress and had escaped from their Confederate persecutors the very first opportunity that offered."[67] Their protest was to no avail. Point number five, as required in their new treaty, stated, "A portion of the lands hitherto owned and occupied by you must be set apart for the friendly tribes now in Kansas, and elsewhere, on such terms as may be agreed upon by the parties, and approved by the government, or such as may be fixed by the government."[68]

While at the peace conference, Armstrong took ill. Never recovering his health, he died in Wyandott City, Kansas, on December 14, 1865. Ironically, he had been principal chief only once before, in 1858, when he served out the term of George I. Clarke upon his death in office. Matthew Mudeater would succeed Silas as principal chief. This again opened the heated debate: Who was the legal chief of the Wyandot? In 1865 that statement was legally moot—yet the government took the question very seriously. With such an unorthodox arrangement the government was perplexed and torn between whom they should support. Knowing that the Citizen Party Council were no longer considered Wyandot, their only legitimate choice was to support the Indian Party Council; however, they had been dealing with the men on the Citizen Party Council for so long that they really didn't know how to continue without them. In addition, this new Indian Party Council was now talking reinstatement of the Wyandot Tribe in Indian Territory. The US government bounced between both parties and finally cast their lot with Tauromee and the Indian Party Council.

Through the tireless work of Tauromee, the Treaty of 1867 was signed on February 23, 1867. Realizing the US Senate would likely ratify the Treaty of 1867, the Citizen Party Council offered the Indian Party Council a compromise. The Citizen Party Council offered to join the Indian Party Council and assist in their efforts to rebuild the Wyandotte Tribe. Tauromee adamantly declined the offer, as he was unwilling to accept the Citizen Wyandots into *his* tribe. Oddly enough, Citizen Wyandots were also serving on the Indian Party Council. It appears that the only thing that mattered is whether Tauromee liked you or not. It also sounds as though bitterness and resentment were getting the best of Tauromee, as was poor advice from some of his advisors. To make matters worse, the offer to merge the two councils was made by Matthew Mudeater. Tauromee's refusal of Mudeater's help allowed for dual Wyandot governments to officially coexist until around 1870.

The Treaty of 1867 was very clear in its wording. First, it reinstated the Wyandotte Tribe, bought land from the Mixed Seneca and Shawnee for a new home, and then defined who could be citizens. The new treaty continued to exclude all Wyandots who had initially accepted US citizenship as given in the Treaty of 1855, including mates and children. An exemption was extended to Incompetents and Orphans—they were now of age and could manage their own affairs. In all fairness the Treaty of 1867 had an inclusionary clause, that is, an escape route for people wanting into the Wyandotte Tribe. If an individual made application for adoption, they could have been adopted through the free consent of the tribe. Initially the Indian Party Council, led by Tauromee and later John Kayrahoo, was given the power and privilege of readmitting Citizen Wyandots into the tribe as though they had never left the tribe. Officially, it was not until July 11, 1872, that the new Wyandotte Tribal Council became stable enough to make the adoptions legal.

It took a lot of time to get the Wyandotte Tribe organized and open for business. By 1872 many Citizen Wyandots were readmitted into the tribe, and more would trickle into Indian Territory over the next several years. Most were readmitted and welcomed into the tribe, including several of the Citizen Wyandots who had served on the former Wyandot Tribal Council. Prominent citizens such as Matthew Mudeater, Isaiah Walker (brother of William Walker Jr.), John Wesley Greyeyes, and Silas W. Armstrong (son of Silas Armstrong) were adopted into the Wyandotte Tribe. All a Citizen Wyandot had to do was ask to be adopted and then physically move to Indian Territory. It was that simple.

Wishing one's name to be placed on the tribal roll, as expressed by William Walker Jr., and actually requesting adoption are two totally different things. Walker and many other Wyandots were never adopted into the Wyandotte Tribe. Why? They never officially asked. There were several Citizen Wyandots who at this time were considered quite wealthy and influential within the greater Wyandott City metropolitan area. For them to have moved to Indian Territory would have come at a great price.

After twelve years of dissolution, only one hundred fifty-one Wyandots initially moved to Indian Territory. Many who did not move eventually stated they were not informed of what was happening. The Wyandot people were not a large tribe, and many families were intertwined with relatives living in Kansas, in Indian Territory, and elsewhere, including Canada. What was happening must have been common knowledge, even though Wyandots were already scattered and displaced throughout the United States and Canada.

They had to have known what was happening, for the conflict between the Citizen Wyandots and the Indian Party Wyandots was just shy of a civil war.

My question is: If a person was truly desirous of remaining a Wyandotte, why did he or she not move to Indian Territory? There are few excuses that can justify their decision. Unless, like Ebenezer Zane who left the Wyandot Purchase and disappeared, someone moved to a deserted island in Antarctica, or crawled under a rock and hid, it would have been nearly impossible not to know what was happening. Yes, it could be that some Wyandots were too incompetent to understand what was happening, but the Incompetents were generally the citizens who could not speak English. John Kayrahoo could not speak English, yet he obviously knew what was happening, because he was then serving the Indian Party Wyandots as second chief and eventually chief of the Wyandotte Tribe. All of what was happening was a pretty big deal. The key thing was it was expected that individuals physically move to Indian Territory. Why?

Not too many years earlier, the Wyandot Tribe was faced with a very similar event. Upon moving west from Ohio and Michigan, there were many Wyandot who chose to stay behind and continue to live in Canada. Many, but not all, Canadian Wyandots denied an open invitation to remain part of the main body of Wyandots and move west across the Mississippi River as a unified tribe. As the Ohio and Michigan Wyandots started their trek south from Upper Sandusky in July of 1843, the inevitable consequences of one hundred years of geopolitical differences were finally fulfilled. The Wyandot Tribe was now technically and officially two independent bands of *Huron*-Wyandots. Tribal leadership did not want a third band of Wyandots.

As people who had accepted US citizenship in 1855 began to trickle south in the years 1867 to 1872, the physical move was both symbolic and purposeful. The first step a Citizen Wyandot had to take was to ask for adoption into the Wyandotte Tribe. Doing so may have been an embarrassment, but both tradition and treaty made it a necessity. Very few people who asked to be adopted were rejected; however, a few former Wyandot citizens were denied Wyandotte citizenship.

Knowing what had happened a meager twenty-five years earlier with the Canadian Wyandot, the new tribal leadership knew it was important to keep the Wyandotte Tribe unified and not repeat another split. Communication with the Wyandots in Canada, who were now a separate and independent tribe, was often difficult and delayed and served no needful purpose. It was known from experiences over the last ten years with Wyandots in both Kansas and Indian Territory that if Wyandottes were allowed to stay in both locations, communication and unity would become an impossible challenge. After all, the Kayrahoo Council was unsuccessfully trying to manage and govern the Wyandotte's affairs in Indian Territory from Quindaro, Kansas. To make matters worse, I do not doubt that rumblings and grumblings from the state of Kansas were making Kansans' intentions clear—Indians were not welcome in their state. A complete and total move of the Wyandotte Tribe south into Indian Territory was the only way to protect and preserve the lives of each citizen. Much like being banned from your clan for the crime of outlawry, if you did not move with the Wyandotte Tribe, a blanket of protection could not be extended. In essence, if you did not move to Indian Territory and ask for adoption, you became an outlaw and lost the protection of the Wyandotte Tribe.

Shortly after the death of Tauromee, Superintendent of Indian Affairs Enoch Hoag directed that an election be held for the Wyandotte Tribe in Indian Territory. Superintendent Hoag was growing tired of watching the progress to nowhere and directed Special Indian Agent George Mitchell to make things happen. The best way to see this accomplished was to hold an election. Those deemed eligible to vote in the upcoming election were all who refused US citizenship in 1855; the Incompetent and Orphan classes, along with their descendants; and those from the Citizen class who were younger than twenty-one upon the signing of the 1855 treaty, and their descendants. These terms did not quite match up to those of the Treaty of 1867, but the decree went uncontested—until after the election. The election was scheduled for May 30, 1871.

Abelard Guthrie became John Kayrahoo's right-hand man and too often did not have the best interest of his adopted tribe at heart, especially after suffering terrible financial losses after the demise of Quindaro—his town, not his wife. As the Indian Party Wyandots were being organized, Tauromee secured the services of Guthrie as tribal attorney and gave him power of attorney over the tribe during his tenure. Guthrie's title and authority remained intact into Kayrahoo's Council. He tried to recover from his financial losses by diverting tribal funds from the selling of Incompetent and Orphan class allotments and negotiated fees paid to the tribe for railroad rights running through the new reservation in Indian Territory. In addition, Guthrie sought the right to claim his mother-in-law's Shawnee allotment. After marrying a naturally born Wyandot citizen and being given full rights the same as she had, he expected that the other tribes would also honor and accept him as their equal, but they did not. He reportedly attempted on multiple occasions to switch his tribal affiliation from Wyandot to Shawnee so that he could possess his mother-in-law's two-hundred-acre allotment.[69] If successful, which he was not, he would have promptly sold the land without hesitation to get his hands on some much-needed cash.

In November of 1870, John Wesley Greyeyes was living in Indian Territory and after the death of Tauromee was recognized by many as the principal chief of the Wyandotte Tribe. In need of a little help to try to inspire the US government to enact the terms of the Treaty of 1867, Greyeyes recruited the assistance of William Walker Jr. and Russell B. Garrett. In an ironic twist, neither of the two men sought or appeared to desire adoption into the Wyandotte Tribe. Organized as a committee with authority to act in the absence of a viable Wyandotte tribal council, Greyeyes took the initiative to finish the work started by Tauromee. At the same time, the committee informed the US government that "Guthrie does not represent the Wyandots and should be disregarded."[70] Greyeyes was himself an attorney. In his younger years he was known to be an alcoholic; however, as he grew older, he defeated the vice and remained sober until his death in Indian Territory.

On May 30, 1871, the first Wyandotte tribal election was held in Indian Territory with only twenty-four people voting, half of them Citizen Wyandots. John Kayrahoo was elected chief. Guthrie protested the voting of Citizen Wyandots. The votes of the Citizen Wyandots were affirmed, and those who voted were allowed to remain on the Wyandotte tribal roll. Because of the unnecessary attention brought to the election, it was considered tainted and caused extensive debate as to who would be considered eligible for Wyandotte citizenship in spite of the Treaty of 1867. Special decrees and statements made by the Superintendent of Indian Affairs led the Wyandotte Tribe to petition that they be the one to determine who would be eligible for Wyandotte citizenship. Their request was successful, and over the next year around one hundred Citizen Wyandots were added to the Wyandotte tribal roll.

Another election was held on July 11, 1872, with forty-four out of fifty-eight qualified to vote present. Thomas Punch was elected chief over John Kayrahoo. Kayrahoo believed that the election from the previous year was for a four-year term, and he protested the results, again to no avail. This election set the precedents of who would be adopted and how elections would be handled within the Wyandotte Tribe for many years to come. Kayrahoo eventually left the Wyandotte Tribe, choosing instead to live with the Seneca. The Seneca had retained and were practicing a more traditional lifestyle. Kayrahoo is considered one of the last of the traditional Breechcloth Band Wyandots—a true traditionalist.

In 1875, after being denied adoption into the Wyandotte Tribe, a few Citizen Wyandots, including Quindaro Nancy Brown Guthrie, are known to have solicited the Canadian Wyandot for inclusion. These people were requesting that they be allowed relocation privileges and receive protection of the Canadian Wyandot. Their requests were denied. The Canadian Wyandots, represented by their agent, told the Citizen Wyandots that since they had accepted US citizenship, they could no longer be considered Wyandots in Canada. Nancy Guthrie, the granddaughter of Adam Brown and cousin to Peter D. Clarke, was also banned from returning to Canada because she had married a white man.[71] The infamous news of her husband's legacy preceded her request to move to Canada and proved a dark fact she could not escape or deny.

The General Allotment Act of 1887, or the Dawes Act, called for the allotment of the Wyandotte's reservation in Indian Territory. In 1888 two hundred fifty-one Wyandottes, not including their dependent family members, received an allotment. The Citizen Wyandots in Kansas were not considered when allotments in Indian Territory were assigned. Without a tribal government that provided protection, the Citizen Wyandots essentially and eventually became unwanted wards of the state of Kansas. They were citizens of the United States, but they were unwanted and unaccepted as being legitimate citizens because in the past they had once identified themselves as Indians! It was the US government that bestowed them citizenship. According to the state of Kansas, US citizenship was a birthright not a decree. In the mid- to late nineteenth century, bigotry and racial discrimination were not crimes. At this point in time Citizen Wyandots were unwanted by just about everyone. The United States did not want them, nor did the state of Kansas, nor did any other Indian tribe. Prior to the allotment of the Wyandotte Reservation in 1888, the Wyandotte Tribe would have adopted them into the tribe, but the Citizen Wyandots did not want the Wyandotte Tribe. After the allotment of the Wyandotte Reservation in 1888, the Wyandotte Tribe would no longer consider adoption of the Citizen Wyandots—they were now Absentee Wyandots and committed the fatal crime of outlawry.

As predicted, a little later, near the close of the nineteenth century, the Citizen Wyandots, who were trying to sustain a lifestyle in Kansas, found it to be impossible. They would begin to lose their land to taxation. Now, when facing the prospects and reality of being homeless, they finally cried foul. However, it was too late. The Citizen Wyandots were shocked by the reality that they were no longer welcome on the Wyandotte Reservation in Indian Territory. Unlike the Pagan Wyandots, who were given a place to live on the Grand Reserve when they sold the Big Spring Reserve, the Citizen Wyandots had denied their heritage. Clearly, the Pagan Wyandots never denied their *Huron*-Wyandot heritage. The Absentee Wyandots were now being dealt with as a separate entity and people by the US government. In an attempt to find concessions and accommodation for the Absentee Wyandots, the Public Act of 1894 became law.

There was one small problem with the Public Act of August 15, 1894: No tribe wanted to share their land with the Absentee Wyandot. As per this act, eighty acres in Indian Territory were to be purchased from the Quapaw, but the Quapaw declined to sell. Another attempt also failed in 1896 when land was to be bought from the Choctaw and Chickasaw nations—they also said no. These Wyandot carried the distinct mark of being US citizens. No tribe was going to accommodate their needs for any reason! If the Wyandottes did not want them, it's no wonder that their plea for land went unheeded. After the Joel T. Olive roll of April 28, 1904, eighty acres of agricultural land, wherever there may be such lands subject to entry, were finally provided to the Absentee Wyandot. Most of the land was found out west and was not located on any tribal lands, as the land was in the public domain. Upon acceptance of the land, the Absentee Wyandots, including their children and descendents, forever forfeited the opportunity to become Wyandotte citizens.

The Oklahoma Indian Welfare act of 1936 called for the reorganization of the Wyandotte Tribe and all the other tribes then in Oklahoma. Through the efforts of tribal leaders, a tribal constitution was written and subsequently adopted by the Nations Council. From the Oklahoma Indian Welfare Act a census was also conducted from which the Wyandotte's tribal roll of 1937 was compiled. Until 2013, the tribal roll of 1937 was the oldest recognized roll the Wyandotte Nation used to determine citizenship status..The census roll of 1881 has since been recognized as the oldest roll that can be used to determine citizen status; however, a majority vote of the nation's council is required if it or any subsequent tribal roll is used by anyone seeking tribal citizenship. The Tribal Constitution of 1937 also called for a name change. The Wyandotte Tribe was thereafter known as the Wyandotte Tribe of Oklahoma.

It was under the leadership of Chief Leonard Cotter, not Leaford Bearskin, that first began the fundamental policy of excluding Absentee Wyandots, or those whose names appeared on the Olive Roll and their descendants, from seeking and obtaining Wyandotte Nation citizenship. The constitution which

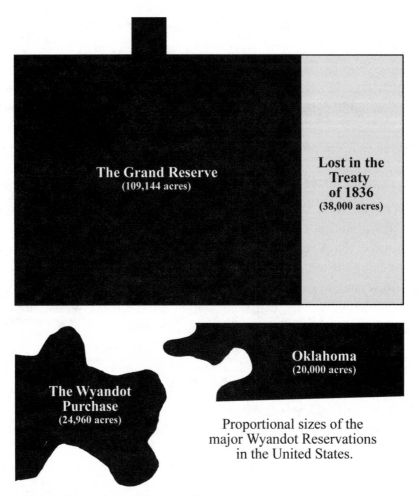

The Grand Reserve
(109,144 acres)

Lost in the
Treaty
of 1836
(38,000 acres)

Oklahoma
(20,000 acres)

The Wyandot
Purchase
(24,960 acres)

Proportional sizes of the
major Wyandot Reservations
in the United States.

MAP 5.3. Comparison of Wyandot Reserves

Chief Cotter helped write simply stated that when citizenship requirements were listed, "all persons of Indian blood whose names appear on the official census roll of the Tribe as of January 1, 1937" would be included. Absentee Wyandots and Wyandots whose names appeared on the Olive Roll would not have been accounted for on the tribal roll of 1937.

Given that federal recognition was reconferred upon the Wyandotte Tribe in 1867, then residing in Indian Territory on land purchased from the Seneca, the historic Wyandot Tribe technically had not ceased to exist. Instead, the historic Wyandot Tribe found new life with a name spelled a little differently—the Wyandotte Tribe. Tauromee, head chief of the historic Wyandot Tribe at the signing of the Treaty of 1855, was the same head chief at the signing of the Treaty of 1867. At this same time an opportunity was extended to the Citizen Wyandot for adoption into the Wyandotte Tribe, but the invitation was not accepted by many former citizens. Therefore, today the proper tribal name for the descendants of these people who did not seek adoption into the Wyandotte Tribe should be the *Citizen* Wyandot Nation of Kansas, or better, the *Absentee* Wyandot Nation of Kansas. This band of Wyandots do not have an unbroken tribal government spanning one hundred years which is required in order to be considered for federal recognition.

The Wyandot Nation of Kansas is relatively new. They were organized for the first time in 1959 as a nonprofit organization due to ongoing battles over the *Huron* Indian Cemetery located in Kansas City.[72] At the time of this writing, they have had only two chiefs: George Zane and Janith (Jan) English. The Wyandot Nation of Kansas was incorporated in 1994; they began their petition with the Bureau of Indian Affairs for federal recognition. The descendants of the Absentee Wyandot then needed additional legal protection to further contest the Wyandotte Tribe of Oklahoma. As of today, the Wyandot Nation of Kansas's bid for federal recognition remains an unsuccessful one.

At the turn of the twentieth century, self-identifying as a Wyandotte in Oklahoma was not an easy choice. Most Wyandottes could not then tell anyone about their amazing heritage, life was full of hardship, and some experienced various degrees of persecution just because they were an Indian. In the next chapter we will meet Hazel Wallace, the niece of BNO Walker. Hazel was a citizen of the Seneca-Cayuga Tribe and she was also a Wyandotte. As a young girl she was beaten at the boarding school in Wyandotte, Oklahoma, for speaking her native language. Back then, to have been an Indian was not something to covet, and many Indians denied their heritage—many Indians lost their lives.

Today many people want to be an Indian because it has a flair of glamor and is rather covetous. There are also many who think they are an Indian; however, most cannot prove they are Indian. Others have proof they are Indian but because of decisions made by their ancestors they are not eligible to be placed on any tribal roll. History can be both glorious and cruel. At times its remembrance can bring much joy and pleasant reminiscing. At times its remembrance can bring much sorrow and painful regret. Such is the case in the history and relationship between the Wyandot Nation of Kansas and the Wyandotte Nation. The decisions we make today can and will affect the lives of our children for many generations to come. If you doubt this, just ask a descendant of an Absentee Wyandot.

CHAPTER 6

"Preserving the Future of Our Past"

I ask more, Great Spirit: watch over my people; protect them; keep them
unharmed in spirit as well as in body. Help me to regard each life as highly
as my own.[1]

—Leaford Bearskin, 1983

Indian Reunion and Barbecue

In 1868 if you were a Wyandotte citizen and living within the boundary of
the Neosho Agency in Indian Territory, it was a purposeful choice. You were
there because you wanted to be there. Unlike the tribe's recent move from the
state of Ohio to Indian Territory, no one was forcing you to leave the state of
Kansas for the Neosho Agency. This time your individual freewill guided your
staying or leaving. The slender strip of land in the northeast corner of Indian
Territory east of the Neosho and Grand rivers and north of the Cowskin River
once belonged to the Osage, then the Cherokee, and most recently the Mixed
Seneca and Shawnee. Now the land belonged to the Wyandotte. It was a land
both copiously abundant and cruelly unforgiving with a varied mix of terrain.
The weather was very unpredictable, making your decision to move that much
more difficult. For the few who chose to move, a little less than half the historic Wyandot Tribe, the move could not be made in a few days or even a few
months. Little by little Citizen Wyandots trickled south from Kansas over the
course of several years, requested adoption, and again became Indian—Wyandotte Indians.

For many citizens this was the third place they would call home in three
short yet turbulent decades. The people were small in number, conspicuously
poor, and hardworking, and many were unknowing of the culture and history

that preceded them. Still they endured and remained defiantly proud to be Wyandotte. They were equally proud to again be recognized as Indians and living among their old Indian friends.

In their poverty the Wyandottes were blissfully unaware of what they did not have. They had a home and land, and familiar old friends surrounded them on three of four sides. What more did they need? The tribal politics that engulfed and nearly suffocated the tribe's move to the Neosho Agency was noticeably present but was ignored by many. Family units huddled together and supplied the network of support once innately given through the clans. Many of the prominent family names found in Ohio, Michigan, and Kansas were noticeably absent. Many chose to stay in Kansas to pursue other adventures and accumulate their treasures. Families were split between Indian and Citizen. There was a swirl of bitterness and forgiveness, acceptance and rejection, justice and injustice; the time was simple, yet unquestionably difficult.

After they had endured the difficult years of Bleeding Kansas, the Civil War, and the Wyandot's own pseudo–civil war, surviving to make the move to Indian Territory must have been invigorating as the people began the process of renewing the old *Huron*-Wyandot traditions. On August 15, 1868, during what was likely the first green corn feast held in Indian Territory, "events include the naming of children, the bestowing of honorary names, and the feast, followed by a traditional Shawnee dance."[2] William Walker Jr. attended this green corn feast as one of the featured speakers. What is the most disappointing revelation from the 1868 green corn feast held in Indian Territory? A reporter for the *Wyandotte Gazette,* a newspaper published in Wyandott City, Kansas, was in attendance, and in her article she favorably compared the green corn feast to similar non-Indian gatherings.[3] The reporter favorably compared the sacred *Huron*-Wyandot feast to a white man's fair—and that is disappointing. The green corn feast of the *Huron*-Wyandot people had become no different from any county fair then being held anywhere throughout the United States.

Times were desperate when in 1874 the tribal council required eligible voters to register by clan. Only seventy-six men from seven clans were found eligible to vote.[4] In a 1911 interview with Dr. Barbeau, Mary Williams Walker stated, "The last green corn feast took place at John Cour's [Coon's] about 1881 at which a large number of people were present."[5] The years 1880 to 1882 were pivotal years for the Wyandotte people. The tribal roll in 1881 listed two hundred eighty citizens who identified themselves as being Wyandotte. If indeed the green corn feast were last celebrated around 1881, it is a strong

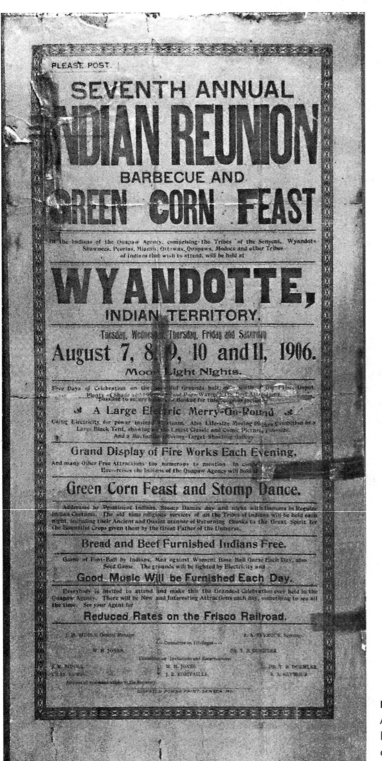

FIGURE 6.1. Poster Announcing 7th Annual Indian Reunion, Barbecue, and Green Corn Feast

indication that the clans had been severely weakened before moving to Indian Territory. It also indicates that with the Wyandotte's small population they could no longer sustain something as culturally important as the clans. There were no longer enough Wyandottes to fully populate the clans; therefore, the clan animals went into hibernation until a time when the Wyandotte people could again sustain the clans.

Why did the Wyandotte people bury their green corn feast? That is an extremely complicated discussion which I do not have time to fully explore in this book; however, the small population mentioned above was a major contributing factor. Without clans and clan mothers, the feast was just another social feast. The Wyandottes still knew how to conduct the feast, but without clans and clan mothers they did not want to dishonor its time-honored sanctity. When the clans came together at the feast, the importance of the health and the unity of the tribe was confirmed and reaffirmed. In 1881 the health of the Wyandotte Tribe wasn't looking very good. The people were struggling, but this was just another enemy they would not turn their backs to and succumb to defeat. At this last green corn feast, an age-old tradition of dropping kernels of corn may not have happened. Eldredge H. Brown stated, "Each person would drop a grain of Indian corn. . . . When each member of the clan was thus represented in the tray by a grain of corn, some specially appointed people . . . would examine the relative strength of each clan by the examination of the number of grains."[6] In time the Wyandotte people will again drop their kernels of corn.

The poster "*Seventh Annual Indian Reunion, Barbecue, and Green Corn Feast*" illustrates how greatly the sanctity of the green corn feast had been insulted by 1906. From the poster it is safe and easy to assume that the feast had been taken hostage by the Quapaw Agency. Much like what was happening across the United States with other tribes, the feast was becoming a show and a public spectacle. With a large electric merry-go-round and grand display of fireworks, the feast must have been nothing less than spectacular. The whites in attendance came to gawk, spend their money, and watch the show. The Indians were on parade, but at least bread and beef were furnished to the Indians for free.

Across the United States, other tribes were coerced to dance by various governmental officials. By doing this, the tribes traditions and cultures became a show and source of entertainment for the whites; hence, the birth of pow-wows. In defiance of many governmental policies then stifling tribal traditions, the tribes danced and openly celebrated their traditions; hence, their traditions thrived and the powwows grew nationwide into an honored and new celebrated tradition. Unfortunately, for the Wyandotte people the tradition of the green corn feast did not survive. Wyandotte citizens who still wanted to dance and feast had to do so as guests of the Seneca-Cayuga Tribe of Oklahoma.

The degradation of the Wyandotte's green corn feast was not a situation unique to the Wyandotte people. William M. Beauchamp in *Indian Corn Stories and Customs* tells how in the late nineteenth century he found disappointment upon attending a green corn feast of the Onondaga. Beauchamp explained, "The green-corn feast is one of the most important of all, formerly lasting four days, when large quantities of corn, beans, and squashes were consumed. It has now degenerated into a public show, as the warm summer time brings many curious visitors."[7] For me personally, it brings sadness and a little comfort knowing the green corn feast of other tribes was also suffering equal compromise and loss.

Potatoes, Hay, and Ham

Over the years I have read many stories of the *Huron*-Wyandot people. One of my favorite is from the time period we are now discussing. The story shows that amid enduring hardship, life went on unabated and the common good found in the Wyandottes never diminished. Jared Silas Dawson in his 1937 interview with Nannie Lee Burns tells the story of his uncle Irvin Patton Long. A studio photograph taken in 1882 by Thomas Concannon gives a priceless look into Irvin's face. The difficult time the Wyandotte Tribe was experiencing is exposed by Long's expression, yet his flinty and chiseled countenance remained unblemished, strong, and determined. Long was principal chief of the Wyandotte Tribe in 1882, and he also served as Chairman of the Intertribal Council consisting of the Wyandotte, Seneca, Ottawa, Shawnee, Peoria, and Quapaw tribes.

In 1937 Dawson was living in Commerce, Oklahoma. Like so many other Wyandottes, he did not live on the former reservation land. At the time of his story, he was a small child. The story was likely handed down to him and retold countless times until it could not be dislodged from his memory. Today when most Wyandotte citizens speak of traditional stories, they often include only the oral narratives as told by their ancestors from their far distant past. These stories are commonly called the *Traditional Narratives*. Yes, I have no doubt that the Wyandottes in Long's day were still telling the old oral narra-

FIGURE 6.2. Irvin Patton Long

tives of their origin; however, I also have no doubt that during Dawson's day those same stories were beginning to grow silent and many forgotten. There were many other stories that began to replace the old, such as the following relatively new story of Irvin Long.

As the Wyandottes sought shade and a cool breeze during the heat of summer, or huddled around a potbelly stove in the cold dark of winter, they did not have distractions to entertain themselves. They only had each other and their stories. I can just see them sitting on a porch or under a big oak tree, smiling and laughing. The stories may have been an odd mix of Wandat and English, for the old language was starting to grow silent. It did not matter which tongue told the stories; everyone would laugh just the same. Dawson retold the story of his famed uncle to Nannie as though he had witnessed the events himself.

One day, Uncle Irving Long, who was then chief was driving a team of mules to an ox-wagon past Mr. Beauchamp's Place (who was digging potatoes). Uncle Irving got out of his wagon without a word and took from the wagon two sacks which he filled with potatoes and loaded them into the wagon and without saying anything relative to the potatoes drove off. Later Mr. Beauchamp needing some hay hitched up to his wagon with a hay frame on it and drove to Uncle Irving's haystacks and helped himself to as much hay as he wanted and drove home with it.

Uncle Irving had a large and very long log smoke house and each year he killed many, many hogs and this or rather the poles would be full of meat. Later when any of his friends were at his house when they left they would find concealed somewhere either in their wagon or in something he had wrapped up and given them a large piece of meat or perhaps a whole shoulder or ham; he didn't have to pen the hogs then. They were ear marked and turned out.[8]

This is what community is all about. This is why the Wyandotte people, in order to remain Indian, chose the difficult life and moved to the Neosho Agency, which was reorganized and renamed the Quapaw Agency in 1871. They chose to share the hard-earned abundance of the land, celebrate life, work hard, and care one for another. Any unspoken and unmerited act of acceptance, respect, and kindness will always exceed the utterance of mere words. For the chief of the Wyandotte Tribe, with all his expected responsibilities, to exert himself and give gifts with no expectation of return is amazing. Long's lead should be an example for all of us today. For Chief Long, Beauchamp, and anyone else to share the abundance of the Great Spirit's blessing was just the natural order of the way they thought and lived.

The Reverend William Martin Beauchamp was an ethnologist and Episcopal minister. In 1889 the US Bureau of Ethnology commissioned Reverend Beauchamp to study the six tribes of the Iroquois in New York. For a short while prior to this commission, Reverend Beauchamp was in Indian Territory and spent time with the Wyandotte and Seneca people. For the Wyandotte it did not matter that Reverend Beauchamp was an outsider: He was equally welcome and fulfilled his role in the Wyandotte community. In 1882, there were no vagabonds on the Wyandotte Reservation, and the elitists were nowhere to be found. However, there were a few from the old breechcloth band—the hard-core traditionalists—who remained true to their traditional heritage.

Unfortunately, the traditionalists became a little intolerant of their brothers and sisters who were struggling to survive. As the common, everyday citizens of the Wyandotte Tribe chose to live and raise their families, a tinge of whiteness inevitably began to settle over their households and the tribe in whole. Year after year, as this became more apparent, the breechcloth band began to preach a divisive message: Stay Indian or become white—you cannot be both. We still hear this same message today. This is good! The preachers of divisiveness still see enough Indian to recognize the Indian—a Wyandotte Indian. On the Wyandotte Reservation in 1882 there were a lot of dirt-covered fingers; bands of muddy beads strung around sweaty necks; bruised, achy knees; tired backs; and smiling faces as the Wyandottes tirelessly worked to turn the unforgiving land into a land of plenty. Their parents had accepted the same challenge and accomplished the same task thirty-six years earlier in Kansas. Failure was not an option then, nor was failure an option now.

The common support of community can mask many fears; mend countless blisters on tired, working hands; and give hope when hope is all but lost. In today's technology burdened and distracted society it seems people have forgotten what uniquely makes us human. We were created to bond and be together, care for and serve each other with little concern for our own personal needs. As a mother cares for the needs of her child, the citizens of a true community are equally concerned and watching for the needs of their fellow citizens. Community is free and freely given from the heart, and it's what people naturally do when a common bond unites them in spirit, faith, hope, trust, and truth.

For many people in our contemporary society, the common theme is a self-centered and entitled *me* and what is *mine*: toys, fancy homes, expensive cars, you know, the stuff that doesn't come close to defining anyone as a person. In contrast there are also many people who are struggling to make ends meet, feed and clothe their children, and not lose hope that tomorrow will still bring another day of hope. Many people, those who have and those who have not, hold little regard to the fact that anything different exists. Both are missing the very essence of community. How lucky Wyandottes are to have the treasure of a heritage they can equally share with others of common heritage where community is alive and well.

In the Wyandot's language there is not a word for please; however, thanks—tižamęh—is very prevalent and still used today in everyday conversations. What can one say about a people who do not have a word for please? Are they demanding, uncouth, discourteous, and disrespectful to their fellow citizens? Absolutely not! I know that it means no one had to ask for anything. They especially did not have to say please in order to receive the help they needed. If you were hungry, it's likely you would find a lovingly smoked and very delicious whole shoulder of hog in your wagon when you returned home from visiting a friend. Maybe you found some flour, corn, fresh eggs or the whole chicken, and some maple syrup. If you possessed an outstanding debt that needed to be paid, but you did not have enough money to meet the debt, it's amazing how a neighbor or two across the way would suddenly have some odd jobs that required your help. Without hesitation, you would heed the requests for help, earn a little extra money, and pay your debt. My debt, my pain, my need, my likes and dislikes, along with my abundance—all were equally shared within my community. My community and I are no different—we are one and the same.

In order for this sense of community to happen, neighbors need to be neighbors and know what's happening in the lives of their neighbors. This can easily be done without imposing or being nosy. It's called trust, respect, and compassion—it's community. If there was abundance, there was freedom to take as needed, just as Irvin Long did with the potatoes—stockpiling and hoarding excluded. No one had to ask for anything. No one took more than they needed. Community existed openly and freely. It naturally existed with the Wyandotte people, and it still exists today. Please was a foreign word that had no place among people who naturally cared about and attended to the needs of their neighbors, *their family,* before the need to ask for anything arose.

I have no doubt that Long had many visitors and gave away many hams. Many stories were told on his front porch. He was "chipped from the flint of Wyandot legend," and thus when he died, his death was a huge loss for his people. The Wyandotte people, much like when Leaford Bearskin died in 2012, grieved and felt alone, without a leader. Jared Dawson, who was a little older when his Uncle Irvin died, vividly remembered the day: "I rode two horses down carrying the news through the country. He was buried at the John Bland Cemetery where my parents and several others of the tribe are."[9]

By 1880, for most citizens life on the Wyandotte Reservation had returned to a sense of normalcy. By then, if an individual or family were planning to move from Kansas or elsewhere to Indian Territory, they would have done so regardless of the hardship. The General Allotment Act, or Dawes Act of 1887, and the ensuing allotment of the Wyandotte Reservation in 1888 were technically the cutoff points for Citizen Wyandots to seek adoption. An individual had to be physically living on the Wyandotte Reservation in 1888 to take possession of the land. If at this time someone had not been adopted back into the Wyandotte Tribe, they were not part of the community, and they did not get their share of the land.

One of the darkest times in Wyandotte history quickly follows the reinstatement of Wyandotte community in the last two to three decades of the nineteenth century. After the turn of the twentieth century, the following fifty years were starkly void of dynamic events. The intrusive and ever-present documentation of the missionaries and imposing government agents that had once followed the lives of the Wyandotte's grandparents dissolved into near nothingness. It seems that an interest in the Wyandotte people after Dr. Charles Barbeau's short stay in and departure from Oklahoma in the years 1911 and 1912 just fizzled away. Even tribal records are starkly barren and silent of the many events that may have transpired after this time. Only three things seem to have commanded the time and attention of the chiefs and tribal councils: the plight of the children in the Indian Schools, the fight over the *Huron* Place Cemetery, and the ongoing battle with the US government to justify the Wyandotte's existence.

One comprehensive report from 1894, titled *Report On Indians Taxed and Not Taxed In The United States,* provides a nice glimpse into the Wyandotte community. The following is the whole of the report, and it needs no deletion of propaganda or fluff. As you read, close your eyes and envision the Wyandotte people living in a community that was a reflection of the old but had been adapted into something new with the intent to survive. By this time the land had been allotted and overrun by whites, but still it was home; it was their land.

> The Wyandotte reservation is on steep land lying north of the Seneca reservation and adjoining it, with Missouri on the east and Grand river on the west. But a very small portion of the land is good for agricultural purposes, as it is hilly and quite rough except along Sycamore and Lost creeks. Along these streams the lands are good for all purposes, and here they have fine farms. The Wyandottes have taken their lands in severalty, but there is so much poor land that now some 25 of them have none. These lands are well watered not only by the streams but by numerous springs. It is really the best watered of any reservation at this agency. There are strong indications to lead and zinc on a great portion of the land, especially in the hills and on the bluffs.
>
> The Wyandottes number 288 in all, 129 males and 159 females; 250 speak English and 157 read it.
>
> These Indians have good farms, which are mostly along the streams. They have some few, however, on the prairie, which are not so large, as they use the prairie land for grass and grazing purposes. Since they have taken their lands in severalty, they have made greater progress than for many years previous, building houses, barns, fences, and all kinds of improvements, and acquiring more stock of all kinds.
>
> Horses and mules, 273; Cattle, 1,028; Swine, 697; Sheep, 138; Fowls of all kinds, 2,875.

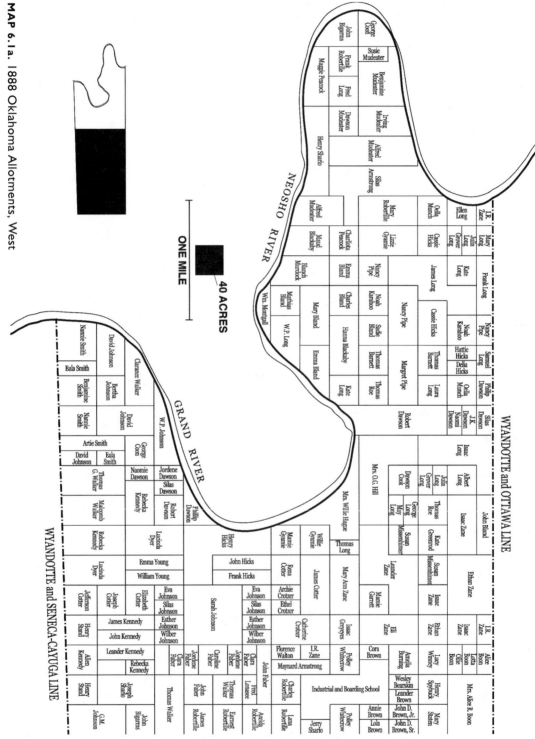

MAP 6.1a. 1888 Oklahoma Allotments, West

ONE MILE

40 ACRES

MAP 6.1b. 1888 Oklahoma Allotments, East

WYANDOTTE and SHAWNEE LINE

WYANDOTTE and SENECA-CAYUGA LINE

WYANDOTTE and STATE of MISSOURI LINE

By the allotment the head of a family received 160 acres, single men and women 80 acres, and children 40 acres.

They are typical Indians in appearance, of a quite dark complexion, and while there are but three or four who claim to be full bloods, most of the older ones have full blood appearance. This is attributed to intermarriage, all the older ones claiming blood relation. The younger generation intermarries with the whites, which gives the children a much whiter appearance. The men are good businessmen and traders, but are not as industrious as the women, some of whom are good housekeepers, neat and tidy, dress well, and make a respectable appearance. All wear citizens' clothes. They are increasing in number, and seem to be in good health. There are but few very old people among them. Their houses are of both log and frame; some are large and well built, with good outbuildings, barns, and stables for stock. Quite a number of new buildings have been erected within the last year. They are exclusively farmers, and although some are able to assist mechanics in erecting buildings none make it a business. Sheep and stock raising is done on a small scale and is growing.

There is one church on this reservation, which belongs to them. It was built by the Methodist missionaries. Services are held here twice in each month. Their religious belief is about equally divided between the Methodists and the Society of Friends, and both of these denominations have missionaries here, who take great interest in their spiritual welfare.

The Wyandottes have entirely lost their old traditions and legends. The last medicine man died about 12 years ago. His record was kept by beads, strung in a peculiar manner, which he alone was able to read. This knowledge he never imparted to any one. Some of these beads are now kept as curiosities.

Many of these Indians use their own language in their families, although nearly all speak English; many, however, will not do so unless to their advantage. In council with the whites they must have an interpreter.

The Seneca boarding school is situated on the Wyandotte reservation. It is attended by children from all the tribes at this agency, and consists of 5 buildings, for schoolrooms, dormitory, dining room, laundry, and carpenter shop, with ample room for employes [sic]. All of these buildings are large, well ventilated, healthy, and capable of accommodating 100 children. The common industries are taught, such as housekeeping, sewing, and fancy work to the girls, and all kinds of farm industries to the boys. The school is well conducted.

The Wyandottes are peaceable and law abiding. Minor offenses are adjusted by the agent. They have an Indian police, and there is little trouble in keeping order. They have entirely abandoned Indian dances. However, some of them will attend the dances of other tribes and take part, more for amusement than to keep up the custom. The making of trinkets, beadwork, and bows and arrows has nearly ceased.

These Indians have a chief, whom they elect every year, but his power is nominal. Polygamy has been abandoned, and the marriage relation is strictly adhered to. Their homes seem pleasant, and they are a contented people. They have no annuity fund. Their lands are allotted, heads of families receiving 160 acres, children under 21, 40, and single persons 80 acres each.[10]

In 1894 there were two hundred eighty-eight Wyandotte citizens residing on 20,000 acres. They were peaceably living on a little strip of land again honeycombed with whites. Artie Nesvold described to me in 1988 how the reservation had been allotted with a grand scheme and purpose. As we sat and visited, she began pointing out names on a map of the 1888 allotments. She told me how the allotments of citizens were haphazardly spread from one end of the reservation to the other. To illustrate what was happening to the Wyandotte's land, let's use my great-great-grandfather, John Bland Jr., as an example. In 1888 John, a twenty-one-year-old unmarried man, received a total of eighty acres. Forty of his acres were located on the northwest boundary of the Wyandotte and Ottawa reservations just west of the Spring River. Another forty acres were located approximately 3¾ miles to the southeast in a hilly area between Lost Creek and Sycamore Valley. John lived in a small, one-room cabin and farmed the Spring River bottomland. The land in the hilly area to the southeast was unfit for farming, and he did not have many cattle to use the land for grazing.

Since John could not physically take possession of both allotments, the agent eventually deemed his southern allotment abandoned and uninhabited land. Artie continued to explain how abandoned land was sold for profit; or used as political collateral and bribes, gifts to family and friends; or used to pay off personal debts. At times the land had squatters, and the agent did nothing to retrieve it back for its rightful owner. Just about every citizen who received land that was not contiguous lost their land in much the same way as John had: by default. Well over 50% of Wyandotte citizens were assigned noncontiguous allotments.

It did not take long for the Wyandotte's reservation to look a lot like a honeycomb with many unfilled and unused cells. The allotments deemed as abandoned land were quickly occupied by whites, and the process of loss began anew, no differently than in Ohio and Kansas. The whites spread throughout the former reservation land until the allotments occupied by the Wyandottes were few and far between. What happened to the Wyandottes in 1888 also happened to just about every tribe who had their reservations allotted. Seemingly overnight across the whole of the United States, Indian land and many of the communities went—*poof*!

Indian School, Quapaw Agency

By the turn of the twentieth century, illegal settlers were boldly coming to the redefined and reestablished Indian Territory and staying. The Oklahoma Land Rush of 1889 opened a floodgate to the unassigned lands, which a few years earlier had been Indian lands. This did not mean that the unassigned lands were now barren of any Indians. People were walking and running into the Indian Territory by the wagon loads. The Dawes Act became law in 1887, quickly followed by the allotment of most, but not all, of the Indian Reservation lands in 1888. The land allotment was followed by the Land Rush of 1889, and Oklahoma Territory was promptly established in 1890. The Wyandotte Reservation was allotted, and technically still in Indian Territory, which was devoid of any public lands. Yet the Wyandotte Reservation land was full of whites who had no legal claim to one small pebble on the land.

Long before the Land Rush of 1889 a large number of settlers—white, black, Texan, Asian, and Hispanic—had already made Indian Territory their home. It's estimated that on April 22, 1889, the first day of the Oklahoma Land Rush, 30,000 to 40,000 Boomers,[11] excluding the Sooners, would stake claim to their small piece of land in the unassigned lands—you know, the land still inhabited by Indians. Amazingly, just a few years earlier the land everyone now wanted had been deemed uninhabitable except by the various Indian tribes who were exiled to the Indian Territory. In 1890 it was hard for many settlers to differentiate between the new Territory of Oklahoma and what was now again restricted Indian Territory.

The US Census Map of June 1, 1890, included this statement: "The total population of the Five Civilized Tribes is 178,097, as follows: Indians, 50,055; persons of negro descent including claimants of citizenship, 18,636; Chinese, 13; whites, including some claimants, 109,393. The population of the Quapaw agency, 1,281, and 804 on military reservations, added to that of the Five Civilized Tribes, would make the population of the Indian Territory 180,182."[12]

The Quapaw Agency was to oversee the tribes in the far northwest corner of Indian Territory. The Oklahoma Organic Act disbanded the Quapaw Agency in 1890 nineteen years of serving the eight tribes. Through the Organic Act, the Territory of Oklahoma was established and the Quapaw Agency was dissolved and incorporated into the greater whole of Indian Territory.[13] With so many tribes in one small area to properly administer and care for their needs, the Quapaw Agency essentially never dissolved. The agent was assigned to the Industrial Boarding School, where he continued to run the Quapaw Agency until it was reestablished in 1920 as a stand-alone agency. In 1947 the Quapaw Agency was again reorganized and its name changed to the Miami Agency, which is now attached to the Muskogee office of the Bureau of Indian Affairs.

According to census, within ten years of the Oklahoma Organic Act, in 1900 there were nine hundred fifteen whites living on Wyandotte tribal lands, with two hundred twenty-four living in the small, unincorporated town of Wyandotte.[14] Remember, there was no public land for the whites to claim, only excess allotments that were deemed uninhabited. Wyandotte tribal lands had not been opened to any land rush, but the whites rushed in just the same. Edward Goldberg, then Indian agent, on June 30, 1900, reported that three hundred thirty-one Wyandottes were scattered among the majority whites. The year before, a report titled *Statistics of Indian Tribes, Agencies, and Schools* accounted for the whole of the eight tribes who resided in what was once known and still commonly referred to as the Quapaw Agency: "In size it is scarcely larger than a county, but several remnants of tribes who were once powerful reside inside its limits. The Quapaw, Peoria, Miami, Ottawa, Shawnee, Modoc, Wyandotte, and Seneca reservations were all included."[15] Today the eight tribes still call the Quapaw Agency home.

It's estimated that in 1906, the year before Oklahoma was granted statehood, the white population had increased to around 8,000 within the Quapaw Agency alone.[16] On November 16, 1907, Oklahoma became the forty-seventh state of the union, at which time all of the Indian Territories were incorporated into the new state and dissolved into history. Conservatively, it's comfortable to say there were eight times the number of whites than there were Indians in the tiny piece of land once known as the Quapaw Agency. As I noted in the preface of this book, a majority of the Indians were now living in towns like Miami, and the whites were living on the Indians' reservation lands.

D. C. Gideon's *Indian Territory* appears to have been written as a prophetic epitaph for the Indian Territory. Gideon indicated in 1901 that Miami was by far the largest town in the Quapaw Agency with 1,200 inhabitants. The illegal community founded in what was still then Indian Territory was destined to become the county seat of Ottawa County. The bustling boomtown also had a federal court and a good school. As the population soared, an immediate problem was noted: Where were all the white children going to get a proper education? A few had begun to attend the Indian boarding schools, but, for obvious reasons, they were not a comfortable fit. The schools were attempting to teach the attending Indian children how to be white, and these children were already white. One public school in the Quapaw Agency was located in Miami. A number of subscription, or district schools, for white children were scattered throughout the agency.[17] A subscription school was different in that parents paid a subscription, or small fee, for their children to attend. The cost was one dollar a month.[18] Many of the Indians began paying the subscription fee to keep their children from having to go to the boarding schools. With the whites overrunning the reservations, the need to care for the white children was beginning to take precedence over the needs of the Indian children.

After the split of the Methodist Church North and South over the issue of slavery, the Methodist missionaries began to lose interest with the minor tribes. The Wyandot Tribe was thereafter considered just a minor tribe. With the Methodists showing little interest in retaining a church or school to serve the Wyandotte people, a door was opened for the Society of Friends. The Quakers, who had entered into an agreement with the US government to manage, staff, and teach the Indian children nationwide, would now be instructing Wyandotte children. The mission school, a government contract school, would open its doors on the Wyandotte Reservation in 1872, on land donated by the Wyandotte Tribe for that purpose. Many Wyandotte children would attend the school and make good progress in their education.

The Quaker curriculum at the Mission School was reflective of what the Methodists missionaries were teaching the children in Ohio. The school was very formal and equivalent to today's sixth-grade education. The children attended from September through most of June. They did not return home except for a brief weekend vacation every six weeks.[19] The children were being taught spelling, reading, writing, arithmetic, natural philosophy, religion, history, the Bible, general knowledge, geography, algebra, grammar, physiology, and botany.[20] Alongside the formal education, the children were taught common, useful, everyday domestic and farming skills—you know, the same skills they already possessed and did as chores around their homes when on vacation from school. If the children already possessed most of the domestic and farming skills, what were the teachers truly teaching the children? They were trying to bleach the Indian children white. Arrell Gibson explained the practical skills being taught the children.

> A member of the staff, the Industrial Teacher, had the major responsibility for supervising the boys and providing them with vocational training. This included harness and shoemaking, woodworking, carpentry, and metal work. The School Farmer assisted the Industrial Teacher in imparting to the boys the elements of farm operation and management, horticulture, and livestock care. Practical training included assignment to routine chores about the school consisting of chopping wood for fuel, milking cows, and feeding and caring for horses, mules, pigs, and poultry kept on the school farm. Also, both boys and girls helped put out the school garden, weed the vegetables, and harvest the crops. Caring for the campus flowers, shrubs, and lawn also was their responsibility.
>
> Girls were assigned to the matron-seamstress who instructed them in hygiene and cleanliness, sewing, home nursing, and other skills which would make them more effective household managers. Practical duties included making beds, sweeping, and helping the school cook and laundress.[21]

With education being a central focus of Wyandotte tribal leadership, many of the tribe's children attended the Mission School and other various non-reservation schools across the United States. A few would attend Carlisle, and seventeen were noted in 1889 as being enrolled at Haskell Institute, located in Lawrence, Kansas.[22] As the children received their education, a few would come back home and teach or work at the Mission School. Others would travel to other schools across Indian Territory and serve in various capacities such as blacksmith, cook, carpenter, and groundskeeper. The most noted pupil to return, and herself be a teacher at the Industrial Boarding School, is Mrs. Naomi Dawson Pacheco. In 1911 she was teaching kindergarten and being paid by the United States a comfortable $600.00 salary.[23]

In 1888 management of the Indian School on Wyandotte land passed from the Quakers to the US government. The contract with the Quakers to manage the schools was cancelled in 1880. The contract was canceled for three primary reasons: poor-quality food, clothing, and shelter. Generally speaking, the children were very well kept and respected by the Quaker missionaries and teachers; however, the Quakers did not have enough resources to adequately take care of the comfort and bare necessities of the children.

Also in 1888 A. B. Upshaw, Acting Commissioner of Indian Affairs, revived a statement first made by Superintendent J. H. Meteer. In his letter, Acting Commissioner Upshaw highlighted an issue that needed to be quickly addressed. Unlike the Quakers, the United States had issues with the children speaking their traditional language. Acting Commissioner Upshaw wrote, "A large proportion of them speak Indian at home, which gives them a great advantage at the beginning of their course of study. The English, however, which they bring from home is not always the purest; so, as in other English-speaking schools, much unlearning must be done."[24]

Acting Commissioner Upshaw quoted Superintendent Meteer, clarifying Indian policy relevant to teaching English or, better stated, the cessation of the children speaking their traditional language. Teaching the children English as their first language meant that speaking their traditional language was now forbidden—including Wandat!

> In government schools, no textbooks and no oral instruction in the vernacular [language] will be allowed, but all textbooks and instruction must be in the English language. No departure from this rule will be allowed except when absolutely necessary to rudimentary instruction in English. But it is permitted to read from the Bible in the vernacular at the daily opening of school when English is not understood by the pupils.[25]

Hazel Wallace, in a 1975 article found in the *Miami News-Record,* described a little of what was happening in the Indian schools. She experienced first-hand the much unlearning that went into removing Wandat and Seneca from her lips. Mrs. Wallace was a niece of BNO Walker and was a Wyandotte and citizen of the Seneca-Cayuga Tribe of Oklahoma. As faith-keeper she held true and honored the traditions of her ancestors, both Wyandotte and Seneca-Cayuga. She stated, "The teachers tried to make white children out of us. We were taught and ordered to forget the old customs and were punished if we spoke our own language."[26]

Joe Jackson described how discipline was administered and order was maintained. The little Indian school that resided on Wyandotte land at the turn of the twentieth century was run like a military school, with harsh discipline for even the smallest infraction of the rules. It's likely that variations of the same disciplinary policies continued until the school was closed in 1980. Jackson explained, "To take care of discipline problems incurred by increased enrollment, both boys and girls were organized into military units at Seneca and were drilled daily by the disciplinarian of the school—a unique policy in that girls in government schools were ordinarily not subjected to such training."[27]

From time to time the reports made to Washington, DC, by the missionaries, agents, and superintendents would include an attendance record. Many of these records did not reflect a favorable or desirable report on the children's attendance. In the early days of the school it would have been understandable, and to a degree acceptable, to see the children not showing up or not staying long after they arrived. In addition, many of the families could not afford to have their children locked away in school during planting and harvesting season. They needed all the help they could muster to make ends meet.

The Quaker missionaries did everything they could to keep the children in school. They would send teachers to retrieve the children, and when this method proved unsuccessful, they sent the Indian police. The children became little Indian outlaws because they were skipping school. Retrieving the children was at times difficult or impossible, even for the Indian police. The terrain around the Mission School in Wyandotte was rough river bottom and very easy to disappear into in less than the blink of an eye. When some families saw the teachers or police coming to retrieve their children, the parents would help their children escape. The Quakers did not appreciate or tolerate the children's running away, skipping school, or blatantly failing to enroll, and the children were disciplined and at times even *spanked* with loving-kindness.

While the children were still under the care of the Quakers, in 1876 Agent Jones wrote to the Bureau of Indian Affairs asking for drastic measures to keep the children in school. Permission would not be granted at that time to garnishee their parents' annuities, but the seed had been planted. Agent Jones stated, "I would recommend that means be adopted to make it compulsory on the parents to place their children in school and keep them there. This would in a great measure be effected by withholding the annuities of children of a suitable age to attend school who are kept out without a reasonable excuse."[28]

By 1881, the Quakers were out! The US government was now in complete control of the schools, and attendance policies changed, seemingly overnight. To a degree the Industrial School was now something a little less than a conscripted prison school. If mom and dad did anything to keep their children from going to school, or tried to get them out without an acceptable reason, they would pay a tremendous price. In 1881 the Commissioner of Indian Affairs sent a specific and pointed directive to Agent D. B. Dyer, stating the following:

Regarding attendance of children at school over the opposition of parents, devise some plan by which . . . the attention of these children can be secured— some distinction should be made, in the distribution of implements, or goods, or whatever gratuities the Indians receive from the government between those families whose children attend school and those who refuse to send them.[29]

The curriculum was about teaching the children the skills they needed to survive in the white man's world. The curriculum was specifically designed and intended to turn the Indian children into respectful white children. If the Indian children were not in attendance, they could not be taught how to be good, respectful white children. If the children did not have the responsibility and initiative to stay in school—and their parents could not have cared less— someone was going to pay, and dearly. As it turns out, the children's parents paid the price. Ultimately, the children were paying the highest price through the discipline they received while in the schools. However, mom and dad's annuity payments, in cash or goods, came under attack and were garnisheed.

Now it's becoming easier to see why by 1920 there were few Indian children from the Quapaw Agency in the Indian School. It was cheaper in many ways for the parents to send their children to a subscription or district school, where they were not being punished for being born into and living the life of an Indian.

What was happening inside the school buildings? It's hard to say, other than the few details of what had happened to Wyandotte children while under the care of the Quakers. In the Indian Pioneer papers, Jared Silas Dawson gave detailed accounts into the way of life the children were expected to live while under the Quaker's care. The organization of military units and punishment for speaking one's traditional language did not come into full consideration until the government closed the contract system in 1880. Dawson indicated that the Quakers "were good to us" in spite of the very poor clothing, food, and quarters.

The boys had red duck pants put together with rivets, hickory shirts of blue and white, brogan shoes, common black hats, no socks and no underwear. The girls wore blue denim all made alike with course canton flannel underwear, heavy shoes and the little girls had copper toes on their shoes.

Our sleeping room or dorm, as you would say today was without fire, hard mattresses, coarse blankets and no sheets. What did we have to eat? For breakfast, we had boiled beef, gravy, light bread, and weak coffee. For dinner, cornbread, beans, gravy and water. For supper, two tubs were filled with sliced light bread, in one tub two slices were put together with New Orleans molasses and there were rows of pegs about two feet apart; we boys took our place at these one boy to a peg with the larger boys in front and these led up to where two women were in charge of the two tubs of bread and as a boy moved up to the peg in front of the tub one of the women would say "With or without" and if he said "with" he was given two slices of the light bread put together with molasses and if he said "without" he was handed two slices of dry bread, these we took and went to where the pump was for water and this was our supper.

Major Redpath who was the agent at the Seneca Agency, came to the mission one evening as we were receiving our supper and shortly after the Government took over the school. I was seven when this happened. After that we had plenty to eat, good clothes, sheets, etc. Then our clothes were grey uniforms with red stripes and the girls received blue flannel dresses.[30]

The Industrial School resided on one hundred sixty acres located on the top of a hill about a mile east of the junction of the Neosho and Spring rivers. The little town of Wyandotte, formerly known as Prairie City, sprang up a little due south of the school. Conveniently located near the center of the Quapaw Agency on the Wyandotte Reservation, the school was initially welcomed, but soon came to be despised by all the various tribes and many of the resident whites. Operating nonstop for one hundred eight years, the school was closed on June 15, 1980; henceforth, the land was promptly returned to the Wyandotte Tribe of Oklahoma on June 27, 1980. The school was commonly known in the area as the Seneca Indian School or the Seneca Indian Boarding School. The name prompted a minor legal challenge by the Seneca-Cayuga Tribe which was quickly dismissed.

Thus closed the long and often maligned history of the Indian Boarding School located on the Quapaw Agency, Ottawa County, Oklahoma. On the surface, the face of the school appeared to be a normal school commissioned with educating the poor Indian children. Unfortunately, as revealed by Hazel Wallace, the school was too often used as a place to continue and enhance the erasure of their cultures. Indian children were taken from the homes of their parents and forced into the schools, many of which were far from their homes. When the children returned home, the parents were often unable to recognize them. Their cultures and personal identities had been stripped from their own children. The tales of horror, deceit, and assimilation abound.

Today in Wyandotte, Oklahoma, it is hard to find any tangible evidence that the US Industrial and Boarding School ever existed. Outside of the memories held by former students and the stories they tell, proof of the school's existence is difficult to find; however, proof is there in the form of old photos, government reports, articles, and books such as this one. Over the course of any given year, a number of people will invariably call or email the Wyandotte Nation asking about records or the whereabouts of a former student. The Wyandotte Nation does not have any records or lists of former students to answer these questions.

High on the hill overlooking the progress below, where the boarding school once stood, now stands the Bearskin Health and Wellness Center alongside the Cultural Center and Museum. The hill that was once dedicated to erasing the existence of the Indian within Wyandotte children has been wholly rededicated to the preservation of the Indian. The Bearskin Health and Wellness Center addresses all the holistic needs of the body, mind, and soul. By keeping the body strong and active, the mind can remain young and allow the soul to venture into unexplored and unimaginable realms. The cultural center and museum will challenge the hearts and minds of Wyandotte citizens to reach out and embrace who they are as Wyandottes by learning of their amazing heritage. Long gone are the days when their great-grandparents denied that they were Indian—denials that were made out of fear of being slapped or enduring other punitive measures when, for example, they spoke Wandat.

Wandat is again being spoken atop the hill where it was once forbidden. Stories of the *Huron*-Wyandot's history and their traditions are again being told to attentive ears both young and old. Beading, finger weaving, flint knapping, and the playing of lacrosse, have replaced the domestic skills that were once taught to better integrate the Indian children into white society. You can try to break the body and erase the mind of the Indian, if you must, but you will never break the spirit and resolve of a Wyandotte Indian.

Sacred Ground

Tauromee's heart was filled with desire for the establishment of a new Wyandot Reservation in Indian Territory. After being taken hostage by Secessionist Indians upon the outbreak of the Civil War, he worked tirelessly to this end until the Treaty of 1867 was finalized. He wanted desperately to get his people out of Kansas so that they could remain Wyandot and again live on land they had claimed as their own. Tauromee died on January 15, 1870, while in Wyandott City, Kansas, and was buried in the *Huron* Place Cemetery. His body now lies at rest in the state of Kansas, the one place he desperately sought to leave and never intended to stay. Many who moved to the new Wyandotte Reservation are buried in small family cemeteries, such as the Walker and Wright cemeteries. Many would also be buried in the much larger Bland Cemetery. The Wyandotte Indian Cemetery, the new tribal cemetery, is near the small town of Wyandotte, Oklahoma. The date of the earliest known burial in the Wyandotte Indian Cemetery is 1870.

Shortly after Tauromee's death, Matthew Mudeater made a permanent move to the Quapaw Agency and new Wyandotte Reservation. There he promptly asked for adoption, and his request was granted on June 3, 1872. The fact that Mudeater had served as chief of the Citizen Party Wyandot had no bearing on his future in the new Wyandotte community. The community had come full circle when in 1875 Mudeater was elected principal chief of the Wyandotte Tribe. He would serve his people for at least two years and make one trip to Washington, DC, before he died on August 20, 1878. Thirty yards due south of my grandparents in Bland Cemetery lie Matthew and Nancy Mudeater.

The earliest known burials in Bland Cemetery were during the Civil War; the exact year is uncertain, but believed to be 1863. At the Hudson Bottom skirmish, five Union soldiers were killed. John Bland Jr. stated, "Old Anthony Hatt [son of Tauromee], a full-blood Wyandotte Indian, told me that there were graves there in the early part of the Civil War. When he first came to this country before that there were six graves there that were piled over with rocks and no one knows whether they were Indians, Spaniards, or who, and we have never known."[31] There has been a long-standing legend that the Union soldiers were buried on the parcel because it had already been chosen as a burial ground by Spanish explorers. As a kid I can clearly remember a pile of stones in the southwest corner of the cemetery. The pile of stones has long been removed.

As life began anew on the new Wyandotte Reservation, citizens obviously held reverence for the small piece of land in downtown Wyandott City that was the final resting place for many family members and fellow citizens. As Wyandottes began to die on the Wyandotte Reservation, new little pieces of land would become equally sacred. The importance of the *Huron* Place Cemetery, known today as the *Huron* Indian Cemetery, was always remembered, but over time the cemetery began to fade as being secondary in importance to other cemeteries. I have family buried in the *Huron* Indian Cemetery, as do all Wyandottes, which makes the cemetery special and sacred. However, for me personally, Bland Cemetery is very special and very sacred.

I can go to Bland Cemetery anytime I want, but going to the *Huron* Indian Cemetery is not as convenient. My immediate family is buried at Bland Cemetery: grandparents, aunts and uncles, and of course my brother. Also at Bland Cemetery are Matthew Mudeater, Irvin Patton Long, and Nicholas Cotter—three Wyandotte chiefs from the time period we are currently discussing. Much like the *Huron* Indian Cemetery we know there are many Wyandottes buried in the Bland Cemetery, but we do not know exactly how many are buried or when and where they were buried.

As community was reestablish on the Wyandotte Reservation, life and the pursuit of happiness trudged onward. For the Citizen Wyandot, who did not make the move to the Quapaw Agency, life trudged onward as well. After the Dawes Act of 1887 and the ensuing allotment of the Wyandotte Reservation in 1888, the fate of the Citizen Wyandots was sealed. The Citizen Wyandot were thereafter known as Absentee Wyandot. The differences and strife between the two bands became much more contentious. Animosities came to the forefront, and dislike, mistrust, and rejection began to grow as a deep cancerous lesion. You could feel that it was there, but seeing the strife was difficult due to the distance that separated the two bands—one recognized as citizens of the Wyandotte Tribe and the other as citizens of the United States of America.

For well over one hundred twenty-five years the Oklahoma Wyandotte and Kansas Absentee Wyandot have shared a relationship that has at times been tenuous. Only in recent years has the relationship found the resolve to set aside most of the differences and just get along. Differences have often heated up over the subjects of tribal recognition, tribal citizenship, and especially the *Huron* Indian Cemetery located in the heart of downtown Kansas City, Kansas. Anger and bitterness have erupted too many times when removal of those buried in the *Huron* Place Cemetery have been proposed in order to perpetuate the selling of the land. I am sad to say that at times the proposals to sell the cemetery have been sanctioned by the Wyandotte Nation. On other occasions third parties bent on eradicating the presumed eyesore and making a lot of money have promoted the selling of the land.

The land where the cemetery lies is extremely valuable real estate in the heart of Kansas City, Kansas. It just so happens that a majority of the buildings of the Unified Government of Wyandotte County and Kansas City dominate the tiny little parcel of land. The names of the Wyandots buried in the cemetery inspire gasps of awe, no less than when one gazes around the circumference of the cemetery and the modern marvel of a large metropolitan city in the heartland of America. Some who look upon the city see an eyesore just as others who gaze upon the sacred cemetery also see an eyesore. It's all in the perspective of where you came from and what you hold sacred. The first attempt to sell the land and move those interred, was instigated in 1890 by then–Kansas Senator Preston B. Plumb. Perl Morgan in *History of Wyandotte County Kansas,* Vol. I, explained that

> Senator Preston B. Plumb, in 1890, introduced a joint resolution in the United States Senate looking forward to the sale of the cemetery. In that resolution it was set forth that the cemetery was a nuisance and a majority of the Wyandots then living desired that their ancestors be removed to a more secluded place. The proposition was to improve the Quindaro cemetery, and it was estimated that the old Huron Place ground would bring $100,000. The resolution raised such a storm of protest from old citizens, members of the Wyandots and the descendants of Wyandots, that it was defeated.[32]

In response to Senator Plumb's attempt to sell the cemetery, a letter to the *Kansas City Gazette,* written by Lucy B. Armstrong on July 4, 1890, served as the rallying cry to defeat the proposed sale: "To remove the burying ground now would be to scatter the dust of the dead to the winds. What a sacrilege! I remember with reverence many of the good Wyandotts buried there, and my heart protests against such a desecration of that sacred ground."[33] The resolution to sell the cemetery was opposed by the Oklahoma Wyandotte and the Absentee Wyandot alike. Unfortunately, the situation would quickly change in just a few short years.

Even though Senator Plumb's resolution was soundly defeated, William Elsey Connelley again revived the proposal in 1899. Connelley, born in Kentucky, was raised in poverty and was self-educated; he worked as a shoemaker, a schoolteacher, and a farmhand. Moving to Wyandott County in 1881 at the age of twenty-six, he would fall into the job of deputy county clerk. Eventually serving two terms as county clerk of Wyandott County, Kansas, from 1883 to 1887, Connelley became familiar with the plight of the Absentee Wyandot when he witnessed the lawful but unscrupulous loss of their land and property to—taxes. It was then that as an amateur historian he began researching the culture and history of the *Huron*-Wyandot people.

Leaving the office of county clerk, Connelley moved to Springfield, Missouri, where he excelled as a businessman in a wholesale lumber company. He accumulated a measure of wealth and moved back to Kansas City in 1892 and connected with the city's elite who had interests in banking.[34] During this time he continued his research both on the Wyandot people in Kansas City, and on the Wyandotte people on the Wyandotte Reservation in Indian Territory. While he was working on his research material in March of 1896, Ebenezer O. Zane, an Absentee Wyandot elder, assisted Connelley as he conducted a survey of the *Huron* Place Cemetery.[35] This survey still serves today as the best accounting of those buried in the cemetery. Connelley, who had been busy studying, researching, and interviewing Wyandots and Wyandottes, focused his attention on the cemetery with noble intents which slowly dwindled into unscrupulous motives. The assessment made by Senator Plumb in 1890 indicated that the cemetery had developed into an eyesore of proportions equaling those of its real estate value. Connelley convinced himself that the failure of Senator Plumb could be reconciled with his efforts. It should be a relatively easy endeavor with his connection in banking, especially if he had the support of the Wyandotte Tribe in Indian Territory. Taking advantage of both friendships, Connelley was determined to sell the cemetery for a sizable profit.

After making many friends within the Wyandotte Tribe in Indian Territory, Connelley was all too familiar with their destitute poverty. Playing upon their emotions, he convinced them to sell the *Huron* Place Cemetery. After all, it was an eyesore that no one truly wanted in the middle of downtown Kansas City. It was in the best interest of everyone, including those buried, to move them to a more secluded and protected place. The Wyandotte Tribe would promptly give Connelley power of attorney to ensure the selling of the cemetery and the collection of the money.

In 1898, Allen Johnson Jr. was twenty-six years old and head chief of the Wyandotte Tribe. With Johnson being so young and inexperienced, Connelley, with his swank and swagger, could have easily manipulated him into doing just about anything he wanted. What Connelley wanted was the blessing of the tribe to act as a paid agent to broker the sale of the cemetery with the ultimate removal of those buried. Clearly, the Wyandotte Tribe was viewing it as a potential source for some badly needed cash. Supporting Connelley were a number of Kansas City businessmen who were determined that the eyesore, as they defined the cemetery to be, be sold for development.[36]

Connelley's task of selling the *Huron* Place Cemetery proved to be unsuccessful. Think about it for a moment. How intimidating would it have been to try to move the resident bodies of the dead Wyandot Indians? Very! Desecrating the burial ground of Indians carried the possibility of dark and ghostly repercussisons that few people understood or desired. It was best to leave such things alone. However, Connelley found new hope in 1906. On June 16, 1906, the US Congress authorized the Oklahoma Territory to become the state of Oklahoma. Connelley was successful in getting a clause inserted and buried deep within the omnibus appropriations bill. The clause addressed every Indian agency, tribe, and school in the country. It stated, "The Secretary of the Interior is hereby authorized to sell and convey, under such rules and regulations as he may prescribe, the tract of land located in Kansas City, Kansas, reserved for a public burial ground."[37]

Obviously the omnibus bill passed, and Oklahoma became the forty-seventh state. The *Huron* Place Cemetery was, now by law, marked as needing to be sold. Again the proposal to sell the cemetery would end in defeat, but not without much heartache and much history that was made in the realization of the defeat. A niece of Ebenezer O. Zane, Eliza "Lyda" Conley, stepped forward and stood in defiance to the bill and Connelley's selling of the *Huron* Place Cemetery. With the assistance and resolve of her sister, Helena, they put padlocks on the gates of the cemetery, erected signs proclaiming "Trespass At Your Peril," and then proceeded to take up residence in a small shack on the grounds. Borrowing their father's double-barrel shotgun, they threatened to shoot anyone entering the cemetery to remove the bodies.

Kimberly Dayton in "Trespassers, Beware" explains many of the influences upon the young life of Lyda who was born a Wyandot in Kansas somewhere between 1865 and 1869. Lyda's family would not move to Indian Territory and seek adoption into the reorganized Wyandotte Tribe; therefore, Lyda was an Absentee Wyandot. In the late nineteenth century the state of Kansas was very progressive in giving women significant constitutionally based rights, and many of the women in the state began challenging the then-established norms of society. With radical female figures such as Populists Mary Elizabeth Clynen Lease and Annie Diggs, along with Jennie Mitchell Kellogg, Lyda began to view her role in society beyond what most women even dared to dream in the late nineteenth century.[38]

Dayton concludes that Lucy B. Armstrong may have also added to Lyda's self-perception and her role of a Wyandot, as well as an aggressive Wyandot woman, in her modern and progressive Kansas community. In 1900 Lyda enrolled in the Kansas City College of Law, from which she graduated in May of 1902. She was promptly admitted into the Missouri Bar on June 21, 1902.[39] At this point in time William's attempt to sell the cemetery had garnished nothing but a few weak nibbles of interest. Now, in 1906, US law clearly decreed that the Secretary of the Interior was obligated to sell the cemetery and move those buried.

Once the bill became public knowledge, Lyda filed suit in Federal Court on June 11, 1907. Named in the suit were James R. Garfield, Secretary of the Interior, and the three appointed commissioners. The suit restrained the men from selling or interfering in any way with the cemetery. Over the following years the case would slowly drag its way through the courts. Lyda and her sister, who had kept a constant vigil at the cemetery, were subjected to harassments. The sisters were arrested and charged with disturbing the peace, threatened by a US Marshal, and charged with contempt by a federal judge. The shack they occupied, which they named Fort Conley, was burned. In defiance the sisters built a new shack in its place and continued their protest.

On July 1, 1907, a counter to Lyda's suit was filed in Federal Court asserting numerous grounds for dismissal. The primary ground was that "Conley was not a citizen of the Wyandotte Tribe, nor of any Indian tribe, but rather a citizen of the United States and therefore had no right or interest stemming from the 1855 Treaty."[40] However, as despairing as this fact was, it did not hinder Lyda from pushing forward with her suit even after it was immediately dismissed on July 2, 1907. Hoping to eliminate a few of the deficiencies found in her original suit, she refiled her suit with a bill of exceptions. The center-piece of her bill of exceptions stated, as explained by Ms. Dayton,

> The 1867 Treaty that reestablished the Wyandotte Tribe in Oklahoma, the newly constituted tribe now seeking to sell the cemetery was not the legitimate successor to the Wyandot Tribe dissolved by the Treaty of 1855. Accordingly, the new tribe retained no authority to sell the cemetery over the objection of a citizen-Wyandot whose ancestors were buried there. In addition, the complaint alleged that the Act of Congress authorizing the sale of the Huron Place Cemetery was unconstitutional under the Fifth Amendment of the United States Constitution because it authorized the taking of property without due process of law.[41]

Lyda's countersuit was for nothing as the district court never considered her amended bill. Lyda promptly petitioned the US Supreme Court. On January 14, 1910, after a long, hard fight, Eliza "Lyda" Conley stood before the US Supreme Court to plead her case. She was acting *in propria persona,* "in her own person,"[42] as she could not stand as a representative of the Absentee Wyandot Tribe since they did not exist as a tribe. After a historic argument, the first woman of American Indian descent to argue a case in front of the US Supreme Court, she rested and waited. Her wait would not take long. In less than three weeks Justice Oliver Wendell Holmes Jr. delivered an opinion. The Supreme Court dismissed Lyda's petition as again summarized by Ms. Dayton: "If the Treaty of 1855 created any right at all, they were tribal rights, not individual ones; Conley, in effect, had no standing to bring an action based on the treaties [sic] provisions."[43]

For two and a half years the Conley sisters had thrown a major curve into the efforts of William E. Connelley and the Wyandotte Tribe to sell the land and move those buried. An ongoing delay, financial burden, and emotional drain for all parties involved needed some fast closure. After a decade had passed, was there still a desire to sell the cemetery? Unfortunately, the answer is yes. With Lyda's defeat in the US Supreme Court, the decree to sell the cemetery was still a foregone conclusion. There were no other options outside of a miracle that could stop the selling of the cemetery.

The plan to sell the cemetery and obtain the much-coveted cash was devised as Connelley was conducting a survey of the cemetery. Throughout his research and study, it is clear that a heartfelt respect and admiration for the Wyandot people was kindled. Connelley's heart was eventually ignited with a true passion for the Wyandot people. The success and history of the tribe, along with its endurance and perseverance, are well beyond admirable. The accomplishments of the men and women buried in the cemetery extend to levels that are nothing less than legendary.

With the amount of time Connelley spent in the cemetery conducting his survey, there is no way he could not have felt admiration for those he sought to identify. I challenge you to visit the cemetery today, walk about and admire its serenity in the middle of a thriving city, absorb its history, read the names on the stones, and remember the lives the people led. If you can leave without being humbled or shedding a tear, you must be made of stone no less than a Stone Giant. Connelley was mortified at the condition of the cemetery and the lack of peace those buried had to endure. The Wyandot people buried in the cemetery were looked upon as an eyesore. Their sweat, blood, and tears accounted for nothing, or for very little. Connelley felt they deserved better and wanted to give them a peaceful rest. Unfortunately, his plan was bringing unnecessary pain to their sleep.

After researching and studying the Wyandot people, Connelley decided to play upon the hearts and emotions of the city's administration and residents. The history of Kansas City cannot under any circumstances overlook or underestimate the historical significance of the Wyandot people. After all, it is without question citizens of the Wyandot Tribe established the little village and then helped massage and manage its growth until it become a major city in the heart of the United States of America.

On September 8, 1911, a series of resolutions confirmed the Wyandotte's previous action authorizing Connelley to sell the cemetery for the benefit of the tribe. An additional resolution was adopted, stating the cemetery needed to become a city park and to be owned outright by the city. City administrators would have to pay the Wyandotte Tribe the going rate for the little piece of land. The land, approximately one and a half acres, was now estimated to carry a street value of $1 million.[44] With the tribe now offering to sell the cemetery to the city, it would eliminate any suspicions of motives for personal gain and seem to express a noble gesture.

> Wyandots in Oklahoma further petition the Honorable Secretary of the Interior: that if it may be in accordance with legislation enacted for the sale of Huron Place Cemetery, to effect a sale of said tract to the municipality of Kansas City, Kansas, that it may be retained and forever held by said municipality as an historic park; that said municipality will remove and re-inter the remains of those Wyandots buried therein in a certain portion thereof, and erect a monument to the memory of said Wyandots, and forever retain and preserve said park; the consent and approval of the Wyandots of Oklahoma for such sale for the aforesaid uses and purposes is hereby given.[45]

The incentive to play upon the heart of the city did not work. In spite of Lyda's loss in the courts, her efforts were finding success. Her stand and argument garnered national attention, which attracted then–Kansas Senator Charles Curtis. Senator Curtis, who would serve as the thirty-first vice president of the United States, was from Topeka and of Kansas (Kaw) descent. After visiting the *Huron* Place Cemetery in 1912, Senator Curtis quickly introduced a bill to Congress to repeal the right of the Secretary of the Interior to sell the cemetery. The bill was passed on February 13, 1913. The battle to sell the *Huron* Place Cemetery came to an immediate halt.

With all of the attention given the *Huron* Place Cemetery, the US Congress went from authorizing its sale to investing in its preservation. In 1916,

$10,000 was appropriated for improvements to the grounds.[46] On March 20, 1918, an agreement with the city of Kansas City was made to ensure that the improvements were implemented. As a signing bonus the government paid the city $1,000 to accept the contract. The cities administrators agreed:

> To forever maintain, care for, preserve the lawns and trim the trees and give the grounds the same and usual attention that it gives to its city parks within the main part of the city, and particularly Huron Park adjoining the Cemetery; and that the City of Kansas City, Kansas, will furnish police protection equivalent to that furnished for the protection of Huron Park; and furnish all electrical energy free of charge for the maintaining of the electric lights, as provided for in the plans and specifications, maintaining and keeping in place all globes and fixtures, and give said Cemetery any and all care that a park of its nature in the heart of a city should demand.[47]

The $10,000 given to Kansas City purchased many noticeable improvements for the cemetery; however, over time, as often happens, distractions grew and emphasis on the cemetery was diverted to other projects. As the city grew, so did the vandalism. The cemetery became a local hangout for the homeless, and the cemetery again fell into disrepair. The eyesore became painfully noticeable, and locals complained, requesting the city to intercede—all to no avail. As the cemetery continued to decline, the Wyandotte Tribe of Oklahoma again expressed an interest to sell the cemetery. The effort to sell the cemetery was challenged from 1947 to 1949 by Kansas Congressman Errett P. Scrivner and local attorney and historian Grant W. Harrington.[48] Facing stiff resistance, the effort to sell the cemetery was eventually dropped. During this attempt the Absentee Wyandot were noticeably *absent* from the process.

A fourth attempt to sell the *Huron* Place Cemetery came as collateral damage when the Wyandotte Tribe of Oklahoma was terminated on August 1, 1956. The financial condition of the tribe had not improved in the last fifty years, and life was just downright difficult. With hope of a little relief, a list of citizens was obtained, and from that list "all or any part of such property . . . a pro rata distribution of the proceeds of sale among the members of the tribe" will be made.[49] One of the stipulations found in the termination decreed that if the *Huron* Place Cemetery could be sold within three years, the proceeds would be distributed among the enrolled citizens of the tribe.

This time the descendants of the Absentee Wyandot, along with Kansas City residents, stood and challenged the sale. The attempt to sell the cemetery failed in part because the Absentee Wyandot and residents' efforts, but more important, the appraised value of the cemetery was deemed too low and the Wyandotte refused to sell the land. In September of 1965, the Wyandotte Tribal Council unanimously adopted a resolution calling for the *Huron* Place Cemetery to be designated as a historic site. With such a profound change everyone took immediate notice, and great things began to happen with the land that no one seemed to want—except for those buried in its dirt.

Coincidentally, about this same time the Kansas City Urban Renewal Agency initiated the Center City Urban Renewal Project, and the decision was made to renovate the *Huron* Place Cemetery. After the cemetery had been renovated, in 1970 the Urban Renewal Agency requested that Kansas City adopt a historic landmarks ordinance. Along with the request, they had only one other recommendation—to designate the *Huron* Place Cemetery as a historic landmark, and the cemetery was promptly distinguished as such. It seems the city had come full circle. When in 1911 William E. Connelley and the Wyandotte Tribe attempted to entice the city to purchase and then turn the cemetery into a city park, the city had shown little interest, and for good reason. Actually, many reasons! Now they had gone one step further, without spending one dollar to purchase the small piece of land, by making it a historic landmark. This designation was followed on September 3, 1971, with the cemetery placed on the National Register of Historic Places.

As usual, delays were abundant, and the dedication of the *Huron* Indian Cemetery did not take place until May 16, 1978. During the dedication ceremony it was announced that President Jimmy Carter had reinstated federal status to the Wyandotte Tribe of Oklahoma not more than twenty-four hours earlier. It was indeed a day of great celebration.

With the cemetery now protected on the National Register of Historic Places, old habits would not change. The cemetery would again begin to decline, as stones were being desecrated and destroyed by the city's homeless population. The Kansas City Urban Renewal Agency was now defunct, and again no one appeared interested in maintaining the cemetery. In recent years the Kansas City Parks Department stepped up with assistance from the Wyandotte Nation to provide direct oversight and care of the cemetery.

Today, ample resources are available to protect and provide for the care and upkeep of the *Huron* Indian Cemetery. However, it is hard to express the feelings held by many when lamenting or cursing the *Huron* Indian Cemetery. Artie Nesvold, in a 1977 interview with Charles Aubrey Buser stated, "One time we had a government official who said we (Wyandots) seemed to be possessed with cemeteries. But they have been the things, which have kept us kind of together, to talk to each other, to keep things going. So maybe it has been important that our cemetery played a large part in our doings."[50] What Artie did not know was that after her death, the cemetery would again play an even larger part in the Wyandot's doings.

We Want Our Land Back

As I look back at the great chiefs of the *Huron*-Wyandot people, Kondiaronk first comes to mind. Nicholas, Pomoacan, Matthew Mudeater, Leonard Cotter, and Leaford Bearskin follow Kondiaronk. I am sure that some are now questioning why I did not include Tarhe and Tauromee on the list. Since I have just mentioned their names, hopefully I will not have to explain my reasoning. Who was the greatest? That is an easy question to answer: The greatest *Huron*-Wyandot chief is the one who stepped forward at the time his people needed him the most. Also William Walker Jr. could arguably be mentioned in this list of chiefs. In spite of his many faults Walker was a much-needed leader when his people needed a leader. The problem is that he served as chief for only a little over a year. His influence upon the Wyandot Tribe came more as a leading man than as chief.

Over the last eighty years eight men have served as head chief of the Wyandotte Nation. Two of these men served as head chief longer than the others combined: Leonard Nicholas Cotter Sr. and Leaford Bearskin together served their people as head chief for fifty-three years. This generation, and many yet to come, will look upon the leadership of Cotter and Bearskin with much respect and honor. Chief Bearskin's influence as head chief easily extends into the lives of every Wyandotte citizen. Thus, I would like to take a moment and look at one of his greatest accomplishments. As we will quickly see, Leaford's legacy is a mix of controversy and heartfelt admiration.

I do not want to recite the long legal history of the battle over the *Huron* Indian Cemetery and Chief Leaford Bearskin's quest to obtain gaming rights on the property, but I must. Some people think history is boring; *if so,* then reading a long legal brief would be absolute torture. The many years during which the process ensued were a very stressful and confusing time in the history of the Wyandotte people. Standing true to just about everything the Wyandotte stood for, Leaford Bearskin engaged in this battle which, like so many others, ended in success.

Everything began in 1994 with an explosive announcement. The Wyandotte Tribe of Oklahoma was going to establish a casino in downtown Kansas City. That wasn't so bad, but what followed caused a firestorm. The casino was to reside on the property where the *Huron* Indian Cemetery was located, and the graves of those buried on the sacred ground would be moved. Larry Hancks in *The Emigrant Tribes* stated the following:

> In February, 1994, the old disagreements flared once again when Principal Chief Leaford Bearskin of the Wyandotte Tribe of Oklahoma, in partnership with Florida gaming interests, proposed the removal of all the graves in the Huron Indian Cemetery to Oklahoma, and the erection of a 40,000 to 50,000 square foot, high-stakes bingo parlor on the site. The proposal was made public on March 7, and immediately raised a storm of protest, not only from Citizen Class Wyandot descend[a]nts and the residents of Kansas City, Kansas, but from some of the younger, more history-conscious members of the tribe as well.[51]

To try to explain everything that happened, detail by detail, over the next fourteen years would be tedious for the reader. However, I will attempt to account for much of what happened without such tedious details and conclusions. When you read many of the opinions found on various websites, you will see that the media unjustly brutalized and demonized Chief Leaford Bearskin. As the lawsuits became numerous and more complex with every new development, the media fell into a frenzy. It is the media's constitutional right to write whatever they choose, as long as it's not libel, but there are always two sides to a story, and the contentious one is what sells papers. It did not help the situation that Chief Bearskin was a very private chief and wholeheartedly believed that the business of the tribe was just that—the business of the tribe and not a public affair. As a result, the media too often speculated on conclusions which just fanned and incited the general public's confusion and anger.

All I will personally say on the matter is back then I was one of the "younger, more history-conscious members of the tribe" and as a member of the Wyandotte Nation Historical Committee, while the battled trudged onward, I focused a lot of time and energy on organizing Culture Days and other cultural projects. This focus proved a blissful distraction to the frenzy that swirled in all directions. The historical committee was fighting their battles. Once the battle over gaming rights in Kansas City concluded and a hard-fought victory was claimed, the resources gained invigorated the efforts of cultural revitalization. The revitalization reiterated and reaffirmed one thing—the Wyandots buried in the cemetery should never be moved.

No, I wish it were that easy to say "end of discussion," but we still need to take a look at what happened. Now, I begin this tale. It all began on or around March 7, 1994, when the initial announcement was made regarding a contractual relationship with gaming interests from Florida. A statement was made that the bodies of the Wyandots buried in the *Huron* Indian Cemetery would be exhumed and moved to Oklahoma, potentially opening the cemetery land for the construction of a large casino on the property. About the same time, an interest was also expressed in the Woodlands Race Track on the far northwest of Kansas City. The problem with the location of the Woodlands Race Track is that it lay outside the boundary of the original Wyandot Purchase. The Indian Gaming Regulatory Act of 1988 allowed gaming only within or on land contiguous to the original reservation land. The act also assumed that the tribe establishing gaming rights occupied the land on which the casino would be operated.

On March 27, 1995, the descendants of the Absentee Wyandot incorporated as the Wyandot Nation of Kansas and began the process of petitioning the Bureau of Indian affairs for federal recognition. The purpose of their primary intent—to obtain incorporation and recognition—was to better combat the efforts of Chief Bearskin and the Wyandotte Tribe of Oklahoma. It was clear: Moving the Wyandots buried in the cemetery would potentially be met with significant opposition. When countered by Chief Janith English of the Absentee Wyandot, Chief Bearskin pushed back even harder, and the mudslinging and silly, hollow threats began. As Larry K. Hancks stated, "The old disagreements flared," but in this rendition the previous disagreements were like child's play compared to what was about to manifest with full fury.

Thereafter, in early 1996, the Wyandotte Tribe began to look for properties that were viable options for the location of a casino. Still expressing their preference for the Woodlands Race Track, the tribe noted that the Scottish Rite Temple adjacent to the *Huron* Indian Cemetery was also a desirable, legitimate, and convenient option. After a request was made by the Wyandotte Tribe of Oklahoma, on June 6, 1996, Secretary of the Interior Bruce Babbitt designated the Scottish Rite Temple as Indian trust land, thereby opening the door for Indian gaming to be held on the property. But no: A long legal battle would ensue before one slot machine could gobble its first token.

A temporary injunction was obtained by the state of Kansas in opposition to Secretary Babbitt's decision; however, the injunction was promptly dismissed. On July 12, 1996, the state of Kansas, along with three of four resident federally recognized tribes, filed a suit challenging the secretary's action. The Wyandot Nation of Kansas also joined the suit. The state of Kansas was opposed to any additional Indian casinos within the state; in addition, the crux of their lawsuit focused on the Wyandotte Tribe of Oklahoma's use of $100,000. In 1998, the US government paid the Wyandotte Tribe of Oklahoma $100,000 as compensation for land ceded in Ohio. Under federal law if this money and no additional tribal funds were used to purchase additional land, the Secretary of the Interior was obligated to place the land into trust. The Wyandotte Tribe of Oklahoma bought the Scottish Rite Temple, and Secretary Babbitt promptly placed the property into trust. The state of Kansas basically said there was no way the Wyandotte Tribe bought the property for $100,000 without commingled funds from other sources; therefore, the land being placed in trust was not guaranteed by law and was rightfully needed to be contested by the state of Kansas.

The Wyandotte Tribe of Oklahoma continued with the plans to turn the Scottish Rite Temple into a casino. However, since there was not an official agreement with the state of Kansas regarding gaming on the property, and one did not appear to be forthcoming, inflammatory comments were again made regarding the moving of those buried in the cemetery. In addition, a proposed compromise to erect a casino above the cemetery on stilts was also suggested by Chief Bearskin. The graves of those buried in the cemetery were to be located with ground-penetrating radar, but the technology was never employed. This latest series of threats from the Wyandotte Tribe of Oklahoma to desecrate the cemetery brought a severe backlash even from the US government. Senator Sam Brownback of Kansas, on October 28, 1997, introduced legislation that was passed which ensured that "the lands comprising the Huron Cemetery are used only . . . as a cemetery and burial ground."[52]

On July 11, 1998, in a much-needed act of reprieve, the Wyandotte Tribe of Oklahoma and the Wyandot Nation of Kansas signed an agreement proposing permanent protection and designation of the *Huron* Indian Cemetery as a—cemetery. From this agreement and renewed relationships outside of the courtroom, the door was opened for the signing of the 1999 Wendat Confederacy. Chief Janith English of the Wyandot Nation of Kansas stated:

> We are thankful that productive interaction between the Wyandot Nation
> and the Wyandotte Tribe of Oklahoma has led to an agreement that, pend-
> ing approval by the Department of Interior, is designed to immediately and

permanently protect the sanctity of the Huron Cemetery as a burying ground, and prohibits any economic development on, over or under its ground.[53]

The agreement also noted that the Scottish Rite Temple would be used for governmental purposes and for a cultural center and museum. A five-member commission would be established to oversee and administer the *Huron* Indian Cemetery. The proposed agreement was pending the securing of another location for the Wyandotte Tribe of Oklahoma's gaming interests, upon which the Wyandot Nation of Kansas would drop their lawsuit against the tribe. The most difficult stipulation to the agreement was the Bureau of Indian Affairs's ultimate approval of the Wyandot Nation of Kansas as a federally recognized tribe. The Wyandotte Tribe of Oklahoma agreed not to openly oppose the application. The Wyandot Nation of Kansas has never obtained federal recognition, which in essence has made the overall agreement null and void.

After nearly a four-year delay, the injunction filed in 1996 by the state of Kansas and three federally recognized tribes was dismissed in March of 2000. The injunction was dismissed on a technicality: Since the Wyandotte Nation is a sovereign nation, tribal leaders had to consent to being sued. Since they did not consent to the suit, the injunction was dismissed. Of course the state of Kansas promptly appealed the decision, and the process began anew.

With the injunction dismissed, construction and renovation began on the Scottish Rite Temple. The first order of business was to dig the foundations for two service towers. As trenches were being dug, the construction was halted over concerns that graves would be found in the area. After an assessment was conducted, it was determined that due to differences in ground elevation, there was no possible way that any graves would be disturbed. As renovation proceeded, the Wyandotte Nation seized a public relations opportunity in order to allow the media and public a view of the restoration efforts. During the event it was noticed that some historic objects in the Scottish Rite Temple had evidently been destroyed. It was then brought to everyone's attention that the Scottish Rite Temple had been listed on the National Register of Historic Places since September of 1985. Another temporary injunction was filed by the state of Kansas, and all construction and renovation efforts were immediately stopped.

On February 27, 2001, a major blow was dealt to the efforts to establish a casino in Kansas City. A three-judge panel in the 10th US Circuit Court of Appeals in Denver overturned the dismissal of the injunction originally filed by the state of Kansas and the three resident Kansas tribes in 1996. The panel stated that Secretary Babbitt did not have any authority to declare the Scottish Rite Temple as Indian trust land since it was to be used for gaming. The panel indicated that the National Indian Gaming Commission had the sole authority to settle the case. After a long legal brief discussing the reasoning behind the original intent of the Indian Gaming Regulatory Act, including the reason why allowing the Wyandotte to take advantage of the opportunity as extended by Secretary Babbitt was dangerously counterproductive, the case was closed. After the US Supreme Court refused to hear the case, all options to securing rights to a casino in Kansas City appeared to have been lost.

I will now reveal the strategic genius of Lieutenant Colonel Leaford Bearskin, USAF Retired, in his response to this dramatic and demoralizing opinion. I will also show his unpredictable nature and strong resolve to win regardless of the cost. Chief Bearskin was the epitome of a fearless and fearsome Wyandotte warrior. Lieutenant Colonel Bearskin loved a challenge and always rose to the challenge. "Now, leaders of the tiny tribe, whose members sell pumpkins to help make ends meet, say that because of a monumental mistake by the government, they may have hit the jackpot."[54] I have never known members, better known as citizens, to have sold pumpkins in order to survive. This is the type of rhetoric that began to come from the media. Unfortunately, the media attacks that began to center on Chief Bearskin also insulted his people.

Chief Bearskin on June 18, 2001, filed a lawsuit indicating that the three sections of land that the Delaware Tribe had gifted to the Wyandot Tribe were never sold or relinquished back to the United States in the Treaty of 1855. Therefore, he demanded that the land be returned to the Wyandottes and if the land was not returned, compensation must be given for its value, along with damages, going back to 1855. Remember, please cannot be found anywhere in the vocabulary of the Wyandotte's traditional language. A June 24, 2001, Washington Post article by William Claiborne summarized the scope of what was happening:

> The land claim is one of about a dozen similar cases pending across the country on behalf of Native American tribes. Some of them acknowledge that their purpose is to leverage big monetary settlements or win the right to build Las Vegas–style casinos rather than take back land that non-Indians have owned for generations.
>
> The Indian Gaming Regulatory Act, enacted in 1988, allows tribes that reclaim historic tribal trust lands far from their present-day reservations to

seek permission to run gambling operations that are exempt from state laws and taxes.

Nearly a third of the 544 federally recognized tribes run some sort of gambling operation, earning $10 billion a year in the process. Although instant riches have not come to all of them, many tribes have used casino revenue to kick-start economic development projects that have pulled reservations out of abject poverty and reversed abysmal social conditions.

Supporters of Native American rights contend that leveraging land claims for casino rights is fair recompense for the nearly 100 million acres that tribes have given up since the Indian wars ended in the late 19th century. Most of that tribal land was lost to policies designed to dissolve reservations and force tribal members to assimilate.

In a telephone interview, Wyandotte Chief Leaford Bearskin would not suggest that the tribe's ultimate intentions have anything to do with gambling rights. When asked if the tribe was seeking a casino via the lawsuit, Bearskin replied: "I can't really talk about that. Let's just say that we put the case in as a part of our effort to get where we want to go."[55]

It just so happened that Chief Bearskin deemed the three sections gifted by the Delaware Tribe began at the confluence of the Kansas and Missouri rivers and extended due west. Of course there was no way anyone could determine that his statement was factual, nor could anyone prove it to be false. These three sections of land are known today as the Fairfax Industrial District. The district is home to the International Paper Company, Owens Corning Fiberglass, and General Motors, just to name a few. Was it by coincidence the new Federal courthouse just happened to also be on the land? It was said, "Neither side in the dispute expects the 3,000-employee GM plant, the Owens-Corning Fiberglass Corp., the International Paper Co. or the other big factories in the Fairfax industrial district in northeast Kansas City to pack up and move. But the lawsuit could result in a huge monetary judgment."[56]

As Hancks stated, "Historically this was nonsense."[57] Very true, but only a few historically minded people knew this, and everyone else was in shock or else too fearful to say anything. Nearly everyone seemed to take Chief Bearskin's threat seriously. Was he bluffing? Perhaps yes, but not likely. Everyone involved was playing right into Chief Bearskin's hands. They were running to and fro trying to figure out what to do. Many of the historically minded people believed and hoped the move was a ploy to better position the Wyandotte Nation for the renewed battle that lay ahead.

Chief Bearskin was settling in and repositioning himself to renew the fight for gaming rights. Knowing Chief Bearskin, yes, he obviously knew the importance of the land in question, and he also knew his claim held little validity. Would he still have pressed forward knowing that his claim to repossess the land was invalid? *Absolutely!* His warrior's training said, Even if you *do not* have any bullets in your rifle, you *still* shoulder it and aim at your combatant. A key tactic was not to blink, which left your combatant not knowing whether you did or did not have any bullets in your rifle. This was five-stud poker with the highest stakes possible. All Chief Bearskin wanted was to play slot machines—not bingo or poker. The only thing your opponent saw was a Wyandotte warrior holding a rifle, and it was pointed right at you. The tactic worked. There was much scrambling, and many were afraid Chief Bearskin would indeed pull the trigger. What many people expected to hear was a boom, not a click.

Did Chief Bearskin seriously want the three sections of land returned to the Wyandotte Nation? No, not really. All he wanted was to establish gaming rights, build a casino, and help the Wyandotte Nation achieve a sense of financial security and stability.

The government blinked, dodged a nonexistent bullet, and offered fifty-two acres in Edwardsville as a bargaining chip, along with the Wyandotte Nation's right to establish a casino. The state of Kansas continued to oppose the measure. The government's promised legislation would never materialize. What did materialize was a sense of disdain from the local residents of Kansas City. Rick Babson, assistant business editor of the Kansas City Star, wrote a commentary that painted a picture of then-local feelings and sentiments toward the Wyandotte Nation.

Typically, when you get caught holding someone or something hostage, the outcome is unpleasant. Apparently that's not so if you happen to be the Wyandotte Tribe of Oklahoma.

The tribe, a thorn in the side of Gov. Bill Graves and the Unified Government of Wyandotte County and Kansas City, Kan., stands to be rewarded for actions tribal representatives and others have described in terms just short of blackmail.

The Unified Government has approved a deal in which the tribe would be allowed to build a casino and hotel in Edwardsville, in western Wyandotte County, south of the Kansas Speedway.

Forget for a moment that it took the commission two days after a hastily called meeting to announce it had approved a tentative deal—an act more befitting of old Wyandotte County than the new Unified Government. The deal, contingent on U.S. Rep. Dennis Moore's ability to get enabling legislation through Congress, could close one Pandora's box while opening another.

The thought of the tribe winning in court forced the Unified Government to the bargaining table. Unified Government Mayor Carol Marinovich said dealing with the Wyandottes left a bitter taste in her mouth.

The deal, however distasteful, is pretty simple. If Moore's legislation passes—no sure thing in the current lame-duck session, which will have higher-priority issues with which to deal, such as the budget—then the Wyandotte Tribe will drop its lawsuit.

Give the tribe credit for outmaneuvering the establishment in Wyandotte County. If Moore is successful, and that's a big if given the known opposition to additional tribal casinos in Kansas by Graves and U.S. Sen. Sam Brownback, the tribe wins. If Moore is not successful, and the tribe presses ahead with its lawsuit, it could gain an even bigger victory.

Combine Sunday booze, Indian gambling and auto racing and you've got the punch line to one of those "you might be a redneck" jokes. But no matter which victory the Wyandotte Tribe claims in this seemingly win-win situation, the joke will be on us.[58]

To add insult to injury, a joint House and Senate committee approved a Department of the Interior spending bill for the 2002 fiscal year. The act contained a clause buried deep in the one-hundred-fifty-four-page bill that reiterated Senator Sam Brownback's bill to protect the *Huron* Indian Cemetery in 1997. The 2002 bill stated, "The lands of the Huron Cemetery shall be used only for religious and cultural uses that are compatible with the use of the lands as a cemetery and as a burial ground."[59] Was this the last spike to be driven into Chief Leaford Bearskin's fight to obtain gaming rights in Kansas? No, not quite, as the bill mentioned only the *Huron* Indian Cemetery. The Scottish Rite Temple was not mentioned in the bill.

Over the next several years a tremendous amount of money and time was spent by the businesses in the Fairfax Industrial District as they pursued their own lawsuits against the Wyandotte Nation. Based on a plea of prejudice, the industries wanted the Wyandotte Nation excluded from all claims to the land. The ramifications of the lawsuit, and Chief Bearskin's claim to the land, were beyond significant. In a July 20, 2002, article by the Associated Press the following was stated: "The lawsuit demands title to the 4,080 parcels of land which the tribe estimated is valued for tax purposes at $1.9 billion and unspecified monetary damages for 150 years of 'lost use, rents, issues, income and profits.'"[60] Shock waves were sent throughout the greater Kansas City metropolitan area and the United States in whole—other tribes were standing tall and taking note of what the Wyandottes were doing.

As quickly and unexpectedly as the lawsuit materialized—it just went away. In August of 2004 the Wyandotte Nation dropped the lawsuit. The hope and the reality of actually getting anything were beyond remote. Tribal attorney David McCullough said, "The lawsuit is over. We'll be looking at whether there is other recourse, besides legal action, against the U.S."[61] In spite of the lawsuit being dropped, the image of the Wyandotte Nation now carried a huge blemish. Could that blemish be erased and the respect of the tribe ever be repaired?

In the middle of the ongoing lawsuits, and there were many, from April 2002 to April 2004, the Wyandotte Nation installed slot machines, not within the Scottish Rite Temple but in mobile units moved onto the property. In essence, as some have said, the tribe operated not a casino but a bingo parlor. For about eight months, commencing on August 28, 2003, the casino was operational until the state of Kansas stepped in on Friday, April 15, 2004, and made the fatal blink—mistake, if you will—in this high-stakes game of poker.

Determined to shut down the tribe's gaming facility and unwilling to wait for the case to travel through proper legal channels, Kansas officials decided to simply bypass the federal court system. They sought and obtained a search warrant in Kansas state court based on suspected violations of state gaming law. On April 2, 2004, armed officials from the Kansas City Police Department, the Kansas Bureau of Investigation, and the Office of the State Attorney General stormed the casino, seized gambling proceeds and files, and confiscated gaming machines. The law enforcement officers arrested Ellis Enyart, the casino's general manager, for violating state gambling laws. That same day, the officers seized a bank account owned by the Wyandotte. In total, the officers seized more than $1.25 million in cash and equipment. Criminal charges were filed against Enyart but a state court rightly dismissed them because Kansas has no authority to enforce its gaming laws on the Shriner Tract.[62]

The raid by the state of Kansas was illegal. According to federal law, a state does not have any jurisdiction over tribal lands held in trust by the US government. The state of Kansas became impatient and responded to what was then illegal gaming activity by the Wyandotte Nation. After ten years of lawsuit after lawsuit it was still clear: "The tribe cannot operate a casino, but the state also cannot claim any jurisdiction over the casino site."[63] An impasse still persisted. The best synopsis of what happened is stated in the 2006 decision of *Wyandotte Nation v. Sebelius*: "However, because the outcome of this case turns on developments in prior and concurrent litigation, it is necessary to review this epic tale of claims and counter-claims, federal regulators and state agents, legislation and lots and lots of law suits."[64]

On October 6, 2004, the Wyandotte Nation filed a motion for a preliminary injunction in *Wyandotte Nation v. Sebelius. OK, OK, I hear you.* This has gone on long enough, and we need to find closure really fast. Just think what it was like: For ten years the lawsuits kept spawning more lawsuits, and more lawsuits, and then more lawsuits on top of the lawsuits. I will always remember Chief Bearskin telling citizens of the heartbreaking setbacks year after year at the annual meetings. Chief Bearskin also kept telling citizens, and encouraging himself, that the tribe was getting closer to winning the battle. Closure finally came one step closer when on April 7, 2006, the injunction against the Wyandotte Nation was dropped.[65] Quickly after, on July 6, 2006, the US District Court for the District of Kansas overturned the National Indian Gaming Commission's final decision, which ultimately approved the Shriner Tract for federal trust status and gaming.[66]

Finally, on September 20, 2007, the Unified Government of Wyandotte County and Kansas City, Kansas, approved and entered into a Memorandum of Understanding with the Wyandotte Nation. This agreement allowed for a "Class III Tribal-State Gaming Compact Agreement that specifically delineates the wording of provisions of interest to the Unified Government, which the Nation will agree to use its best efforts to ensure are included in the Class III Tribal-State Gaming Compact."[67] The agreement also called for the provision of all public services to be given to the casino. Of course the Wyandotte Nation would have to reimburse the Unified Government of all incurred expenses.

In September the Unified Government accepted a revenue-sharing agreement with the Wyandotte Nation, which gave 3.5 percent of the first $10 million; 1 percent of the next $10 million; and 0.3 percent of the third $10 million from casino revenues.[68] Thereafter, the Unified Government was not scheduled to receive any additional resources from generated revenues. The decision of US District Judge Richard D. Rogers "dismissed a state lawsuit challenging the legality of a casino in downtown Kansas City, Kan., opening the door for the Wyandotte Nation to upgrade and possibly expand the operation."[69] This decision was made public in September of 2008.

Gaming at the 5th Street Casino officially commenced on Thursday, January 10, 2008. At 6:00 PM many local dignitaries attended the opening ceremony. Chief Bearskin performed a smoking ceremony followed by the official ribbon cutting. "After years in court," Chief Bearskin said, "the fight is over and the tribe won. We went by all the rules and regulations set up by Washington. We went by the law and came out on top. We're going to stay on top. The people of Kansas City will never be sorry the Wyandotte are here."[70]

The Gathering of Traditions

From 1911 to 1912 the majority of Wyandotte citizens were still living in the general area of Wyandotte, Oklahoma. Many of the essential elements of a thriving Native community were becoming scarce—the traditional language, stories, songs, and dances. The Wyandotte people were not forsaking their heritage; it was just becoming harder and harder for them to retain and sustain due to a number of extenuating circumstances.

At this time the young and adventurous Dr. Charles Marius Barbeau, a trained ethnologist, was commissioned by the newly established anthropological division of the Geological Survey of Canada to collect material on the Huron of Lorette. The Huron, cousins of the Wyandotte, lived in the small village of Lorette outside Quebec City, Canada. The village was close and convenient for the young Dr. Barbeau, who in 1911 was twenty-eight years old. His first assignment should have been easy, but it turned out to be logistically difficult and the adventure of a lifetime. While collecting Huron folklore and songs in April and May of 1911 from Abbe Prosper Vincent, Dr. Barbeau came to learn of the Wyandotte living in Oklahoma. He promptly contacted Bertrand Nicholas Oliver (BNO), or Bertie Walker, chief clerk of the Quapaw Agency.[71]

By luck's chance, BNO was a Wyandotte citizen and had connections in the agency and Indian world. While communicating with BNO, Dr. Barbeau came to learn of Mary McKee, BNO's elderly cousin, who lived on the Anderdon Reserve near Amherstburg in Ontario, Canada. This was too convenient and an opportunity the young ethnologist could not ignore or refuse. Amherstburg was just fifteen miles south of Windsor, Ontario, and a day's trip by train from Quebec. Learning that McKee could still speak Wandat, Dr. Barbeau, on June 10, 1911, set out to meet her and make recordings of her speaking and singing Wyandot songs. Dr. Barbeau stayed with her through most of June and July, for he was in much need of data for his research. There was not much to collect in Lorette.

Upon arriving at Amherstburg, Dr. Barbeau stated, "I heard for the first time the Huron language spoken by an old woman named Mary McKee."[72] It was quickly determined that McKee did not remember many Wyandot songs, but she remembered the language. She also proved invaluable as an informant when she gave Dr. Barbeau a lot of background on tradition, history, and valuable contacts in Oklahoma. Dr. Barbeau was in quest of traditional Wyandot songs and stories. McKee was hesitant to tell Dr. Barbeau many Wyandot stories because it was against tradition to tell many stories during the summer. If a Wyandot traditional story spoke of an animal, it was disrespectful to mention its name harshly or in jest, which many stories did. If the animal felt it had been insulted or disrespected, it always had the right to claim and seek retribution for the misdeed. This is why traditional Wyandot stories, which have animals as main characters, are told only in winter while the animal is sleeping. What the animal does not hear leads to no insult and no need for retribution.

After meeting Mary McKee, Dr. Barbeau began to make plans to visit Oklahoma. He was duly commissioned to preserve the songs and folklore of the Wyandotte people. Spending about nine months—September 14 through November 18, 1911, and April 20 through August 3, 1912—Dr. Barbeau collected a vast and varied assortment of Wyandotte cultural treasures. One of his greatest contacts, who proved invaluable for social and logistical purposes, was BNO Walker. In early 1911 BNO informed Dr. Barbeau there were fewer than two hundred descendants of the Absentee Wyandot living in and around Kansas City. In 1910 the US Census recorded three hundred seventy-one Wyandotte, many of whom were still residing on their allotted lands within the old reservation near Wyandotte, Oklahoma. The population of Wyandottes in Oklahoma was increasing. The population of Wyandots in Kansas was decreasing. Without the protection of the Wyandotte community, the Absentee Wyandots were being absorbed by the white community.

BNO also indicated that about a dozen citizens did not speak fluent English, which was perfect for Dr. Barbeau. Many citizens who spoke only Wandat were living and intermingled with the Seneca. BNO stated his greatest fear: "The prospective field for research here is almost barren; yet it is the sole remaining place where even the shreds of anything pertaining to the past of the Wyandots can be found."[73] In defiance of the warning, Dr. Barbeau arrived in Oklahoma on September 14, 1911. BNO Walker had been called away on business, and his eighty-two-year-old mother took Dr. Barbeau under her wing. Without any delay Dr. Barbeau went to work.

Toward the end of the month, Dr. Barbeau attended a three-day feast at the stomp ground at Bassett's Grove on the Seneca Reservation. The Seneca-Cayuga, with the Wyandotte as their guests, hosted the feast, which was the green corn feast, where Dr. Barbeau indicated he met many interesting people and saw many varieties of dances. Dr. Barbeau indicated in a report that everybody was nice and friendly, but they are "thick-headed or deaf or drunkards."[74]

At this point Dr. Barbeau had been introduced to three Wyandotte informants: Eldridge H. Brown, Hiram Young, and Naomi Dawson. Dawson was the kindergarten teacher at the Indian Boarding School and proved to be more than just an informant. Throughout Dr. Barbeau's stay on the Wyandotte Reservation, he and Naomi spent a lot of time together. The couple's *special relationship* would stay with Naomi for the rest of her life, but not so much with Charles. That's what sometimes happens when a dazzling foreigner comes to town. The hearts of the women are swept away, and then the man just goes away. Dr. Barbeau was insensitive to the fact that Dawson's young heart had become smitten by his charm. He unknowingly took Naomi's heart back to Canada, along with wax recordings, artifacts, and notebook after notebook of strangely written characters and words. These notebooks were priceless because they preserved much of the Wyandotte's native language and oral narratives.

On his first return trip to Canada, Dr. Barbeau wrote to his father stating, "Oklahoma is the most barbarous and uncivilized country I have yet visited."[75] After comfortably returning to civilization and having a chance to review his collection from the uncivilized country, he came to the realization that "I have succeeded beyond my hopes in obtaining ethnographic material of great value and in great abundance."[76] What Dr. Barbeau took back to Canada was a treasure trove of the history of the incomparable cultural wealth of the Wyandotte people.

Dr. Barbeau returned to Oklahoma on April 20, 1912, and immediately picked up where he left off. Remembering a comment made the previous year by Naomi Dawson regarding how poor many Wyandotte citizens were, Dr.

Barbeau commissioned several citizens to make new artifacts for which he paid a very nice commission. Dr. Barbeau also purchased many old artifacts that were then revered as having obvious cultural and sentimental value. Old or new, it did not matter: The artifacts were artifacts made and used by, and representative of, the Wyandotte people when they still knew many of the old ways of making things. Bought and paid for, they are Wyandotte treasures now belonging to the Canadian Museum of Civilization.

Preceding Dr. Barbeau's first visit to Oklahoma, BNO Walker was unable to assemble all the informants as hoped, yet the trip proved to be an overwhelming success. With ample time before the second trip, BNO's list of informants had become longer. In addition, their familiarity with Dr. Barbeau ensured a better understanding of what was needed and expected. Dr. Barbeau met Smith Nichols on the first trip, and he proved to be a very valuable informant on the second.

Nichols was the leader and eldest survivor of the conservative breechcloths, Wyandotte traditionalists dedicated to the old way of doing things. Speaking Wandat almost exclusively, he associated with John Kayrahoo on the Seneca Reservation. Kayrahoo spoke exclusively Wandat and, after serving as head chief of the Wyandotte Tribe, left office amid controversy. As a result of the controversy, he rarely ever ventured among his fellow citizens. Nichols had three wives,[77] and Nichols operated on Nichols time, yet nothing was ever rushed or delayed—if that makes any sense. It just so happened that it was corn-planting season when Dr. Barbeau arrived in Oklahoma, upon which he sent Nichols a letter of invitation. Nichols replied from his farm at Turkey Ford, "I have my corn to plant next Monday and Tuesday and I can't possibly get away from here until after my planting is done."[78] So Dr. Barbeau waited until it was convenient for him, and the wait was well worth the delay. Smith Nichols, along with his niece Catherine Johnson, provided the best material for Dr. Barbeau's collection.

Returning to Canada on August 3, 1912, Dr. Barbeau never returned to Oklahoma, and the treasures he took became stories of folklore in their own right. *Huron*-Wyandotte traditional stories, a token of the language, became accessible when Barbeau's *Huron and Wyandot Mythology* was published in 1915. Greater access to the Wyandotte's traditional language was gained in 1960 when his *Huron-Wyandot Traditional Narratives* was published. The wax recordings of the traditional language, including many songs sung by a few of the last native speakers, became hollow echoes in the vaults of the Canadian Museum of Civilization. After a fire in the vaults, wax cylinders became warped, making the precious language that much more difficult to hear and understand. Photos of citizens and the artifacts eventually began to show up on the internet; however, the copyright held by the Canadian Museum of Civilization made it nearly impossible for anyone to use the photographs.

Many attempts have been made to access the Wyandotte's culturally relevant material, with frustrating success. Little bits and pieces would be surrendered over the years, yet the restrictions placed on its use were stifling. When a contract was presented to the Wyandotte Nation for use of the material, there were many restrictions. One such restriction expressed the following:

> Works to appear on an internal page of the Wyandotte Nation web site (wyandotte-nation.org), for a period of ten (10) years, beginning October 2006. This web site will be a password protected site, restricted to Wyandotte language researchers and students in the Wyandotte Nation of Oklahoma and Kansas (currently approximately one hundred (100) users, not to exceed five hundred (500).[79]

The Wyandotte Nation chiefs, board of directors, and tribal leadership have decreed that no person or entity can place a copyright on *Huron*-Wyandot traditional culture, including the language, stories, and songs as collected by Dr. Charles Marius Barbeau. The Wyandot people are grateful for the Canadian Museum of Civilization's guarded stewardship of the collection over the last 100-plus years; however, the condition of the Wyandotte Nation has greatly improved since 1911 and 1912, and the Wyandotte Nation will freely use, only for the benefit and betterment of citizens, what rightfully belongs to the people—their culture. How can a contract limiting the use of a culture be placed upon a people who own and live that culture? It cannot be done! Shame on anyone who tries!

Not long after Dr. Barbeau returned home to Canada, many of his informants died. They were the Wyandotte's last living connection to knowledge of the old ways and customs of the *Huron*-Wyandot people. Shortly thereafter, the Great Depression and the Dust Bowl hit Oklahoma and the Wyandotte people hard. Many Wyandotte citizens were scattered, with the tribe's survivability again placed in jeopardy. World War II engulfed the world, and it was then that Leaford Bearskin and his twin brother Leland left the former reservation to go fight as Wyandotte warriors protecting their homeland. After Germany's and Japan's surrender, the entire world changed, and that change would eventually find its way to the Wyandotte Tribe.

During the presidency of Dwight David Eisenhower, in August of 1956, a letter was delivered to the Wyandotte Tribe of Oklahoma telling of the tribe's termination. At the time, Wyandotte chiefs and tribal leaders worked from their homes. The tribe did not have a council house, administrative building, health clinic, gymnasium, education building, or cultural center. There were barely enough Wyandotte citizens attending the annual meetings to hold a quorum. The letter did not come as a surprise, but its words were nonetheless heart-wrenching. The feelings and emotions would have been numbing. The anger, confusion, and inability to do anything would have been nearly paralyzing; however, Wyandottes do not turn their back on a fight, and a fight was declared to again obtain recognition.

What happened to the Wyandotte Tribe in 1957 also happened to many other tribes across the United States. The 1950s are often referred to as the *termination era*. During Eisenhower's presidency a three-pronged policy was employed to terminate all federal obligations to the various tribes. The first prong was a relocation program whereby Indians were taken from their villages and reservations for relocation to larger metropolitan cities. In these cities the Indians were to be given training and employment opportunities. The program started in 1953, and it is estimated that by 1960, 33,466 American Indian and Alaska Natives had been relocated.[80] Many did not survive the stress inflicted by the relocation.

The second prong was the termination of federally recognized tribes. In total, one hundred tribes were terminated. Along with termination, over one million acres of land were removed from trust status.[81] Only the tribes and villages who resided in Alaska escaped termination because Alaska did not become a state until 1959.

The third prong extended deep into Indian Country. Public Law 280, passed in 1953, transferred federal law enforcement over the various tribes to the states. The states were unhappy with the new law due to the "failure of the Act to provide funding for their new authority to enforce criminal law in Indian country."[82] The tribes saw the act as undermining tribal sovereignty. The law was imposed without the consent of the various tribes.

With leadership from Chiefs Leonard Cotter, Sam Long, Mont Cotter, and Lawrence Zane, the Wyandotte Tribe of Oklahoma attempted to conduct business as usual. Oklahoma Senators and Congressmen joined the fight and assisted in getting the Wyandotte Tribe reinstated in 1978. The injustice of termination was rescinded. The announcement was made during the dedication ceremony of the *Huron* Indian Cemetery in Kansas City. Public law

95-281 stated, "Be it enacted by the Senate and House of Representatives of the United States of America in Congress assembled, That, (a) Federal recognition is hereby extended or confirmed with respect to the Wyandotte Indian Tribe of Oklahoma."

Wytopia

I will never forget when, ten years later, in 1988, Artie Nesvold invited me into her home. She gave me a wonderful history lesson and allowed me to photograph her map of the 1888 allotments. As she searched for the map, she began pulling box after box of documents from under her bed. It was then that I realized whom I was sitting with. Over the decades of serving the Wyandotte Tribe, many during the years of termination, Artie had collected and preserved everything. In much the same way as Tauromee and his wooden chest of wampum belts, Artie's tribal treasures were stuffed in cardboard shoeboxes. Also in much the same way as Tauromee, after Artie died, too many of the documents in her care disappeared.

In the absence of Wyandotte clan mothers, Artie became the grandmother of the Wyandotte Tribe of Oklahoma. In spirit, and through her many acts of service, Artie was in essence the Wyandotte Tribe's faith-keeper. She played a tremendous role in the Wyandotte's fight for reinstatement. She stared the Stone Giant of termination straight in the face and did not blink. Actually, she took the Stone Giant by the nose and twisted. Now that's pretty impressive, scary, and a little funny, especially since she was rather small in stature. Artie was a fiery little Wyandotte lady whom no one in their right mind chose to challenge. Even the legendary warrior Chief Bearskin yielded a tremendous amount of respect and right-of-way when she entered a room. Artie's death in 1993 was a tremendous loss for the Wyandotte people. She represents just one of the many Wyandotte women who have quietly and gracefully strengthened the whole of the *Huron*-Wyandot people through their selfless service. It may have been the men who graced the history books, but it was the women who graced the *Huron*-Wyandot people.

When the historical committee first began talking about reinstating traditional *Huron*-Wyandot culture, a search was made for Wyandotte elders who were willing to help. Not many were found; however, Juanita McQuistion and Hazel Wallace stepped forward and immediately began to help. Remember Hazel from several pages back? Hazel was the little girl at the Industrial

FIGURE 6.3. Artie Sarah Nesvold

Boarding School who was spanked for speaking her native language. No matter how often or hard the spankings were, the schoolmasters could not beat the Indian out of the little girl. Each whack and bruise only confirmed what Hazel already knew: She would never release or allow to be taken away the privilege of being a little Indian girl. Hazel became faith-keeper of the Seneca-Cayuga Tribe—she never gave up, lost hope, or surrendered her faith—the little girl won!

I remember that as the search began for traditional Wyandotte culture, a lot of talk was initiated by Chief Bearskin in the years 2001 to 2003. After the Annual Meetings in September, Chief Bearskin would invite interested parties to a second meeting after lunch. In these informal meetings traditional Wyandotte culture was discussed, including what could be done to initiate its reinstatement. Second Chief Jim Bland was in charge of organizing culturally related projects, and from these meetings the first annual Culture Week was held May 31 through June 4, 2004.

Several months prior to the first Culture Week, known today as the Annual Gathering, an online Wendat Yahoo eGroup was established. The purpose of this online discussion board, facilitated and administered by Richard Zane Smith, was to unite citizens from the Wyandotte Nation, Wyandot of Anderdon Nation, Wyandot Nation of Kansas, and Huron-Wendat of Wendake. Smith, a tribal member of the Wyandot Nation of Kansas, used this forum to generate excitement for the upcoming Culture Week. The discussion board, as its name clearly shows, outwardly promoted all four nations as being Wendats.

The discussions facilitated by Chief Bearskin were all about reinstating Wyandotte culture and had nothing to do with Wendat culture. At that time the concept of the Wyandotte being Wendat had not been explored, discussed, cussed, embraced, or denied. Everyone just went along with the notion being presented, for it appeared to be serving a purpose and was definitely garnering some good talk. From January through February of 2004, there were many discussions and much activity on the Wendat Yahoo eGroup, but, unfortunately, the discussions eventually devolved into arguments. Thankfully, all of this was short-lived. Efforts to reinstating lost Wyandotte, or should I say Wendat, culture became more a philosophical debate between Wendake and Oklahoma than a pursuit of tangible and sustainable efforts to reinstate anything.

The Wendat Yahoo eGroup is now defunct and has been replaced with other forms of social media. From this initial setting the name Wendat was formally carried into discussions of the Wyandotte Nation Culture Committee, or Historical Committee, as it was then known. An invitation was extended to Smith to attend the meetings and represent the interests of the Wyandot Nation of Kansas. It was believed that his attendance would continue the reconciliation process which began after the signing of the 1999 Wendat Confederacy.

As the Historical Committee started planning Culture Days, interested parties told me we must prove ourselves and humbly submit to "the traditional way of doing things." I was told this had to happen before Wyandotte elders would come out of hiding and consent to help. Prove ourselves? Come out of hiding and submit to what or whom? The people telling the historical committee to submit were telling them to submit not to Wyandotte elders but to their own agenda. Juanita McQuistion and Hazel Wallace, the two elders who sought out the committee, did not request that the committee submit to anything—they submitted to the committee!

Initially I was told that the committee was going too fast in its quest to reinstate traditional culture. Now, well over a decade later, I have been told the committee is going too slowly. You will never please everyone, and just about everyone will have a different idea as to what traditional culture entails. Some will think traditional culture can be found only in the establishment of Wytopia. Still others will think it's learning Wandat, the Wyandotte's traditional language. For me, it's researching and writing about *Huron*-Wyandot history. Others may want to tell traditional stories or dance socially or competitively during powwow. Still others may want to bead, finger-weave, make regalia, or feast and socialize. Is anyone wrong?

The interested parties demanding that the Historical Committee prove itself were self-appointed neotraditionalists seeking the reinstatement of a traditional Wyandot-Wendat culture. The neotraditionalists were, in essence, promoting the creation of Wytopia—a utopian world where Wyandot-Wendat traditions were to be reinstated as though something was wrong with contemporary Wyandotte traditions. Reinstating traditional *Huron*-Wyandot culture and creating a Wyandot-Wendat Wytopia are two totally different matters. I obviously support the reinstatement of as much traditional *Huron*-Wyandot culture as possible; however, I do not support the creation of a Wytopia, as it would be a very divisive place where no one could live. Divisiveness is not limited to the creation of a Wytopia. Divisiveness can be simple ideas and unachievable expectations imposed upon people who do not meet a standard determined by an individual, committee, or council of people. When legalism, in addition to divisiveness, is disseminated, an impossibly difficult environment exists. Wytopia becomes suffocating. The intoxicating euphoria of Wytopia loses its fun even for its founders and organizers who must now constantly police the people.

During many of the discussions, it was easy to see that the neotraditionalists were promoting Wendat universalism. This universalism demanded a return to Wytopia. In this return all Wyandots were to be divided into good Wyandots and bad Wyandots, as determined by a personal commitment and loyalty to the concept and philosophy of Wytopia. After nearly a decade of personality and philosophical conflicts, the ideas of how Wytopia was to be reinstated became one-sided, which began to take a terrible toll. Any potential use of the name Wendat was rejected after it was determined to have no historical legitimacy for the *Huron*-Wyandot people. After the name Wendat was rejected, the universalism and divisiveness just rolled over into the name Wyandot.

I am very conscious of what John Kayrahoo said in 1911: "Could one still live after the customs of long ago? No, that is not possible. That time is gone."[83] Kayrahoo was a last link to the old ways of the *Huron*-Wyandots. He was a traditionalist, and thus almost everything he said that was recorded by

Dr. Barbeau has been examined with impeccable detail and scrutiny. Kayrahoo died in 1913. It appears that today's neotraditionalists want to be selective in what they wish to learn from his traditional knowledge and wisdom.

What is being demanded by the neotraditionalists is a return to a matrilineal clan–based society where *Huron*-Wyandot clan mothers are in charge of nearly all aspects of life. I do not have a problem with this, but I just have to ask—how do we get there? Should we rebuild the palisades? The best advice I have heard thus far has been "What I would like you to do is to break the wall and cross to the unseen world."[84] If only it were this easy. I do not believe that Wytopia is a tangible world but an unseen world and a personal choice to be made. As philosophical, sociological, and cultural differences were being debated, "crossing to the unseen world" is one of the few things discussed that actually makes sense in a rather strange, but understandable, way.

In contrast to the way many neotraditionalists now demand, Wytopia is a personal spiritual commitment more than a tangible physical commitment. It is a way of life, a chosen lifestyle. What was the lifestyle of the old *Huron*-Wyandots? It was a clan-based, shamanistic lifestyle. Could Wyandottes again embrace certain elements of tradition, reinstate many of their old ways, and leave behind elements they no longer want to embrace? Can many of the old ways be reinstated without taunting high governmental authorities and challenging contemporary tradition? Should the Wyandottes care what the government thinks? Yes, they should. Tarhe did back in his day, and Wyandottes should do the same today—it's called wisdom. Tarhe did build his palisades of isolationism, but he did not taunt the government officials to come and tear them down.

A physical Wytopia would be built upon two things: clan mothers and shaman. Since the Wyandotte people currently have neither, where are the neotraditionalists going to find them? In the past, *Huron*-Wyandot women from each of their respective clans chose their clan mother from among themselves. Today the clans are not fully assembled and are thus unable to choose their clan mothers; therefore, appointments must first fill the vacancies. OK, who, then, is making the appointments? An individual or a committee does, and they are the ones who are truly in charge of Wytopia.

Dr. Georges Sioui, a Huron-Wendat citizen and coordinator of the Aboriginal Studies Program at the University of Ottawa, recently said, "We are rediscovering the way to bring up children to recognize their relationship with the natural world, to speak with nature, to greet a flower, to relate to a tree, to relate to a wild animal or an animal he or she is eating. It's also the idea just to be more sensitive to life itself."[85] This is a large part of what makes Wytopia—Wytopia. For some Wyandottes their personal convictions and current life choices would make this a difficult territory for them to traverse. I propose that we do not have to travel anywhere. Many Wyandottes are already innately embracing the discoveries being made by Dr. Sioui. For citizens who want to reside in Wyandotte, Oklahoma, they can stay. Other citizens who live in Seattle, Dallas, Tulsa, Baltimore, or Jackson, South Carolina, and anywhere else across the Great Island, they likewise do not have to leave their homes and move somewhere else. In our contemporary world there are many modern conveniences that can keep every citizen easily connected. But do not get soft! Always be alert! There may again come a time when all Wyandottes need to come together in order to survive.

I once saw a billboard that read, "Stop looking for your happy place and make one here." I really liked that. I submit it would be better for all of us to come together and stop looking for our happy place and just make one here. Actually, when you look back at the lives the ancestors of the Wyandottes lived, you can see they were filled with war and injustices, and the hope for a better future in which to raise their children. Why are the neotraditionalists looking backward with the hope of reinstating a time that was filled with constant struggles? Yes, we currently have our own struggles and misgivings; however, all generations are supposed to remember the past but make preparations for future generations to have a better place to live. In comparison to the way the Wyandotte's ancestors were living back in their day, we are indeed now living in Wytopia.

Many generations of the *Huron*-Wyandot people have been filled with glorious accomplishments, remarkable leadership, and an all-encompassing intelligence, even in light of all the injustices. The ancestors of the Wyandotte people did not complain; they endured and conquered with a forward-looking stance. I would advise the neotraditionalists to keep looking forward and not look back with the thought that anyone has failed. Do not be discouraged when you look back and compare how the old Wyandots lived to the way Wyandottes live today. Do not think for a moment that anyone has failed. Big Tree could not easily live in our contemporary Wyandotte culture. Likewise, you could not easily go back and live in Big Tree's contemporary Wyandot culture. A living, breathing culture will change and adapt to and at times follow different paths in order to survive. That's OK—*it's called life*—and the Wyandotte people have a lot of life yet to live.

If a Wyandotte citizen wants to learn about who he or she is and the history that rightfully belongs to them, no Wyandotte elder will ever hold their heritage hostage or make demands for anything. Neotraditionalists, on the other hand, will make and have already made some pretty ridiculous demands. In much the same way as Mononcue and the choices he made, the best thing you can do is quietly listen, be aware there are competing voices, and *choose wisely* whom you listen to. Many of the old Wyandots did not listen to the voice of Handsome Lake, Tenskwatawa, or even John Stewart. Be aware that there are new voices speaking an old message that is not very different from the one many old Wyandots rejected back in their day.

Today in Wyandotte, Oklahoma, Billy Friend is Chief of the Wyandotte Nation. The tribe is growing under his leadership, as is most citizens' desire to learn their history and traditions. A short while ago I was encouraged to hear that a Wyandotte teenager was telling traditional stories to the children in the Wyandotte Nation's daycare program. The reinstatement of tradition must start at the very beginning, with the children. I have always said, "We need to learn to walk before we talk." The telling of traditional stories is a first and easy step all Wyandottes can make. Maybe one of my daughters will step forward to continue the tradition of correcting the men on historical matters. Maybe it's your daughter, or your son, who will step forward. Encourage them. Support them. In the future there will still be plenty of Stone Giants in need of defeat. May all *Huron*-Wyandot generations find the courage to stand face to face with the monsters and kill a Stone Giant or two.

It was not all that long ago that Naomi Dawson, like most of the young people of her day, ignored the old *Huron*-Wyandot traditions. She taught her kindergarten students what white society at that time wanted the children to know, including how they should behave as bleached white children. Today all Wyandottes are surrounded by a culture tinged with many colors and beliefs; therefore, parents must be diligent in teaching their children who they are as Wyandottes. All Wyandotte families must build individual yet invisible palisades around their homes scattered coast to coast and elsewhere. We cannot again easily come together and collectively build one palisade for all *Huron*-Wyandots. But no one can stop the Wyandottes from building hundreds of palisades everywhere they now choose to live.

In June of 2009 the Historical Committee was officially recognized by the Wyandotte Nation Board of Directors as the Cultural Committee. In our first official meeting on July 11th we started with a round table discussion on how the purpose of the Cultural Committee could be summarized into a short motto. After several suggestions Sherri Nesvold Clemons, the Tribal Heritage Department Director, simply stated, "Preserving the future of our past." The statement was perfect and immediately adopted as our motto and has been used ever since. Use of the motto is not limited to just the Cultural Committee. It will take more than a committee to revive and preserve traditional *Huron*-Wyandot culture—it will take a community, the whole of the Wyandotte people. It will take Wyandotte households integrating into their daily lives what they feel is appropriate *Huron*-Wyandot tradition for their families to embrace. No committee can demand that anyone must live a certain way and think or believe certain things. It will take contemporary Wyandotte citizens to ensure a future for Wyandotte citizens yet to be born. It's through everyone's selfless preservation of our *Huron*-Wyandot culture that future generations can live the honor of being Wyandotte. It's through the preservation of our future that the memory and honor of our generations past will also continue to live.

Not all that long ago it was a sacred tradition for the old *Huron*-Wyandots to recite the history of their nation and their wars. It was also a sacred tradition for the old *Huron*-Wyandots to repeat the traditions of their fathers. It's important for Wyandottes to do the same today so that the *Huron*-Wyandot people will forever live *On the Back of a Turtle*.

NOTES

Notes to the Preface

1. Carton, "Historical Work after The War," 340.
2. Connelley, "The Wyandots," 98.
3. McQuistion, *Letter to Charles Garrad,* 27 Feb. 1973.
4. Thwaites, *How George Rogers Clark Won the Northwest,* 100.
5. Hancks, *The Emigrant Tribes,* 453–55.
6. Tooker, "Wyandot," 406.
7. Clarke, *Origin and Traditional History of the Wyandotts,* 148.
8. Trigger, "The Liberation of Wendake," 10.
9. Finley, *History of the Wyandott Mission,* 57.

Notes to Chapter 1

1. Hewitt, "Huron," 589.
2. Dr. Charles Marius Barbeau, in *Huron and Wyandot Mythology,* indicates there were nine versions or fragments of *Huron*-Wyandot cosmological myths (37). These oral narratives of the *Huron*-Wyandot people go beyond telling not only the story of Creation but also the structure of the universe in which they lived. With so many different versions of the oral narratives, this narration undoubtedly originates from the fact the *Huron*-Wyandot people are a mixture of several different people groups. The differences within the stories are minor, and the key elements in each narrative remain essentially unchanged. Each of the narratives contains the Woman Who Fell from Above, the animal gods, a world Created upon the back of a turtle, the good and bad twins, the destruction of the world, and the Creation of the world after its destruction with a compromise of both good and bad.

    The old *Huron*-Wyandot's faith and trust in these stories reflected their dedication over the course of hundreds of years. Over time their stories remained amazingly unaltered. In 1899 William Connelley published "Notes on the Folk-Lore of the Wyandots. I. Religion." Connelley concluded the essay by stating, "At the present time the opportunity for such studies has passed away, inasmuch as the old Wyandots from whom this information was received, with one exception, have died, and the present generation is wholly ignorant of the ancient beliefs. No folk-lore could be obtained from any Wyandot now living, and few can speak the language" (125). If Connelley were alive today, he would be surprised to learn that these stories are still very much alive and are being told with fascinating creativity.

The sources used in my compilation are woven primarily around and within Bertrand Nicholas Oliver (BNO) Walker's rendition of "The Origin of the World," recorded by Dr. Barbeau in Wyandotte, Oklahoma, twelve years after Connelley stated, "No folk-lore could be obtained from any Wyandot now living." BNO's story was published in Barbeau's *Huron* and is one of the most complete renderings of the *Huron*-Wyandot creation story ever recorded.

When reading Connelley's work, one can become a little confused as he tries to incorporate many of the noted variances to the *Huron*-Wyandot's oral narratives within his different writings. Thus, his stories do not flow well from publication to publication and at times do not make good sense of what is happening. Connelley used at least eleven different informants when he collected the stories. Some of the informants were in Kansas and some in Oklahoma. His collection and compilation of the stories was an incredible task that stands second to none. Unfortunately, because of the magnitude of material he collected, and his desire to publish it all, it can be confusing to the casual reader.

3. Trigger, *The Children of Aataentsic,* 77.

4. Barbeau, *Huron,* 38.

5. Barbeau, *Huron,* 40.

6. Connelley, *Wyandot Folk-Lore,* 71.

7. Connelley, *Wyandot,* 45.

8. How did the young woman become pregnant? Several different theories are presented within the oral narratives. Some say she was pregnant before she fell from the Sky-world (Hale, "Huron I," 180), and others believe she became pregnant upon eating the flower from the tree of light (Connelley, "Religious Conceptions," 116–17). One of the most fantastic beliefs is that she simply wanted and chose to become pregnant. This belief is likely a late addition to the oral narratives and reflects an influence from Christianity. Walker simply stated, "The woman felt that she was with child" (Barbeau, *Huron,* 44). Walker did not give an explanation as to how the young woman became pregnant, and after all it really doesn't matter.

9. Barbeau, *Huron,* 44.

10. Barbeau, *Huron,* 44.

11. Schoolcraft, *Oneóta, or Characteristics of the Red Race of America,* 210.

12. Hale, "Huron Folk-Lore I," 181.

13. Connelley, *Indian Myths,* 125–26.

14. Connelley, "Religious Conceptions," 120.

15. The names of the Twins—what a mess! In this text I have chosen to present the names of the Twins with a modern translation. Dr. Craig Kopris, former linguist of the Wyandotte Nation, has rewritten the Twins' names as tséhsta? and tawéskare. These spellings are based upon Walker's telling of the Twins' names to Dr. Barbeau, but the names in this story are presented in a way that is much easier to read, reproduce, and pronounce. Walker stated in "The Origin of the World," found in Dr. Barbeau's *Huron and Wyandot Mythology,* that the Twins' names were tsɛ′(sta)—the Good One—and tăwɛ′skärɛ—the Evil One (Barbeau, *Huron,* 45). After making a case for the complexity and variance of the Twins' names I am going to simply call them the Good Twin and the Bad Twin. As the stories are told today by most Wyandottes, the Twins are simply referred to as the Good Twin and the Bad Twin.

Connelley created a long, complex presentation of the Twins' names. The first-born is Tsēh′-sĕh-howh′-hŏŏhⁿgk—Made of Fire, or The Man Who Was Made of Fire. The second-born is Täh′-wĕh-skäh′-rŏŏhⁿgk—Made of Flint, or The Man Who Was Made of Flint ("Notes on the Folk-Lore," 123). Published also in 1899, *Wyandot Folk-Lore* presents the Twins' names as Tsēh′-stäh, the Good One, and Täh′-wĕh-skäh′rĕh, the Bad One (47). Yet still again in 1922 Connelley published "Religious Conceptions" in which he states that the first-born was called "Tsesta," "Tsesehhowngk," or "Tsesehhowoongk," "the Man of Fire." The second one was called "Taweskareh," or "Taweskaroongk," "the Man of Flint"" (121). In Connelley's last publication of Wyandot oral narratives, in 1928, he adapted the stories into a reader for third through fifth graders. Here he modified, simplified, and shortened the Twins' names to Sē′stä, Fire, and Skä′rĕh, Ice or Stone (*Indian Myths,* 18). Horatio Hale indicated the Twins were named Tijuskeha, which means something like "savior," or "good man," and Tawiskarong, meaning flinty, or flint-like ("Huron Folk-Lore I" 181). Regardless of the spelling of the names, in all accounts the Twins' roles, personalities, and deeds were the same.

16. Connelley, *Wyandot Folk-Lore,* 40.

17. Hale, "Huron Folk-Lore. I," 181.

18. Connelley, "Religious Conceptions," 118.

19. Connelley, "Religious Conceptions," 123.

20. Connelley, "Religious Conceptions," 123.

21. Schoolcraft, *Oneóta,* 209.

22. Finley, *Life among the Indians,* 326–28.

23. Schoolcraft, *Oneóta,* 210.

24. Connelley, "Religious Conceptions," 124.

25. Bruce, "The Petuns," 34.

26. Buser, "Our Great Chiefs."

27. Blair, *The Indian Tribes of the Upper Mississippi Valley,* Vol. 1, 252–53.

28. Hale, "The Fall of Hochelaga," 7.

29. Hale, "The Fall," 7.

30. Wright, "Before European Contact," 21.

31. Parkman, *The Conspiracy of Pontiac,* Vol. I, 6th ed., 22.

32. Schoolcraft, *Historical and Statistical Information,* Vol. I, 305.

33. Hewitt, "Huron," 585.

34. Hewitt, "Huron," 584.

35. Warrick, *A Population History of the Huron-Petun,* 9

36. Hewitt, "Hurons," 585.

37. Charlevoix, *History and General Description of New France,* Vol. 2, 71.

38. Trigger, *Children,* 27.

39. Hewitt, "Huron," 584.

40. Charlevoix, *History and General Description of New France,* Vol. 2, 71.

41. Hewitt, "Huron," 584.

42. Barbeau, *Huron,* ix.

43. Trigger, "The Original Iroquoians: Huron, Petun and Neutral," 41.

44. Trigger, *Children,* 58.

45. Trigger, *Children,* 30.

46. L. Sioui, "Huron to Huron-Wendat."

47. Sioui, *The Reaffirmation of Wendat/Wyandotte Identity in a time of Globalization,* 47, 68.

48. Hewitt, "Huron," 584.

49. Kopris, "Wendat A Universal Social Identity."

50. Trigger, *Children,* 27.

51. Peace and Labelle, eds., *From Huronia to Wendakes,* 10.

52. Trigger, "Liberation," 3–4.

53. Kathryn Magee, *Dispersed but Not Destroyed: Leadership, Women, and Power within the Wendat Diaspora, 1600–1701,* 16.

54. Warrick, *Population,* 9.

55. Garrad, "Commemorating the 350th Anniversary of the Dispersal," 4.

56. Trigger, "The French Presence in Huronia," 109.

57. Sayre, *Sauvages,* xii.

58. Buser, Unpublished manuscript two.

59. Clifton, *Re-emergent,* 8.

60. Hewitt, "Huron," 591.

61. Thwaites, *Early Western Travels 1748–1846,* Vol. I, 28–29.

62. Thwaites, *Early,* Vol. I, 30.

63. Barbeau, "Huron-Wyandot Dictionary," 436.

64. Pearson, *The Wyandotte Language: Handbook and Dictionary,* 1.

65. Clifton, *Re-emergent,* 13.

66. Trigger, "The Original Iroquoians: Huron, Petun, and Neutral," 59.

67. Hewitt, "Huron," 585.

68. Trowbridge, "Wyandots—C. C. Trowbridge's Account," 6–8.

69. Schoolcraft, *Oneóta,* 54–57.

70. Warrick, *Population,* 3.

71. Garrad, "Emailing_Divine2015."

72. Schoolcraft, *Oneóta,* 211.

73. Warrick, *Population*, 4.

74. Trigger, *Children*, 588.

75. Barbeau, "How the Huron-Wyandot Language Was Saved from Oblivion," 226.

76. Trigger, "The Original Iroquoians: Huron, Petun, and Neutral," 46.

77. Trigger, "Original," 46.

78. Trigger, "Original," 46.

79. Trigger, *Children*, 632–33.

80. Hewitt, "Wenrohronon," 932.

81. Garrad and Steckley, "Craigleith and the Birth of the Wyandot Tribe," 3.

82. Hawkins, "Genoa Frilled Pottery," 17.

83. Garrad and Steckley, "Craigleith," 3.

84. Garrad, "The Planter-Fleming BdHb-2 Site: A Review," 19.

85. Hawkins, "Genoa," 33.

86. Hewitt, "Wenrohronon," 933.

87. Trigger, "Original," 53.

88. Trigger, *Children*, 562.

89. Hewitt, "Wenrohronon," 933.

90. Hewitt, "Wenrohronon," 934.

91. Hawkins, "Recreating Home?" 77.

92. Trigger, "Original," 44.

93. Hewitt, "Hurons," 585.

94. Johansen, "Dating the Iroquois Confederacy," 62.

95. Parkman, *Conspiracy*, Vol. I, 6th ed., 21.

96. Trigger, "Liberation," 3.

97. Garrad, *Petun to Wyandot*, 159.

98. Trigger, *Children*, 403.

99. Trigger, *Children*, 522.

100. Trigger, *Children*, 522.

101. Trigger, *Children*, 524.

102. Trigger, *Children*, 546.

103. Otterbein, "Huron," 151.

Notes to Chapter 2

1. Thwaites, *Collections of the State Historical Society of Wisconsin*, Vol. XVI, 354.

2. Otterbein, "Huron," 143.

3. Garrad and Steckley, "Craigleith," 4.

4. Thwaites, *Jesuit Relations*, Vol. XXXIV, 15.

5. Thwaites, *Jesuit Relations*, Vol. XXXIV, 16.

6. Garrad, *Petun*, 49–50.

7. Shea, "An Historical Sketch of the Tionontates," 263.

8. Thomas, "Some Indian History," 160.

9. Thomas, "History," 161.

10. Thwaites, *Collections*, 350.

11. Thwaites, *Collections*, 354.

12. Thwaites, *Collections*, 14.

13. Thwaites, *Collections*, 11–13.

14. Thwaites, *Collections*, xiv.

15. Thwaites, *Collections*, 14–15.

16. Thwaites, *Collections*, xiv.

17. Thwaites, 14.

18. Shea, "Sketch," 264.

19. Shea, "Sketch," 264.

20. Thwaites, *Clark*, 239.

21. Thwaites, *Clark*, 244.

22. Gordon, *History of Barron County Wisconsin*, 30.

23. Stewart, *Rene Menard, 1605–1661*.

24. Stewart, *Menard*.

25. Stewart, *Menard*.

26. Stewart, *Menard*.

27. Gordon, *History*, 30.

28. Shea, "Sketch," 264.

29. Thwaites, *Clark*, 210.

30. Thwaites, *Collections*, 17–19.

31. Shea, "Sketch," 264.

32. Shea, "Sketch," 264.

33. Parkman, *Count Frontenac*, 159–60.

34. Shea, "Sketch," 264.

35. Parkman, *Count Frontenac*, 74–75.

36. Parkman, *Count Frontenac*, 77.

37. Parkman, *Count Frontenac*, 145.

38. Parkman, *Count Frontenac*, 122.

39. Shea, "An Historical Sketch of the Tionontates," 264.

40. Thwaites, *Collections*, 167.

41. Shea, "Sketch," 265.

42. Parkman, *Count Frontenac*, 173–78.

43. Thwaites, *Collections*, 166.

44. Shea, "Sketch," 265.

45. Shea, "Sketch," 265.

46. Shea, "Sketch," 265.

47. Shea, "Sketch," 266.

48. Schoolcraft, *Oneóta*, 56–57.

49. Mansfield, *History of the Great Lakes,* Vol. I, 62–63.

50. Thwaites, *Collections*, 166–67.

51. Shea, "Sketch," 266.

52. cbc.ca/history/EPCONTENTSE1EP3CH2PA2LE.html.

53. Parkman, *Count Frontenac*, 444–48.

54. Parkman, *Count Frontenac*, 142.

55. Parkman, *Count Frontenac*, 452.

56. Shea, "Sketch," 266.

57. Laut, *Cadillac*, 158.

58. Laut, *Cadillac*, 52.

59. Burton, *The City of Detroit Michigan 1701–1922,* Vol. II, 866.

60. Burton, *Detroit,* Vol. II, 867.

61. Dubuisson, *Official Report Made by the Commanding Officer.*

62. Thwaites, *Collections*, 268.

63. Thwaites, *Collections*, 269.

64. Thwaites, *Collections*, 271.

65. Thwaites, *Collections,* Vol. XVI, 271.

66. Thwaites, *Collections*, 272.

67. Thwaites, *Collections,* Vol. XVI, 274.

68. Thwaites, *Collections*, 275.

69. Thwaites, *Collections*, 277.

70. Thwaites, *Collections*, 278.

71. Thwaites, *Collections*, 280.

72. Thwaites, *Collections*, 284.

73. Burton, *Detroit,* Vol. II, 870–71.

74. Trowbridge, "Wyandots," 15–16.

75. Shea, "Sketch," 268.

76. Winter, *A History of Northwest Ohio*, 10.

77. Steckley, "The 1747 Wyandot Elders Council," 29.

78. Clifton, "Re-emergent," 1.

79. Frohman, "Searching for the Forts and Indian Villages of Sandusky Bay."

80. Shea, "Sketch," 268.

81. Shea, "Sketch," 268.

82. Shea, "Sketch," 268.

83. Winter, 11.

84. Shea, "Sketch," 268.

85. Shea, "Sketch," 268.

86. Clifton, "Re-emergent," 1.

87. Clifton, "Re-emergent," 1.

88. Walton, *Conrad Weiser and the Indian Policy*, 187–88.

89. Shea, "Sketch," 269.

90. Walton, *Weiser*, 242.

91. Walton, *Weiser*, 154.

92. Walton, *Weiser*, 252.

93. Croghan, *A Selection of George Croghan's Letters and Journals*, 48.

94. Pritts, *Incidents of Border Life*, vii.

95. Eid, "The Ojibwa-Iroquois War," 298–99.

96. Parkman, *Defeat*, 8.

97. Parkman, *Defeat*, 8.

98. Parkman, *Defeat*, 13.

99. Martin, "Confrontation at the Monongahela," 125.

100. Martin, "Confrontation," 134.

101. Barr, "A Road for Warriors," 20.

102. Parkman, *Braddock's Defeat*, 28.

103. Tyler, *The Literary History of the American Revolution 1763–1783*, 133.

104. Shannon, *Iroquois Diplomacy on the Early American Frontier*, 138.

105. Parkman, *Defeat*, 29.

106. Shannon, *Iroquois Diplomacy on the Early American Frontier*, 140.

107. Shannon, *Diplomacy*, 141.

108. Shannon, *Diplomacy*, 141.

109. Martin, "Confrontation at the Monongahela," 149.

110. Lawson, *Bravest of the Brave*, 67.

111. Draper, *Collections of the State Historical Society of Wisconsin*, 130.

112. Martin, "Confrontation," 149.

113. Lawson, *Bravest of the Brave*, 68.

114. Parkman, *Defeat*, 48.

115. Parkman, *Defeat*, 48.

116. Lawson, *Bravest*, 86.

117. Washington, memory.loc.gov.

118. Lawson, *Bravest*, 90–91.

119. Cohen, "Sparke," 549.

120. britishbattles.com/braddock.htm.

121. Cohen, "Sparke," 546.

122. Parkman, *Pontiac*, Vol. 1, 169.

123. Stone, *The Life and Times of Sir William Johnson, Bart*, Vol. II, 133.

124. avalon.law.yale.edu/18th_century/paris763.asp.

125. Stone, *The Life and Times of Sir William Johnson, Bart*, Vol. II, 134.

126. Parkman, *Conspiracy*, Vol. 1, 151.

127. Stone, *The Life and Times of Sir William Johnson, Bart*, Vol. II, 140.

128. Stone, *Bart*, Vol. II, 151.

129. Eaggleston and Seelye, *Brant and Red Jacket*, 170.

130. Stone, *Bart*, Vol. II, 152.

131. Stone, *Bart*, Vol. II, 152.

132. Burton, *Detroit*, Vol. II, 885.

133. Stone, *Bart*, Vol. II, 196–97.

134. Stone, *Bart*, Vol. II, 197.

135. Parkman, *Conspiracy*, 180.

136. Parkman, *Conspiracy*, Vol. I, 187.

137. Lawson, *Bravest*, 181.

138. Parkman, *Conspiracy,* Vol. II, 9.

139. Gladwin, *The Gladwin Manuscripts,* 665.

140. Gladwin, *Manuscripts,* 665.

141. Gladwin, *Manuscripts,* 665.

142. Gladwin, *Manuscripts,* 665.

143. Gladwin, *Manuscripts,* 665.

144. Lawson, *Bravest,* 182.

145. Parkman, *Conspiracy,* 570–71.

146. Parkman, *Conspiracy,* 572.

Notes to Chapter 3

1. F. Drake, *The Indian Tribes of the United States,* Vol. 1, 400.

2. William Pitt, qtd. in Thackeray, *A History of the Right Honorable William Pitt,* 335.

3. Taylor, "The Ohio Indians," 73–74.

4. Pritts, *Incidents,* v–vi.

5. Thwaites, *Chronicles of Border Warfare,* 96.

6. Thwaites, *Chronicles,* 96.

7. Thwaites, *Chronicles,* 96.

8. Connelley, *The Provisional Government of Nebraska Territory,* 234–35.

9. Pritts, *Incidents,* 76.

10. Smith, *An Account of the Remarkable Occurrences,* 150–54.

11. Butterfield, *An Historical Account of the Expedition Against Sandusky,* 164–65.

12. Barbeau, *Huron,* 275–80.

13. Elliott, *Indian Missionary Reminiscences,* 95.

14. Trowbridge, "Wyandots," 39–40.

15. Trowbridge, "Wyandots," 40–41.

16. Trowbridge, "Wyandots," 54–55.

17. Elliott, *Reminiscences,* 114.

18. Parkman, *Defeat,* 64.

19. Kappler, *Indian Affairs. Laws and Treaties,* Vol. II (Treaties), 22.

20. Thwaites and Kellogg, eds., *Frontier Defense on the Upper Ohio 1777–1778,* 166–67.

21. Finley, *Wyandott Mission,* 46–47.

22. Thwaites, *Chronicles,* 217.

23. Wimer, *Events In Indian History,* 207–8.

24. Baxter, *The British Invasion From the North,* 235–37.

25. D. Wilson, *The Life of Jane McCrea,* 2–3.

26. Thwaites and Kellogg, eds., *Frontier,* xii–xiii.

27. Thwaites and Kellogg, eds., *Frontier,* 67.

28. Thwaites, *Chronicles,* 217–26.

29. Thwaites, *Chronicles,* 230.

30. Marshall, *The History of Kentucky,* Vol. 1, 130.

31. Marshall, *Kentucky,* Vol. 1, 127.

32. Z. Smith, *The History of Kentucky, From Its Earliest Discovery,* 189–91.

33. Chapin, *The Missionary Gazetteer,* 138.

34. Chapin, *Gazetteer,* 139.

35. Loskiel, *The History of the Moravian Mission,* 219.

36. Loskiel, *Moravian,* 231–32.

37. Loskiel, *Moravian,* 233.

38. Chapin, *Gazetteer,* 139.

39. Loskiel, *Moravian,* 239–41.

40. Loskiel, *Moravian,* 245.

41. Sipe, *The Indian Wars of Pennsylvania,* 639.

42. Loskiel, *Moravian,* 247–51.

43. Doddridge and Doddridge, *Notes on the Settlement and Indian Wars,* 206.

44. Butterfield, *Expedition,* 60.

45. Butterfield, *Expedition,* 76.

46. Butterfield, *Expedition,* 77.

47. Roosevelt, *The Winning of the West,* Part III, 24.

48. Butterfield, *Expedition,* 94.

49. Butterfield, *Expedition,* 126–27.

50. Butterfield, *Expedition,* 128.

51. Brown, "The Battle of Sandusky," 137.

52. Butterfield, *Expedition,* 166.

53. Butterfield, *Expedition,* 194.

54. Butterfield, *Expedition,* 187.

55. Butterfield, *Expedition,* 216.

56. Brown, "Battle," 146.

57. Butterfield, *Expedition,* 330–31.

58. Brackenridge, *Narratives of a Late Expedition Against the Indians,* 10–13.

59. Brown, "The Fate of Crawford Volunteers," 338–40.

60. Douglass, *History of Wayne County Ohio,* 832.

61. Sipe, *Wars,* 631.

62. Frost, *Border Wars of the West,* 214.

63. Douglass, *Wayne,* 832–34.

64. Finley, *Wyandott Mission,* 254–55.

65. Martzofff, "Big Bottom and Its History," 4–10.

66. woosterhistory.org/exhibits/show/indigenoushistory/beaverhattown.

67. woosterhistory.org/exhibits/show/indigenoushistory/beaverhattown.

68. woosterhistory.org/exhibits/show/indigenoushistory/beaverhatmassacre.

69. Douglass, *Wayne,* 161–65.

70. Douglass, *Wayne,* 170.

71. Brooke, "Anthony Wayne," 388–89.

72. Kappler, Affairs, Vol. II, 7.

73. Meek, "Tarhe—The Crane," 64.

74. Brooke, "Anthony Wayne," 389–90.

75. Clarke, *Origin and Traditional History of the Wyandotts*, 63.

76. Clarke, *Origin*, 63.

77. Clarke, *Origin*, 65.

78. Winter, *Northwest Ohio*, 84.

79. Stone, *Brant*, Vol. II, 293–94.

80. armyhistory.org/the-battle-of-the-wabash-the-forgotten-disaster-of-the-indian-wars.

81. Voorhees, "General George A. Custer," 351.

82. Voorhees, "Custer," 352.

83. armyhistory.org/the-battle-of-the-wabash-the-forgotten-disaster-of-the-indian-wars.

84. Winter, *Northwest Ohio*, 59.

85. Winter, *Northwest Ohio*, 59–62.

86. S. Hunt, "General Anthony Wayne," 217.

87. Brooke, "Anthony Wayne," 392.

88. Dodge, *Red Men of the Ohio Valley*, 19–20.

89. Brooke, "Anthony Wayne," 392.

90. Hunt, "General Anthony Wayne," 222.

91. Brooke, "Anthony Wayne," 394–95.

92. Hunt, "General Anthony Wayne," 222–23.

93. Dodge, *Red Men*, 19–20.

94. Hunt, "General Anthony Wayne," 231.

95. Hunt, "General Anthony Wayne," 232.

96. Schoolcraft, *Indian Tribes*, Part VI, 343–34.

97. Benton, "Northern Ohio During the War of 1812," 29–30.

98. Benton, "Northern," 31.

99. Benton, "Northern," 32.

100. Benton, "Northern," 32.

101. Cass, *Remarks on the Policy and Practice*, 61.

102. Elliott, *Reminiscences*, 163–65.

103. Burton, *The City of Detroit Michigan 1701–1922*, Vol. II, 1000–03.

104. Elliott, *Reminiscences*, 167.

105. Cass, *Remarks*, 64.

106. Drake, *The Book of Indians*, 130.

107. Drake, *Book*, 127.

108. Parkman, *Conspiracy*, Vol. II, 109.

109. Elliott, *Reminiscences*, 149.

110. Elliott, *Reminiscences*, 150.

111. Finley, *Wyandott Mission*, 406–7.

Notes to Chapter 4

1. Elliott, *Reminiscences*, 155.

2. Brackenridge, *Narratives*, 3.

3. E. Elliott, *Hugh Henry Brackenridge*.

4. Schomburg, *Two Negro Missionaries to the American Indians*, 402.

5. Finley, *Life Among the Indians*, 20.

6. Trowbridge, "Wyandots," 63.

7. Finley, *Wyandott Mission*, 403.

8. Trowbridge, "Wyandots," 63.

9. Mitchell, *The Missionary Pioneer*, 4.

10. Elliott, *Reminiscences*, 7.

11. Finley, *Wyandott Mission*, 74.

12. Mitchell, *The Missionary Pioneer*, 19–20.

13. Elliott, *Reminiscences*, 35.

14. Elliott, *Reminiscences*, 29–30.

15. Bangs, *History of the Missions*, 70.

16. Finley, *Wyandott Mission*, 415.

17. Finley, *Wyandott Mission*, 107.

18. Bangs, *An Authentic History of the Missions*, 63.

19. Finley, *Wyandott Mission*, 115–16.

20. Finley, *Wyandott Mission*, 119–20.

21. Finley, *Wyandott Mission*, 238.

22. Finley, *Wyandott Mission*, 167–68.

23. Finley, *Wyandott Mission*, 168.

24. Elliott, *Reminiscences*, 43.

25. Elliott, *Reminiscences*, 53.

26. Elliott, *Reminiscences*, 86–88.

27. worthington.org/index.aspx?nid=82.

28. L. Smith, *The Life of Philander Chase*, 124.

29. Connelley, *Provisional Government*, 12.

30. Lemon, *Seneca White Dog Feast*, 319.

31. Finley, *Wyandott Mission*, 83–84.

32. Allen, Personal handwritten letter to James B. Finley.

33. Finley, *Wyandott Mission*, 323.

34. Elliott, *Reminiscences*, 155.

35. Elliott, *Reminiscences*, 200.

36. *The Declaration of Independence*.

37. Jefferson, "*President Thomas Jefferson to William Henry Harrison*."

38. Finley, *Wyandott Mission*, 35.

39. Trowbridge, "Wyandots," 20–21.

40. Trowbridge, "Wyandots," 21.

41. Trowbridge, "Wyandots," 26.

42. Finley, *Life*, 443–45.

43. Finley, *Life*, 447–49.

44. Biographical Sketch of Rutherford B. Hayes, *rbhayes.org*.

45. Jackson, "Transcript of President Andrew Jackson's Message to Congress"

46. Oliphant, "The *Report of the Wyandot Exploring Delegation, 1831*," 259–60.

47. Oliphant, "*Exploring Delegation*," 248.

48. Oliphant, "Exploring Delegation," *1831*, 249.

49. museum.bmi.net/Picnic%20People%20A.L/Disaway%20Mary.htm.

50. museum.bmi.net/Picnic%20People%20A.L/Disaway%20Mary.htm.

51. Chapman, *The Story of Oregon and its People*, 67.

52. Walker, "W. Walker to G. P. Disosway."

53. Oliphant, "Exploring Delegation," *1831*, 254–57.

54. Oliphant, "Exploring Delegation," *1831*, 259.

55. Oliphant, "Exploring Delegation," *1831*, 258.

56. Kappler, *Affairs*, Vol. II, 339.

57. Kappler, *Affairs*, Vol. II, 340.

58. Armstrong, "Letter to Lucy Billow."

59. Kappler, *Affairs*, Vol. II, 340.

60. Hancks, *Emigrant Tribes*, 114.

61. Map of the Huron Reserve.

62. Kappler, *Affairs*, Vol. II, 340.

63. Smith, *The Wyandot Exploring Expedition of 1839*, 2.

64. Hancks, *Emigrant Tribes*, 127.

65. Hancks, *Emigrant Tribes*, 134.

66. Hancks, *Emigrant Tribes*, 134.

67. Hancks, *Emigrant Tribes*, 141.

68. Smith, *The Wyandot Exploring Expedition of 1839*, 4.

69. Smith, *Wyandot Exploring*, 4.

70. Smith, *Wyandot Exploring*, 4.

71. Smith, *Wyandot Exploring*, 5.

72. Smith, *Wyandot Exploring*, 7.

73. Smith, *Wyandot Exploring*, 8.

74. Hancks, *Emigrant Tribes*, 143.

75. *United States Office of Indian Affairs*, "#741, Vol. 34," 153.

76. Smith, *Wyandot Exploring*, 9.

77. Evers, *Many Incidents and Reminiscences of the Early History of Wood County*, 46–51.

78. Buser, "*Great Chiefs*, 12.

79. Finley, *Life*, 546–48.

80. Evers, *Wood County*, 46.

81. "Charles Elliott: Methodist Preacher, Editor and President of Iowa Wesleyan University."

82. Wheeler, "Letter to Brother Elliott."

83. Kappler, *Affairs*, Vol. II, 460.

84. Wheeler, "Letter."

85. Dickens, *American Notes for General Circulation,* Vol. II, 168.

86. Dickens, *American Notes,* Vol. II, 168–69.

87. Kappler, *Affairs,* Vol. II, 536.

88. Klopfenstein, "The Removal of the Wyandots From Ohio," 131.

89. Hancks, *Emigrant Tribes,* 154.

90. Greyeyes, *"Farewell to a Beloved Land."*

91. Hancks, *Emigrant Tribes,* 171.

92. Klopfenstein, "Removal," 133.

93. Klopfenstein, "Removal," 134.

94. Wheeler, "Journal Accounts: 10–20 July 1843."

95. Wheeler, "Personal Letter: 28 July 1843."

96. Klopfenstein, "Removal," 133.

97. Klopfenstein, "Removal," 134.

98. Klopfenstein, "Removal," 134.

99. Love, "The Old Mission," 129.

Notes to Chapter 5

1. Walker, "Personal Letter to John Carey 22 Oct. 1843."

2. Winter, *Northwest Ohio,* 175.

3. Connelley, *Provisional Government,* 23–24.

4. L. Armstrong, *"Armstrong's Account of Travel from St. Louis to Kansas."*

5. westbottoms.com/history.htm.

6. Klopfenstein, *Removal,* 135.

7. Warren, *Anderdon: Some Folks Down the Road,* 350.

8. Swan, *Descendants of Wyandot Chief Live Here.*

9. Swan, *Warrow Family Kin of Wyandot Chiefs.*

10. Unified Government, "Full Commission Meeting Agenda," 170.

11. Speise, "Huron Indian Cemetery," 1.

12. Connelley, *Provisional Government,* 280.

13. Clarke, *Traditional History of the Wyandotts,* 132.

14. Andreas, *History of the State of Kansas,* 292.

15. Andreas, *History,* 292.

16. Unified Government, "Meeting Agenda," 353.

17. Connelley, *Provisional Government,* 303.

18. P. Morgan, ed., *History of Wyandotte County Kansas and Its People,* Vol. I, 129–30.

19. Connelley, *Provisional Government,* 58.

20. Connelley, *Provisional Government,* 60.

21. Manuscript, "Wyandotte Nation to the American Congress."

22. Root, "Joseph Root to William Hutchinson," 4.

23. Connelley, *Provisional Government,* 316.

24. Connelley, *Provisional Government*, 341.

25. Connelley, *Provisional Government*, 68.

26. Phillips, *Conquest*, 15.

27. Morgan, *History,* Vol. I, 130.

28. Connelley, *Provisional Government*, 31.

29. Connelley, *Provisional Government*, 290.

30. Connelley, *Provisional Government*, 275.

31. Connelley, *Provisional Government*, 112.

32. Connelley, *Provisional Government*, 363.

33. Connelley, *Provisional Government*, 345.

34. Connelley, *Provisional Government*, 105.

35. Connelley, *Provisional Government*, 27.

36. Connelley, *Provisional Government*, 384.

37. Hancks, *Emigrant Tribes*, 217.

38. Gladstone, *The Englishman In Kansas*, 29.

39. Crouch, "A 'Fiend in Human Shape,'" 149.

40. Connelley, *Quantrill and the Border Wars*, 198.

41. Connelley, *Quantrill and the Border Wars*, 198.

42. Burns, "An Interview With Mr. William Long," 1.

43. Crouch, "'Fiend,'" 153.

44. Burns, "Interview with J. S. Dawson."

45. Phillips, *Conquest*, 16.

46. Phillips, *Conquest*, 12.

47. Phillips, *Conquest*, 11.

48. Abel, *Slaveholding Indians,* Vol. II, 206.

49. Abel, *Slaveholding Indians,* Vol. II, 206.

50. Abel, *Slaveholding Indians,* Vol. II, 206.

51. Blair, *Indian Tribes,* Vol. I, 189.

52. Burns, "Interview with Percy Ladd Walker, Wyandotte," 9.

53. Burns, "Percy Ladd Walker," 10.

54. Andreas, *History*, 184.

55. Bremer, "*A Species of Town-Building* Madness," 160.

56. Connelley, *Provisional Government*, 114.

57. "Anderdon Reserve—Application by Mrs. Nancy Guthrie . . ." collectionscanada. gc.ca.

58. Bremer, "Madness," 163.

59. Connelley, *Provisional Government*, 104.

60. Kappler, *Affairs,* Vol. II, 536.

61. Socolofsky, *Floats*, 245.

62. Socolofsky, *Floats*, 246.

63. Kappler, *Affairs,* Vol. II, 681.

64. Socolofsky, *Floats*, 286.

65. *Wyandott Indian Council Records*, 218.

66. Abel, *Slaveholding Indians,* Vol. III, 182.

67. Abel, *Slaveholding Indians,* Vol. III, 191.

68. Abel, *Slaveholding Indians,* Vol. III, 189.

69. Hancks, *Emigrant Tribes,* 225.

70. Hancks, *Emigrant Tribes,* 403.

71. "Anderdon Reserve—Application by Mrs. Nancy Guthrie," collectionscanada.gc.ca.

72. Belt, *"Wyandots Seek Tribal Status."*

Notes to Chapter 6

1. wyandotte-nation.org/community/tribal-profiles/bearskin/chiefs-prayer.

2. Hancks, *Emigrant Tribes,* 391.

3. Hancks, *Emigrant Tribes,* 391.

4. Hancks, *Emigrant Tribes,* 453–55.

5. Barbeau, *Field-Notes B-G-88.5,* 8.

6. Barbeau, *B-G-88.5,* 3.

7. Beauchamp, *Indian Corn Stories and Customs,* 198.

8. Burns, "Interview with J. S. Dawson," 9–10.

9. Burns, "J. S. Dawson," 10.

10. "Wyandotte Reservation," *Report On Indians Taxed and Not Taxed,* 248–49.

11. history.com/this-day-in-history/the-oklahoma-land-rush-begins.

12. U.S. Census Office Map of Indian Territory and Oklahoma, 1890.

13. Everett, "Organic Act (1890)."

14. rootsweb.ancestry.com/~okottawa/quapawlands.txt.

15. Gideon, *Indian Territory,* 87.

16. Jackson, "Schools Among The Minor Tribes In Indian Territory," 66.

17. Jackson, "Schools Among The Minor Tribes In Indian Territory," 66.

18. Jackson, "Schools Among The Minor Tribes In Indian Territory," 66.

19. Gibson, "Wyandotte Mission: The Early Years," 146.

20. Gibson, "Wyandotte Mission: The Early Years," 141.

21. Gibson, "Wyandotte Mission: The Early Years," 142.

22. Jackson, "Schools Among The Minor Tribes In Indian Territory," 60.

23. Fisher, "Expenditures For Indian School Buildings, Etc., 1911," 10.

24. Gibson, "Wyandotte Mission: The Early Years," 141.

25. Gibson, "Wyandotte Mission: The Early Years," 141.

26. Nieberding "The Moccasin Telegraph," 11.

27. Jackson, "Schools Among the Minor Tribes In Indian Territory," 62–63.

28. Gibson, "Wyandotte Mission: The Early Years," 147.

29. Gibson, "Wyandotte Mission: The Early Years," 148.

30. Burns, "J. S. Dawson," 4–5.

31. Burns, "John Bland," 4.

32. P. Morgan, *History,* Vol. I, 83.

33. Hancks, *Emigrant Tribes,* 422.

34. Connelley, *A Standard History of Kansas and Kansans,* Vol. 5, 2,731.

35. Hancks, *Emigrant Tribes,* 421.

36. Hancks, *Emigrant Tribes,* 421.

37. Kappler, *Indian Affairs: Laws and Treaties,* Vol. III, Laws, 554.

38. Dayton, "'Trespassers, Beware,'" 16.

39. Dayton, "'Beware,'" 17.

40. Dayton, "'Beware,'" 20.

41. Dayton, "'Beware,'" 21–22.

42. Dayton, "'Beware,'" 1–2.

43. Dayton, "'Beware,'" 25–26.

44. "Ancestral Cemetery," 34.

45. "Ancestral Cemetery," 33.

46. Hancks, *Emigrant Tribes,* 423.

47. Hancks, *Emigrant Tribes,* 423.

48. Hancks, *Emigrant Tribes,* 424.

49. Public Law 887 | Chapter 843, August 1, 1956 | [S. 3970] 70 Stat. 893.

50. R. Armstrong, *The Descendants of Robert Armstrong,* 25.

51. Hancks, *Emigrant Tribes,* 425.

52. Hancks, *Emigrant Tribes,* 426.

53. Carras, "Wyandotte Wyandot Peace Pact Signed."

54. Claiborne, "Kansas City and Tribe Locked in Casino Duel."

55. Claiborne, "Casino Duel."

56. Claiborne, "Casino Duel."

57. Hancks, *Emigrant Tribes,* 427.

58. Babson, "Distasteful Dealings with Wyandotte Tribe."

59. "Congress Kills Wyandotte Casino Project."

60. Associated Press, "KCK Land."

61. Associated Press, "Tribe Ends K.C. Land Ownership Lawsuit."

62. *Wyandotte Nation* v. *Sebelius,* Nos. 04-3431, 04-3432.

63. Hanna, "Tribe Seeks Assets Seized in KCK Casino Raid."

64. *Sebelius,* 04-3431, 04-3432.

65. *Sebelius,* 04-3431, 04-3432.

66. Hogan, "Re: Wyandotte Nation Gaming Ordinance."

67. Unified Government, "Meeting Agenda," 4.

68. The Associated Press, "Wyandotte Plan to Open Casino in Kansas City, Kan., This January."

69. The Associated Press, "State Case."

70. wyandotte-nation.org/tribal-news/7th-street-casino.

71. Nowry, *Man of Mana: Marius Barbeau,* 103.

72. Nowry, *Marius Barbeau,* 104.

73. Nowry, *Marius Barbeau,* 107.

74. Nowry, *Marius Barbeau,* 110.

75. Nowry, *Marius Barbeau,* 113.

76. Nowry, *Marius Barbeau,* 113.

77. Nowry, *Marius Barbeau,* 114.

78. Nowry, *Marius Barbeau,* 114.

79. Richard, "Draft Agreement Concerning Use of CMC Material."

80. tm112.community.uaf.edu/unit-2/termination-era-1950s-public-law-280.

81. tm112.community.uaf.edu/unit-2/termination-era-1950s-public-law-280.

82. tm112.community.uaf.edu/unit-2/termination-era-1950s-public-law-280.

83. Barbeau, *Huron,* 36

84. C. Sioui, "Politics & Religion."

85. Bond, "Georges Sioui on Spiritual Reawakenings."

BIBLIOGRAPHY

Abel, Annie Helouise. *The Slaveholding Indians. The American Indian as Participants in the Civil War,* Vol. II. Cleveland: The Arthur H. Clark Co., 1919. *gutenberg.org.* 27 Sept. 2012.

―――. *The Slaveholding Indians. The American Indian Under Reconstruction,* Vol. III. Cleveland: The Arthur H. Clark Co., 1915. *archive.org.* May 28 2013.

Abing, Kevin. "A Holy Battleground: Methodist, Baptist, & Quaker Missionaries among Shawnee Indians, 1830–1844." *Kansas History,* Vol. 21. No. 2 (Summer 1998): 118–37. *kshs.org.* 3 Apr. 2015.

Allen, S. M. Personal Handwritten Letter to J. B. Finley.

"An Ancestral Cemetery." *The Twenty-Ninth Annual Report of the Executive Committee of the Indian Rights Association, For The Year Ending December 14, 1911.* Philadelphia: Office of the Indian Rights Association, 1912. 32–34. *books.google.com.* 14 Aug 2015.

"Anderdon Reserve—Application by Mrs. Nancy Guthrie to be Restored to Membership in the Wyandot Band, 1875." *Library and Archives of Canada,* Inventory No. 10-5, Microfilm Reel C-12777, File 5729. *collectionscanada.gc.ca.* 27 June 2013.

Andreas, Alfred Thayer. *History of the State of Kansas.* Chicago: A. T. Andreas, 1883. *columbia.edu.* 23 July 2015.

Armstrong, John McIntire. "Letter to Lucy Biglow: 29 Aug. 1837." *wyandot.org.* 8 Aug. 2010.

Armstrong, Lucy B. "Lucy B. Armstrong's Account of Travel from St. Louis to Kansas on the Missouri Riverboat Nodaway." *wyandot.org.* 8 Aug. 2010.

Armstrong, Ralph W. *The Descendants of Robert Armstrong, Indian Captive.* Wilmington: Self-Published, 1980.

Arrowsmith, Aaron. *Ohio.* Philadelphia: John Conrad & Co., 1804. *davidrumsey.com.* 5 Feb. 2013. Map.

The Associated Press. "Judge Drops State Case against KCK Casino." *ljworld.com/ news/2008/sep/14/judge_drops_state_case_against_ kck_casino/*. 14 Sept. 2008. 22 Aug. 2015.

The Associated Press. "Tribe Ends K.C. Land Ownership Lawsuit." *ljworld.com/ news/2004/aug/18/tribe_ends_kc/* 18 Aug. 2004. 21 Aug. 2015.

The Associated Press. "Tribe Files Lawsuit for KCK Land." *ljworld.com/news/2002/ jul/20/tribe_files_lawsuit/*. 20 July 2002. 21 Aug. 2015.

The Associated Press. "Wyandotte Plan to Open Casino in Kansas City, Kan., This January." *indiancountrynews.com/index.php/news/26-mainstream-politics/2255- wyandotte-plan-to-open-casino-in-kansas-city-kan-this-january.* 22 Aug. 2015.

Babson, Rick. "Distasteful Dealings with Wyandotte Tribe." *citizensalliance.org.* 13 Nov. 2002. 22 Aug. 2015.

Baldwin, Charles Candee (C. C.). "Early Indian Migrations In Ohio." *Western Reserve Historical Society,* Vol. II. Tracts 37–72 (1888). 81–95. *books.google.com.* 10 Oct. 2012.

Bangs, Nathan. *An Authentic History of the Missions.* New York: The Methodist Episcopal Church, 1832. *books.google.com.* 4 Aug. 2104.

Barbeau, Charles Marius. *Field-Notes B-G-4.12 (Personal Names).* Canadian Museum of Civilization. Barbeau Collection. 1911–12.

———. *Field-Notes B-G-88.5.* Canadian Museum of Civilization. Barbeau Collection. 1911–12.

———. *Field-Notes B-G-96.2.* Canadian Museum of Civilization. Barbeau Collection. 1911–12.

———. *Field-Notes B-G-183.4.* Canadian Museum of Civilization. Barbeau Collection. 1911–12.

———. "How the Huron-Wyandot Language Was Saved from Oblivion." *Proceedings of the American Philosophical Society,* Vol. 93. No. 3 (1949): 226–32. *jstor.org.* 2 May 2010.

———. *Huron and Wyandot Mythology.* Ottawa: GPB, 1915. *archive.org.* 25 Nov. 2009.

———. *Huron-Wyandot Dictionary.* Canadian Museum of Civilization. Barbeau Collection. 1911–12.

———. *Huron-Wyandot Traditional Narratives, In Translations and Native Texts.* Ottawa: GPB, 1960.

———. "Iroquoian Clans and Phratries." *American Anthropologist, New Series,* Vol. 19. No. 3 (1917): 392–402. *jstor.org.* 2 May 2010.

———. "On Huron Work, 1911." *Summary Report of the Geological Survey Branch of the Department of Mines For The Calendar Year 1911.* Ottawa: C. H. Parolee, 1912. 381–86. *books.google.com.* 11 Sept. 2016.

———. "On Iroquoian Field-Work, 1912." *Summary Report of the Geological Survey Branch of the Department of Mines For The Calendar Year 1912.* Ottawa: C. H. Parolee, 1914. 454–60. *archive.org.* 11 Sept. 2016.

———. "Supernatural Beings of the Huron and Wyandot." *American Anthropologist, New Series,* Vol. 16. No. 2 (1914): 288–313. *jstor.org.* 2 May 2010.

———. "Wyandot Tales, Including Foreign Elements." *The Journal of American Folklore,* Vol. 28. No. 107 (1915): 83–95. *jstor.org.* 2 May 2010.

Barr, Daniel P. "'A Road For Warriors'; The Western Delawares and the Seven Years' War." *Pennsylvania History,* Vol. 73. No. 1 (2006): 1–36. *journals.psu.edu.* 15 Oct. 2015.

Baughman, Abraham J., ed. *Past and Present of Wyandot County, Ohio. A Record of Settlement, Organization, Progress and Achievement.* Chicago: The S. J. Clarke Publishing Co., 1913. *books.google.com.* 24 May 2013.

Baxter, James P. *The British Invasion From the North: The Campaigns of Generals Carleton and Burgoyne from Canada, 1776–1777, with the Journal of Lieut. William Digby, of the 53d, or Shropshire Regiment of Foot.* Albany: Joel Munsell's Sons, 1887. *archive.org.* 12 May 2016.

Beauchamp, William Martin. "Indian Corn Stories and Customs." *The Journal of American Folklore,* Vol. 11. No. 42 (1898): 195–202.

Belt, Mike. "Wyandots Seek Tribal Status." *Kansas City Kansan.* 16 Apr. 1995. *wyandot. org.* 17 Oct. 2012.

Benton, Elbert J., ed. "Northern Ohio During the War of 1812." *Western Reserve Historical Society,* Tract No. 92. 27–107. Cleveland: Leader Printing Co., 1913. *books. google.com.* 26 Oct. 2015.

Bieloh, Christina. "Bad Water and Epidemics: The Wages of Neglect at the Seneca Indian School." *The Chronicles of Oklahoma,* Vol. 87. No. 1 (2009): 56–75.

Blair, Emma Helen, ed. *The Indian Tribes of the Upper Mississippi Valley and Region of the Great Lakes as described by Nicholas Perrot, French commandant in the Northwest; Bacqueville de la Potherie, French royal commissioner to Canada; Morrell Marston, American army officer; and Thomas Forsyth, United States agent at Fort Armstrong,* Vol. I. Cleveland: The Arthur H. Clark Co., 1911. *books.google.com.* 7 Mar. 2013.

Bond, Araina. "Georges Sioui on Spiritual Reawakenings." *Research Matters.* 24 Oct. 2014. *yourontarioresearch.ca/2014/10/spiritual-reawakening.* 11 Feb. 2015.

Bourne, A., B. Hough and J. Melish. *State of Ohio.* Chillicothe: B. Hough & A. Bourne, and J. Melish, 1815. *davidrumsey.com.* 17 Jan. 2013. Map.

Bowes, John P. *Land Too Good for Indians: Northern Indian Removal.* Norman: University of Oklahoma Press, 2016.

Brackenridge, Henry, ed. *Narratives of a Late Expedition Against the Indians; With An Account of the Barbarous Execution of Col. Crawford; and the Wonderful Escape of*

Dr. Knight and John Slover From Captivity, In 1782. Philadelphia: Francis Bailey, 1782. *archive.org.* 23 June 2012.

Brainerd, Ezra. "Jeremiah Hubbard, Hoosier Schoolmaster and Friends Missionary among the Indians." *Chronicles of Oklahoma,* Vol. 29. No. 1 (1951): 23–31. *digital. library.okstate.edu.* 4 May 2010.

Brandão, J. A. and William A Starna. "The Treaties of 1701: A Triumph of Iroquois Diplomacy." *Ethnohistory,* Vol. 43, No. 2 (Spring 1996): 209–44. *jstor.org.* 28 Feb. 2014.

Bremer, Jeff R. "A Species of Town-Building Madness." *Kansas History: A Journal of the Central Plains,* Vol. 26 (2003): 156–71. 19 Apr. 2013.

Bricker, David D. "George Foulkes: The Story of an Unsung Legend." *earlyamerica. com.* 8 Apr. 2015.

Brooke, John. "Anthony Wayne: His Campaign Against the Indians of the Northwest." *The Pennsylvania Magazine of History and Biography,* Vol. 19. No. 3 (1895): 387–96. *jstor.org.* 28 Feb. 2014.

Brown, Parker B. "The Battle of Sandusky, June 4–6, 1782." *Western Pennsylvania Historical Magazine,* Vol. 65 (Apr. 1982): 115–51. *journals.psu.edu.* 7 Apr. 2015.

———. "The Fate of Crawford Volunteers Captured by Indians Following the Battle of Sandusky in 1782." *Western Pennsylvania Historical Magazine,* Vol. 65 (Oct. 1982): 323–40. *journals.psu.edu.* 7 Apr. 2015.

Bruce, G. W., "The Petuns." *Ontario Historical Society. Papers and Records,* Vol. VIII (1907): 34–39. *books.google.com.* 22 Mar. 2013.

Burns, Nannie Lee. "Interview with John Bland—7176." *University of Oklahoma Libraries Western History Collections,* Vol. 8. 1937. *digital.libraries.ou.edu.* 2 Nov. 2011.

———. "Interview with J. S. Dawson—6539." *University of Oklahoma Libraries Western History Collections,* Vol. 23. 1937. *digital.libraries.ou.edu.* 2 Nov. 2011.

———. "Interview with Mark C. Crotzer—12300." *University of Oklahoma Libraries Western History Collections,* Vol. 22. 1937. *digital.libraries.ou.edu.* 2 Nov. 2011.

———. "Interview with Mr. William Long—7549." *University of Oklahoma Libraries Western History Collections,* Vol. 55. 1937. *digital.libraries.ou.edu.* 2 Nov. 2011.

———. "Interview with Percy Ladd Walker—5171." *University of Oklahoma Libraries Western History Collections,* Vol. 94. 1937. *digital.libraries.ou.edu.* 2 Nov. 2011.

Burton, Clarence M., ed. *The City of Detroit, Michigan 1701–1922,* Vol. I. Detroit: Chicago: S. J. Clarke Publishing, 1922. *archive.org.* 31 Oct. 2015.

———. *The City of Detroit, Michigan 1701–1922,* Vol. II. Detroit: Chicago: The S. J. Clarke Publishing, Co., 1922. *books.google.com.* 20 Oct. 2015.

Buser, Charles Aubrey. *Our Great Chiefs.* Wyandotte Nation Cultural Archives.

————. *Some of the Names Given to the Wyandot Tribe of Indians.* Wyandotte Nation Cultural Archives.

————. *Tarhe: Grand Sachem.* Wyandotte Nation Cultural Archives.

————. Unpublished manuscript one. "We Do Not Know." *library.osu.edu.*

————. Unpublished manuscript two. "Wendat." *library.osu.edu.*

Butterfield, Consul Willshire (C. W.). *An Historical Account of the Expedition Against Sandusky Under Col. William Crawford In 1782.* Cincinnati: Robert Clarke & Co., 1873. *archive.org.* 28 June 2012.

Carras, John. "Wyandotte Wyandot Peace Pact Signed." *Kansas City Kansan.* 15 July 1998. *wyandot.org/agreement.htm.* 21 Aug. 2015.

Carton, Augustus C. "Historical Work after The War." *Michigan History Magazine,* Vol. III. Lansing: Michigan Historical Commission, 1919. *books.google.com.* 31 July 2017.

Cass, Lewis. *Remarks on the Policy and Practice of the United States and Great Britain in Their Treatment of the Indians.* Boston: Frederick T. Gray, 1827. *archive.org.* 31 Oct. 2015.

Chapin, Walter. *The Missionary Gazetteer: Comprising a View of the Inhabitants, and a Geographical Description of the Countries and Places, Where protestant Missionaries Have labored; Alphabetically Arranged, and so Constructed as to Give a Particular and General History of Missions Throughout the World.* Woodstock: David Watson, 1825. *books.google.com.* 25 Oct. 2015.

Chapman, Charles H. *The Story of Oregon and its People.* Chicago: O. P. Barnes, 1909. *books.google.com.* 22 Mar. 2015.

"Charles Elliott: Methodist Preacher, Editor and President of Iowa Wesleyan University." *homepages.rootsweb.ancestry.com/~eelliott/Gannon/celliott-minister.html.* 17 Feb. 2013.

Charlevoix, Pierre François Xavier de. *History and General Description of New France,* Vol. I. Ed. John Gilmary Shea. New York: John Gilmary Shea, 1866. *archive.org.* 9 Oct. 2013.

————. *History and General Description of New France,* Vol. II. Ed. John Gilmary Shea. New York: John Gilmary Shea, 1866. *archive.org.* 9 Oct. 2013.

Christie, Robert. *The Military and Naval Operations in the Canadas, During the Late War With the United States.* Quebec: n.p., 1818. *books.google.com.* 26 Oct. 2015.

Claiborne, William. "Kansas City and Tribe Locked in Casino Duel." *washingtonpost. com.* 24 June 2001. 21 Aug. 2015.

Clarke, Peter Dooyentate. *Origin and Traditional History of the Wyandotts, and Sketches of Other Indian Tribes of North America. True Traditional Stories of Tecumseh and His League in the Years 1811 and 1812.* Toronto: Hunter, Rose & Co., 1870. *archive. org.* 13 Sept. 2010.

Clifton, James A. *Hurons of the West: Migrations and Adaptions of the Ontario Iroquoians, 1650–1704.* Ottawa: Canadian Ethnology Service, 1977. Draft.

———. "The Re-emergent Wyandot: A Study in Ethnogenesis on the Detroit River Borderland, 1747." *The Western District: Papers from the Western District Conference.* Windsor, ON: University of Windsor, 1983.

Clifton, James A., George L. Cornell, and James M. McClurken. *People of the Three Fires: The Ottawa, Potawatomi and Ojibway of Michigan.* Grand Rapids: The Michigan Indian Press, 1986. *files.eric.ed.gov.* 24 July 2016.

Cohen, Sheldon S. "Major William Sparke along the Monongahela: A New Historical Account of Braddock's Defeat." *Pennsylvania History,* Vol. 62. No. 4 (Oct. 1995): 546–56. *journals.psu.edu.* 11 Oct. 2015.

"Congress Kills Wyandotte Casino Project." *indianz.com.* 21 Aug. 2015.

Conley v. *Ballinger,* 216 U. S. 84 (1910). *supreme.justia.com.* 1 July 2015.

Connelley, William E. *A Standard History of Kansas and Kansans,* Vol. I. Chicago: Lewis Publishing Co., 1918. *archive.org.* 29 Jan. 2010.

———. *A Standard History of Kansas and Kansans,* Vol. V. Chicago: Lewis Publishing Co., 1918. *archive.org.* 10 Sept. 2012.

———. *Indian Myths.* Chicago: Rand McNally & Company, 1928.

———. "Kansas City, Kansas: Its Place In the History of the State." *Collections of the Kansas State Historical Society 1919–1922,* Vol XV. Ed. William E. Connelley. Topeka: Kansas State Printing Plant, 1923. 181–91. *archive.org.* 11 Dec. 2012.

———. "Notes on the Folk-Lore of the Wyandots' Religion. I. Religion." *Journal of American Folk-Lore,* Vol. 12. No. 45 (Apr.–June, 1899): 116–25. *jstor.org.* 2 May 2010.

———, ed. *The Provisional Government of Nebraska Territory and the Journals of William Walker Provisional Governor of Nebraska Territory.* Lincoln: State Journal Co., 1899. *archive.org.* 17 Jan. 2010.

———. *Quantrill and the Border Wars.* Cedar Rapids: The Torch Press, 1910. *books.google.com.* 27 Sept. 2012.

———. "Religious Conceptions of the Modern Hurons." *The Mississippi Valley Historical Review,* Vol. 9. No. 2 (1922): 110–25. *jstor.org.* 2 May 2012.

———. "The Wyandots: The Clan System of the Wyandots." *Archaeological Report 1899.* Toronto: Warwick Bros. & Rutter, 1900. 92–123. *books.google.com.* 10 June 2017.

———. *Wyandot Folk-Lore.* Topeka: Crane & Company, 1899.

———. "Wyandot and Shawnee Indian Lands in Wyandotte County, Kansas." *Collections of the Kansas State Historical Society 1919–1922,* Vol XV. Ed. William E. Connelley. Topeka: Kansas State Printing Plant, 1923. 103–80. *archive.org.* 11 Dec. 2012.

Cox, Michael Leonard. *The Ohio Wyandots: Religion and Society on the Sandusky River, 1795–1843.* Diss. University of California Riverside, 2016.

Cram, George Franklin. *Map of Oklahoma and Indian Territory.* New York: G. F. Cram, 1901. *davidrumsey.com.* 8 Aug. 2015. Map.

Crouch, Barry A. "A 'Fiend in Human Shape'? William Clarke Quantrill and His Biographers." *Kansas History,* Vol. 22 (Summer 1999): 142–56. *kshs.org.* 20 May 2013.

Currey, William L. "The Wyandot Chief, Leather Lips: His Trial and Execution." *Ohio Archaeological and Historical Publications,* Vol. XII. Columbus: Fred J. Herr, 1903. 30–36. *books.google.com.* 30 Sept. 2015.

Dayton, Kim. "'Tresspassers, Beware!'": Lyda Burton Conley and the Battle for Huron Place Cemetery." *Yale Journal of Law and Feminism,* Vol. 8. No. 1 (1996): 1–30. *wmitchell.edu.* 5 July 2015.

"The Declaration of Independence." Washington, DC: U. S. National Archives & Records Administration. *ourdocuments.gov.* 5 Feb. 2013.

Dickens, Charles. *American Notes For General Circulation,* Vol. II. London: Chapman and Hall, 1842. *archive.org.* 19 Feb. 2013.

Divine, Lloyd Eldon Jr. "The Gathering of Traditions Dedication." Sam Noble Museum: University of Oklahoma, Norman. 6 Sept. 2012. Address.

———. "The Giving of Wyandotte Names—Traditional and Contemporary." *Gyah´ - Wish Atak-Ia: The Turtle Speaks,* Vol. 18. No. 4 (2014): 4.

———. "John Bland, Jr." *wyandotte-nation.org.* 11 Sept. 2012.

———. "Re: Your text Part 5." Email from the author to Mr. Charles Garrad. 13 Jan. 2015.

———. "Wyandotte Clans the DNA of Life." *Gyah´ -Wish Atak-Ia: The Turtle Speaks,* Vol. 12. No. 2. (2008): 1, 4–5, 7.

Doddridge, Joseph and Narcissa Doddridge. *Notes on the Settlement and Indian Wars of the Western Parts of Virginia & Pennsylvania From 1763 to 1783, Inclusive, Together With A Review of the State of Society and Manners of the First Settlers of the Western Country.* Ed. John S. Ritenout and William T. Lindsey. Pittsburgh: The New Werner Co., 1912. *archive.org.* 19 July 2012.

Dodge, J. R. *Red Men of the Ohio Valley: An Aboriginal History of the Period Commencing A.D. 1650, and Ending at the Treaty of Greenville, A.D. 1795; Embracing Notable facts and Thrilling Incidents In The Settlement By The Whites of the States of Kentucky, Ohio, Indiana and Illinois.* Springfield: Ruralist Publishing Co., 1860. *archive. org.* 18 July 2012.

Douglass, Ben. *History of Wayne County, Ohio, From the Days of the Pioneers and the First Settlers to the Present Time.* Indianapolis: Robert Douglass, 1878. *archive.org.* 7 Apr. 2015.

Dowd, Gregory Evans. "The French King Wakes Up in Detroit: 'Pontiac's War' in Rumor and History." *Ethnohistory*, Vol. 37. No. 3 (Summer 1990): 254–78. *jstor.org*. 28 Feb. 2014.

Drake, Francis S. *The Indian Tribes of the United States: Their History, Antiquities, Customs, Religion, Arts, Language, Traditions, Oral Legends, and Myths,* Vol. I. Philadelphia: J. B. Lippincott & Co., 1884. *archive.org*. 2 Feb. 2011.

Drake, Samuel Gardner. *The Book of Indians; or, Biography and History of the Indians of North America, From Its First Discovery to the Year 1841.* Boston: Benjamin B. Mussey, 1845. *books.google.com*. 31 Oct. 2015.

Draper, Lyman Copeland, ed. *Report and Collections of the State Historical Society of Wisconsin, for the Years 1873, 1874, 1875 and 1876,* Vol. VII. Madison: E. B. Bolens, 1876. *wisconsinhistory.org*. 18 Oct. 2015.

Dubuisson, Jacques-Charles Renaud. *Official Report Made by the Commanding Officer, Mr. Dubuisson, Governor General of Canada, of the War Which Took Place At Detroit, In 1712, Between the French and Their Allies, and the Ottagamie and Mascoutins Indians.* Detroit: Harsha & Wilcox, 1845. *books.google.com*. 24 Sept. 2015.

Eggleston, Edward and Lillie Eggleston Seelye. *Brant and Red Jacket. Including An Account of the Early Wars of the Six Nations, and the Border Warfare of the Revolution.* New York: Dodd, Mead & Company, 1879. *books.google.com*. 22 Oct. 2015.

Eid, Leroy V. "'A Kind of Running Fight': Indian Battlefield Tactics in the Late Eighteenth Century." *The Western Pennsylvania Historical Magazine*, Vol. 71. No. 2 (Apr. 1988): 147–71. *journals.psu.edu*. 1 Nov. 2017.

———. "The Ojibwa-Iroquois War: The War the Five Nations Did Not Win." *Ethnohistory*, Vol. 26. No. 4 (Autumn 1979): 297–324. *jstor.org*. 28 Feb. 2014.

Elliott, Charles. *Indian Missionary Reminiscences, Principally of the Wyandot Nation.* New York: T. Mason & G. Lane, 1837. *archive.org*. 17 June 2012.

———. "Wyandot Mission." *The Methodist Magazine, Designed as a Compend of Useful Knowledge, and of Religious and Missionary Intelligence, For the Year of Our Lord 1823,* Vol. VI. New York: Methodist Episcopal Church, 1823. 36–37. *books.google. com*. 2 May 2017.

Elliott, Emory B. "Hugh Henry Brackenridge." *princeton.edu*. Princeton: Princeton University Press, 1978. 13 Feb. 2013.

English, Janith (Jan) K. "Wendat Confederacy." *wyandot.org*.

Everett, Dianna. "Organic Act (1890)." *The Encyclopedia of Oklahoma History and Culture*. *okhistory.org*. 5 Aug 2015.

Everett, Edward G. "Pennsylvania's Indian Diplomacy 1747–1753." *The Western Pennsylvania Historical Magazine*, Vol. 44. No. 3 (Sept. 1961): 241–56. *journals.psu.edu*. 25 Feb. 2015.

Evers, Charles W. *Many Incidents and Reminiscences of the Early History of Wood County, Together With Some of the Historic Events of the Maumee Valley Contained In This Pioneer Scrap-Book.* Bowling Green, OH: The Democrat, 1910. *archive.org.* 11 Nov. 2009.

Farmer, Silas. *The History of Detroit and Michigan or The Metropolis Illustrated.* Detroit: Silas Farmer & Co., 1884. *books.google.com.* 21 Dec. 2014.

Feng, Patrick. "The Battle of the Wabash: The Forgotten Disaster of the Indian Wars." *armyhistory.org.* 15 Dec. 2015.

Fenton, William N. "Masked Medicine Societies of the Iroquois." *Annual Report of the Board of Regents of the Smithsonian Institution 1940.* Washington: GOP, 1941. 397–429. *archive.org.* 6 July 2015.

Finley, James Bradley. "Account of the Work of God Among the Wyandott Indians at Upper Sandusky." *The Methodist Magazine, For the Year of Our Lord 1820,* Vol. III. New York: Methodist Episcopal Church, 1820. 431–37. *books.google.com.* 2 May 2017.

———. *Autobiography of Rev. James B. Finley; Or, Pioneer Life In The West.* Ed. W. P. Strickland. Cincinnati: R. P. Thompson, 1854. *archive.com.* 17 Jan. 2010.

———. *History of the Wyandott Mission, At Upper Sandusky, Ohio, Under the Direction of the Methodist Episcopal Church.* Cincinnati: R. P. Thompson, 1840.

———. *Life Among the Indians; Or, Personal Reminiscences and Historical Incidents Illustrative of Indian Life and Character.* Ed. D. W. Clark. Cincinnati: R. P. Thompson, 1860. *archive.com.* 17 Jan. 2010.

———. "Mission Among the Wyandots." *The Methodist Magazine, For the Year of Our Lord 1822,* Vol. V. New York: Methodist Episcopal Church, 1822. 188–93. *books. google.com.* 2 May 2017.

———. "Wyandot Mission." *The Methodist Magazine, Designed as a Compend of Useful Knowledge, and of Religious and Missionary Intelligence, For the Year of Our Lord 1823,* Vol. VI. New York: Methodist Episcopal Church, 1823. 152–54. *books.google. com.* 2 May 2017.

———. "Wyandot Mission and School." *The Methodist Magazine, Designed as a Compend of Useful Knowledge, and of Religious and Missionary Intelligence, For the Year of Our Lord 1823,* Vol. VI. New York: Methodist Episcopal Church, 1823. 115–17. *books.google.com.* 2 May 2017.

——— and Joshua Soule. "Progress of Religion Among the Wyandott Indians at Upper Sandusky." *The Methodist Magazine, For the Year of Our Lord 1822.* Vol. V. New York: Methodist Episcopal Church, 1822. 29–33. *books.google.com.* 2 May 2017.

Fisher, Walter L. "Expenditures For Indian School Buildings, Etc., 1911." *House Documents,* Vol. 142. Washington: GPO, 1912. *books.google.com.* 1 Aug. 2015.

Frohman, Charles E. "Searching for the Forts and Indian Villages of Sandusky Bay." *The Hayes Historical Journal,* Vol. 1. No. 1 (Spring 1976). *rbhayes.org.* 4 Nov. 2015.

Frost, John. *Border Wars of the West: Comprising the Frontier Wars of Pennsylvania, Virginia, Kentucky, Ohio, Indiana, Illinois, Tennessee, and Wisconsin; and Embracing Individual Adventures Among the Indians.* Auburn: Miller, Orton & Mulligam, 1856. *archive.org.* 4 Oct. 2015.

Garrad, Charles. *Commemorating the 350th Anniversary of the Dispersal of the Wyandots from Ontario, and Celebrating Their Return.* North York, ON: The Petun Research Institute, 2003.

———. "Emailing_ Divine2015." Email to the author. 24 Feb. 2015.

———. "The Planter-Fleming BdHb-2 Site: A Review." *Arch Notes.* No. 89-3 (1989): 7–25. *ontarioarchaeology.on.ca.* 8 Feb. 2015.

———. "Your text Part 4." Email message to the author. 12 Jan. 2015.

Garrad, Charles. "Petun to Wyandot: The Ontario Petun from ca. 1580 A.D." Ed. Michael W. Kirby. North York, ON: The Petun Research Institute, 2011. Prepublication version in PDF.

———. *Petun to Wyandot: The Ontario Petun from the Sixteenth Century.* Ed. Jean-Luc Pilon and William Fox. Ottawa: Canadian Museum of History and University of Ottawa Press, 2014.

——— and Conrad E. Heidenreich. "Khionontateronon (Petun)." *Handbook of North American Indians,* Vol. 15 Northeast. Ed. Bruce G. Trigger. Washington: GPO, 1978. 394–97.

——— and John Steckley. *Craigleith and the Birth of the Wyandot Tribe.* North York, ON: The Petun Research Institute, 1998.

———, Thomas S. Abler, and Larry K. Hancks. "On the Survival of the Neutrals." *Ontario Archaeological Society Arch Notes.* Mar.–Apr. 2003: 12–21.

Gibson, Arrell M. "Wyandotte Mission: The Early Years, 1871–1900." *Chronicles of Oklahoma,* Vol. 36. No. 2 (1958): 137–54. *digital.library. okstate.edu.* 4 May 2010.

Gideon, D. C. *Indian Territory: Descriptive Biographical and Genealogical Including the Landed Estates, County Seats, Etc., Etc. With A General History of the Territory.* New York: The Lewis Publishing Company, 1901. *archive.org.* 5 Aug. 2015.

Gilruth, James. "Memoir of Between-The-Logs." *The Methodist Magazine, Designed as a Compend of Useful Knowledge, and of Religious and Missionary Intelligence, For the Year of Our Lord 1827,* Vol. X. New York: Methodist Episcopal Church, 1826. 382–85. *books.google.com.* 2 May 2017.

———. "Wyandot Mission." *The Methodist Magazine, Designed as a Compend of Useful Knowledge, and of Religious and Missionary Intelligence, For the Year of Our Lord 1827,* Vol. X. New York: Methodist Episcopal Church, 1826. 481–82. *books.google. com.* 2 May 2017.

Gladstone, Thomas H. *The Englishman In Kansas or, The Squatter Life and Border Warfare.* New York: Miller & Company, 1857. *archive.org.* 19 May 2013.

Gladwin, Henry. *The Gladwin Manuscripts; With an Introduction and a Sketch of the Conspiracy of Pontiac.* Ed. Charles Moore. Lansing: Robert Smith Printing, 1897. *archive.org.* 21 Oct. 2015.

Gordon, Newton S., ed. *History of Barron County Wisconsin.* Minneapolis: H. C. Cooper, Jr. & Co., 1922. *books.google.com.* 4 Sept. 2015.

Greenleaf, Jeremiah. *United States (Massive Huron and Missouri Territories).* New York: Jeremiah Greenleaf, 1841. *raremaps.com.* 12 Oct. 2017. Map.

Gregg, Josiah. *Indian Territory, Northern Texas and New Mexico.* London: Wiley and Putnam, 1844. *davidrumsey.com.* 11 Oct. 2012. Map.

Greyeyes, Squire. "Farewell to A Beloved Land: The Wyandot's Last Ohio Church Service July 9, 1843." *wyandot.org/farewell.htm.* 8 May 2009.

Guthrie, Abelard. "Abelard Guthrie to Hiram Hill: 11 Nov. 1858." *kansasmemory.org.* 23 Jan. 2013.

———. "Abelard Guthrie to Hiram Hill: 18 Jan. 1859." *kansasmemory.org.* 23 Jan. 2013.

Hakluyt, Richard. *The Principal Navigations, Voyages, Traffiques, and Discoveries of the English Nation,* Vol. XII: America Part I. Ed. Edmund Goldsmid. Edinburgh: E. & G. Goldsmid, 1889. *books.google.com.* 16 Nov. 2017.

———. *The Principal Navigations, Voyages, Traffiques, and Discoveries of the English Nation,* Vol. XIII: America Part II. Ed. Edmund Goldsmid. Edinburgh: E. & G. Goldsmid, 1889. *books.google.com.* 16 Nov. 2017.

Hale, Horatio. "The Fall of Hochelaga: A Study of Popular Tradition." *The Journal of American Folk-Lore,* Vol. 7. No. 24. Jan.–Mar. (1894): 1–14. *jstor.org.* 2 May 2010.

———. "Huron Folk-Lore. I. Cosmogonic Myths. The Good and Evil Minds." *The Journal of American Folk-Lore,* Vol. 1. No. 3. Oct.–Dec. (1888): 177–83. *jstor.org.* 2 May 2010.

———. "Huron Folk-Lore. II. The Story of Tijaiha, the Sorcerer." *The Journal of American Folk-Lore,* Vol. 2, No. 7. Oct.–Dec. (1889): 249–54. *jstor.org.* 2 May 2010.

———. "Huron Folk-Lore. III. The Legend of the Thunderers." *The Journal of American Folk-Lore,* Vol. 4. No. 15. Oct.–Dec. (1891): 289–94. *jstor.org.* 2 May 2010.

Hancks, Larry K. *The Emigrant Tribes: Wyandot, Delaware & Shawnee: A Chronology,* In Three Volumes. Kansas City, KS, 1998. *wyandot.org.* 20 Dec. 2012.

Hanna, John. "Tribe Seeks Assets Seized in KCK Casino Raid." The Associated Press. *cjonline.com.* 19 July 2004. 21 Aug. 2015.

Harrison, Daniel F. "Change amid Continuity, Innovation within Tradition: Wampum Diplomacy at the Treaty of Greenville, 1795." *Ethnohistory,* Vol. 64. No. 2 (Apr. 2017): 192–215. *ethnohistory.dukejournals.org.* 26 July 2017.

Hawkins, Alicia L. "Genoa Frilled Pottery and the Problem of the Identification of the Wenro in Huronia." *Ontario Archaeology,* No. 72 (2001): 15–37. *academia.edu.* 7 Feb. 2015.

———. "Recreating Home? A Consideration of Refugees, Microstyles and Frilled Pottery in Huronia." *Ontario Archaeology,* No. 77/78 (2004): 62–80. *academia.edu.* 7 Feb. 2015.

Heckewelder, John. *History, Manners, and Customs of the Indian Nations Who Once Inhabited Pennsylvania and the Neighbouring States, 1819.* Ed. William C. Reichel. Philadelphia: The Historical Society of Pennsylvania, 1876. *archive.org.* 23 Sept. 2012.

Heidenreich, Conrad. *Huronia: A History and Geography of the Huron Indians, 1600–1650.* Toronto: McClelland and Stewart, 1971.

Hewitt, John N. B. "Huron." *Handbook of American Indians North of Mexico,* Part 1. Ed. Frederick W. Hodge. Washington: GPO, 1912. 584–91. *books.google.com.* 18 Jan. 2015.

———. "Neutrals." *Handbook of American Indians North of Mexico,* Part 2. Ed. Frederick W. Hodge. Washington: GPO, 1910. 60–62. *books.google.com.* 18 Jan. 2015.

———. "Wenrohronon." *Handbook of American Indians North of Mexico,* Part 2. Ed. Frederick W. Hodge. Washington: GPO, 1910. 932–34. *books.google.com.* 18 Jan. 2015.

Hinton, J. "An Accurate Map of Canada, with the Adjacent Countries." *Universal Magazine.* London (1761). *raremaps.com.* 6 Oct. 2012. Map.

The History of Wyandot County Ohio, Containing a History of the County: Its Townships, Towns, Churches, Schools, etc.;. Chicago: Leggett, Conway & Co., 1884. 1–31. *archive.org.* 17 Aug. 2012.

Hodge, Frederick Webb, ed. *Handbook of American Indians North of Mexico,* Part 1. 4th ed. Washington: GPO, 1912. *books.google.com.* 18 Jan. 2015.

———. *Handbook of American Indians North of Mexico,* Part 2. Washington: GPO, 1910. *books.google.com.* 18 Jan. 2015.

Hogan, Phillip N. "Re: Wyandotte Nation Gaming Ordinance." Letter to Chief Leaford Bearskin, 28 Sept. 2007. *nigc.gov/LinkClick.aspx?fileticket=K%2FF6Zcn5sEc%3D&tabid=122.* 22 Aug. 2015.

Hollands, Hulda T. *When Michigan Was New.* Chicago: A. Flanagan Co., 1906. *books.google.com.* 24 Sept. 2015.

Honsberger, Lonnie L. *A Book of Diagrams and Index of Indian Landholders on the Wyandot Reservation Wyandot County, Ohio at the Time of Cession.* Upper Sandusky: Self Published, 1989.

Hubbard, Jeremiah. *Forty Years Among the Indians.* Miami: The Phelps Printers, 1913. *archive.org.* 26 July 2013.

Huber, Donald L. "White, Red, and Black: The Wyandot Mission at Upper Sandusky." *Timeline,* Vol. 13. No. 3 (1996): 2–17.

Hultkrantz, Ake. "North American Indian Religion in the History of Research: A General Survey. Part IV." *The History of Religions* (Nov. 1967): 113–48. *jstor.org.* 5 Feb.
2010.

Hunt, George T. *The Wars of the Iroquois: A Study in Intertribal Trade Relations.* Madison: The University of Wisconsin Press, 1940.

Hunt, Samuel F. "General Anthony Wayne and the Battle of "Fallen Timbers." *Ohio
Archaeological and Historical Quarterly,* Vol. IX. Columbus: Fred J. Herr, 1900. 214–
37. *books.google.com.* 13 Feb. 2015.

*Index to the Senate Executive Documents for the Second Session of the Forty-First Con-
gress of the United States of America. 1869–70. In Three Volumes.* Washington: GPO,
1870. 635–89. *books.google.com.* 7 June 2010.

Jackson, Andrew. "Transcript of President Andrew Jackson's Message to Congress 'On
Indian Removal' (1830)." Washington, DC: U.S. National Archives & Records
Administration. *ourdocuments.gov.* 5 Feb. 2013.

Jackson, Joe C. "Schools among the Minor Tribes in Indian Territory." *Chronicles of
Oklahoma,* Vol. 32. No. 1 (1954): 58–69. *digital.library.okstate.edu.* 4 May 2010.

Jefferson, Thomas. "President Thomas Jefferson to William Henry Harrison." University of Houston: Digital History. *digitalhistory.uh.edu.* 5 Feb. 2013.

Johansen, Bruce E. "Dating the Iroquois Confederacy." *Akwesasne Notes New Series,*
Vols. 1, 3, 4 (Oct./Nov./Dec. 1995): 62–63. *ratical.org/many_worlds/6Nations/
DatingIC.html.* 19 Dec. 2014.

Kappler, Charles J., ed. *Indian Affairs. Laws and Treaties,* Vol. I (Laws). Washington:
GPO, 1904. *books.google.com.* 13 Oct. 2012.

———. *Indian Affairs. Laws and Treaties,* Vol. II (Treaties). Washington: GPO, 1904.
books.google.com. 7 June 2010.

———. *Indian Affairs. Laws and Treaties,* Vol. III (Laws). Washington: GPO, 1913.
books.google.com. 16 Nov. 2009.

Klopfenstein, Carl G. "The Removal of the Wyandots from Ohio." *The Ohio Historical
Quarterly,* Vol. 66 (Apr. 1957): 119–36. *publications.ohiohistory.org.* 19 Feb. 2013.

Kopris, Craig Alexander. *All Wandat Word List,* 2012 Edition. *Word List.* Email to the
author. 1 Aug. 2012.

———. "Further Notes on the Name 'Wyandot.'" *Society for the Study of the Indigenous
Languages of the Americas Newsletter* XXI (4) (2003):10–11.

———. "Hypothetical Connections." Email to the author. 10 Jan. 2015.

———. "Wendat A Universal Social Identity." Email to the author. 16 Dec. 2014.

Labelle, Kathryn Magee. *Dispersed but Not Destroyed: A History of the Seventeenth-Century Wendat People.* Vancouver, BC: UBC Press, 2013.

Lajeunesse, Earnest J., ed. *The Windsor Border Region: Canada's Southernmost Frontier, A Collection of Documents.* Toronto: University of Toronto Press, 1960. *archive.org.* 9 Feb. 2015.

Laut, Agnes Christina. *Cadillac. Knight Errant of the Wilderness, Founder of Detroit, Governor of Louisiana from the Great Lakes to the Gulf.* Indianapolis: Bobbs-Merrill, 1931. *gutenberg.ca.* 6 Sept. 2015.

Lawson, Publius Virgilius. *Bravest of the Brave: Captain Charles de Langlade.* Menasha, WI: George Banta Publishing Company, 1904. *books.google.com.* 19 Oct. 2015.

Leib, John L. "Wyandot Mission—Upper Sandusky." *The Methodist Magazine, Designed as a Compend of Useful Knowledge, and of Religious and Missionary Intelligence, For the Year of Our Lord 1827,* Vol. X. New York: Methodist Episcopal Church, 1826. 414–15. *books.google.com.* 2 May 2017.

Lemon, J. S. "Seneca White Dog Feast." *The Journal of American Folklore,* Vol. 18. No. 71 (1905): 317–19. *jstor.org.* 23 July 2013.

Loskiel, George Henry. *The History of the Moravian Mission Among the Indians In North America From Its Commencement to the Present Time With A Preliminary Account of the Indians.* London: T. Allman, 1838. *archive.org.* 23 Oct. 2015.

Love, N. B. C. (Nathaniel Barrett Coulson). *History of the Central Ohio Conference of the Methodist Episcopal Church.* Cincinnati: Methodist Book Concern, 1913. *archive.org.* 23 Sept. 2016.

———. "An Indian Camp Meeting." *Ohio Archaeological and Historical Publications,* Vol. XV. Columbus: Fred J. Herr, 1906. 163–81. *books.google.com.* 30 Sept. 2015.

———. *John Stewart Missionary to the Wyandot.* New York: The Missionary Society of the Methodist Episcopal Church, 1900. *archive.org.* 25 Sept. 2016.

———. "The Old Mission." *The Ladies' Repository: A Monthly Periodical, Devoted to Literature, Arts, and Religion,* Vol. 3. Issue 2 (Feb. 1869): 127–29. *quod.lib.umich.edu/m/moajrnl/acg2248.2–03.002/139.* 24 Sept. 2016.

———. "The Wyandot's Bride." *Ohio Archaeological and Historical Publications,* Vol. XV. Columbus: Fred J. Herr, 1906. 182–88. *books.google.com.* 30 Sept. 2015.

Lutz, J. J. "The Methodist Missions Among the Indian Tribes In Kansas." *Transactions of the Kansas State Historical Society, 1905–1906,* Vol. IX. Ed. Geo. W. Martin. Topeka: State Printing Office, 1906. 160–230. *archive.org.* 11 Nov. 2014.

Magee, Kathryn. *Dispersed but Not Destroyed: Leadership, Women, and Power within the Wendat Diaspora, 1600–1701.* Columbus: The Ohio State University, 2011. Diss. *etd.ohiolink.edu.* 24 July 2015.

Mansfield, John Brandt, ed. *History of the Great Lakes,* Vol. I. Chicago: J. H. Beers & Co., 1899. *books.google.com.* 5 Sept. 2015.

Marsh, Thelma R. *Moccasin Trails to the Cross. A History of the Mission to the Wyandott Indians on the Sandusky Plains.* Upper Sandusky: John Stewart United Methodist Church, 1974.

Marshall, Humphrey. *The History of Kentucky. Exhibiting An Account of the Modern Discovery; Settlement; Progressive Improvement; Civil and Military Transactions: and the Present State of the Country,* Vol. I. Frankfort: Geo. S. Robinson, 1824. *books.google.com.* 7 Jan. 2013.

———. *The History of Kentucky. Exhibiting An Account of the Modern Discovery; Settlement; Progressive Improvement; Civil and Military Transactions: and the Present State of the Country,* Vol. II. Frankfort: Geo. S. Robinson, 1824. *books.google.com.* 7 Jan. 2013.

Martin, Ronald D. "Confrontation at the Monongahela: Climax of the French Drive into the Upper Ohio Region." *Pennsylvania History,* Vol. 37. No. 2 (Apr. 1970): 133–50. *journals.psu.edu.* 4 Oct. 2015.

Martzofff, Clement L. "Big Bottom and Its History." *Ohio Archaeological and Historical Publications,* Vol. XV. Columbus: Fred J. Herr, 1906. 1–38. *books.google.com.* 30 Sept. 2015.

Mason, Ronald J. "Archaeology and Native North American Oral Traditions." *American Antiquity,* Vol. 65. No. 2 (Apr. 2000): 239–66. *jstor.org.* 5 July 2017.

———. "Rock Island. Historical Indian Archaeology in the Northern Lake Michigan Basin." *MidContinental Journal of Archaeology,* Special Paper No. 6. Kent, OH: Kent State University Press, 1988.

McKendree, William. "Sandusky Mission." *The Methodist Magazine, Designed as a Compend of Useful Knowledge, and of Religious and Missionary Intelligence, For the Year of Our Lord 1827,* Vol. X. New York: Methodist Episcopal Church, 1826. 371–73. *books.google.com.* 2 May 2017.

McQuistion, Juanita. Letter to Charles Garrad. 27 Feb. 1973. TS. Personal library of Charles Garrad. North York, ON.

Meek, Basil. "General Harmar's Expedition." *Ohio Archaeological and Historical Publications,* Vol. XX. Columbus; Fred J. Heer, 1911. 74–108. *books.google.com.* 13 Dec. 2015.

———. "Tarhe—The Crane." *Ohio Archaeological and Historical Publications,* Vol. XX. Columbus: Fred J. Heer, 1911. 64–73. *books.google.com.* 13 Dec. 2015.

Melish, John. *Ohio.* Philadelphia: Palmer, Thomas & George, 1812. *davidrumsey.com.* 3 Oct. 2015. Map.

Mitchell, Joseph. *The Missionary Pioneer or A Brief Memoir of the Life, Labours, and Death of John Stewart, (Man of Colour,) Founder, Under God of the Mission Among the Wyandotts At Upper Sandusky, Ohio.* New York: J. C. Totten, 1827. *archive.org.* 28 Apr. 2010.

Mononcue. "A Sketch of the Life of Ma-nuncu." *The Methodist Magazine, Designed as a Compend of Useful Knowledge, and of Religious and Missionary Intelligence, For the Year of Our Lord 1827,* Vol. X. New York: Methodist Episcopal Church, 1826. 470. *books.google.com.* 2 May 2017.

Morgan, Lewis H. *Ancient Society.* Chicago: Charles H. Kerr & Company, 1910. *archive. org.* 5 Feb. 2010.

Morgan, Perl W., ed. *History of Wyandotte County Kansas and Its People,* Vol. I. Chicago: The Lewis Publishing Co., 1911. *archive.org.* 16 Nov. 2009.

Mulkearn, Lois. "Half-King, Seneca Diplomat of the Ohio Valley." *The Western Pennsylvania Historical Magazine,* Vol. 37. No. 2 (Summer 1954): 65–81. *journals.psu.edu.* 4 Nov. 2015.

Munson, Bishop S. *United States.* Cincinnati: Doolittle, Munson & Sherer, 1845. *davidrumsey.com.* 10 Feb. 2013. Map.

Nieberding, Velma. "The Moccasin Telegraph." *Miami News-Record.* 7 Sept. 1975: 11.

Nowry, Laurence. *Man of Mana: Marius Barbeau.* Toronto: NC Press Ltd., 1995.

Oliphant, J. Orin, ed. "The Report of the Wyandot Exploring Delegation, 1831." *Kansas Historical Quarterly,* Vol. 14. No. 3 (1947): 248–62. *kshs.org.* 27 Sept. 2012.

Otterbein, Keith F. "Huron vs. Iroquois: A Case Study in Inter-Tribal Warfare." *Ethnohistory,* Vol. 26. No. 2. (1979): 141–52. *jstor.org.* 16 Apr. 2010.

Parkman, Francis. *Braddock's Defeat. 1755. The French and English In America.* New York: E. Manynard, 1890. *archive.org.* 25 Aug. 2015.

———. *The Conspiracy of Pontiac and the Indian War After the Conquest of Canada,* 6th ed., Vol. 1. Boston: Little, Brown and Co., 1870. *archive.org.* 8 Oct. 2012.

———. *The Conspiracy of Pontiac and the Indian War After the Conquest of Canada,* 9th ed., Vol. 2. London: Macmillan and Co., 1885. *books.google.com.* 8 Oct. 2012.

———. *Count Frontenac and New France Under Louis XIV.* London: Macmillan and Co., 1885. *books.google.com.* 2 Sept. 2015.

———. *France and England In North America.* Boston: Little, Brown and Company, 1892. *books.google.com.* 2 Aug. 2016.

———. *History of the Conspiracy of Pontiac, and the War of the North American Tribes Against the English Colonies After the Conquest of Canada.* New York: A. L. Burt Company, 1851. *archive.org.* 21 Oct. 2015.

Parmenter, John William. "Pontiac's War: Forging New Links in the Anglo-Iroquois Covenant Chain, 1758–1766." *Ethnohistory,* Vol. 44. No. 4 (Autumn 1997): 617–54. *jstor.org.* 28 Feb. 2014.

Peace, Thomas and Kathryn Magee Labelle, eds. *From Huronia to Wendakes: Adversity, Migration, and Resilience, 1650–1900.* Norman: University of Oklahoma Press, 2016.

Pearson, Bruce L. *The Wyandotte Language: Handbook and Dictionary*. Bloomington: Yorkshire Press, 2007.

Phillips, William. *The Conquest of Kansas by Missouri and Her Allies. A History of the Troubles in Kansas, From the Passage of the Organic Act Until the Close of July 1856*. Boston: Phillips, Sampson and Company, 1856. *books.google.com*. 27 Feb. 2013.

Pitt, William. "Speech on the Proposed Address to the Throne." *Liveblogging the American Revolution: November 18, 1777: The Earl of Chatham*. 18 Nov. 2015. *bradford-delong.com*. 18 May 2016.

Powell, John Wesley. "Wyandotte Government: A Short Study of Tribal Society." *First Annual Report of the Bureau of Ethnology to the Secretary of the Smithsonian Institution 1879–80*. Washington: GPO (1881): 57–69. *gallica.bnf.fr*. 25 Apr. 2010.

Pownall, Thomas et al. *Map of the Middle British Colonies in North America. 1755*. London: John Almon, 1776. *davidrumsey.com*. 11 Oct. 2012. Map.

Pritts, Joseph, ed. *Incidents of Border Life: Illustrative of the Times and Conditions of the First Settlements in Parts of the Middle and Western States, Comprising Narratives of Strange and Thrilling Adventure-Accounts of Battles-Skirmishes and Personal Encounters With the Indians—Descriptions of Their Manners, Customs, Modes of Warfare, Treatment of Prisoners*. Lancaster: C. Hills, 1841. *archive.org*. 25 Aug. 2015.

Redford, A. H. *A History of Methodism in Kentucky*, Vol. I. Nashville: Southern Methodist Publishing House, 1868. *archive.org*. 6 July 2017.

Report of the Commissioner of Indian Affairs to the Secretary of the Interior For The Year 1871. Washington: GPO, 1872. 208. *archive.org*. 7 June 2010.

Richard, Tanya. "Draft Agreement Concerning Use of CMC Material." *WyandotNation(web).doc*. Personal email to the author. 5 Sept. 2006.

Roosevelt, Theodore. *The Winning of the West, Part III: The War in the Northwest*. New York and London: G. P. Putnam's Sons, 1900. *archive.org*. 7 Nov. 2015.

Root, Joseph. "Joseph Root to William Hutchinson—Wyandott City Ks Ty, Tuesday eve Nov 17th 1857 Wm Hutchinson Esq." *kansasmemory.org*. 23 Oct. 2014.

Rowley, A. E. "'Uncle Jim.' The Last of the Wyandots." *The Firelands Pioneer*, New Series, Vol. VIII (Oct. 1895). Norwalk: E. J. Lee & Co., 1895. *archive.org*. 7 July 2017.

Royce, Charles C. "Indian Land Concessions in the United States." *Eighteenth Annual Report of the Bureau of American Ethnology to the Secretary of the Smithsonian Institution 1897–97*, Part 1. Ed. J. W. Powell. Washington: GPO, 1899. *archive.org*. 9 Apr. 2015.

Sayre, Gordon M. *Les Sauvages Américains: Representations of Native Americans in French and English Colonial Literature*. Chapel Hill: University of North Carolina Press, 1997.

Sayer, Robert. *A New Map of North America, with the British, French, Spanish, Dutch & Danish Dominions on That Great Continent; and the West India Islands.* London: Robert Sayer, 1750. *loc.gov.* 16 Oct. 2015. Map.

———— and John Bennett. *The American Military Pocket Atlas (1776).* London: Sayer and Bennett, 1776. *dartmouth.edu.* 17 Oct. 2015.

Schomburg, Arthur A. "Two Negro Missionaries to the American Indians, John Marrant and John Stewart." *The Journal of Negro History,* Vol. 21. No. 4 (1936): 394–405. *jstor.org.* 2 May 2010.

Schoolcraft, Henry R. *Historical and Statistical Information Respecting the History, Condition and Prospects of the Indian Tribes of the United States,* Part I. Philadelphia: Lippincott, Grambo & Co., 1851. *archive.org.* 3 Feb. 2011.

————. *History of the Indian Tribes of the United States: Their Present Condition and Prospects, And A Sketch of Their Ancient Status,* Part VI. Philadelphia: J. B. Lippincott & Co., 1857. *archive.org.* 3 Feb. 2011.

————. *Notes On The Iroquois; or Contributions to American History, Antiquities, and General Ethnology.* Albany: Erastus H. Pease & Co., 1847. *books.google.com.* 6 Nov. 2017.

————. *Oneóta, or Characteristics of the Red Race of America.* New York: Wiley & Putnam, 1847. *archive.org.* 23 Nov. 2014.

Shannon, Timothy J. *Iroquois Diplomacy on the Early American Frontier.* New York: Penguin, 2008. *books.google.com.* 15 Oct. 2015.

Shea, John Gilmary. "An Historical Sketch of the Tionontates or Dinondadies Now Called Wyandots." *The Historical Magazine and Notes and Queries Concerning the Antiquities, History and Biography of America,* Vol. 5. New York: Charles B. Richardson & Co., 1861. 262–69. *books.google.com.* 9 Oct. 2012.

Sioui, Claudine. "Politics & Religion." *Wendat Yahoo Forum* (16 Feb. 2004).

Sioui, Georges E. *Huron Wendat, The Heritage of the Circle.* East Lansing: Michigan State University Press, 1999. *books.google.com.* 5 Aug. 2013.

Sioui, Linda. "Huron to Huron-Wendat." Personal email to the author. 2 Feb. 2014.

————. *The Reaffirmation of Wendat/Wyandotte Identity in a Time of Globalization.* Wendake: Les éditions Hannenorak, 2012.

Sipe, C. Hale. *The Indian Wars of Pennsylvania.* Harrisburg: The Telegraph Press, 1929. *archive.org.* 25 Feb. 2015.

Smith, James. *An Account of the Remarkable Occurrences In the Life and Travels of Col. James Smith, (Now a Citizen of Bourbon County, Kentucky,) During His Captivity with the Indians, In the Years 1755, '56, '57, '58, & '59.* Lexington: John Bradford, 1799. *archive.org.* 31 Dec. 2015.

Smith, Laura Chase. *The Life of Philander Chase: First Bishop of Ohio and Founder of Kenyon and Jubilee Colleges.* New York: E. P. Dutton and Co., 1904. *archive.org.* 23 Nov. 2016.

Smith, Robert Emmett. "The Clash of Leadership at the Grand Reserve: The Wyandot Subagency and the Methodist Mission, 1820–1824." *Ohio History Journal,* Vol. 89. No. 2 (Spring 1980): 181–205. *ohiohistory.org.* 30 Nov. 2017.

———. "Thomas Moseley, Jr. and the Last Years of the Wyandot Subagency." *Pacific Historian,* Vol. 21. No.1 (1977): 1–20.

———. "The Wyandotte Exploring Expedition of 1839." Manuscript. Wyandotte Nation Historical Archives. *Chronicles of Oklahoma,* Vol. 55. No. 3 (1977): 282–93.

Smith, Zachariah F. *The History of Kentucky, From Its Earliest Discovery and Settlement, to the Present Date.* Louisville: The Prentice Press, 1895. *archive.org.* 3 June 2016.

Socolofsky, Homer E. "Wyandot Floats." *Kansas Historical Quarterly,* Vol. 36. No. 3 (1970): 241–304. 2 June 2013.

Soule, Joshua. "Wyandot Mission." *The Methodist Magazine, Designed as a Compend of Useful Knowledge, and of Religious and Missionary Intelligence, For the Year of Our Lord 1825,* Vol. VIII. New York: Methodist Episcopal Church, 1825. 32–38. *books. google.com.* 2 May 2017.

Speck, Frank Gouldsmith. "The Delaware Indians as Women: Were the Original Pennsylvanians Politically Emasculated?" *Pennsylvania Magazine of History and Biography,* Vol. I. No. 70. Issue 4 (Oct. 1946): 377–89. *journals.psu.edu.* 30 Oct. 2017.

Speise, Steve. *Huron Indian Cemetery: Wyandot National Burying Ground, 1843 et seq.* Kansas City: Unified Government of Wyandotte County and Kansas City, Kansas, 1979. *wycokck.org.* 23 Mar. 1999.

St. Clair, Arthur. *A Narrative of the Manner in Which the Campaign Against the Indians, in the Year One Thousand Seven Hundred and Ninety-one, Was Conducted, Under the Command of Major General St. Clair, Together With His Observations on the Statements of the Secretary of War and the Quarter Master General, Relative Thereto, and the Reports of the Committees Appointed to Inquire Into the Causes of the Failure Thereof.* Philadelphia: Printed by Jane Aitken, 1812. *archive.org.* 13 June 2016.

Statistics of Indian Tribes, Agencies, and Schools. Washington: GPO, 1899. *archive.org.* 5 Aug. 2015.

Steckley, John L. *The Eighteenth-Century Wyandot: A Clan-Based Study.* Waterloo: Wilfrid Laurier University Press, 2014.

———. "Linguistically Linking the Petun with The Southern Bear." *Arch Notes,* Vol. 93. No. 2 (Mar./Apr. 1993): 20–26.

———. "The 1747 Wyandot Elders Council." Email to the author. 2 Aug. 2011.

———. "Wendat Dialects and the Development of the Huron Alliance." *Northeast Anthropology,* Vol. 54 (Sept. 1997): 23–36. Email to the author. 7 Oct. 2012.

———. "Why Did The Wenro Turn Turtle?" *Arch Notes,* Vol. 85. No. 3 (May/June 1985): 17–19. 15 Jan. 2014.

Stewart, Alexander McGinn. *Rene Menard, 1605–1661; A Life Story Which Connects the Finger Lakes Region of New York with France, Québec, Georgian Bay and Wisconsin.* Rochester: Heindel Print, 1934. *bikexprt.com/menard/menardfr.htm.* 5 Sept. 2015.

Stone, William L. *Life of Joseph Brant—Thayendanegea: Including the Border Wars of the American Revolution and Sketches of the Indian Campaigns of Generals Harmar, St. Clair, and Wayne. And other matters connected with the Indian relations of the United States and Great Britain, from the peace of 1783 to the Indian peace of 1795,* Vol. I. New York: A. V. Blake, 1838. *archive.org.* 12 Dec. 2015.

———. *Life of Joseph Brant—Thayendanegea: Including the Border Wars of the American Revolution and Sketches of the Indian Campaigns of Generals Harmar, St. Clair, and Wayne. And other matters connected with the Indian relations of the United States and Great Britain, from the peace of 1783 to the Indian peace of 1795,* Vol. II. New York: A. V. Blake, 1838. *archive.org.* 12 Dec. 2015.

———. *The Life and Times of Sir William Johnson, Bart,* Vol. I. Albany: J. Munsell, 1865. *archive.org.* 12 Dec. 2015.

———. *The Life and Times of Sir William Johnson, Bart,* Vol. II. Albany: J. Munsell, 1865. *books.google.com.* 22 Oct. 2015.

Swan, Isabella. "Descendants of Wyandot Chief Live Here." *The Ile Camera* (22 Apr. 1957): 2.

———. "Warrow Family Kin of Wyandot Chiefs." *The Ile Camera* (17 June 1957: 4-B.

Sweet, William Warren. *Circuit-Rider Days Along the Ohio, Being the Journals of the Ohio Conference From Its Organization in 1812 to 1826.* Cincinnati: The Methodist Book Concern, 1923. *archive.org.* 6 July 2017.

Taylor, Edward Livingston. "The Ohio Indians." *Ohio Archaeological and Historical Publications,* Vol. VI. Columbus: John W. Trauger, 1898. 72–94. *books.google.com.* 30 Sept. 2015.

Thackeray, Francis. *A History of the Right Honorable William Pitt, Earl of Chatham: Containing His Speeches In Parliament; A Considerable Portion of His Correspondence When Secretary of State, Upon French, Spanish, and American Affairs, Never Before Published: With An Account of the Principal Events and Persons of His Time Connected With His Life, Sentiments, and Administration,* Vol. II. London: Printed for C. and J. Rivington, 1827. *books.google.com.* 4 July 2016.

Thomas, T. C. "Some Indian History." *The American Antiquarian and Oriental Journal,* Vol. XXXV. Toledo: The Antiquarian Publishing Co., 1913. 158–61. *books.google. com.* 4 Mar. 2017.

Thwaites, Reuben Gold, ed. *A Selection of George Croghan's Letters and Journals Relating to Tours Into the Western Country—November 16, 1750–November, 1765.* Cleveland: The Arthur H. Clark Company, 1904. *archive.org.* 8 Oct. 2015.

————. *Chronicles of Border Warfare or, A History of the Settlement by the Whites, of North-Western Virginia, and of the Indian Wars and Massacres in That Section of the State With Reflections, Anecdotes, &c by Alexander Scott Withers.* Cincinnati: Stewart & Kidd Company, 1912. *books.google.com.* 8 Sept. 2015.

————. *Collections of the State Historical Society of Wisconsin,* Vol. XVI—*The French Regime in Wisconsin, 1634–1727.* Madison: Published by the Historical Society of Wisconsin, 1902. *books.google.com.* 27 Jan. 2015.

————. *Early Western Travels 1748–1846,* Vol. I. Cleveland: The Arthur H. Clark Company, 1904. *books.google.com.* 25 Feb. 2015.

————. *Early Western Travels 1748–1846,* Vol. XVII. Cleveland: The Arthur H. Clark Company, 1904. *archive.org.* 12 Apr. 2015.

————. *How George Rogers Clark Won the Northwest: And Other Essays In Western History.* Chicago: A. C. McClurg & Co., 1903. *archive.org.* 25 Aug. 2015.

————. *The Jesuit Relations and Allied Documents 1610 to 1791,* Vol. XXXIV. Cleveland: The Burrows Bros. Co., 1896. *archive.org.* 13 Apr. 2010.

————. and Louise Phelps Kellogg, eds. *Frontier Defense on the Upper Ohio, 1777–1778.* Madison: Wisconsin Historical Society, 1912. *books.google.com.* 14 Jan. 2013.

————. *The Revolution on the Upper Ohio, 1775–1777.* Madison: Wisconsin Historical Society, 1908. *books.google.com.* 7 Mar. 2013.

Tooker, Elisabeth. "An Ethnology of the Huron Indians, 1615–1649." *Bureau of American Ethnology,* Bulletin 190. Washington: GPO. 1964. *repository.si.edu.* 15 Jan. 2014.

————. "Wyandot." *Handbook of North American Indians,* Vol. 15 Northeast. Ed. Bruce G. Trigger. Washington: GPO, 1978. 398–406.

Trigger, Bruce. *The Children of Aataentsic: A History of the Huron People to 1660.* Montreal: McGill-Queen's University Press, 1976.

————. "The French Presence in Huronia: The Structure of Franco-Huron Relations in the First Half of the Seventeenth Century." *Canadian Historical Rev.,* Vol. 49, No. 2 (1968): 107–41. *utpjournals.metapress.com.* 14 Feb. 2015.

————. "The Liberation of Wendake." *Ontario Archaeology,* No. 72 (2001): 3–14. *ontarioarchaeology.on.ca.* 18 Jan. 2015.

————. "Settlement as an Aspect of Iroquoian Adaptation at the Time of Contact." *American Anthropologist,* Vol. 65. No. 1 (Feb. 1963): 86–101. *onlinelibrary.wiley.com.* 7 Nov. 2017.

Trigger, Bruce G. "The Original Iroquoians: Huron, Petun, and Neutral." *Aboriginal Ontario: Historical Perspectives on the First Nations.* Ed. Edward S. Rogers and Donald B. Smith. Toronto: Dundurn Press Limited, 1994. 41–63. *books.google.com.* 2 Dec. 2014.

Trowbridge, C. C. (Charles Christopher). "Wyandots—C. C. Trowbridge's Account." *Wyandot History: A Guide to Original Sources and Current Scholarship. wyandothistory.com.* 24 Oct. 2014.

Tyler, Moses Coit. *The Literary History of the American Revolution 1763–1783,* Vol. I. New York: G. P. Putnam's Sons, 1898. *books.google.com.* 16 Oct. 2015.

Unified Government: Wyandotte County and Kansas City, Kansas. "Full Commission Meeting Agenda Thursday, September 20, 2007." *wycokck.org.* 22 Aug. 2015.

United States Office of Indian Affairs, Central Superintendency: Correspondence. St. Louis, Missouri, and William Clark Papers Coll. #741, Vol. 34: 153. *kansasmemory.org.* 23 Oct 2014.

U.S. Census Office. *Map of Indian Territory and Oklahoma.* New York: Julius Bien & Co., 1890. *davidrumsey.com.* 8 Aug. 2015. Map.

Voorhees, Richard M. "General George A. Custer." *Ohio Archaeological and Historical Quarterly,* Vol. XV. Columbus: Fred J. Herr, 1906. 342–54. *books.google.com.* 3 Oct. 2015.

Walker, Bertrand Nicholas Oliver and Czarina C. Conlan. "Sketch of B. N. O. Walker." *Chronicles of Oklahoma,* Vol. 6. No. 1 (March 1928): 89–93. *digital.library.okstate. edu.* 4 Feb. 2010.

Walker, Matthew. "Personal Letter to John Carey 22 Oct. 1843."

Walker, William. "W. Walker to G. P. Disosway." *kansasmemory.org.* 23 Jan. 2013.

———. "W. Walker to J. M. Armstrong." *kansasmemory.org.* 23 Jan. 2013.

Wallace, Paul A. W. *Conrad Weiser: Friend of Colonist and Mohawk.* Philadelphia: University of Pennsylvania Press, 1945.

Walsh, Martin W. "The "Heathen Party": Methodist Observation of the Ohio Wyandot." *American Indian Quarterly,* Vol. 16. No. 2 (1992): 189–211. *ebscohost.com.* 9 Oct. 2012.

Walton, Joseph Solomon. *Conrad Weiser and the Indian Policy of Colonial Pennsylvania.* Philadelphia: G. W. Jacobs & Co., 1900. *archive.org.* 30 Aug. 2015.

Warner, Michael S. "General Josiah Harmar's Campaign Reconsidered: How the Americans Lost the Battle of Kekionga" *Indiana Magazine of History,* Vol. 83. (Mar. 1987): 43–64. *scholarworks.iu.edu.* 14 Dec. 2015.

Warren, Mark. *Anderdon: Some Folks Down the Road. Anderdon1812.com.* Web. 2012.

Warrick, Gary. *A Population History of the Huron-Petun, A.D. 500–1650.* New York: Cambridge University Press, 2008. *cambridge.org.* 19 Mar. 2013.

Wheeler, James. "Letter to Brother Elliott." *The Western Christian Advocate. 1843. Wyandot.org.* 23 Nov. 2011.

———. "Journal Accounts: 10–20 July 1843." *wyandot.org.* 23 Nov. 2011.

———. "Personal Letter: 28 July 1843." *wyandot.org.* 23 Nov. 2011.

———. "Personal Letter: 30 Sept. 1843." *wyandot.org.* 23 Nov. 2011.

Wilson, David. *The Life of Jane McCrea with an Account of Burgoyne's Expedition in 1777.* New York: Baker, Godwin & Co., 1853. *archive.org.* 12 May 2016.

Wilson, Frazer E. "The Treaty of Greenville." *Ohio Archaeological and Historical Publications,* Vol. XII. Columbus: Fred J. Herr, 1903. 128–59. *books.google.com.* 30 Sept. 2015.

Wimer, James. *Events in Indian History, Beginning With the Account of the Origin of the American Indians; and Early Settlements In North America, and Embracing Concise Biographies of the Principle* [sic] *Chiefs and Head-Sachems of the Different Indian Tribes, with Narratives and Captives.* Lancaster: G. Hills & Co., 1841. *archive.org.* 12 May 2016.

Winter, Nevin O. *A History of Northwest Ohio: A Narrative Account of Its Historical Progress and Development from the First European Exploration of the Maumee and Sandusky Valleys and the Adjacent Shores of Lake Erie, Down to the Present Time.* Chicago: The Lewis Publishing Company, 1917. *archive.org.* 2009.

Withers, Alexander S. *Chronicles of Border Warfare: or, A History of the Settlement by the Whites, of North-Western Virginia: and of the Indian Wars and Massacres, In That Section of the State; With Reflections, Anecdotes, &c.* Clarksburg: Joseph Israel, 1831. *archive.org.* 9 Oct. 2015.

Wright, James V. "Before European Contact." *Aboriginal Ontario: Historical Perspectives on the First Nations.* Ed. Edward S. Rogers and Donald B. Smith. Toronto: Dundurn Press Limited, 1994. 21–38. *books.google.com.* 2 Dec. 2014.

Wyandot Tribe. "Wyandot Indian Council Records: 1855–1871." *kansasmemory.org.* 23 Jan. 2013.

———. "Wyandot Nation to the American Congress: 27 Oct. 1848." *kansasmemory.org.* 23 Jan. 2013.

Wyandotte County and Kansas City, Kansas. Historical and Biographical. Chicago: The Godspeed Publishing Company, 1890. *archive.org.* 170, 353. 23 July 2015.

Wyandotte Nation v. Sebelius, No. 04-2140-JAR 6 Oct. 2004. *law.justia.com/cases/federal/district-courts/FSupp2/337/1253/2470076/.* 21 Aug. 2015.

Wyandotte Nation v. Sebelius, Nos. 04-3431, 04-3432 7 Apr. 2006. *caselaw.findlaw.com/us-10th-circuit/1431470.html.* 21 Aug. 2015.

"Wyandotte Reservation." *Report On Indians Taxed and Not Taxed In the United States (Except Alaska) at the Eleventh Census: 1890.* Washington: GPO (1894): 248–49. *archive.org.* 17 June 2015.

ILLUSTRATION CREDITS

Figures

Maps

INDEX

ABOUT THE AUTHOR

Lloyd Divine Jr. is a citizen of the Wyandotte Nation who has served on his tribe's cultural committee for over twenty-five years. The committee's primary task is to search out and teach tribal citizens their traditions and history. As Lloyd began his personal quest to fulfill this commission and better understand who his ancestors are, he quickly realized there are many misunderstandings in the *Huron*-Wyandot's written history. Many of these misunderstandings have proven to be points of confusion since the early days of the tribe's dispersal during the French and Iroquois Wars of the seventeenth century. With a desire to tell the complete and often confusing *Huron*-Wyandot story, Lloyd spent many years researching and writing *On the Back of a Turtle: A Narrative of the* Huron-*Wyandot People*. His book is a full-length, all-encompassing history of the *Huron*-Wyandot people from their oral account of Creation to the present day. Within his book Lloyd tells his people's story with an undeniable passion that is a reflection of his grandfather six-times removed. In *History of the Wyandott Mission,* The Reverend James B. Finley described Mononcue, Lloyd's grandfather, as "vehement." Lloyd carries this same passion for his people's history into his writings, public speaking, and profession as a paramedic. Living and serving his community within the greater Springfield, Missouri, area, Lloyd is an EMS educator and field paramedic who teaches new paramedics how to be paramedics. With a wife and four daughters, a generational family blessing, Lloyd spends all of his time living the glorious life of husband, father, tribal historian, and paramedic.